THE HOLLAND
HANDBOOK

CONTENTS

ABOUT THE HOLLAND HANDBOOK

Welcome, expat, to the Netherlands! After the very successful previous editions we are proud to present you with the sixth edition of *The Holland Handbook*, which we hope will prove to be as good a friend to you during your stay in the Netherlands as it has been to numerous other expats over the past five years.

This book has been compiled for a very mixed group of readers who have one thing in common and that is that they want to find their way in the Netherlands: the expat EMPLOYEE, the expat's PARTNER, foreign ENTREPRENEURS and the many foreign STUDENTS who have come to the Netherlands to train or study. For PROFESSIONALS who want to keep abreast of the latest developments in expat affairs this book has also proved to be a very welcome source of information.

The Holland Handbook has come to be thanks to the enthusiastic efforts of more than 30 authors, organizations and proofreaders of various nationalities and with very different backgrounds. Most of them are specialists who work for international companies and organizations and who have an impressive amount of know-how when it comes to providing expatriates with information.

The fact that the editorial team is such a 'hotchpotch' of people cannot go unnoticed when reading the book. You will find technical information on practical subjects interspersed with personal experiences, background information and columns. *The Holland Handbook* may at times take an unexpected turn – however, as this book is primarily meant as a reference book and not one to be read in one go, we hope this will only serve to make it a more interesting read.

Though *The Holland Handbook* contains a lot of information, we do not have the illusion that it is at all complete. It is meant as an introduction, or orientation if you will, into the various subjects that can be of interest to you. By referring you to the relevant literature, addresses and websites, we have provided you with as many sources of additional and/or more in-depth information as we can think of. Undoubtedly we have forgotten a few subjects, websites or books. If you feel that we have left out something that should not have been missed, we would greatly appreciate it if you let us know about this, for instance by sending an e-mail to editor@xpat.nl.

On our website www.xpat.nl you will find a short summary of the chapters of *The Holland Handbook*, as well as of the current issue of our quarterly magazine *The XPat Journal* and the option to order copies of our other publications on the Netherlands.

We hope you have a pleasant, enriching and successful stay in the Netherlands. Should you suffer from culture shock every now and then, we suggest you read Connie Moser's opening article, in which you will be sure to recognize a few symptoms and which will help you to remember that ... YOU ARE NOT ALONE. Nor do you have to go through this alone. You have *The Holland Handbook*, the many organizations and information sources mentioned in this book and about 250,000 other expatriates to turn to for information, entertainment and understanding.

Bert van Essen and Gerjan de Waard
Publishers

THE HOLLAND HANDBOOK

YOUR GUIDE TO LIVING IN THE NETHERLANDS

When attempting to understand another culture, there are many areas where we need to pause and consider how our own culture and the host culture differ. Whatever has contributed to our background, to how and why we are here, we all come into this new experience with some preconceived ideas and expectations. Art, music, architecture, folklore, foods and dress, our roles and relationships, body language, gestures, greetings and partings, all weave together to form a rich cultural diversity. Our reactions vary when confronted with so many new and unknown experiences. It is not always easy to keep an open mind. In fact, it can be a real shock!

Culture Shock! & Cultural Enrichment!

BY CONNIE MOSER AND STEPHANIE DIJKSTRA

CULTURE SHOCK – MANAGING EXPECTATIONS

Everyone who moves to a foreign country has some ideas about what it's going to be like. When people think of Holland, the 'typical Dutch' stereotypical objects that come to mind are windmills, wooden shoes, lots of cheese and cows and chocolate. As well as fields full of beautiful flowers, bicycles, quaint villages and exciting Amsterdam.

These preconceived ideas are in part based on traditional elements of the Dutch culture, but the Netherlands is much more complex. Beyond what meets the eye, is a multi-cultural society of tolerant, frugal, hardworking, sober and single-minded people. Looking from a historical perspective, we can see many influences shaping the character of the Dutch culture – the religious impact of Calvin, the struggle of many centuries of fighting water, the determination in Dutch character in building the dikes, a few bouts with foreign occupation and two world wars. Today, the Dutch are still building the reclaimed land resulting in the proud claim that indeed the 'Dutch made Holland'.

COPING WITH REALITY – THE VISUAL AND EMOTIONAL VERSUS THE EXPERIENTIAL

By taking a look at various customs and the daily life of the Dutch, you can better begin to understand and perhaps appreciate some of the new and different things you will be confronted with during your stay in this small and surprising country.

When adjusting to life in a new country, we refer to a strange phenomenon called 'culture shock'. If you've ever had an electric shock, you know what a surprise that is to your system! In the same way, what you 'see' may not correspond with what you 'know' and what you experience may not correspond with what you are feeling at the time. When you do not understand what you are seeing, or the language you are hearing, this can be very confusing. You might feel like your mental wires are crossed and that you are receiving mixed signals from your senses.

What you know to be true may not be valid in your new situation. Things look different from what you are used to, the sound of the language may be incomprehensible gibberish, and the smells may be penetrating or sweet or even disgusting. There may be a lot of disturbing noises, making it difficult to concentrate. The foods you know (and love!) may not be readily available (if at all) and many new foods may smell odd and taste even stranger!

In all this confusion of your senses, you also have your emotions at work, and you may be feeling overwhelmed by all the new input, surprised or shocked, delighted or distressed, frustrated that everything takes longer to do or impatient with yourself that you don't understand many things. You may also be experiencing some 'homesickness' and sadness in missing loved ones and familiar places and comforting things from 'home'.

DEALING WITH TRANSITION

Finding your way through all of your physical, mental and emotional changes is part of the challenge of living abroad and coping with culture shock. Each person's experience is unique.

Being aware of the stages your adjustment will go through can help you in realizing that 'This too shall pass' in time. Though culture shock can be emotionally painful, you will learn to manage the stress, cope with the many frustrations and learn to appreciate a varied and culturally enriching life in your new country.

THE PHASES

The phases of transition you will encounter form a typical pattern:

Tourist Phase – When you first arrive, everything is new, exciting, charming or otherwise so different and interesting you may find yourself saying 'Oh, I love it here!' You will enjoy exploring your new country and be so fascinated by the quaint or radically

16

INTRO

different sights and sounds that your new life seems like one big adventure! Amazed and amused, you enthusiastically embrace each new experience you encounter.

I-Hate-This-Country-Phase – The fun may end when the newness wears off and you find yourself disenchanted and entering this rather negative phase.

Suddenly all the differences become irritating. Life is frustrating; you may have difficulty understanding the language. It takes forever to find things, which makes you weary. Or you feel incompetent and inadequate in your new role often as stay-at-home spouse who may have given up his/her own career or as a student at a new school with a different curriculum and lots of strange faces, quite possibly also from other nations. The sense of competence, efficiency and identity you knew in your own culture may not translate into your new situation. You strain and struggle to re-establish yourself within an unfamiliar system. Weariness sets in.

Life is confusing, you feel disoriented. Where do you fit in? You may feel depressed, anxious and even hostile. Some people experience a lethargic cloud and sleep a lot in order not to have to deal with all the difficulties life now demands, others have difficulty sleeping. Headaches, stomachaches and general 'not feeling well' are not uncommon complaints. Sometimes you will feel quite angry with the Dutch, at yourself, at your partner, or at your parents (if a student or child) or even your employer for bringing you here. You may find yourself thinking 'What have we done in coming here? What in the world were we thinking?' 'What am I going to do? How do I cope?'

Occasionally you may also feel afraid, and not want to leave the house because it takes so much extra energy to cope. This is referred to as 'transition fatigue'; the tiredness that comes from being continually asked to deal with too many changes within a short time-span.

You might be scared of asking questions, or you might not trust the foreign language for fear of not being understood, or, you may be devastated at the idea of 'getting lost'. (Note: You are never really 'lost', you are always 'somewhere' and the possibility always exists to get to 'somewhere else', even the place you need to be! Don't panic.) Always carry a map and a list of phone numbers and/or address of hotel, school, or your new home as well as a phone card if you do not have a mobile phone.

Culture Shock – In this phase you may seek the company of other expatriates or your fellow countrymen. You may be highly critical of the host culture and voice your negative feelings towards the local people. Typically you may avoid contact with the new culture. This is a natural response as you attempt to hold on to your own cultural framework. Each new culture you encounter will be judged by comparing it to your own frame of reference.

What makes the challenge of an international move even more complex is that you are immersed in an unfamiliar culture where the people's values, attitudes, and ways of relating to one another are very different from those to which you are accustomed. Some differences are quite obvious and expected (for instance language, customs, laws, governmental systems) but many differences are less obvious but still very real – such as values guiding people's actions, their attitudes, concepts and their historical impact. Frustrations in understanding another culture also stem from the

hidden or submerged differences, which most often occur in areas where we inadvertently assume that all people think in a similar manner, or share like-minded universal standards, so that differences may clash with our ideas of what is 'true' or 'right' or 'polite' in our home culture.

We need to learn to 'decode' or culturally translate these differing meanings in attitudes, values and concepts, to pick up on the signals to sense what is appropriate in specific situations, and to also realize which actions are inappropriate or 'just not done'. It takes some time to pick up the signals. Even gestures specific to one culture can confuse us when used in a new setting with a different interpretation.

We move beyond criticism to acceptance of 'just another way of life' when we begin to acclimatize to our new situation. This acceptance of the norms of the host culture and our own sensitivity to the people and their customs will greatly benefit us in our integration process, to function more effectively, and enjoy our foreign adventures.

Acceptance and Adjustment Phase – This is the next step. Life improves when you begin to find your way around, make new friends, settle into a regular routine and adjust to daily life in your new environment. You become involved in some activities, be it social, sports, or sharing group fellowship in a place of worship. You take some risks, explore with curious interest, even try some new foods! Perhaps you make some Dutch friends who share their experiences and provide you with some more insight into appreciating many of the wonderful things the Dutch culture has to offer.

As time goes on, you will no doubt take part in festivities surrounding Dutch holidays. You will know what to do in social situations, be less judgmental and regain your sense of humor. As you gain some language skills, you will feel less awkward and come to accept the Dutch culture on its own merits. This 'global perspective' helps you to look at your world in view of a much 'bigger picture'. You actually really begin to enjoy quite a few new things and may even feel at home. Yes, even at home in Holland!

THE DUTCH THROUGH THE EYES OF EXPATS

YONINA (USA)
On social niceties: 'I love the social amenities of the Dutch culture: people are attentive, they give you flowers, they offer you cookies with your coffee, they see you to the door and, when you leave, they stand waving in the street till they can't see you anymore. I think that is just wonderful'.'

On society: 'There is a difference between giving one of my motivational talks in Holland or in the US. Holland has an older society and more advanced forms of culture. This makes them less spontaneous and less willing to show their emotions. I have to build up slowly to audience participation. Also, the people here are more auditive; they want an explanation as to the why, who and where.'

DIEDRA ATKINSON (USA)
On truth and honesty: 'The Dutch have this thing about truth and honesty. They'll tell you the truth even though it rips you up one side and down the other.'

FEDERICO CHERI (ITALY)
On the need for an agenda to make a social appointment: 'You don't just call and say *hey, let's go to a movie tonight*, no, you have to take out your agenda and *make an appointment* – most likely for two or three weeks hence. *Over twee weken heb ik wel een plekje,*' he quotes (I can make a spot for you in two weeks). 'In Sardinia, if you make an appointment to meet in two weeks, you *forget*.'

MARCELO BENDAHAN (SPAIN)
On religion: 'In some countries, religion has a great influence, but in Holland, for instance, I feel there is no religion in everyday life. This is a very free society, a free country. People trust in their own opinion here, they want to be 'themselves', 'master of their own destiny'. But if you trust your own opinion, are you always right? How do you know you are right? Don't you need guidance; from parents, teachers or maybe someone spiritual?'

On family ties: 'It's great that the children here leave the house when they are 17 or 18, but when they go away, they really go away. From then on, they make an *appointment* to see their parents. Their parents are *guests* at their wedding.'

AHARON NAFTALI (ISRAEL)
On being direct: 'You know how many people comment that the Dutch are very direct, but I am an Israeli. So when I meet a Dutchman I say: 'You may be direct, but I am an Israeli, so I am more direct than you are.' That usually sets us off in the right direction. The Dutch like it when you are direct; if it is clear who is across from them, they are more accepting: they like it, they know there is no fooling around.'

RUDI GOLDMAN (USA)
On consensus: 'What to me seems a bit problematic is that the Dutch tend to move slowly, because they need to reach consensus. The consensus model, of course, tends to be strong model, because everyone involved has, as the Dutch say, 'their noses pointing in the same direction'. But it takes such a long time, that it is not always very productive. This led to my first bout with culture shock. We had very long meetings, with something like 20 people. They'd pick my brain and take suggestions. Then we'd have a second meeting, where they would cut back on everything I suggested. And then we'd have a third meeting, where they would cut back even more on everything I suggested.'

On responsibility: 'Due to this rule of *doe maar gewoon* (just act normal), whereby no one is allowed to stick out above the rest, it is hard for people to take responsibility, because it is always shared. It would be refreshing if someone said: 'Right or wrong, this is my responsibility'.'

LYDIA PIETERNELLA (CURAÇAO)
On politics: 'I am a bit concerned about the direction the country is taking. On the one hand, I am glad that people are finally able to open up and talk and acknowledge that there are problems. It is true that in the past – when it came to politics – the Dutch did not say what they really felt. On the other hand, the new policies are a bit fragmented and uncoordinated. There has been so much 'if we take two of yours and two of mine and we stick them together' – not only regarding ministers and state secretaries but also regarding ideas – that the outcome of this has not been very consistent. A lot of continuity is being lost.'

STEVEN NG (SINGAPORE)
On consensual management style: 'The consensual style of managing does send a positive message to employees; it gives people a sense of belonging, a sense that they have a place and a say. And I understand what it is like to be recognized, to have a say in a lot of things. But as a manager I can see also that it can be hard if you want to please a thousand people – or ten thousand people.'

YOU HAVE ARRIVED IN THE NETHERLANDS
BY HAN VAN DER HORST

What does it mean to be in the Netherlands? You crawl ahead on the highway behind laboring windshield wipers, watching the ragged horizon of apartment buildings go by as the gray clouds are chased along by a strong southwestern wind.

As the slowly moving traffic jams come to another halt, you have the chance to focus on your fellow drivers. Your first conclusion is obvious: you are in a wealthy country. This is evident from the newness of the cars. There are many trucks, which are well-kept and loaded with valuable goods. These goods are seldom raw materials, but rather finished industrial goods. The prominent phone numbers and e-mail addresses that can be found on the sides of the trucks are witness to the fact that this country has a good network of electronic communication and that the electronic highway is fully in place. Your fellow drivers, incidentally, appear to be talking to themselves. You can see that they are keeping it short. Probably they are telling someone that they will be late, due to traffic. In the past, they would have reached for their mobile phones, but they don't do that anymore – it is no longer allowed. Nowadays, you are expected to use a hands-free system, or else the police will redirect you to a road stop, where they will present you with a hefty fine after having courteously introduced themselves and shaken your hand.

However, there is an apparent contradiction to the perceived wealth, if you look around you: the cars are far from luxurious. You are surrounded by middle class cars, and you can see how strongly the Asian market is represented on the European car market. Where is the top of the market? Where are the Rolls Royces, Cadillacs, Daimlers and Jaguars? You won't even find them in the business centers or the upper-class neighborhoods. In the Netherlands, if you want to see one of these cars, you will have to visit a dealer. The most expensive cars you will see are the standard Mercedes, Audis and BMWs. Should you actually spot a Rolls Royce trying to make its way through traffic, you will notice that it does not really command any respect. To the contrary. It even seems as if the middle class cars want to block this show of wealth, as if they think it inappropriate for such a showpiece to be on the road and they want to prove, by the way they drive, that they are worth just as much as the fellow in the Rolls.

On both sides of the highway, you will see many towns and little cities. There are no real metropolises with millions of people in Holland.

The largest city, Amsterdam, does not have more than about 750,000 inhabitants. Still, Holland is a highly urbanized country. Every few kilometers, there is an exit to one, two or three places that have a couple of thousand to not many more than 100,000 inhabitants. These cities and towns all have their own character and are all equally picturesque. In the urban areas you will find neither hovels nor palaces. What you will find is primarily middle class houses.

Even Wassenaar, Aerdenhout or Rozendaal, the Dutch equivalents of Miami Beach and Beverly Hills, look comparatively modest. There is an undeniable air of wealth, but none of the glitter of excessive opulence.

You will also not find harbors filled with expensive yachts. Those who buy a pleasure yacht in the Netherlands will have a hard time finding a spot for it, as the harbors are all filled. Not with luxurious threemasters and a regular crew, however, but rather with motor and sail boats of all shapes and sizes. And should there be one that sticks out above the rest, chances are it is flying a foreign flag.

You would almost think that socialism reigns here, even more so than in the countries of the former East Bloc. However, economic statistics show the opposite. When it comes to per capita income, the Netherlands is securely situated towards the top of the European Union.

After being hit quite hard by the oil crises in 1974 and 1979, it resumed its growth after five years – a growth to which only towards the end of 2001 there appeared to come an end, when the economy slowly but surely started to go into a recession ... Despite all this, corporate life in the Netherlands is resilient. There are several multinationals of various sizes – most noticeably Philips, the electronics company, while there are also the banking giants ING, Rabo and ABN-Amro. Shell and Unilever are British-Dutch companies.

If this is the case, there must be large concentrations of wealth in the hands of individual persons somewhere in this country. And, indeed, there are more than one hundred thousand millionaires among the more than sixteen million inhabitants – and they have been on the rise over the last ten years or so. Apparently, the wealthy Dutch do not buy castles. Or Rolls Royces.

A PESSIMISTIC CLIMATE

BY HAN VAN DER HORST

He who spends more than a few days in the Netherlands and connects with its inhabitants, will soon notice that there is a certain fear for the future. This became painfully apparent after the murder of film maker Theo van Gogh by a Muslim terrorist, which reminded people instantly of the murder of the populist politician Pim Fortuyn – shot to death in May 2002. How is it that two murders spread over a period of a few years can so shock Dutch society? Just as in the case of the assassination of President Kennedy and of 9-11, almost every Dutchman can tell you precisely where he was when he heard of the murder of these two men.

Why did these murders take place? It is interesting to note that the motivations for these two murders, though they could have been the same (both men had expressed anti-Muslim sentiments), the reasons were quite diverse. Pim Fortuyn was murdered by an environmental activist who felt that Fortuyn was a threat to his ideologies. Theo van Gogh was murdered because he had made a short film, together with Somali-born VVD-parliamentary member Ayaan Hirsi Ali, that illustrated and narrated the repression of women on the basis of the Koran. (Not as an attack on the Islam, but as a first step in their aim to make people aware of how women are repressed the world round. Nonetheless, particularly the Muslim world took exception to this movie.) Both Fortuyn and Van Gogh were men who did not shy away from controversial opinions – and were considered by some to be a champion of free speech and by others as simply trouble-makers.

Nevertheless, both incidents can be considered a violent attack on the freedom of speech – which is very serious matter. But not something that could shatter an old democracy and warrant such nervousness. Let's just say that the two murderers placed themselves outside of civilized society, and that society has its own legal means to deal with this...

For the Dutch, however, this is not the only issue – which will help me explain the general fear and anger. The Dutch have always been deeply divided along religious, political and – during the last few decades – life-style lines. Still, through this all, they managed to maintain unity and peace. This had to do with mutual respect. Everyone had their own deep and sometimes radical convictions, but did not live by them too expressly or strongly. Those who were too extreme were banned to the margins of the debate. 'Everyone has a right to an opinion' and 'live and let live' were and are important philosophies; stay true to who you are and try not to rock the boat.

Tolerance is a mutual thing: I will respect your points of view, so that you will respect mine. Part of this philosophy is that, when in public space, people don't dress or behave in a way that expresses too obviously what their life philosophy is. Catholics don't 'look' like Catholics and Protestants don't look like Protestants. At school, little Catholic children learn that it is a good idea to keep your rosary in your pocket and your amulet of Maria under your shirt. If you are in an accident,

The murder of film maker Theo van Gogh leads to a 'noisy' protest by the people. Text banner:
Multicultural society vs. fundamentalism.

then the ambulance staff will recognize your religion and bring you to Catholic hospital. Better to express your religion this way than to advertise it.

The moment someone does not respect these silent agreements, he starts chopping at the roots of internal peace. If you don't have to tolerate me, then I don't have to tolerate you, either. In October, 2004, fundamentalist Muslims issued a manifesto against the visible presence of homosexuals in the streets. What they didn't realize was that the tolerance that allowed homosexuals to freely be themselves was the same tolerance that allowed their daughters to openly express their religion by means of wearing a head scarf. And when Van Gogh's killer appealed to Allah when he murdered him, this was, to some, an invitation to attack mosques and Muslim schools – as, with this act, he had broken the covenant of mutual tolerance.

When this happens, extremists are no longer marginalized; all of a sudden, they are at the center of the debate – making it impossible to resolve and avoid conflicts by creative communications, negotiation, compromises and ego-soothing.

That is why the Dutch are so afraid for the future. That is why the actions of one person can so upset the balance and generate so much insecurity.

Technical research team at work.

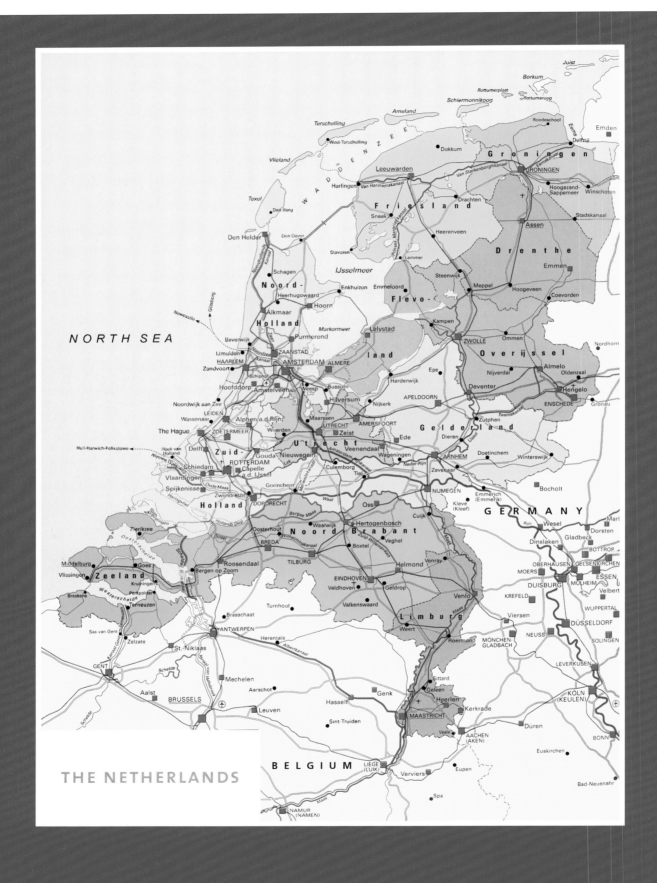

THE NETHERLANDS

THEY MUST BE GIANTS
BY STEVEN STUPP

One of my first observations about the Netherlands was how tall the Dutch are. Actually, tall doesn't do them justice. They are really tall. Damn tall. I am not used to thinking of myself as short; I'm above the average, adult-male height in my native land. But after a few introductions, where I looked up and found myself staring the person in the throat, the point hit home.

According to the statisticians, the Dutch are currently the tallest people on the planet. The average height for men is 6 foot, 0.4 inches (1.84 meters); the women come in at a res-pectable 5 foot, 7.2 inches (1.71 meters). Cold averages, however, don't convey the entire picture. Connoisseurs of numbers know to look at the tails of a distribution. There are quite a few Dutch men, and even a few women, who are over seven feet tall (2.10 meters). This poses some interesting problems. For example, they are taller than the height of many doorways in the Netherlands; I have no doubt that the risk of accidental concussions is now a painful reality. On the other hand, size does offer some advantages: the Dutch are already a volleyball powerhouse, and if basketball ever catches on in the somehow misnamed Low Countries, they'll give the Michael Jordans of this world a run for their money.

What is truly remarkable is the Dutch are getting taller. While the average height in all first-world countries increased dramatically in the last century, this growth spurt has slowed down of late and seems to be leveling off. The increase in the average height of the Dutch, however, shows no sign of abating. In the last decade alone, the average height of 18 to 39-year-old men and women has increased by 0.9 (2.3) and almost 0.7 inches (1.7 centimeters). It is in this context that height has taken on an interesting significance in Dutch society. Enhancing one's stature has become surprisingly important. Techniques range from the large hats Dutch police-women wear – it makes them appear taller – to surgery. The Dutch are often critical – and rightly so – of cosmetic surgery, such as face-lifts, tummy-tucks and breast implants. That stated, every once in a while a particularly short Dutch man or woman (typically, shorter than five feet tall or some 1.5 meters) undergoes a fairly radical surgery called the Ilizarov procedure, in which a patient's femurs are broken and the bone ends are separated using a metal frame. Over time, the bones grow together and fuse, thereby increasing the patient's height. Aside from the pain and the risk of infection, there is nothing fundamentally wrong with the procedure and the patients usually seem pleased with the results. A similar technique is used in other countries, but it is reserved for cases of exceptional dwarfism. What defines that, I suppose, is a question of perspective.

Male tourists will encounter this quote-unquote difference in perspective the first time they go into a public bathroom. The urinals are mounted sufficiently high on the walls to make it almost impossible to use them, unless you stand on your tip-toes. Unfortunately, there are no boxes or phone books in the bathrooms to level the porcelain playing field and to give foreigners a much needed leg up! As a consequence, I always enjoy the look of shock on the faces of many male visitors in the Netherlands as they return from the wc (the Dutch phrase for toilet).

An exchange I once had with a Dutch friend is also illustrative. She was reading a Dutch magazine when I suddenly heard 'Tsk, tsk, tsk, tsk, tsk.' (A sound the Dutch like to make. In this case it conveyed sympathy.) 'That's terrible,' she said. I asked her what was wrong. 'There's a letter here from a mother whose daughter is only twelve years old and is already 183,' she replied. That seemed unremarkable, so I asked, 'Pounds or kilograms?' A bewildered look crossed her face and her head recoiled in shock. It took a few seconds for what I had said to sink in. Finally, she blurted out, 'No, *centimeters!*' (While there is nothing inherently wrong with being very tall, the Dutch mother was concerned that her daughter might be teased or could encounter other social problems.)

That conversation also emphasizes that, no matter how hard you try, you remain a product of your country of origin. People in many countries (in particular, Americans), even if they don't have the problem personally, are obsessed with weight. The Dutch are plagued by their size, although they seem to deal with their affliction better than most. As an aside, the Dutch still don't really have a weight problem. While there are overweight people in the Netherlands (the overall trend quali-tatively mirrors that found in other countries), obesity is less prevalent, and frankly, is never carried to the extremes that occur in places like the United States. How is this possible? Simple: they don't eat as much and what they do eat contains a lot less sugar and fat. If anything, some of the Dutch have the opposite problem with regard to weight. I know a few Dutch women, and even a few men, who are not anorexic, but do have an odd problem: they can't gain weight. They eat lots of junk food and still can't gain weight. What do you say to someone who tells you, with complete sincerity, that they have always wanted to know what it feels like to go on a diet? Welcome to a different world.

Aside from the general improvement in the standard of living over the last half-century and the more even distribution of wealth in Dutch society, the best explanation I've come across for the remarkable growth spurt in the Netherlands is their diet. Specifically, the infant diet. In a laudable program, the government-subsidized consultatiebureau provides regular advice to parents about their children's health and nutrition through four years of age. The objective is to improve the well-being of newborns. It has been an admirable success. The hypothesized impact on the height of the general population is apparently unintended. Alternatively, in a new twist to the age-old, nature-nurture argument, a few British colleagues once proposed a theory over beers in a pub. 'It's all a simple matter of natural selection,' they said. 'How's that?' I asked. 'What with all of those floods, only the tall could survive.'

1

The windmills of your mind are not playing tricks on you. You have (or your Dearly Beloved has) accepted that job in the Netherlands. The dust, created by the whirlwind consequences of this decision, has started to settle and you are beginning to wonder what type of country you have come to. Having read about culture shock in the preceding introduction, you now know that the best step towards familiarizing yourself with this new culture is knowing more about it. First off, relax in the knowledge that the Netherlands has one of the highest standards of living in the world. But what kind of people are the towering Dutch? What about their government and economy, religion, the climate, their customs and etiquette, particular ways of celebrating holidays and special occasions, and their oh-so-challenging language? This chapter will help you navigate through some of the canals of these riddles. In the end, the effort you put into rowing through uncharted territory will matter more than which way the wind is blowing.

The Netherlands in a Nutshell

CONTRIBUTING AUTHORS: SHIRLEY AGUDO, STEPHANIE DIJKSTRA, BEN VAN DER HAVE, MARK HOOKER, HAN VAN DER HORST AND STEVEN STUPP

HISTORY AND ITS INFLUENCE ON THE DUTCH OF TODAY

In the Middle Ages, there were many countships and the occasional duchies on the territory of the Netherlands, which for the larger part coincide with the current provinces. By way of a long historic process, the King of Spain inherited all of these in the second half of the 16th century. However, his hands were tied by the many privileges that the cities and rural districts had acquired in the time of the counts and dukes. These had to do with autonomy and other regulations, as a result of which the King was obligated to nominate the local governors from a predetermined select group of persons, recommended by the local prominent families.

Philip II's intention was to end these privileges. For his day and age, he was a modern ruler who believed in a powerful central authority that maintained the same procedures everywhere, and who based his decisions on the ethical and ideological principles of one sole religion, that of the Roman Catholic Church. However, in the Netherlands, there was much sympathy for Protestantism, especially that of John Calvin.

Philip II's ideas were therefore not met with much enthusiasm. There was a successful uprising – in which a central role was played by William of Orange, the patriarch of the Dutch royal family. William of Orange was a stadtholder – a representative of the king – in one of the countships, Holland, and he found he could not agree with the loss of the existing privileges nor with the persecution of the Protestants, which was a central element in the royal politics.

The uprising against Philip II resulted in the Republic of the Seven United Netherlands, in which the old privileges and local autonomy remained of central importance. This republic could be seen as a union of states – such as the CIS, the Commonwealth of nations that came into being after the dissolution of the USSR – in which the independent members were also part of a federal union. In such a system, no one could muster enough power to conquer a position of dominance in this republic and one only created enemies if one was too much of a braggart or made too much of a show of wealth and power. A high position could only be based on influence and not on power. Even the stadtholders, who were always recruited from the House of William of Orange – and who managed to make their position a hereditary one – could not do this. They had the authority originally vested in them by Philip II, subject to the many constraints that also came with the system of privileges and old rights.

To get something done in the old Republic required the formation of coalitions with others, while also making sure not to unnecessarily offend one's opponents. Central conditions to being successful were: respect for others, a modest life style, a willingness to listen and the capacity to restrain oneself. Calvinism, the source of this philosophy, was embraced in a liberal way by a majority of the elite, and was very influential.

The Netherlands is no longer a union of states, but rather a democratic state of which the unity is symbolized by the Queen, who is a descendant of William of Orange. However, the mentality of the Dutch has remained the same. Even though Dutch society has become strongly secularized, it is still greatly influenced by the Calvinistic philosophies. Still evident today is the strong Protestant work ethic with overtones of moderation in all aspects of life, decision-making by consensus, and the stymieing of individualism. In a country where ostentatiousness and boastfulness are akin to sinfulness, and where orderliness and cleanliness are next to godliness, showing off your wealth is still considered equal to showing a lack of respect, decisions are not taken without giving all those involved a chance to voice their opinion, and in most houses, the curtains are left open after dark, signifying that there is nothing to hide, as secretiveness is looked upon with suspicion. This is further reflected in the way in which the country is run, a system generally referred to as the 'Poldermodel'.

POLDERMODEL

A piece of land that is completely surrounded by a dike for the purpose of protecting it against high waters is called a polder in Dutch. You can find them in all shapes and sizes. The largest in the Netherlands, Flevoland (also the Netherlands' youngest province), measures 48,000 hectares. The management of such a polder requires a tight cooperation between the users. The smallest mis-take can result in disaster, as a dike is as strong as its weakest point.

Life behind the dikes has influenced the Dutch culture. It might be going too far to say that it has made the Dutch a democratic people, however, it is clear that they are partial to detailed agree-ments, to which they must strictly adhere. Foreigners never fail to notice the large degree of organization and planning in Dutch society.

This coming together to reach a consensus, this give and take in all the various areas, all characterize Dutch society and Dutch politics. It has resulted in, for instance, the downward adjustment of wage demands, the tolerance of drugs and the legalization of prostitution. This attitude can be summarized in a new word, invented by the British press in 1997: Poldermodel. This word represents all that makes Dutch society a successful one: a society in which the people literally and figuratively try to keep their feet dry.

THE DUTCH POLITICAL SYSTEM
IN BRIEF

THE GOVERNMENT
The Dutch government is what one calls a 'monarchical govern-ment', meaning that it is not only comprised of the ministers and the state secretaries, but also the monarch, Queen Beatrix. Another term for describing this is: a constitutional monarchy with a par-liamentary system, whereby the constitution has determined how the powers are divided between the Queen and the other institutions of the government. For instance, the parliament has been given certain rights allowing them to check the power of the government (listed further on in this chapter). However, though the Ministers are accountable to Parliament, the Queen, who has no political responsibility, is not.

THE CABINET
The cabinet's responsibilities are: preparing and implementing legislation, overseeing the local government, carrying out the day-to-day business of government and maintaining internation-al relations. There are currently 15 ministers and a Prime Minister (Jan-Peter Balkenende of the CDA). Furthermore, there are state secretaries (10) who are not members of the cabinet, but who do

(continued on page 30)

POLDERMODEL ON ITS WAY OUT?

A recent example of how the Poldermodel works, was given by the Minister of Social Affairs Aart Jan de Geus. Shortly after the second cabinet of Balkenende was installed, he announced sharp cuts and a sobering of the welfare state. He also observed that the Dutch would have to work longer in order to be able to maintain the current pension system. At the same time he made the rather vague announcement that the situation might be less dire if the increase in the wages – to which the Dutch has become accustomed during a decade of growth and welfare – could be reduced.

The unions had a fit. The two largest unions – the social-democratic and the Christian-based – called Minister De Geus every bad name they could think of; even the feared words 'anti-social' fell. Lodewijk de Waal, president of the social-democratic FNV, announced that we were in for a long, hot autumn. Upon which the Minister grumbled solemnly about the even greater cuts – not to mention an increase in unemployment – that would result from this attitude. Thus, the summer continued, with heated discussions, usually by means of the media, while, in the meantime, the research bureaus continued to publish somber statistics on the development of the economy.

De Waal got pretty worked up – he even organized warning strikes and mass demonstrations – and he uttered the most damning observation imaginable: namely, that apparently Minister De Geus was not interested in discussion.

If you didn't know any better, you would have thought the long, hot autumn was really on its way.

Those who really knew the Netherlands, however, knew better.

And then it was over. The Minister and the unions sat around the table, which, despite all the somber predictions on the outcome, produced acceptable results. The Minister postponed a number of measures and the unions promised – in connection with the unfortunate times – to not submit any wage increase demands for the time being.

And so the good relations were maintained, without any loss of face for any of the parties.

And this is how the Poldermodel works – though critics remarked that this was a case of sacrificing the long term to the short term, because the only thing the Minister really did was turn back measures that had once been introduced to allow early retirement. One day – they said, using a typical Dutch expression – the shore would turn back the ship.

Would you like to 'polder'? This takes some practice, and a lot of advice from a weary and wise Dutch expert. The central point is: you have to know exactly at which point to make concessions. If you do this too early, you will end up having to give away too much. If you are too late, an essentially un-Dutch conflict might be unavoidable. And the problem is; the poldering Dutch are not very good at restoring relations, once things have gone awry. Take, for instance, the relations between the Muslims and rest of the Dutch population in the after-math of the murder of film maker Theo van Gogh. The Dutch term for this shows how bad this really is: blood on the pole...

POLDERMODEL ON ITS WAY OUT?

According to many political experts, politicians in other countries can't wait to adopt the *Poldermodel*. Where there is much strife and discontent in politics and in the negotiations between employers and employees (unions) in other countries, the Netherlands is known for its lack of conflict. All thanks to the *Poldermodel* – a term coined abroad, as you read earlier.

However, the Dutch themselves are not as wild about the *Poldermodel* as one would expect them to be. This is not half as shocking as it may sound. The lack of conflict, the sharing of decision-making, the compromises – they are not the result of the *Poldermodel*. They are, if you will, the cause of the *Poldermodel*. They are inherent to the Dutch, who are very much inclined to consult, seek an agreement – and speak up.

That which constitutes the official *Poldermodel* is the plethora of middle level advisory bodies – and these are the ones that have been under fire for quite some time. Already in the early nineties, complaints could be heard about the 'treacly' nature of decision-making, thanks to the advisory bodies. Since then, many of them have disappeared or have been stripped of a great deal of their power. On the other hand, many responsibilities have been delegated directly to lower government levels, providing them with more leverage and an increased sense of effectiveness. In other words, the various forms of deliberation have been removed from the heading of *Poldermodel*, and simply been given a 'new coat', as the Dutch would say.

Consequently, should the *Poldermodel* officially be abolished, this will not make much of a difference in how things are done in the Netherlands – either politically, or in business – at all. When abolishing the *Poldermodel*, the Dutch will not be rejecting their atmosphere of deliberation, but simply weeding out a few (or, conceivably, many) redundant factors: a few committees, government bodies and *adviesorganen* (advisory bodies). But if these have proven themselves redundant, they would have disappeared under any system.

THE WATER BOARDS

Speaking of the Poldermodel and a tight cooperation between the inhabitants of the polder, is this just history or is water still being managed today? The answer is: it is just as important today as it was centuries ago and this responsibility rests on the shoulders of the water boards.

The Dutch water boards are responsible for everything that has to do with water; not only the maintenance of dikes and the draining of the lands, but also the quality of the water. Water boards thus play an important role in the environmental management of the country and are run by councils that are elected through a very complicated election system.

Whoever lives in the Netherlands becomes acquainted with the water boards by means of their utility bill, where they will find what they are to pay (in the form of an assessment) in connection with the purification of the water. If you are the owner of water systems, such as ditches, for instance, then you will make a more personal acquaintance with the water boards – which is the case for most Dutch farmers. Every year, they come and check the situation on your grounds, to see if your ditches are deep enough to fulfill their role in the draining of the land. If not, you can expect a hefty fine. This often leads to unpleasant conflicts between the water boards and landowners, who do not want their picturesque dike to be modernized and reinforced – at the expense of the landscape. Meanwhile, the water boards' concern is with safety.

In the future, the role of the water boards will become even greater, as the climate becomes increasingly wetter due to global warming, causing the water levels to rise, and thereby threatening one third of the Netherlands, which lies below sea level.

HOLLAND OR THE NETHERLANDS?

Now there's a good question: why is this country sometimes referred to as Holland and sometimes as the Netherlands? The official name of the country you have come to live in is the Netherlands, or *de Nederlanden*, also known as *Les Pays Bas* in French, and *Los Países Bajos* in Spanish. Literally translated, it means 'the Low Lands'; a country where 60% of the people live below sea level.

Then why is this country so often referred to as Holland? The answer to this question lies in its history. A few centuries ago, the province of Holland (which included today's North and South Holland provinces) was economically the strongest of all the Dutch provinces, and the one from which virtually all foreign trade originated. Most of the Dutchmen that foreign traders dealt with were Hollanders, literally from Holland. Hence, when talking about the Netherlands, this became the accepted way of referring to the country and its people. Over the years, both names have come to be accepted, although the preference seems to lean in favor of the official name, the Netherlands, when referring to the entire country.

SENSITIVITY

This is maybe a good time to give you, the unsuspecting 'expat', a little tidbit of information. Though it is generally accepted that the Netherlands is referred to as Holland, those who are not from the provinces of North or South Holland do not like to be referred to as Hollanders. The other Dutch provinces are: Friesland, Groningen, Drenthe, Limburg, Utrecht, Gelderland, Overijssel, Noord-Brabant, Zeeland and Flevoland (the latter came into existence only twenty-some years ago and consists entirely of reclaimed land). For a map of the provinces, see page 22.

RANDSTAD

Nowadays, it is of course no longer the case that the Holland provinces are the most advanced, though most businesses are still located in the provinces of North and South Holland and Utrecht – an area that is commonly referred to as the Randstad. The rest of the Netherlands is just as well developed and houses many international businesses and expatriates, and the infrastructure (road, rail, water and telephone) is excellent, no matter where you are in this country.

carry out some ministerial duties. The observant follower of Dutch politics will notice that the number of ministers tends to change from one cabinet to the next: for instance, in this cabinet, there are more ministers than in the former. This can be due to the introduction of a new post that resorts under an existing ministry, but that is considered sufficiently important under the current circumstances to warrant its own minister. A case in point is the Minister of Integration and Alien Policy. But it can also be due to the introduction of an entirely new ministry, such as that of Governmental Renovation and Deregulation.

THE PARLIAMENT

The Netherlands has a representative democracy and its parliament (*Staten Generaal*) is made up of two chambers: the Upper House (*Eerste Kamer*), whose 75 members are elected by the members of the provincial councils; and the Lower House (*Tweede Kamer*), whose 150 members are elected directly by the people.

The two Houses of Parliament have been given four rights: the right to set a budget; the right of interpellation; the right to put questions to ministers and state secretaries; and the right of inquiry. The Lower House has been given two further rights: the right of amendment and the right to propose legislation.

Until 1917, the Netherlands made use of the district system for elections. This was then replaced by proportional representation, making the country, province or municipality one single borough. And then there is the quota; if you divide the total number of votes collected by the number of seats in the representative body, you have a quota. In order to win a seat, you must attain this quota. For instance, the Lower House has 150 seats; in order to win a seat, one has to have won 1/150 of all votes. In this system, voters vote for a party that submits a list of candidates.

Since its foundation in 1966, the liberal left party D66 – the smallest partner in the current center-right cabinet – has been arguing for the reintroduction of the constituency voting system. This would bring the representatives of the people closer to their constituents. It has taken until now for them to achieve some of what they were aiming for; the government is looking to introduce a form of constituency voting, giving voters two votes, one according to the system of proportional representation and one for their district. The party has also achieved that, as of 2007, mayors will no longer be appointed, but elected. At the same time, their powers will be limited. Both proposals are considered very controversial in the Netherlands.

THE POLITICAL PARTIES

The Dutch Lower House of Parliament is elected by proportional representation and currently there are nine political parties in the Lower House. Traditionally, the three largest are the PvdA (Labor Party), the CDA (Christian Democrats) and the VVD (Liberals). The Labor Party, the Liberals and one of the smaller parties, D66 (the left-oriented Liberal Democrats), joined hands in 1994, giving the Dutch government its nickname: the Purple Government (*paarse regering*). This forced the CDA into the opposition, the first time since the beginning of the 20th century that there were no Christian politicians in the Dutch cabinet. 2002, election year, saw the introduction of a new major party: the LPF (*Lijst Pim Fortuyn*) which created great upheaval by becoming the second largest party in the country – after the CDA – generating a wholly differ-

ent division of votes among the parties. What happened next can be read under *Surviving the Recession*.

In summary, the PvdA is a social democratic party that has its roots in the trade union movement; the CDA is a merger of three confessional parties and bases its ideas on religious principles; while the VVD is a liberal party. The LPF was created by Pim Fortuyn, in reaction to the congested political culture of the Netherlands (reaction being the operative word here). The smaller parties that can be found in Parliament are: D66, Groen Links (a combination of greens, pacifists and communists), the Socialistische Partij and the fundamentalist protestant parties SGP, GPV and RPF. At the start of 2004, VVD-parliamentary member Geert Wilders was forced to leave his party, when he refused to accept his party's policy on aliens and their support for the admission of Turkey to the European Union. Wilders refused to relinquish his seat in the parliament, but announced his intention to start a new, rightist, political party aiming for the Pim Fortuyn-voters. The current prognoses for him are good, particularly since the murder of film maker Theo van Gogh. Towards the end of 2004, the polls predicted 20-30 seats for him, but Wilders was the first to acknowledge this sounded better than it necessarily was. Pim Fortuyn's experiences taught us that a large political constituency can easily evaporate under the glaring sun of political amateurism and inexperience.

Because there are so many political parties in the Netherlands, there are numerous coalition possibilities. Generally speaking, several months pass after the elections, during which, after extensive deliberation, a cabinet is formed with a program to which the majority of the members of parliament can give their approval. In the meantime, the prime minister tenders the resignation of the entire cabinet – which the Queen 'answers' by requesting the cabinet to stay on until there is a new one. The same happened in 2002, with the added excitement that, after few months, the new government collapsed and the Netherlands was left with a cabinet that was forced to tender its resignation (again) – resulting in new elections held on January 22, 2003.

Does this mean that the Netherlands does not have a government in the meantime? Of course not. After the cabinet's resignation, the incumbent ministers continue to run the country – until the new cabinet is formed (as the case may be: after a new election). However, decisions that might lead to extensive discussions in parliament are delayed until the new cabinet is in power. Any policies that the parliament approved of before the elections are continued. This seldom gives rise to any problems. In fact, it has often happened that the government that was on the way out approved a new budget, though it must be said that this is often a colorless document that mostly reflects a very careful management of the purse. When the 'real' cabinet then enters into power, it colors between the lines of the budget. The entering into power of the new cabinet, incidentally, happens from one day to the next, making it seem as if the 'old' ministers have but a morning to clear out their desks.

THE THREE LEVELS OF GOVERNMENT

The Netherlands not only has a central government, but also provincial and municipal governments and the water boards. The central government occupies itself with matters of national interest. The provincial governments concern themselves with social

SOME STATISTICS AND FACTS FROM 2004

- The total land surface area is 33,948 km²/21,218 mi². This excludes all inland and territorial waters wider than 6 meters/20 feet. If all the water surface area is included, the Netherlands has an area of 41,526 km²/25,954 mi²
- The Netherlands' North Sea coastline is longer (642 km) than its border with either Belgium (407 km) or Germany (556 km)
- About 60% of the population lives below sea level
- The highest point in the Netherlands is the Vaalserberg in the province of Limburg. It is 321 meters/1,053 feet above sea level
- The lowest point in the country is 6.76 meters/22.18 feet below sea level. It is in the Prince Alexander Polder northeast of Rotterdam (Nieuwerkerk a/d IJssel)
- Head of State: Queen Beatrix
- Type of state: constitutional monarchy
- Seat of government: The Hague
- Capital: Amsterdam
- Population: 16.3 million
- Non-native Dutch: 3,090,000 (19%)
- 'Western' non-natives: 1.4 million (0.9%)
- Number of households: a little over 7 million
- Average life expectancy men: 76.2 years, women: 80.8 years
- Average age: 38.7 (gradually increasing: in 1990, it was 36.6)
- Population growth: 40,000
- Immigrants: 90,000
- Emigrants: 110,000
- Seeking asylum: approximately 16,000 requests in 2004

- Labor force: 7.55 million
- Unemployment 2004: 681,000 (6.5% of the labor force)
- Unfit for work: 765,000
- Inflation 2004: 1.4%
- Economic growth 2004: 1.4%
- Expected growth 2005: 1.5%
- Gross National Product: approximately € 445 billion
- Religion: 6 out of 10 persons profess to being religious
- Exports: € 255 billion (+1.1%)
- Imports: € 227 billion
- Savings: increased by € 11 billion
- Most important trade partner: Germany
- Average income: € 23,000 net
- Average price of a house: € 218,000
- Number of cows: 19.4 million
- Number of pigs: 11 million
- Number of chickens: 80 million
- Number of farms: 85,000 (1995: 113,000)

work, cultural affairs, environmental management, spatial planning, energy and sports. The municipal governments occupy themselves with traffic, housing, social services, health care, sports, culture, water supply, public schooling and recreation. In order to help fund these activities, the provinces and municipalities receive government funding and levy their own local taxes. You can read more about the local taxes that may affect you and about the water boards on pages 93 – 94.

VOTING AND STANDING FOR ELECTION AS A NON-DUTCH NATIONAL
Voting
If you are an EU citizen, you are allowed to vote in municipal elections under the same conditions as Dutch nationals. This means that you must be at least 18 years of age on the day of the election and you must be a resident of a particular municipality on the day on which the candidates are nominated. If you are a non-EU national, you may vote under the same conditions; however, you must also have been a legal resident of the Netherlands for a continuous period of at least five years. For more information on whether you can be considered a legal resident for voting purposes, you can call the Ministry of Home Affairs (see the end of the chapter).

If you are a member of consular or diplomatic staff, you are not allowed to vote in the Netherlands, nor is your spouse/partner or children (if they are members of your household).

If you are an EU citizen, and a resident of the Netherlands, you are allowed to vote in elections for the European Parliament provided you do not vote in the same election in your home country, are 18 years of age or older, and are not disqualified from voting in the Netherlands or your home country.

Standing for Election
You can stand for election to *municipal councils* under the same conditions as stated above for voting. The only difference is that you must satisfy these conditions not on the day of nomination, but on the day you are admitted to the municipal council. You can also stand for election in Dutch elections to the European Parliament, provided you do not stand for election elsewhere.

SURVIVING THE RECESSION

The Netherlands is a country of even-tempered people. Its inhabitants are proud of their emotional sobriety and lack of the extreme emotions that can mark life so. The German poet Heinrich Heine once remarked that, if the world were to come to an end, he would emigrate to the Netherlands, as everything takes place 50 years later there. A remark that was considered something of a compliment here.

A YEAR OF EMOTIONS
For a while it seemed as if all this had changed, in 2002. This was a year of strong emotions, with crowds of people filling the streets of Rotterdam, expressing anger and mourning; a political about-face was made; there was scandal; there were more emotions. By the end of 2002, almost all political leaders had left the scene – the majority with a strongly damaged reputation. A political murder

had taken place. Highly-placed people – interestingly enough, from the world of politics and soccer – received bullets by mail. A new cabinet was formed – only to collapse within a matter of months. Suddenly, the Netherlands didn't feel safe anymore and a restitution of morals and values was urgently called for. The attitude towards the minorities and particularly immigrants became unpleasantly negative. It was almost as if the formerly cosmopolitan Netherlands was turning itself away from the world, to work on the restitution of its dreamed past in isolation. And for the first time in the history of the hitherto honorable parliament, common epitaphs were hurled at fellow politicians.
And all this was so unexpected.

BORING, PREDICTABLE FUTURE

At the start of the year, the political and economic establishment was still basking in the general appreciation it had been receiving towards the end of the century. Wim Kok, the social-democratic leader of the second *paarse* (purple – referring to the composition of the coalition – see earlier on) government was preparing a dignified exit. It was expected that the elections, which were to be held on May 15, would – with the exception of a few possible shifts – result in continuity and that Kok's crown prince and the esteemed leader of the PvdA in parliament, Ad Melkert, would take over where Kok left off. The Dutch people, who were very much accustomed to increasing prosperity, were headed towards a boring, predictable future of satisfied consumption.

BIRD OF PARADISE

Until a bird of paradise entered the Dutch political skies, a phenomenon, a man who contradicted everything people expected of politicians in the Netherlands: dr. Pim Fortuyn. Fortuyn was, above all, a flamboyant man. He lived in a mansion (at least according to Dutch standards) in Rotterdam, called Palazzo di Pietro. He had a butler called Herman, who also acted as his chauffeur, driving Pim Fortuyn to his appointments in his Daimler. Mostly, these were well-paid lectures for a financially well-off audience.
Fortuyn was a great performer, an inspirer, someone who could summarize what was on the minds of his followers. He also had a radar for societal trends.
His antenna for what occupied the people picked up on the undercurrent of dissatisfaction in society: the quality of life was not improving, people were starting to feel less and less safe in the streets and they felt surrounded by dangerous and unfathomable threats.

FUNDAMENTALIST ISLAM

These threats all of a sudden had a name, after September 11, 2001: fundamentalist Islam. Fortuyn had already written a booklet on the threat that Islam posed for Dutch society – which had been ridiculed in the press and shoved aside as the ideas of a misinformed xenophobe.

Body guards for VVD-parliamentary member Ayaan Hirsi Ali. Even in the bookstore where she is signing her book. She was also a target for the murderer of Theo van Gogh.

FIFTIES

But he came back with a vengeance. He declared openly that he wanted to become Prime Minister of the Netherlands – and soon. He would then immediately solve the country's big problems, as follows: a radical stop to immigration, followed by a strong integration policy. Anyone who came to live here, was expected to subscribe to the traditional norms and learn the language. Fortuyn also focused on the tremendous waiting lists for health care and the perceived lack of safety in the streets: the police, which had lost much of its authority, needed to win that back. His rhetoric held a lot of nostalgia for the fifties, when structures were clear and everyone knew where he stood.

LIJST PIM FORTUYN – LPF

After a short stint as the leader of a new political party, Leefbaar Nederland, Pim Fortuyn was dismissed and chose to continue campaigning under his own name; with a few friends from the business world, he started his own party, called Lijst Pim Fortuyn, or LPF.

MELKERT

The new party became a gathering point for the dissatisfied. The incumbent politicians hardly knew how to deal with the oratorical phenomenon. Some compared him to Haider and Le Pen – which Fortuyn denounced as demonization. In nothing flat, he wrote another booklet called *The Mess of Eight Years Purple* (the 'purple' cabinet) – which sold by the tens of thousands. He also zeroed in on his favorite enemy, Ad Melkert, who was to succeed Wim Kok – and who was everything Pim Fortuyn was not.
Melkert was an apparatchik, who strongly controlled his party and who – in Fortuyn's eyes – excelled in badly worded and meaningless pronouncements. Fortuyn managed to transform him into the manifestation of evil.

POLITICAL MURDER

However, there was one particular person to whom this was exactly what Pim Fortuyn was; a threat that should be eliminated. On May 6, 2002, Fortuyn was shot to death outside a radio station, ten days before the elections.
This was the first political murder in the Netherlands since the golden age.

COUNTER-THREATS

From the start it was pretty clear that the perpetrator had been acting of his own accord, but it took Fortuyn's followers a while to believe this. In their eyes, even if there had been no conspiracy, then the 'demonizing' of Fortuyn had created the atmosphere for this political murder. The counter-threats aimed at Ad Melkert and Paul Rosenmöller, the leader of the radical GroenLinks-party, were such that special protection had to be arranged for them.

ELECTIONS

Prime Minister Kok left it up to Fortuyn's survivors and the LPF, whether the elections should be postponed. They were of the opinion that they should go ahead as planned. Subsequently, the discredited purple cabinet was thrown out: both PvdA and VVD were reduced to half their former size. The CDA benefited from all this and became the largest party with 44 seats. One might say that the Dutch norms and values had won.

A new coalition was formed with the VVD and the LPF, which together held a huge majority, and the young Christian Democrat leader Jan Peter Balkenende, former professor of Christian-Social philosophy at the Calvinistic Vrije Universiteit, became the new Prime Minister.

HETEROGENEOUS LPF

Who, in the meantime, was in the LPF? Pim Fortuyn had, by means of a hurried recruitment process, put together a very heterogeneous list of characters. Number 2 on his list, for instance, was a young man from Cape Verde, who had rung his doorbell to express his admiration. Other people on the list were the owner of sex-websites and a former editor-in-chief of the weekly magazine *Elsevier*. His party also included politicians who had not quite made it in other political parties, as well as the leader of the union of pig farmers, an assortment of entrepreneurs and a few of the more individualist medical specialists. Their only common denominator was a rejection of 'purple' politics. They called themselves the inheritors of 'Pim's convictions'. What these convictions were, exactly, could be found in eleven little booklets and left plenty of room for disagreement, if only because Fortuyn had not been the most consistent of people and had been known to change his mind.
Mat Herben was chosen to be the party's political leader. Herben had been a civil servant with the Ministry of Defense, and had, until that point, acted a spokesman for Pim Fortuyn.

SCANDALS AND CONFLICT

It was therefore not easy for the LPF to find candidates for the cabinet. Well-known politicians and businessmen (and women) procrastinated. In the end, the party had to settle for acquaintances of some of the party members – leading to a scandal or two. Prime Minister Balkenende was forced to stand by and watch as the LPF was riddled by internal – personal – conflict.

RESIGNATION AND NEW ELECTIONS

Towards the end of October, Balkenende gave up, after it became clear that the cabinet could not continue like this. He tendered the its resignation and Queen Beatrix advised him to call a new election, which took place in January, 2003.

BACK TO BUSINESS

As soon as Balkenende's cabinet had imploded, the politicians of the other parties declared smugly how clear it was that politics was not something for amateurs, but for professionals. They started to prepare for what they considered business as usual – after a short aberration during 2002.
The question is, of course, whether that will be possible. For starters, Fortuyn's presence had made an end to the career of a number of old political leaders. Ad Melkert (PvdA) went to the World Bank in Washington, Paul Rosenmöller (GroenLinks) decided to leave politics altogether, Hans Dijkstal, of the VVD, disappeared from the scene after the elections of May 15 and Thom de Graaf, whose party, D66, was punished by the voters, was subjected to heavy criticism.

NEW GOVERNMENT

It would appear that the January 2003 elections proved the professional politicians right. PvdA, which had suffered much dis-

THE ROYAL FAMILY

THE MEMBERS

In the Netherlands, the Dutch Royal Family and the 'Royal House' are not the same. Not every member of the Orange Nassau family is a member of the Royal House. The Royal Family is made up of Queen Beatrix, her sisters, their spouses and their children and grandchildren. Who becomes a member of the Royal House has been determined by law and consists of the Head of State (currently, Queen Beatrix), her children and their spouses (with the exception of Prince Johan Friso and his wife Mabel, see further on) and grandchildren, as well as one of her sisters and her husband, and their children and their spouses.

Members of the Royal House who marry without the official approval of the parliament, lose the right to succeed to the Throne – an issue that came to bear when Crown Prince Willem-Alexander announced his engagement in 2001 and again when and his brother Johan Friso announced his engagement in 2003. Johan Friso as well as two of Queen Beatrix's sisters lost the right to the throne by marrying without this permission.

POLITICAL POSITION

The King (or Queen, as it turns out), together with the ministers, forms the government. It was determined in 1848 that the ministers, and not the King, are responsible for acts of government. Laws that have been passed by the parliament, and Royal Decrees, are signed by both the King (Queen) and the minister in question, lending it the authority of the Head of State and placing the responsibility for it with the minister.

After elections, the Queen, upon the recommendation of the Vice President of the Council of State, the Presidents of both Houses of the States-General, the presidents of the parliamentary groups of the political parties and sometimes the Minister(s) of the State, appoints the so-called (in)formers (*formateurs* or *informateurs*) who are to form a new cabinet, based on the outcome of the election. Once the political parties have reached an agreement on the program of the new cabinet, the Queen appoints and swears in the new ministers and state secretaries. Every year, on the third Tuesday of September, called *Prinsjesdag*, the Queen and members of her family ride in the royal Golden Coach from her palace on the Noordeinde to the Binnenhof, where the government is housed. Here the Queen holds her famous speech, called the *Troonrede*, before the members of the Upper and Lower House, in which government's policies of the coming year are set out. Prinsjesdag is a popular outing for schools, but also for grown-ups and tourists, who come to The Hague to admire the beauty of the royal procession and the atmosphere of yesteryear.

2002: A YEAR OF MILESTONES

February of 2002 saw the wedding between Crown Prince Willem Alexander and his beautiful bride Máxima Zorreguieta. This wedding was preceded by a few political complications, as the Constitution requires that the parliament approve any royal weddings in advance, due to the fact that the Crown Prince and his wife (will) fill a civic function. Máxima Zorreguieta's father fulfilled the position of Under-Secretary of State for Agriculture in the military regime of Argentina of the 1970s, a time during which many were persecuted in that country. Could the daughter of a man who might be held politically responsible for such actions become the wife of the Crown Prince of the Netherlands? The Dutch are generally of the opinion that the sins of the fathers may not be visited upon their children; on the other hand, the question remained whether father Zorreguieta was a person who could be included and welcomed at the State ceremonies. Prime Minister Kok made it clear that Mr. Zorreguita – who bowed out graciously – would not be present at the wedding ceremonies. The wedding was subsequently approved almost unanimously by the parliament.

Had things gone differently, Willem Alexander could still have married his fiancée, only he would have lost his right to the throne and seen one of his brothers become King. This was not the only event in 2002: in June, Queen Beatrix's and Prince Claus's first grandchild was born to Prince Constantijn and Princess Laurentien – a girl named Eloise. And, to the sorrow of the Dutch population, Prince Claus passed away on October 6, after years of deteriorating health. Prince Claus was a man of dignity and modesty, who managed to fulfill a very public but obligatorily un-political position with dedication and success, pouring much of his energy and convictions into translating his love for Africa, where he had lived as a child, into developmental aid for the African countries. For several days, tens of thousands of people went to the Queen's working palace – where his body lay in state – to pay Prince Claus their last respects.

2003: ANNUS HORRIBILIS

In 2003, Queen Beatrix had an *annus horribilis*, as her colleague Queen Elizabeth II of the United Kingdom might call it. Twice – just after the death of her husband Prince Claus – the family was brought into the spotlight in an unpleasant way. In both cases, the subject was the choice of partner of members of the Royal Family.

In the spring of 2003, Princess Margarita (daughter of Queen Beatrix's younger sister Irene) and her husband Edwin de Roy van Zuydewijn, sought publicity in order to utter strong accusations towards the Queen and her father, Prince Bernhard. To this purpose, they used the magazine *HP/De Tijd*, which was loudly proclaiming its newfound conservatism at that time. The couple had a lot to tell about the various relations within the Royal Family. They accused the Queen and Prince Bernhard of trying to sabotage their marriage and subsequently – when this failed – to ruin De Roy van Zuydewijn's company. They also claimed that the Queen had used the RVD (the National Government Information Service) to investigate De Roy van Zuydewijn. They announced that they would bring the Royal Family to court.

The Prime Minister, Jan Peter Balkenende, was forced to admit that the services of the National Government Information Service had indeed been enlisted, which put the Royal Family in a painful position. On the other hand, Princess Margarita and De Roy van Zuydewijn lost quite a bit of credibility by acting overly paranoid and ending up in conflict with their own lawyers.

And then, in the fall, Queen Beatrix announced that her second son, Prince Johan Friso, was to marry Mabel Wisse Smit. Mabel Wisse Smit was well known in the world of human rights and the Queen made it apparent that she was quite pleased with this union.

Just as Crown Prince Willem-Alexander before him, Johan Friso had to ask the parliament permission to marry Mabel. However, in the meantime, the media had been digging around in Mabel's past and produced evidence of the fact that, while at university during the eighties, she had had a rather intimate relationship with a well-known Dutch criminal, who was eliminated by his competition in 1991.

This was news to the Prime Minister, who was quite vocal of his disapproval. He decided to not even give Johan Friso the opportunity to ask permission for the marriage, so that the prince lost his right to the throne.

The marriage still went through, however, and Queen Beatrix let it be known that she had not lost faith in Mabel.

THE FUTURE QUEEN

The year ended on a happy note. On December 7, Princess Máxima, the wife of Crown Prince Willem-Alexander, gave birth to a daughter, Princess Catharina-Amalia. As the Dutch Constitution does not allow discrimination on the basis of sex, she will succeed Prince Willem-Alexander to the throne, even if he were to have sons after her. The good news is, that it became apparent, towards the end of 2004, that Princess Máxima is once again pregnant.

2004: THE LOSS OF A FORMER QUEEN AND HER HUSBAND

In the spring of 2004, Princess Juliana, former Queen of the Netherlands (from 1948-1980) passed away at the respectable age of 95. As had her mother before her, she had indicated that she preferred the title 'Princess' to that of 'Queen Mother', after her abdication. Queen Juliana had been known for her concern for social issues, particularly children, and had donated great sums of money to national and international causes for the support and protection of children. The Netherlands remembers its former Queen – an informal, caring and motherly monarch – with tenderness, which was clearly evident during her funeral.

In December, her widower-husband, Prince Bernhard, passed away, too. Prince Bernhard had always been a bon vivant with excellent business contacts (to the great benefit of this country during the reconstruction years after the Second World War) – and was a man not inclined keeping his thoughts to himself. At least, not as much as one would normally expect from a constitutional prince. Despite his German heritage, the Prince clearly sided with the Netherlands during the Second World War, earning him great appreciation among the members of the underground resistance.

In keeping with his wishes, the Prince's funeral had a strong military character. After the funeral, a number of interviews appeared in the media, which he had only given permission to publish after his death.

In these, he shared with us his views on the various (corruption) scandals he had been involved involved in during his long life. The Dutch people, however, were clearly willing to forgive him – and not only that, they rather enjoyed the old scoundrel's confessions.

And none of it damaged the reputation of the Royal Family.

Palace Soestdijk in 1976. Prince Claus, far left, died in 2002. Princess Juliana and Prince Bernhard passed away in 2004. Queen Beatrix has been the Head of State since April 30, 1980 and will be celebrating her 25th anniversary in 2005.

pleasure, returned, still going strong, under Wouter Bos. Also the VVD regained a lot of its votes – while the LPF was reduced from 26 to eight seats. At least this allowed the political establishment to work on a more conventional type of coalition. In their eyes, the LPF had proven itself to be negligible.

After long negotiations, a coalition government was created under Jan Peter Balkenende, with ministers from CDA, VVD and D66. It was clearly a conservative cabinet, which – with power and conviction – continued with the cuts that had been introduced in 2002. Several of the ministers declared that the reasons for this were not only common sense but also ideological; it was time for the people to take responsibility and to no longer hide under the protective umbrella of the state.

POLDERMODEL GOING STRONG

In the meantime, the Poldermodel-approach continued to go on strong, as was evident from the agreement reached between the government and the unions in the autumn of 2003. The summer of 2004 saw a new conflict between the unions and the government – whereby the employer organizations appeared to have more sympathy for the employees than for the government. Harsh words were exchanged – which was immediately labeled as un-Dutch – and the unions reacted to the 2005 budget with a series of strikes and a mass demonstration, attended by 200,000 people, in Amsterdam. This was the largest demonstration in almost 25 years. It was clear that the participants were simply demanding new negotiations and a return to the Poldermodel. Which is precisely what happened. After long and difficult negotiations, with the help of intermediaries, the relationship of trust between the unions, the employers and the government was restored, as the Minister of Social Affairs mitigated the proposed measures aimed at discouraging early retirement and at reducing certain benefits and the unions guaranteed social 'calm' and agreed to a maintaining of the current salaries. And this was precisely what everyone had hoped for.

FORTUYN'S CONVICTIONS

Still, the convictions of the LPF remained visible in the new cabinet's program. Law and order, the virtues of being strict and the need for safety played a main role in the ministerial communications. Polls showed that the discontent, on which Pim Fortuyn had built his spectacular success, continued to exist. There was still some rightist-populist grumbling, and the magazine HP/De Tijd acquired a lot of new subscribers after a printing the solemnly official confession to being conservative on its cover: 'Help, we've become rightist!'

IMMIGRANT POLICY

The Dutch government tried to prove itself a reliable heir to Fortuyn's ideas but introducing a strict admission policy for immigrants. Rita Verdonk, Minister of Immigration and Integration, worked on a plan that forced all who spoke insufficient Dutch and/or was otherwise 'undereducated' to follow a familiarization course. To be paid for out of their own pocket. If the person in question passed the exam, then he could expect a restitution of the course fees – which could amount to several thousand euros.

ANOTHER MURDER

Still, xenophobia appeared to be on the increase – though it appeared to be primarily aimed at Muslims, so much so that it became more an ethnic term than a religious one. Furthermore, Muslims became synonymous with Moroccans, even though the Moroccans only constitute a minority of the Dutch Islamic community. The murder of Theo van Gogh gave it all a nastier twist, convincing the Dutch that this country was not immune to Muslim terrorism and strengthening the point of view that terrorism is inherent to Islam. The government and the media hastened to point out that Islam deserved as much respect and appreciation as all other religions and that an entire community could not be held accountable for the acts of a handful of fanatic individuals. And during the Dutch presidency of the European Union in the second half of 2004, Prime Minister Balkenende and Minister Bot of Foreign Affairs successfully pleaded for a long-term admission of Turkey to the EU.

ECONOMY

The Netherlands is in the world top ten in export volume and it ranks in the world's top twenty for GNP, even though, in terms of square kilometers, it is one of the smallest countries of the world. Though it is true that, in population density, it is on a par with countries such as India and Japan, nonetheless this only amounts to a population of almost 16.3 million.

GATEWAY TO EUROPE

The Netherlands owes its favorable ranking, among others, to its advanced transport infrastructure, with, at its hub, both the port of Rotterdam and Schiphol Airport, and its advanced telecom infrastructure, which help support the Netherlands position as *'the gateway to Europe'* (Rotterdam is the world's largest seaport – fourth largest in terms of container activity – and Schiphol Airport is the fourth largest airport of Western Europe).

MONEY FROM ABROAD

Traditionally, the Netherlands has been a country that other countries were eager to invest in, which has been reflected by the huge investments made over the years. This willingness to invest in the Dutch economy is largely due to the country's stable and flexible work environment (thanks to the Poldermodel), its central geographic location, its well-educated multilingual work force and the amount of know-how available here.

PEOPLE FROM ABROAD

Individuals, often enticed while traveling here to stay and find jobs, are as motivated as companies are to settle in the Netherlands, particularly since the opening of the frontiers within the European Union.

ECONOMIC GROWTH

Over 2004, the Netherlands managed a modest bounce-back. Its import and export volume increased – already in the third quarter, the economic growth was the highest in three years – restoring some of this country's European trade partners in popularity. It is said that the Netherlands is relatively slow to adjust to the developments of worldwide economy – both upswings and downswings – partially due to the costs of labor (wages and pension premiums). Annually, measures are taken to encourage those who are long-term unfit for labor or receive some other benefit to re-enter the labor market and one of the newer measures is the removal of fiscal encouragement to go into early retirement in order to miligate the effect.

The Netherlands, as a country of trade, is dependent on the economic well-being of the rest of the world, and overall the world appears to be feeling better. Consequently, the export of goods and services increased and volume in the trade and transport sectors went up. Also, the yield of the land was better, not only in terms of crops (agriculture contributed the most to the economic growth) but also of gas, which was subsequently exported. However, when looking at which sectors contributed to the improved economic situation of the country, it is clear that all sectors, with the exception of the construction industry, experienced an upswing. Imports in particular from Slovakia, Malta and Lithuania increased, as did exports to Argentina, Taiwan and China.

SECTORS

As the 'gateway to Europe', the Netherlands' most dominant sector is the services sector, accounting for approximately two-thirds of both its GNP and its work force. Another important sector is the agricultural and food sector; it generates approximately 10% of the GNP and 75% of the agricultural produce is exported. This year, the agricultural sector fared better than in the recent past, but still farmers are choosing to leave this industry at a some-times alarming rate: some say that only a year ago an average of eight to ten farmers a day closed their gates behind them.

Which sectors are growing, momentarily? At the moment trade and transportation are faring well, while there is also a slight increase in the commercial services sector. The non-commercial services sector – government, education and health care – has been the fastest growing sector over the last several years but appears to be stabilizing right now.

CHEMISTRY AND FUEL

Other factors that continue to influence the Dutch economy favorably are the fact that the world's largest chemical companies are based here, while the Netherlands is one of Europe's largest suppliers of high-tech goods for both the industrial and the consumer market. Additionally the Netherlands is also Europe's largest producer of natural gas, as witnessed by its reserves in the north of the country, while Rotterdam imports and refines huge amounts of crude oil that is shipped to the rest of western Europe. Thanks to these offshore installations and refineries, the Netherlands has many activities in the oil and gas industries, including a strong research and development technology and a specialized construction industry.

FARING WELL AND WELFARE

All in all, this makes the Netherlands a wealthy country, with a high per capita GDP boosted by social security measures guaranteeing a minimum income, health care and education. When, a few years ago, it became apparent that the country would not be able to sustain its level of welfare, support and tax cuts, it introduced a number of measures aimed at reducing the government's contribution to some of these programs. Also Balkenende's two cabinets have given further spending cuts and revenue-generating measures priority. Yet, though there are undeniably people

POPULATION: the population is still growing, though the pace is definitely slowing down. In 2004, the Netherlands saw 40,000 new inhabitants, 25,000 fewer than in 2003 – which was already down 29,000 from 2002. This was caused by a decrease in the number of immigrants (even fewer than last year, which was already at its lowest level since 1995) and an increase in the number of emigrants (the highest ever, surpassing even last year).

ASYLUM SEEKERS: the number of persons seeking asylum went down by 44% over 2002, by 30% over 2003 and yet another approximately 25% over 2004. This has to do with the stricter asylum policies in the Netherlands. By far the greatest number of asylum seekers are from Iraq, then Afghanistan.

UNEMPLOYMENT: 2002 saw the end to a long period of decreasing unemployment – a trend that continued throughout 2004. The prognosis for 2005 and beyond is that not only will the number of job-seekers increase, but also the number of vacancies and new jobs, creating possibilities for the placement of (long-term) unemployed persons. Some predictions even state that the number of jobs in some sectors will increase by as much as 20% – such as in retail, the medical (care) sector and 'other' business services (real estate, employment agencies and security). The number of persons disabled for work has gone down; for the first time since 1994, there was not only no increase, but a decrease.

CONSUMPTION: over the first eight months of 2004, general expenditures showed a modest increase of 0.4%. After that, they more or less stagnated. The expenditures on food and alcohol remained more or less the same, while expenditures on durable goods, such as clothes, furniture and cars, went down.

INFLATION: inflation was at its lowest in 16 years! This was largely due to the low prices for food and non-alcoholic beverages, thanks to the competitive price war between supermarkets. It also helps that the prices for audio and video equipment, computers and software went down by almost 11%. The price of tobacco products went up by 16.1% and the price of fuel by 7.9%. A variety of municipal and other levies were also raised over 2004.

ECONOMY: in 2004, the Netherlands experienced modest economic growth in increasing percentages over the four quarters of the year. It did not achieve the growth of the surrounding countries, due to a variety of factors listed elsewhere in this chapter. Judging by the Amsterdam Stock Exchange, the sectors that did well were construction, insurances and, in particular mineral exploration. Others, such as transportation, trade and (non) financial services, showed moderate increase, while capital goods performed poorly.

TRADE: trade (import and export) with both EU and non-EU countries, with the exception of January, showed tremendous increase, over some months by as much as 20%. In particular, 2004 saw an increase in imports from Malta, Lithuania and the Slovakia (in terms of percentage) and in exports to Argentina, Taiwan and China (in terms of percentage). In terms of volume, China – for the first time – obtained a place in the top-5 trade partners (for imports) of the Netherlands, after Germany, Belgium, the US and the UK.

FINANCES: after initially going up, the Amsterdam stock market started to go down; reaching its lowest point for 2004 in August. After this, it started to climb again, ultimately coming out higher than it had been at the start of the year.

PRICES OF HOUSES: on average, the price of houses went up by 2.5% over 2004 (0.9%) over the last quarter). Particularly around the city of Eindhoven and in the province of Groningen, the housing market did well. There were, of course, also areas where the price went down, such as around Zutphen and Almere.

who are less well off, and who have to scrimp and save to make ends meet, life here is very good. All you have to do is pick up a magazine or turn on the television to know how good life is here.

PREDICTIONS 2005

2004 was a year of modest improvement and economic growth for the Netherlands; however, the expectations are that over 2005, the economic growth will experience a slight setback, due to a worldwide 'pause' in growth, the increase in the value of the euro, an increase labor unit costs and a slight fallback in consumer spending. Exports are still expected to increase – though not in the same volume as they did over 2004. It is also unclear what the effect of the tsunami of December 26, 2004 will be; particularly India was a country where a reasonable percentage of the Netherlands' exports went to, while Dutch imports from Thailand have also been substantial. Analysts note that the world economy has been resilient in the face of disasters and terrorism and that the economies of in particular India, Thailand and Indonesia – thanks to three years of economic growth – are in a relatively strong position for recovery. Nonetheless, all the effects of the disaster are not yet clear and it is, of course, to be expected that spending patterns in these countries will be different over 2005 from what might have been initially planned.

As for inflation; as was expected, inflation went under the 2%-mark in 2004, to 1.2%. Inflation will remain more or less the same over 2005, thanks to the increase in oil prices in 2004, the decreasing effect of the so-called supermarket-wars (who competed by openly and, sometimes, dramatically lowering prices), and the announced raise in fuel prices overall. These upward effects will be somewhat mitigated by the increase in the value of the euro, making imported goods relatively cheaper and the beginning decreases in labor prices. Both the number of new jobs and the number of vacancies is expected to increase; however, so is the number of new persons entering the labor market. A good sign is the fact that the number of temp jobs is on the increase, which would seem to indicate that business are starting to look for new employees – carefully, through employment agencies first. Unemployment is expected to be around 6.75%.

CLIMATE

BORING!

The Netherlands does not have the most exciting of climates. Of course, there are magnificent winter and glorious summer days but, if truth be told, just not too many. This can be very hard to take for those who have not grown up here (and even for those who have!). Many expats comment on how the gray skies make it all so much harder to get up and go out in the mornings and how, during several months of the year, it is still dark when you have to get up and dark again by the time the breadwinner comes home for dinner. What are the facts and how do you get through this?

WINTER

Let's take December. During the last three decades of the 20th century, the average temperature during that month was 4° C – hardly North Pole conditions. The last very cold December days of that century were in 1995, when the average temperature was -0.9° C

(also not very shocking). However, in the winter of 2001-02 and the next, the temperature somewhere in Groningen did go down to -17° C – which was more like it.

And how about January? January is known as the month of ice – but does it deserve this name? Not according to the Dutch Meteorological Institute (KNMI); only the occasional January has been good and cold – notably in 1996 and 1997, giving the Netherlands its last *Elfstedentocht* (see page 235) of the century in 1997.

WESTERN WINDS

Dutch winters have been heating up over the course of the 20th century. This is blamed on the uncommon strength of the western winds over the last couple of years, allowing the warm temperatures of the seas (7° C) to influence the winter temperature, rather than the winds that come in from the north-east. Unfortunately, this also means more precipitation, which, due to the fact that the winters are momentarily quite mild, amounts to an awful lot of rain. Hence the dreary, bleak, rainy, insufficiently cold winters.

SUMMERS

And the summers? They say July 1994 was the warmest July in 300 years and certainly in the 20th century. On third place for the century was July '95, with July '99 and July '91 on sixth and seventh place respectively. However, 2003's summer was so sunny that it broke all records since 1901! There was a two-week heat wave and temperatures reached 37.8° C in some places – among the highest ever.

The Netherlands is known for its wishy-washy summers in both senses; warm and dry one year, cool and wet the next – or warm and dry this week, cool and wet the next. Whether or not you can pack up your tent and enjoy the local vacation spots depends entirely on your luck. A note: though cool and wet summers immediately spark the global change discussion, Dutch summers have been this way since before the Middle Ages, assures the KNMI (Dutch Meteorological Institute).

THE DUTCH MENTALITY

The Dutch position on the international market is a strong one. This is not necessarily because the Dutch are the cheapest; it is not easy to be the cheapest, coming from a country where the wages are high and the social provisions the same. What the Dutch need to focus on is an optimal ratio between quality and price and their legendary dependability.

You can find daily proof of this mentality of dependability. At the bus stops, the time the bus will be there is specified to the minute. For instance, 18.06, 17.46 and 19.08. This is not a statement of intent. It is an aim the buscompany will seek to achieve that will be sought with all possible means. Should the bus be late due to a traffic jam or any other form of delay, the atmosphere among the passengers will plummet. They will steal quick, irritated glances at their watches. They will start to pace restlessly. If they have a mobile phone, they will make a call. And when the bus arrives, five minutes late, the transportation company will have scored badly.

This reaction of the passengers is less irrational than it seems. Arriving on time and keeping an appointment are key issues in Dutch society. Now that the bus is late, you might miss the tram or the train and thus be delayed even further. This can mean trouble for you, but also for the others who are expecting you. They will not be able to make optimal use of the time allotted to the appointment, or the appointment might go overtime, which will further upset their agenda.

Nonetheless, this notorious system of appointments and agendas is surprisingly flexible and efficient, if you keep the main rules in mind: you must make an appointment for everything and you must stick to the agreed time.

P.S. On the NS (railway)-website, they even keep score of their weekly punctuality over a period of five weeks; www.ns.nl, click on *over NS* ...

SURVIVING

So, how do you survive? Step one is to simply accept the facts, rather than fight them or hope for anything else. As for the summers, you simply make a choice: either you go find a place where the sun is guaranteed to shine (home?) or you decide you want to see more of the country and will take the weather as it comes. As for the winters; December is easy. This is the month of lights and candles for the holiday season – and they will presumably brighten your spirits considerably. And January, February and March? If you are not off skiing or vacationing, this is a good time to light the fire in the fireplace (if you have one) and settle down for some good reading. Get together often with friends, have sinful 'high teas' of your own making, eat good hearty meals, turn on all the lights, paint a wall in the living room a yellowish/orange-ish color, so that the light reflecting off of it will feel like sunlight. In short, go in search of some *gezelligheid*. (For things to do with kids, check out chapter 7). And spend a lot of time by the window. Though this will unfortunately expose you to the gray winter skies, it will also expose you to whatever sunlight there is to be had – an absolutely necessary ingredient in combating the winter blues. And whenever the sun comes out: go for it!

2004

During 2003, seven months ended in the top ten of the list of sunniest months of each type (i.e. February and March were the sunniest February and March ever), spoiling us a little for 2004...

In 2004, the average temperature was 10.3° C, making this the eighth year in a row in which it exceeded 10° C. Still, though we had an official heat wave between August 2 and 11, last year can be looked back upon with mixed feelings: whereas April and August generated above average temperatures, May and July were below average – causing us all to store, take out and store away again our warmer sweaters. Furthermore, July and parts of August were so wet that we had the wettest summer since 1951. All in all, it more or less depends on who you are talking to, how they qualify the weather of 2004:

3 days of ice (maximum temperature < 0° C) (*6 in 2003*)
65 days of frost (minimum temperature < 0° C) (*75 in 2003*)
89 warm days (maximum temperature > 20° C) (*116 in 2003*)
25 summer days (maximum temperature > 25° C) (*48 in 2003*)
3 tropical days (maximum temperature > 30° C) (*12 in 2003*)

CUSTOMS AND ETIQUETTE

Before you put your proverbial foot in your proverbial mouth, here are some lessons picked up at the school of hard knocks, where the price of tuition is a lot higher than learning it here.

PERSONAL SOCIAL SPACE

Dutch social space is determined in great part, it is deemed, by the lack of physical space that is available in Holland. Granted, everything and everyone is very close together. Holland has the highest average population density in the world: 452 inhabitants per km^2. (Japan's average population density is only 334 inhabitants per km^2.)

Theory has it that the Dutch compensate for this lack of physical space by making their personal social space wider, so that they can better deal with the problems of living in such a crowded society.

Observe, however, the Dutch standing in line, if you can find one. They normally stand much closer together than Americans do. Americans tend to feel uncomfortable if you stand that close to them in line. American social connections, on the other hand, are much more intimate than Dutch social connections. While Americans interact with people with seeming informality and call everyone by his or her first name, Dutch interaction is generally stylized and formal. Calling a Dutch person by first name when you are not supposed to is like talking to an American with your nose three inches from his. You are invading his space and that makes him feel uncomfortable.

The extended Dutch social space is viewed by many foreigners as standoffishness, but to the Dutch it is just a way of coping with life in a small shoebox. As long as you are polite enough to respect other people's social space, they will politely respect yours and tolerate almost anything you want to do – testimony to a nation dually praised and criticized for its tolerance – as long as you keep it inside your social and personal space and out of theirs.

GETTING A WORD IN EDGEWISE

Oddly enough, the amount of time that the Dutch pause at the end of a sentence to indicate that they have finished talking and someone else can take a turn is a lot less than it is in English. Even when they speak English, the Dutch still use the same short 'change-speakers' pause to give others a chance to join the conversation. Until you get used to it, you may not get much said, because you may not recognize the shorter pause as a signal to say something, and thereby miss your turn, feeling like they're rudely cutting you off. The cue to change speakers is something that you normally perceive subconsciously, based on years of experience listening to other people talk. Just being aware that there is a difference between cultural modes is usually all you need to reset the length of time that you recognize as a change-speakers' cue, so that you can get a word in edgewise.

VISITING

Generally, the Dutch do not like company to stop by informally, if they just happen to be 'in the neighborhood'. If you know someone very well, you can call in the morning to ask if you can come by that evening, but normally you should call further in advance. The greater the social distance between you, the longer in advance you need to call. Grown children even call their parents – and vice versa – to see if it is all right to come by for a visit.

FASHIONABLY LATE

Conversely, do not invite Dutch acquaintances to 'drop by anytime'. Set a specific time, date and specify what you intend to serve. 'Come by next Tuesday at two for coffee' and they will be there at the stroke of two. 'Fashionably late' in Holland is waiting for the bell on the tower clock to finish ringing before you ring the doorbell.

COFFEE

Since the Dutch do not like 'surprise' company, the coffee will be ready to pour when you arrive. Yours should be too. An offer of coffee (or tea) is the absolute minimum expected when someone visits your home. Even the workmen who come to fix a leaky faucet will be offered a cup of coffee. Suffice it to say that there will also be cookies, or, if this is a special occasion like a birthday or anniversary, pastries. *ALWAYS WAIT TO BE SERVED*. It's considered very impolite to help yourself. Conversely, do not forget to offer your Dutch guests a second round of coffee, tea, or cookies; they will not help themselves.

A couple we know, who speak no Dutch, went to visit friends in Holland and when they came back, they were proud to announce that they had learned the Dutch word for 'Hello'. *Koffie?* he said

PROSTITUTION, DRUGS AND EUTHANASIA

High on the to-do list of every visitor to the Netherlands, right up there with the famed museums, is a walk on the wild side of seemingly sedate Dutch society: a tour of the red-light district in Amsterdam. The wallen ('the walls'), as that part of town is known, lives up to its billing. Everything you expect is there. Teeming crowds juxtaposing businessmen and tourists; prostitutes publicly ensconced in the windows of the numerous business establishments; the quote-unquote coffee shops that sell everything from Thai stick to space cakes – coffee is definitely not the specialty of the house.

POINT OF VIEW

After soaking in the sights for a few minutes, you may notice an unexpected aspect of human nature: the only thing that makes the goings-on into a spectacle is your point of view. Having spent some time in the Netherlands, you probably aren't surprised that everything is well organized (the Dutch police even have an English-language how-to-guide to help tourists safely explore the steamier side of the city); but you probably did not expect it to be 'dead normal', as the Dutch say. The only difference between the streets of the red-light district and other shopping districts in the city is the merchandise. While there are prostitutes and drugs in every large city, Dutch or otherwise, in the Netherlands both businesses are given an air of legitimacy that exceeds that found in most other countries. Like so many other visitors, you marvel at the tolerant Dutch in action.

CLICHÉS

Noting that the Dutch are tolerant, however, is not exactly a radical discovery. Social experiments in the Netherlands are sufficiently renowned that such comments are almost clichés. But there is more to this than just being open-minded. Most visitors are shocked when they learn that until recently prostitution was illegal and that the possession or sale of recreational drugs remains against the law. After one day in Amsterdam, it is hard to believe that any of this ever was a criminal offense – which, in a sense, is correct: even when illegal, these activities occurred and thrived with the tacit approval of the local community and the Dutch government.

TURNING A BLIND EYE

How does one reconcile the contradiction? Activities were or are illegal yet officially tolerated at the same time. The superficial answer, in a tradition that is centuries old, is that the laws in the Netherlands are intentionally enforced in a selective manner via a practice called *gedogen*, which means something like turning a blind eye. When it comes to social policy, the underlying reason is the Dutch are not just tolerant; they are incredible pragmatists.

TOLERANCE VS. ACCEPTANCE

Don't confuse Dutch realism with loose mores. As individuals, most are principled; a fair number are very religious. When asked, the overwhelming majority indicates that they don't use drugs or prostitutes, and the statistics bear this out. Remarkably, the Dutch make a distinction between their values and what they expect from others. While there is general agreement that recreational drugs and prostitution are social evils, there is also a strong consensus that they are going to occur whether they are illegal or not; prosecution often results in social ails worse than the original malady. Thus, it is better to mitigate the negative aspects of these activities with regulation (what could be more Dutch than that?) than to drive them underground through futile attempts at eradication. That these vices were or are still technically illegal is mostly a reflection on the consensus building that is implicit to Dutch public policy: it is one thing to passively accept certain activities as inevitable; it was or is another to actively endorse them. In short, there is a big difference between tolerance and acceptance.

A WORK IN PROGRESS

Sounds great. But how well do these Dutch approaches work? The answer depends on your priorities. In the case of prostitution, the public-health accomplishments are impressive. Thanks to access to medical care and routine testing, the physical well-being of most prostitutes and their clients is significantly better in the Netherlands than in many other countries. Unfortunately, rules only protect those who are a part of the system, and even then, only those who are able to understand and use them. In particular, many of the prostitutes are thought to be illegal immigrants, including an unknown number who were coerced into the trade and work in de facto slavery. Due to fear of reprisals or deportation, it is less likely that foreign prostitutes will contact the authorities for help if they need it. Recent attempts to expand government control by legalizing brothels may have made things worse: the added expense has driven some activity underground. While such problems are not unique to the Netherlands, the abuse of these individuals, in spite of the existing rules and regulations, is, to say the least, extremely troubling to the Dutch.

DRUG TOURISM

There are also some notable achievements associated with the recreational drug policies. While the drug business undoubtedly accentuates the petty theft that is prevalent in the Netherlands (Hey! Where's my bicycle?!?), the fears of critics have not come to pass. The streets of the country are not clogged with addicts; and while most Dutch teenagers go through a period of exploration, where some experiment with drugs, most move on: teenage and adult drug usage rates are relatively low. The biggest problems with Dutch drug policy are associated with foreigners, including a thriving business in drug tourism. Many of these visitors are the source of much of the drug-related theft and the less frequent acts of violence. Other countries in the European Union that have stricter drug policies have pressured the Dutch to modify their approach. To date the Dutch have largely resisted these demands.

EUTHANASIA

New ground-breaking social policies, often controversial and influential, continue in the Netherlands. A recent example is the legalization of euthanasia. Legislative experiments in this regard date back more than two decades. The old law offered the usual subtle compromises, where euthanasia was technically illegal but physicians were rarely prosecuted. Once again, the fears of critics were largely unfounded: euthanasia was reserved as a treatment option of last resort (most were terminally ill cancer patients) and studies confirmed that there was no systematic abuse of the system. However, the same studies showed that the majority of euthanasia cases went unreported, presumably out of fear of prosecution. The new law attempts to correct these and other deficiencies. While the requirements are similar, oversight is now after the fact and a doctor's actions are now presumed legal unless there is evidence that the guidelines have been severely violated. As with some other recent Dutch experiments, the efficacy of the new law remains to be seen.

TOO PRAGMATIC?

All of this leads some to conclude that the Dutch are too pragmatic. The foreign press invariably carries stories that make you shake your head in wonder, such as the one about the Dutch parents who ran the coffee shop in their town: if their children were going to experiment with controlled substances, they felt better knowing who was selling them the drugs! Nonetheless, in spite of the occasional excesses and the remaining problems, rational social policies as well systematic and open education about sex, drugs and alcohol have successfully encouraged responsible behavior. As a consequence, most Dutch teenagers choose abstinence or practice safe sex, as evidenced by the low sexually transmitted disease, teen pregnancy and national abortion rates. (Even dictionaries for Dutch tourists propagate the party line. When it comes to sex, the content is restricted to such useful phrases as 'Only with a condom' and 'Let's not take any chances'.) While it may not be politically or culturally feasible for other countries to adopt their policies or approaches, one cannot help but admire what the Dutch have accomplished.

DUTCH NATIONAL HOLIDAYS AND MAIN FESTIVITIES – 2005

January 1	New Year's Day
February 14	Valentine's Day
March 25	Good Friday
March 27	Easter Sunday
March 28	Easter Monday
April 1	April Fool's Day
April 30	*Koninginnedag* (Queen's Birthday)
May 1	Labor Day
May 4	*Dodenherdenking* (Commemoration of the Dead)
May 5	*Bevrijdingsdag* (Liberation Day)
May 5	*Hemelvaartsdag* (Ascension Day)
May 8	Mother's Day
May 15	*Pinksteren* (Whit Sunday)
May 16	Pinkster Monday (Whit Monday)
June 19	Father's Day
September 20	*Prinsjesdag* (Opening of Parliament)
October 4	*Dierendag* (International Animal Day)
December 25	Christmas Day
December 26	Boxing Day
December 31	New Year's Eve

with no accent at all, and he was right. The first thing any Dutch host(ess) says when someone comes into the house is not 'Hello', but: 'Koffie?' (Do you want a cup of coffee?).

HOSPITALITY GIFTS

A visit to someone's home invariably calls for a hospitality gift. Flowers, cookies, or candy are almost always appropriate. If you think that your host(ess) might be dieting or diabetic, take flowers. Flowers are quite inexpensive in Holland, as the world's largest flower exporter, and are a welcome present.

(Hint: buy flowers with the blooms still closed. Not only do they last longer, but fully open flowers have an aura of cheapness about them. The impression will either be that the florist took advantage of your being a foreigner and palmed them off on you, or you took advantage of their lower price to skimp on your hospitality gift.)

KISSING

The arrival ritual for good friends and family members at a Dutch home catches many foreigners by surprise. Ladies enter first to a round of three – the number is significant – kisses on the cheek (right-left-right) with each person there. The men follow, shaking hands with the other men and fashionably kissing all the ladies lightly on the cheek three times (right-left-right). As a foreigner you can get by with shaking hands instead of kissing.

Stating your name – both first and last or just last name only – as you greet someone is considered basic protocol. Understanding the name that they've just told you is another matter.

SPECIAL OCCASIONS – THE DUTCH WAY

BIRTHDAYS

Nearly all Dutch people celebrate all of their birthdays with great enthusiasm. On that day they can usually expect family and friends to visit them at home, or to telephone or send a birthday card. It is considered rather anti-social for a person to ignore his or her own birthday (verjaardag). Contrary to American custom, for example, where the birthday celebrant is catered to, the Dutch celebrant plans and hosts the festivities, inviting and catering to friends and family, most often at home. The custom in the workplace is to bring pastries for colleagues at work to enjoy over coffee. Likewise, children bring treats to school for all their classmates.

Birthday calendars (verjaardagkalenders), which are usually hung prominently in the bathroom, help people to keep track of the dates on which they have to pay visits or send cards. A word of advice: don't overlook a Dutch person's birthday; such forgetfulness borders on insolence.

Curiously, it is customary to congratulate not only the person whose birthday it is, but also his or her relatives, friends and even neighbors. To say 'Congratulations (Gefeliciteerd!) on the birthday of your brother-in-law' would be quite normal. By the same token, don't be caught off guard if someone congratulates you whenever it's your spouse's or child's birthday. You'll now understand what you did to deserve the kudos!

TURNING FIFTY: 'ABRAHAM AND SARA'

The fiftieth birthday is a milestone that the Dutch are particularly keen to celebrate. The person in question is then referred to as Abraham (for men) or Sara (for women), a tradition that originates from a reference to the Bible where Jesus is explaining that Abraham had 'seen' the day on which Jesus would become the Messiah. Skeptics thought he meant that he had actually 'met' Abraham and sarcastically said, 'Not yet fifty years of age, but you have already met Abraham!' Hence the tradition in the Netherlands, that when you reach the age of fifty, you see Abraham or Sara. A life-size doll, with a big sign hung from its neck indicating one or the other constituent, is often placed in front of the celebrant's house. Unlike some cultures that tend to hide or bury the aging process, the Dutch seem uncharacteristically proud of reaching a ripe old age. In their view, the more the merrier.

WEDDINGS

The pre-wedding custom of a bridal shower is one that supposedly originated in Holland. It is said that the daughter of a miller wanted to marry a man her father didn't approve of, and he wouldn't provide her with a dowry. The villagers took pity on the girl and 'showered' her with gifts, enabling her to marry the man of her choice. If this is true, however, it is certainly one custom that left the Netherlands along with settlers to the New World, as it definitely does not exist in the Netherlands of today.

Strangely enough, a church ceremony alone does not constitute a legal marriage here. A civil ceremony, often conducted in the town hall by a local official, is required for a couple to be legally married (see more on page 116). As such, a Dutch wedding could easily consist of both a civil and a church wedding in one day. Following the ceremony, the celebrations may take place in three parts: a receptie, diner, and a feest (reception, dinner and party). Unusual as it may seem, it is quite common to invite different people to different parts of the celebrations. Family and very close friends may be invited to everything, whilst colleagues and neighbors may be invited to the receptie only.

WEDDING ANNIVERSARIES

Though not always customary, the Dutch will at times succumb to the temptation to celebrate a wedding anniversary with a large group of friends and family, usually on the 12 1/2, 25th or 50th anniversary. In such cases, the appropriate gifts are typically flowers, wine or a joint gift by a group of friends, colleagues or relatives. Often you are approached in a letter by one of the children or a family friend, inviting you to sing a song, give a speech or contribute to a joint gift.

BIRTHS

That pink or blue balloon-decked stork in your neighbor's garden means that a new baby boy or girl has arrived. Friends, colleagues and relatives, even those that the parents may have long since forgotten, call to make an appointment, no less, to come and admire the little darling, and bring along a gift – usually a toy or some item of clothing. Visitors are served tea or coffee and beschuit met muisjes (rusks or crisp-bread) covered with sugared aniseeds (sweets resembling mice), pink for girls and blue for boys. (You can read more about this on page 182.)

GIFTS, CARDS AND PARTY ETIQUETTE

Dutch people routinely give each other gifts on various occasions. These include birthdays, visits to someone's home for a meal, and parties to celebrate weddings, anniversaries and graduations. Gifts are generally small and not lavish, unless they are for a family member. Bouquets of flowers, bottles of wine and boxes of chocolates are common gifts. In fact, a group of friends might even put their money together and buy what is considered a larger gift, such as a book or a CD.

A Dutch person generally presents a gift as soon as he sees the recipient, and the recipient generally opens the gift immediately. Not to do so would be considered impolite. Don't, however, expect effusive thanks, as the Dutch are not generally known for their ebullience. Over-enthusiasm can be viewed as pretentious behavior.

Greeting cards are sent on many occasions. In addition to birthday cards, there are cards of congratulations for such events as passing exams, moving to a new home, and taking early retirement. Millions of postcards are also sold, and not just to tourists. While people on holiday send postcards to family and friends back home, many Dutch people also send them as thank-you cards after they have enjoyed a meal at a friend's home, for example.

DEATHS

When a member of the family passes away, the family sends out cards, usually with black borders, announcing the death, and often place an obituary in the newspaper. When you hear about the death of a friend, or a dear one of a friend, it is greatly appreciated if you write a short note of condolence. If the friend is a close one, you can visit the family to pay your respects (do not do this unannounced) or give them a short phone call. The Dutch traditionally go to the funeral service (which is most often held in the funeral home and not in a church) and, depending on their close ties with the deceased, have a flower arrangement delivered by a florist, to be placed on the casket, to which a ribbon or card is attached with a few final words and the names of the sender(s). Sometimes, the announcement already states that the family does not wish to be disturbed before the funeral (*bezoek is niet gewenst* – we would prefer no visitors) or that the funeral will be held for only the immediate family (*de overledene wordt in besloten kring begraven*). Some families prefer that you donate money to a charity rather than give flowers, and the card will then suggest the charity of choice. After the funeral, a reception is held, where you will be given the opportunity to pay your condolences in person to the family.

TYPICAL DUTCH FESTIVITIES

CARNIVAL – FEBRUARY

Carnival, the Dutch either love it or hate it. Those who live *beneden de rivieren* (below the rivers, in other words in Noord-Brabant or Limburg) love it and celebrate it with a passion. Virtually all businesses close (except cafés and restaurants of course) in a three-day celebration of life, spring, beer and friendship, though in the province of Limburg there is an added element of poking fun at the government and politics. In the provinces *boven de rivieren* (above the rivers) the general attitude towards carnival is one of aloofness – adding to their reputation among the Southerners as a dour and 'un-fun' people – a gray dividing line that,

What with the Queen's Birthday, Commemorating the Dead and Liberation Day, all three of them days on which the flags are hung out and the attention of the Dutch is focused on the Dutch Royal Family and Dutch history, the beginning of May appears to be steeped in Dutchness. Especially the older generation *Nederlanders* feel that this is not a bad thing as they fear that the younger generation will forget how their (grand)parents fought for a very precious commodity: freedom.

THE HEATHEN ORIGINS OF SINTERKLAAS AND CHRISTMAS

Research has shown that Sinterklaas and Zwarte Piet have even older origins than commonly assumed; they are, in fact, the Christian version of the heathen Germanic God Wodan who, on his horse Sleipnir and accompanied by his goblin servant, rode across the skies and peered down the chimneys to see what the people were doing.

The missionaries who came to the Netherlands in the sixth century were given instructions by Pope Gregory the Great to give a Christian character to as many existing customs as they could. Thus Wodan became Saint Nicholas (Sinterklaas) who rode a white horse and sent his moor servant to peer down chimneys to see if children were behaving well – and, if so, brought them gifts. Why Saint Nicholas? For a nation whose history and welfare, thanks to its central location, have always been linked to trade, it was wise to select a saint who could count on the interest and dedication of its people, and so they chose Saint Nicholas – the patron saint of traders, as well as of children.

The missionaries also took it upon themselves to convert the Germanic 'Feast of the Light', which celebrated the impending lengthening of the days, into a celebration of the arrival of the 'Light of the Earth', Jesus Christ. This became what has remained to this day one of the most important family holidays in the Netherlands: Christmas. The customs of the Feast of Light are still evident in the lights and candles used to decorate trees, houses and shop windows.

some would say, smacks of a still Protestant-based north and a predominantly Catholic south.

Dutch carnival has the same origins as carnival in Rio (the period of excess preceding the period of self-deprivation of Lent) and is about as wild, though you must bear in mind of course, that it is celebrated by the 'cold-blooded' Dutch rather than the 'hot-blooded' Brazilians, not to mention the general difference in temperature at that time of year! People get dressed up and go from café to café, singing songs, participating in parades and consuming large quantities of beer. There is no need to be afraid of this being a local festivity at which strangers are not accepted: strangers *are* accepted, and it is a great way to meet new people. Breda, Maastricht and 's Hertogenbosch are three of the major venues.

KONINGINNEDAG – THE QUEEN'S BIRTHDAY: APRIL 30TH

Although not necessarily known to be royalists, the Dutch are extremely fond of their queen. Throughout history, the Dutch Royal Family has been very popular and their birthdays have been celebrated with enthusiasm. As of 1898, Queen Wilhelmina's 18th birthday, the holiday has been officially referred to as *koninginnedag* (literally Queen's Day). April 30th officially became *koninginnedag* when Queen Juliana changed the date to her own birthday. Queen Beatrix, whose birthday is actually on January 31st, left April 30th as the official day to celebrate her birthday as the weather would then (theoretically) be much better than at the end of January.

You can celebrate the Queen's birthday either by visiting one of the two annually chosen towns or cities the Queen visits on this day – and witness some true old-fashioned entertainment – or you can visit some of the bigger cities. Amsterdam, in particular, goes all out on this day, with a *vrijmarkt*, a free market, whereby the streets in the center of Amsterdam are filled with stands run by people age 5 – 105, selling anything and everything. People from all across the world come to Amsterdam (including an annual influx of gays from San Francisco hyped on the suggestive nomenclature of Queens' Birthday) to enjoy this special atmosphere. Another option is to visit the traditional *koninginnemarkt* (Queen's Market) of your own town, where the locals sell just about anything for a song, a great opportunity for bargain hunters and antique buffs – but be there early for the best values (6 A.M.)!

COMMEMORATING THE DEAD: MAY 4TH

More a day of national significance than of festivity, May 4th is the day on which the Dutch remember those who died during the Second World War: soldiers, people in the Resistance and those who did not survive concentration camps in Europe as well as in Indonesia. Between 8 P.M. and 8:02 P.M., a two-minute silence is observed nationally. People stop whatever they are doing (often pulling their cars over to the side of the road) to reverently remember those who did not make it through the war. Even local radio and television broadcasts are halted. In many municipalities, people come together for short ceremonies and speeches, particularly in The Hague, on the Waalsdorpervlakte, and in Amsterdam, on the Dam Square. Flags are hung half-mast throughout the country.

LIBERATION DAY: MAY 5TH

Following the sober day of May 4th, the Dutch celebrate their total liberation from the occupying forces in 1945 (some parts of the

Netherlands had been liberated in November 1944). On Liberation Day, May 5th, flags are hung full-mast and the streets take on a festive look. Because remembering the dead and celebrating liberation deserve individual and equal attention, they have been set on different days. Unfortunately, this memorable day is not celebrated as extensively as it used to be: some businesses and most government offices are closed for the day (in keeping with the collective labor agreement), but most are not. However, there is always some celebration going on somewhere. Furthermore, movies and documentaries about this period are broadcast around these days, while many of the older generation sit with glasses of Dutch *jenever* (gin) and relate bittersweet tales of the past.

TRICK OR TREATS – SINT MAARTEN

Increasingly, the trick or treats day of November 11 is being reintroduced. On this day, children (often accompanied by parents) come by your door, carrying lanterns and singing songs such as '*Sint Maarten, Sint Maarten, de koeien hebben staarten, de meisjes hebben rokjes aan, daar komt Sint Martinus aan*' (St. Martin, St. Martin, the cows have tails, the girls wear skirts, there comes St. Martin – who *knows* what the one has to do with the other). This day is a 'treats'-day – no tricks – the treats being anything from tangerines to cookies to candy. The children do not get dressed up for this occasion, either; it is a simple – though friendly and *gezellige* – neighborhood event.

SINTERKLAAS

You might have already met up with a typical Dutch personality called Sinterklaas, or St. Nicholas. You might too have observed that he has many similarities with that white-bearded, redclothed man you tend to run into towards the end of December in other countries (as well as in the Netherlands). However, Sinterklaas has made considerably better arrangements for himself. Santa Claus may live on the North Pole, but Sinterklaas lives in the South of Spain. Santa Claus flies in from the North Pole on his sleigh, high through the freezing skies; Sinterklaas takes a leisurely cruise from the South of Spain to the Netherlands (hence the song: *Zie ginds komt de stoomboot uit Spanje weer aan* – or, 'See the steamboat coming from Spain'). Santa Claus has to squeeze down and back up all those chimneys himself; Sinterklaas has a whole crew of helpers named Zwarte Pieten, or Black Petes, to do that for him. The phenomenon of Zwarte Piet is an element that tends to surprise visiting foreigners. In this era of anti-apartheid and desegregation, what exactly do the Dutch think they're doing with black face-painted helpers? Well, Zwarte Pieten actually represent Moors; chased into the Sierra Nevada by the Catholic Spaniards in the 15th century, they apparently sought gainful employment in the services of St. Nicholas. As a matter of fact, and this is the God's honest truth, if you drive along the coast of Southern Spain, between Motril and Málaga, you run into a tiny little sign, pointing up a narrow winding road into the hills, saying San Nicolás... Incidentally, there is no evidence whatsoever that the presence of Zwarte Piet at Sinterklaas' side has in any way influenced children's perception of people of another race. It's just not an issue here.

December 6th is St. Nicholas's birthday (or as some claim, the anniversary of his death) when, according to legend, this 4th-century Saint gave gifts of gold to three poor girls for their dowries, a tradition the Netherlands emulates (children still receive chocolate coins around this time). Throughout the centuries, Sinterklaas has been considered the patron saint of children, as well as traders. Consequently, on December 5th, the evening before his birthday, he brings them gifts that are surreptitiously dropped off in a sack on the doorstep of each household. During the evening, families exchange gifts and traditionally drink hot chocolate and eat *banketstaaf*, a Christmas pastry made of marzipan, gingerbread and almond paste. On December 6th, as a birthday present to himself, some would say, Sinterklaas high-tails it back to warm, sunny Spain for another 11 1/2 months.

However, it is not only a holiday for children, and grown-ups like to participate in the fun too by means of a gift (serious, silly or, often, homemade – the latter type is called *a surprise*) with an accompanying poem which summarizes the receiver's past year, intermingled with surprising habits and silly mistakes – often in a slightly ridiculing tone. (Bear in mind that the Dutch love to tease and the more they make fun of you, the more they like you, although it has been known to happen that the unsuspecting receiver of such a lovingly and amusingly composed poem has rushed out of the room in tears.)

For more on Sinterklaas, see page 182.

CHRISTMAS DAY AND NEW YEAR'S EVE

Christmas Day itself is normally reserved for religious observances and family get-togethers (see more about this on page 182). Likewise, the stroke of midnight on New Year's Eve signals that it's time to pay a quick visit to your neighbors with good wishes for the coming year. New Year's Day is a quiet continuation of the same.

THE DUTCH LANGUAGE

First off, be thankful that almost everyone speaks virtually fluent English in the Netherlands. The Dutch are enviable linguists who switch from one language to another with the greatest of ease. In the beginning, the Dutch think it's perfectly fine if you speak English, and they will respond in English. But don't be fooled into thinking that their own language is not so important to them. If, after a year, your Dutch is still non-existent or barely so, they will become considerably less tolerant. Thinking that you are not doing your best to accept their culture, they may hold this against you – either explicitly or implicitly.

Like it or not, you must realize that *you* are a guest in *their* country, not the other way around, and that, by right, you should learn your host's language if you're going to live here for any length of time.

WHY SHOULD YOU LEARN DUTCH?

Maybe you think: 'I'm only going to be in Holland for a few years, and everyone understands me at work – why should I make the effort of learning a language I am not going to need for the rest of my life?' Experience shows that you will not only feel more acclimated if you learn the language of your host culture, but that you will generally be more accepted and appreciated for having made the effort, especially with such an obscure and sufficiently difficult language.

Moreover, if you are the partner or spouse of the employee who has been placed in the Netherlands, your life is probably quite different. If you do not have a job, you run more of a risk of becoming isolated, particularly if you can't speak the local language. If you remain an outsider, you will miss out on the finer subtleties of the language and, therefore, the culture itself. In short, you will simply feel more comfortable with your life in Holland if you can understand what's going on around you. You'll quickly realize that having a command of Dutch will go a long way towards being able to decipher all those packages in the supermarket, for example, not to mention being able to read the local newspaper. Learning Dutch may, consequently, be of unexpected significance to both you and your children, though they will most likely pick up the language more easily through immersion in daily life, or what seems to adults as pure osmosis. Survival of the fittest is key to any expatriate experience, and language adaptation is no exception.

HOW DIFFICULT IS DUTCH?

Dutch is not an easy language for English speakers – we simply do not have the capacity for those throaty, guttural sounds on which Netherlandish children are weaned. Sentence structure is awkwardly reversed, and the Dutch seem to have imposed no limit on word length. (*Levensverzekeringsmaatschappijen*, translated as 'life insurance companies', and *projectontwikkelingsmaatschappijen*, meaning 'property development companies', at 32 and 34 letters each, are the two longest official words in the Dutch language, although there are even much longer unofficial, makeshift conglomerations of words used in everyday language.) If your native language is similar to Dutch, or you've studied a parallel language, you'll be one step ahead of the game.

THE FIRST STEPS

Decide whether you would prefer to follow an established course or take private lessons. The Netherlands has a national network of language institutes that offer courses in Dutch to foreigners (usually, these courses are referred to as NT2, Nederlands als tweede taal – Dutch as a second language). The local city or town hall will advise you as to where the nearest institute is, so that you can make an appointment. During an interview, they will probably ask you what type of school you went to at home, what diplomas you have, whether you interact with a lot of Dutch people, whether you have time to go to a school and to do homework, etc. They may also ask you to take a placement exam to determine what level you should pursue. Depending on your specific needs, the institute may suggest an intensive course for quicker immersion. Caution: don't be tempted to buy a Dutch phrasebook as these are generally geared to tourists and often don't accurately reflect common usage. Invest instead in a good Dutch dictionary and a basic 'Dutch for beginners' book to get you started.

Of primary importance is learning the numbers in Dutch, as you'll quickly discover that such everyday tasks as shopping and making appointments rely on this basic knowledge. Dutch numbers require some mental gymnastics – '21' is expressed as 'one and twenty', for example – so be prepared.

SOME PRELIMINARY WORDS OF ADVICE

- *Let everyone know that you don't (or hardly) speak any Dutch.*
  Do this before the other overestimates your capacity to understand him or her, and starts off too quickly and with too complicated a vocabulary. Don't, however, insist on only English conversation as you'll never learn Dutch that way. Simply employ the following sentence if need be: *Ik wil Nederlands leren.* (I want to learn Dutch). The reactions will vary. Some will turn up the volume, others will revert to a type of pidgin Dutch, as if talking to a child. Don't be offended; it's a natural reaction.
- *Do not be afraid to make mistakes.*
  Many expatriates want to master Dutch as well as they do their native language – and it annoys them if they can't converse quickly. Though this is understandable, patience is of the essence. Fluency takes much time, and all that matters at first is basic communication.
- *Don't make it unnecessarily hard.*
  Try to avoid difficult subjects at first. Keep your initial conversations simple.
- *Don't pretend to understand.*
  If the other person has already explained something twice and you still don't understand, the temptation is great to nod enthusiastically as if you get it. You do not want to appear stupid or impolite. However, it is best to admit defeat; have them repeat it again. Who knows what you will learn?
- *Absorb all day.*
  As you hear Dutch in your daily activities, pay attention to what others are saying and how they say it. If you don't know the words, look them up for future reference and try to use them yourself. Attempt to read local or national newspapers and to decipher Dutch television. It's a great way to practice.

WHICH DUTCH?

Not all Dutch people speak the same Dutch language. There is a standard language: Algemeen Beschaafd Nederlands (ABN), which translates into the somewhat pompous-sounding 'General Civilized Dutch'. Well-educated Dutch people who live in the Randstad (the area comprising Amsterdam, The Hague, Rotterdam, Utrecht and everything in between) speak this, as it is the old dialect of the District of Holland, which was once was the most powerful province. Hollands thus became the most widespread dialect and the basis for the standard language that was spoken by the Queen (though, if truth be told, almost no one speaks the way the Queen does), the members of parliament, teachers and preachers, and on radio and television.

The other regions of the Netherlands speak the same language, but the pronunciation can be quite different and hard to understand at first: there is Zeeuws (spoken in Zeeland), Twents (spoken in Twente – in the east), Gronings (spoken in Groningen), Drents (spoken in Drenthe), Brabants (spoken in Noord-Brabant) and Limburgs (spoken in Limburg) – and even within these dialects, there can be considerable variation. And then the people from the four cities all have their very distinct way of pronouncing the language, too. The Dutch can tell within a sentence whether someone is from The Hague, or Amsterdam, or Limburg or Groningen.

In Friesland, a province in the northwest of Holland, there is even an entirely different language called 'Fries', or Frisian, which is spoken in addition to Dutch. Unless you're a die-hard linguist, however, it would be highly unlikely for you to need or want to learn this unique language unless, of course, you intend to live in that region for a lengthy period of time. Even then, Dutch would suffice, as everything is signposted in both languages there.

YOUR AIM

In the end, how far you progress with Dutch will depend on the amount of time you put into it, your ambition and your talents. You might attain the highest level: speaking with ease, making virtually no mistakes, understanding complicated speeches and articles and writing a nearly faultless proposal. Or maybe you will never get any further than a sort of tourist Dutch enabling you to at least carry on a semblance of a conversation. In a country where English is second nature, it will require some determination on your part to plunge hook, line and sinker, into learning Dutch. Chances are you won't regret it.

RELIGION

Although modern Dutch society is very secular, and not many Dutch people identify with an organized religion, you will see plenty of churches and other places of worship, and you will have plenty of opportunities to practice your own religion if you wish.

THE CHURCHES YOU SEE

Before the Protestant Reformation, most Dutch people were Roman Catholics. Churches were built as Catholic churches, full of altars, images and decoration.

The religious reforms of the 16th century took place in the Low Countries against a background of resistance against Spanish domination. The Spanish were militant Catholics, and their persecution of Protestant 'heretics' sharpened the economic and political conflict. It also sharpened the fury with which the Dutch reformers stripped their churches of all the trappings of the Catholic Church. All statues and decorations were removed, and altars were either removed or replaced by burial monuments for lead- ing citizens. Only the pulpits were left standing. The more sober and democratically furnished interiors suited the beliefs of the Calvinists. Today most of the churches built before the Reformation are still Protestant and sober. Only in the southern provinces, where Catholics accounted for a larger percentage of the population, did they succeed in regaining control of the old churches.

The people who remained Catholic after the Protestant Reformation were never systematically persecuted in the Netherlands, but they were discriminated against and hindered in the practice of their religion. For centuries they kept a low profile, getting together for services in hidden, or semi-hidden churches. They were called Papists (Papen), and even today you see traces of their neighborhoods reflected in names of streets and towns. Only in the middle of the 19th century, with the start of the industrial revolution, did the Catholics have enough confidence and resources to start building their own large churches again. Most of these were built in neo-Gothic style. Their newer-looking, machine-made bricks distinguish them from the older churches.

Except for Maastricht and other cities in the south, nearly all large churches you see in Dutch city centers fall into one of these two categories: Protestant and dating from between the 13th and 16th centuries, or Catholic and dating from the 19th century. Churches that date from the 17th, 18th or 20th centuries were usually built on a modest scale.

DUTCH DENOMINATIONS

Of the Dutch people who nowadays claim church affiliation, about half are Roman Catholic and half are Protestant. Only about 20% of the population attends services regularly, however. The southern provinces of Brabant and Limburg are predominantly Catholic, and the other provinces are predominantly Protestant.

PROTESTANTS

At the time of the Reformation, some Dutch Protestants followed the teachings of Martin Luther, but most followed the more radical John Calvin, of Switzerland. The main feature of Calvinism, in addition to its sobriety, was its belief in predestination – the belief that some people are destined for a place in heaven and others are not. These ideas have evolved, and different streams and communities have developed through the years.

The two main categories of Protestantism in the Netherlands today are *Nederlands Hervormd* (Dutch Reformed) and *Gereformeerd* (Reformed). But there are other groups as well – Evangelical, Lutheran, Baptist, Apostolic, Pentecostal and many more.

CATHOLICS

In the 1960s and 1970s, the Dutch Catholic Church was extremely progressive. A series of conservative appointments by the current Pope has made it less so, but you can still find a range of communities – at one end of the spectrum parishes still using the Latin liturgy, and at the other end parishes committed to the most modern ideas and practices. There are also Byzantine Catholic communities.

A little-known group is the so-called Old Catholics; in 1723 – in protest against the concentration of power in Rome – they 'broke' with the city by choosing their own bishop. When, in 1870, the infallibility of the of the Pope was announced, many Old Catholics and others of similar conviction came together and, in 1889, formed the Union of Utrecht. Currently, the Old Catholic Church has approximately 8,000 members in 26 parishes in the Netherlands, however, worldwide there are over 500,000 members.

PHILOSOPHICAL GROUPS

Instead of being members of churches, some people in the Netherlands belong to groups that share a particular philosophical outlook on life. There are of course many of these, but the main ones that are also known outside the Netherlands are: Anthroposophists, Humanists, New Age and the Sufi Movement.

ISLAM

With approximately 1 million (practicing) Muslims living in the Netherlands (6.25% of the population), Islam has become one of the country's main religions. Mosques have been built in most of the larger cities by communities of immigrants from Turkey, Morocco and Indonesia. It is projected that by the year 2020 Islam will be the second largest religion in the Netherlands. By that time, 7% of the populace should be Muslim, while only 10% is expected to be Catholic. The Dutch public is also gradually learning more about Islam – enough to make allowances for colleagues and pupils who are fasting for Ramadan, for example.

Though many believe that Islam is the fastest growing religion in the Netherlands, that is not necessarily the case; the method of counting applied to the group of Muslims and the group of Christians is different. Only church-registered Christians are taken into account, versus all immigrants from Muslim-countries. If Christians (immigrants) were to be counted in the same manner, then this would prove to be the fastest growing religious group.

What is 'popularly' referred to as 'Islam-terrorism' has not contributed to the overall popularity of Muslims among the non-Muslim Dutch. As is the case for any large and diverse group, it is very hard to find an agreed-upon spokesperson for this group who could improve relations and their reputation, making it a difficult task to bridge the current gap of misunderstanding. An excellent explanation of the social forces active in the Netherlands at the moment can be found on page 21, *A Pessimistic Climate.*

JUDAISM

Before and during the Second World War, when Hitler's anti-Semitism took hold in Europe, many Jews came to the Netherlands. Aside from the fact that there already was a large Jewish community in the Netherlands, this country had remained neutral during the First World War, and more importantly, had (has) a centuries-long tradition of religious tolerance. The Jews hoped that these factors would allow them to find a safe haven here – but unfortunately the Netherlands was occupied during the war and could not be the safe haven they had hoped for. Still, a sizeable Jewish community remains in the Netherlands, of which the center is in Amsterdam, though synagogues can also be found in other cities.

OTHER RELIGIONS

Other religious affiliations that have active communities in the Netherlands include Hinduism, Buddhism and Baha'i. For addresses, check the end of this chapter.

YOU CAN'T FIND A COMMUNITY THAT PRACTICES YOUR RELIGION?

Try telephoning the Netherlands Center for Foreigners (NCB or *Nederlands Centrum voor Buitenlanders*) in Utrecht, tel.: 030 239 49 59). They will know whom you should call.

REFERENCES

SUPPORT ORGANIZATIONS

ACCESS
Non-profit making foundation which aims to help English speakers of all nationalities to settle in and make the most of life in the Netherlands. Maintains a comprehensive database of information and a telephone information service, runs educational seminars and workshops on all manner of topics and has various publications designed to meet the needs of the English-speaking community.
Address The Hague office: 2nd floor, Sociëteit de Witte, Plein 24, 2511 CS The Hague
Tel.: 070 346 25 25, fax: 070 356 13 32
Address Amsterdam office: Herengracht 472 3rd floor, 1017 CA Amsterdam
Tel.: 020 423 32 17, fax: 020 423 34 80
Internet: www.access-nl.org

OUTPOST Expatriate Information Center
The center of a worldwide spouse-to-spouse network providing Shell families with practical information about living conditions in expatriate locations around the world.
Address: Carel van Bylandtlaan 16, 2596 HT The Hague
Tel.: 070 377 65 30, fax: 070 377 14 87
E-mail: outpost@si.shell.com
Internet: www.outpostexpat.nl

INPOST Welcome Group
A group of Shell Volunteers welcomes newly arrived or returning Shell families to The Hague, Rijswijk, Pernis or Schiedam areas.
Contact Outpost at tel.: 070 377 65 30
The Outpost Assen Welcome Committee can be reached at tel.: 0592 36 30 64
Internet: www.outpostassen.nl

RECOMMENDED READING

HERE'S HOLLAND
Comprehensive guide to Dutch cities, villages, out-of-the-way places, museums, gardens, castles, dining out and settling in - with cultural and historical background. Recognizes the needs of families with children. Full of ideas for planning interesting excursions.
Internet: www.heresholland.com
ISBN 90 801255 2 0

AT HOME IN HOLLAND
Published by The American Women's Club of The Hague.
A practical guide for foreigners moving to the Netherlands. Provides up-to-date information on the Dutch people, their country and customs, plus practical information about housing, banking, driving, shopping, community and recreation.
Internet: www.awcthehague.org
ISBN 90 5166 863 5

HANDLING HOLLAND
By Janet Inglis
Published by xPat Media
A manual for international women in the Netherlands.
This book contains a wealth of tips and suggestions on how to enrich your life in Holland. It covers job hunting, education, going freelance, remaining fit and healthy, making this new home your home, doing volunteer work, taking in culture, focusing on your family, and finding friends and having fun
Internet: www.xpat.nl
www.hollandbooks.nl
ISBN 90 5594 232 4

THE UNDUTCHABLES
By Colin White and Laurie Boucke
Published by White - Boucke Publishing Inc.
A tongue-in-cheek observation of the Netherlands, its culture and its inhabitants.
Internet: www.undutchables.com
ISBN 1 888580 22 4

THE LOW SKY, UNDERSTANDING THE DUTCH
By Han van der Horst
Published by Scriptum
The book that makes the Netherlands familiar.
A detailed exploration of the reasons for desire of the Dutch for independence, their sense of respect and their business sense
Internet: www.scriptum.nl
www.hollandbooks.nl
ISBN 90 5594 199 9

THE LOW SKY IN PICTURES
Text: Han van der Horst
Photography: Freek van Arkel, George Burggraaff, Ben Deiman, Etienne van Sloun, Gregor Ramaekers, Karel Tomei
Published by Scriptum

A pictorial supplement to the above, a perfect present for relatives back home
Internet: www.scriptum.nl
www.hollandbooks.nl ISBN 90 5594 114 X

HOLLAND HORIZONS - VIEW OF THE DUTCH
Text: Han van der Horst
Photography: Freek van Arkel, Ben Deiman, Ineke Dijkstra, Karel Tomeï and Thijs van Tuurenhout
Published by Scriptum
English-language text and photo book about the Netherlands but without the traditional pictures of windmills and clogs
Internet: www.scriptum.nl
www.hollandbooks.nl
ISBN 90 5594 404 1

ONLY IN HOLLAND, ONLY THE DUTCH
By Marc Resch
Published by Rozenberg
An in-depth look into the culture of Holland and its people.
Internet: www.rozenbergps.com
ISBN 90 5170 800 9

HOLLAND, LIVING WITH WATER
Various authors and photographers
Published by Scriptum
This book is about the relationship between the people of the Netherlands and the water that surrounds them. It is filled with beautiful photographs of life above, at and below sea level, with views from the dikes, the beach, the water and the sky
Internet: www.scriptum.nl
www.hollandbooks.nl
ISBN 90 5594 220 0

.NL
Photography: Ben Deiman and Karel Tomeï
Text: Martin Bril
Published by Scriptum
Two inches thick with 720 pages about the Netherlands
Internet: www.scriptum.nl
www.hollandbooks.nl
ISBN 90 5594 356 9

FOR MORE BOOKS ON HOLLAND VISIT:
www.hollandbooks.nl

REFERENCES

DUTCH LANGUAGE EDUCATION BOOKS

DUTCH TONGUE
Text by Dr. Ben van der Have
Illustrations by Djanko
Published by Scriptum
Internet: www.scriptum.nl
ISBN 90 5594 212 X

AN IRISHMAN'S DIFFICULTIES WITH THE DUTCH LANGUAGE
By Cuey-Na-Gael
Published by De Boekerij
The tortuous attempt of an Irishman to learn and apply the Dutch language at the turn of the former century.
Information, tel.: 020 535 31 35
ISBN 90 72763 033

INTRODUCTION TO DUTCH
By W. Z. Shetter
Published by Martinus Nijhoff
ISBN 90 01 81990 7

DUTCH FOR SELF-STUDY
By Hinke van Kampen
Published by Het Spectrum
This book and two cd-roms provide the basic structures of the Dutch language
Internet: www.spectrum.nl
ISBN 90 274 7379 X

CULTURE SHOCK BOOKS

THE ART OF CROSSING CULTURES
By Craig Storti
ISBN 0933662858

CULTURE SHOCK NETHERLANDS
By Hunt Janin
Published by Graphic Arts Center Publishing
ISBN 155868400X

THE THIRD CULTURE KID EXPERIENCE - THE EXPERIENCE OF GROWING UP AMONG WORLDS
By David C. Pollock and Ruth E. Van Reken
Internet: www.interculturalpress.com
ISBN 1 85788 295 4

WHEN ABROAD DO AS LOCAL CHILDREN DO - ORI'S GUIDE FOR YOUNG EXPATS
By Hilly van Swol-Ulbrich and Bettina

Kältenhauser
Published by XPat Media
This book reaches out to international mobile families with children between 8 and 12 years old.
The activities and assignments in the book encourage the taking of initiatives in exploring the opportunities connected with the new environment.
Internet: www.xpat.nl
www.hollandbooks.nl
www.ori-and-ricki.net
ISBN 90 5594 262 6

A MOVEABLE MARRIAGE: RELOCATE YOUR RELATIONSHIP WITHOUT BREAKING IT
By Robin Pascoe
Published by Expatriate Press Ltd.
Website: www.expatexpert.com
ISBN 09 6867 602 2

HOMEWARD BOUND - A SPOUSE'S GUIDE TO REPATRIATION
By Robin Pascoe
Published by Expatriate Press Ltd.
Website: www.expatexpert.com
ISBN 09 6867 600 6

WEBSITES

GENERAL

www.holland.com - The Holland website of the Netherlands Board of Tourism & Conventions
For useful and fun information on what's on in the Netherlands.

www.rootsinholland.com - Find out what it means to be Dutch, wherever you are.

www.expatica.com - News and community portal for expats in the Netherlands, Belgium, France, Germany and Spain.

www.elynx.nl - A directory for expats in the Netherlands.

www.xpat.nl - The information platform for expatriates in the Netherlands

www.britain.nl - British Embassy website, with extensive information on the Netherlands

www.usemb.nl - Official website of the US Government, with extensive information on the Netherlands

www.minbuza.nl/english - Comprehensive information on the Netherlands in many languages, including Holland Horizon magazine. Also: news, ethical issues, foreign policy and contact information for all ministries and diplomatic missions.

www.outpostexpat.nl - Website of OUTPOST Expatriate Information Center with practical information about living conditions in a.o. the Netherlands.

www.howtosurviveholland.nl - Activities, tips to survive, things to do, 'crash course' and more by Undutchables Recruitment Agency.

CULTURE SHOCK WEBSITES

TRANSITION, CULTURE SHOCK AND RELOCATION
www.tckworld.com
www.tckinteract.net
www.career-in-your-suitcase.com
www.expatexpert.com
www.branchor.com

THE NETHERLANDS

DUTCH GOVERNMENT
Access to the websites of the Dutch Government Departments and Ministries.
www.overheid.nl
Ministry of Foreign Affairs:
www.minbuza.nl/english
Comprehensive information on the Netherlands in many languages. Also: news, ethical issues, foreign policy and contact information for all ministries and diplomatic missions.

THE DUTCH URBAN EXPERT CENTRE (DUTCH EUC): established jointly by twenty-five of Netherlands largest towns and cities and nine government departments. The Centre's purpose is to gather, enrich and disseminate knowledge of urban policy in the Netherlands and in the wider European context: www.dutcheuc.nl

THE DUTCH ROYAL FAMILY
www.koninklijkhuis.nl:
in Dutch, English, German and French

EVD (NETHERLANDS FOREIGN TRADE AGENCY)
www.evd.nl
www.hollandtrade.com

STATISTICS NETHERLANDS (CBS)
www.cbs.nl/en

WEATHER INFORMATION
www.knmi.nl
www.weer.nl

LANGUAGE TRAINING
www.berlitz.com
www.ita-talen.nl
www.kit.nl
www.learndutch.org
www.language-unites.org
www.linguarama.nl
www.reginacoeli.nl: the 'Nuns'
www.nederlandsalstweedetaal.nl

DUTCH HISTORY
www.studybuddy.nl ,
StudyBuddy provides chronological over-
views of history and historical maps
organized by country and contains a concise
history of Holland in English: on the map
click on Europe and select *The Netherlands*.

RELIGION

ORGANIZATIONS

BUDDHIST CENTER AMSTERDAM
Boeddhistisch Centrum Amsterdam
Palmstraat 63, 1015 HP Amsterdam
Tel.: 020 420 70 97
Internet: www.dharmanet.org

COUNCIL OF CHURCHES IN THE NETHERLANDS
Raad van Kerken in Nederland
Koningin Wilhelminalaan 5, 3818
HN Amersfoort
Tel.: 033 463 38 44

DUTCH COUNCIL OF CHRISTIANS AND JEWS
OJEC, Overlegorgaan van Joden en
Christenen in Nederland

Nieuwstraat 3, 1381 BB Weesp
Tel.: 0294 45 22 11
www.xs4all.nl/~ojec/

ISLAMITISCHE STICHTING NEDERLAND
Javastraat 2, 2585 AM The Hague
Tel.: 070 365 37 02

LIBERAL JEWISH COMMUNITY
Liberaal Joodse Gemeenschap
Jacob Soetendorpstraat 8,
1079 RM Amsterdam
Tel.: 020 642 35 62

DUTCH ORTHODOX JEWISH COMMUNITY
Tel.: 020 644 38 68
Internet: www.joods.nl

MUSLIM INFORMATION CENTER
MIC, Moslim Informatie Centrum
Beeklaan 207, 2562 AE The Hague
Tel.: 070 361 44 63

NETHERLANDS REFORMED CHURCH
Nederlandse Hervormde Kerk
Overgoo 11, 2266 JZ Leidschendam
Tel.: 070 313 11 31

**REFORMED CHURCHES IN THE NETHER-
LANDS GKN**, De Gereformeerde Kerken in
Nederland
De Beaufortweg 18, 3833 AG Leusden
Tel.: 033 496 03 60

**ROMAN CATHOLIC CHURCH IN THE
NETHERLANDS**
Rooms Katholiek Kerkgenootschap in
Nederland
Biltstraat 121, 3572 AP Utrecht
Tel.: 030 232 69 00
Internet: www.omroep.nl/rkk

SALVATION ARMY
Leger des Heils
Spoordreef 10, 1315 GN Almere
Tel.: 036 539 81 35
Internet: www.legerdesheils.nl

ANTHROPOSOPHISTS
Anthroposophic Association in the
Netherlands
secretariat, Boslaan 15, 3701 CH Zeist
Tel.: 030 691 82 16

HINDUISM
www.hindustani.nl

HUMANISTS
Humanistisch Verbond
Sarphatikade 13, 1017 WV Amsterdam
Tel.: 020 521 90 00

SUFI MOVEMENT
Soefi Beweging Nederland
Anna Paulownastraat 78, 2518 BJ The Hague
Tel.: 070 346 15 94

INTERNATIONAL CHURCHES

Afrikaanse Kerk (South African Church)
Gruttersdreef 106, 7328 DN Apeldoorn
Tel.: 055 543 18 93
Internet: www.afrikaansekerk.nl

Anglican Church - Christ Church
Groenburgwal 42, 1011 HW Amsterdam
Tel .: 020 441 03 55
Internet: www.christchurch.nl

English Reformed Church
Begijnhof 48, 1012 WV Amsterdam
Tel .: 020 672 22 88

The Blessed Trinity
Zaaiersweg 180, 1097 ST Amsterdam
Tel.: 020 465 27 11

Jewish Community
Van der Boechhorststraat 26,
1081 BT Buitenveldert
Tel.: 020 646 00 46

Liberal Jewish Community
J. Soetendorpstraat 8, 1079 RM Amsterdam
Tel.: 020 642 35 62

American Protestant Church
Esther de Boer van Rijklaan 20,
2597 TJ The Hague
Tel.: 070 324 44 90

Church of St. John´s and St. Philip
Ary van der Spuyweg 1, 2585 HA The Hague
Tel.: 070 355 53 59

Crossroads International Church of The
Hague
Bezuidenhoutseweg 249, 2594 AM The
Hague
Tel.: 070 322 24 85
English Speaking Catholic Church of The

REFERENCES

Hague - Church of our Saviour
Parish House
Ruygrocklaan 126, 2597 ES The Hague
Tel.: 070 328 08 16
Internet: www.parish.nl
St. Aloysius College
Oostduinlaan 50, 2596 JP The Hague
Tel.: 070 328 08 16

Church of Christ
De Gaarde 61, 2542 CH The Hague
Tel.: 070 329 73 80

Liberal Jewish Community of The Hague
Prinsessegracht 26, 2514 AP The Hague
Tel.: 070 365 68 93

Baptist Community
Vier Heemskinderenstraat 91,
2531 CA The Hague
Tel.: 070 380 0318

Reformed Community The Hague
Diamanthorst 187, 2592 GD The Hague
Tel.: 070 385 87 07

Salvation Army (Leger des Heils)
Haversmidtstraat 57, 2522 VT The Hague
Tel.: 070 399 01 46

Trinity Baptist Church
Bloemcamplaan 54, 2244 EE Wassenaar
Tel.: 070 517 80 24

Trinity International Church
Gruttolaan 23, 2261 ET Leidschendam
Tel.: 070 517 80 24
Internet: www.trinitychurch-nl.com

The English Church of St. James
Koninklijke Marinelaan 53,
2251 BA Voorschoten
Tel.: 071 561 15 28

The Scots International Church
Markt 25, Schiedam
Tel.: 010 414 43 38

Hope International Baptist Church
Schiedamse Vest 121, 3021 BH Rotterdam
Tel.: 010 447 25 51

St. Mary´s Anglican Episcopal Church of
Rotterdam
Pieter de Hoochweg 133,

3024 BG Rotterdam-Delfshaven.
Tel.: 010 476 40 43
Internet: http://home.hetnet.nl/~anglican

Holy Trinity Church
Van Hogendorpstraat 26, 3581 KE Utrecht
Tel.: 030 251 34 24

Trinity Church Eindhoven
Pensionaat Eikenburg, Aalsterweg 289,
5644 RE Eindhoven
Tel.: 040 244 81 49
Internet: http://tce.dse.nl

Many of you have come to the Netherlands as an expatriate – placed or transferred here by your employer – so that many of the important things have been taken care of. On the other hand, many of you have not come here with the full company support system behind you. If this is the case, there are a number of things you need to know before entering the job market, such as: the make-up of the Dutch employment market, finding a job here as an expatriate, the Dutch social security system, the possibilities of continuing the social insurance legislation of your country of origin in the Netherlands and how to go about setting up your own business.

Going through this chapter will help you prepare for your ventures, by giving an overview of these topics as well as, on the reference page, the addresses, phone numbers and websites of those organizations that can help you along the way.

Working in the Netherlands

CONTRIBUTING AUTHORS: RUUD BLAAKMAN, RINA DRIECE, STEPHANIE DIJKSTRA, HAN VAN DER HORST, PETER KRANENBURG, BERT RIETMEIJER, YVONNE SØRENSEN, ANTON STEIJN AND ERNO TONKES

THE DUTCH EMPLOYMENT MARKET

THE DUTCH WORKFORCE

There are approximately 16.3 million people living in the Netherlands and in 2004, the total labor force consisted of 7.46 million employees. About 53.8% of those employees has a full time job, and works directly for employers.

SECTORS

In the Netherlands, most jobs that are being fulfilled are in the commercial services sector, industry and 'non-commercial' services. As you can read in chapter 1, the predictions for the coming five years are that, in particular, the number of jobs in the retail, the medical (care) sector and 'other' business services (real estate, employment agencies and security) will increase – some say by as much as 20%. The education level of those working in the Netherlands has been steadily rising over the last decade: 27% has either a university or a 'university of professional education'-degree (you can read more about the distinction between these two in chapter 8). During the '90s, greatly aided by the excellent economy, the age of job-hopping also arrived in the Netherlands – formerly a nation of life-long employment contracts. Now that the economy is recovering from quite an extensive slump, it can be expected that employees will be switching jobs less often – however, this is likely to be the same across the globe. One difference with some other countries is that this slump may not lead to a wave of mass dismissals; the Netherlands champions the protection of the underdog (in this case, the employees) and (large) dismissals are only possible on the basis of a few, specifically given, legal grounds, such as economic instability or bankruptcy.

EMANCIPATION?

The Netherlands is known abroad as a greatly 'emancipated' country, where women share an equal standing with men. To a large degree this is true, in fact, many expats comment on how the Dutch women are the ones 'who wear the pants at home' – to use a Dutch expression. However, the workforce does not reflect this emancipation, particularly not in the full-time or highest paid jobs sectors. Several reasons have been given for this (insufficient government support for child care, the Dutch social values emphasize the need to devote time to raising the children, Dutch men are closet machos) – and probably all have an element of truth to them. Many expat women find themselves quite dismayed at how few women are in top positions, though it may be some consolation that, over the last few years, the amount of women holding down a job has gone from 41% to more than 55%. Still, most women are still in part-time positions – and consequently not in the businesses' top echelons nor among the top earners. Research, carried out towards the end of the 2004, shows that the only increase to be detected was in the number of women on management boards, from 1.9% to 3.3%, a representation that seems to be spilling over into the two layers below. Notably, women are far better represented in the non-profit sector than they are in the business sector.

EMPLOYMENT AGENCIES

The Netherlands, where the first employment agencies started over thirty years ago, was one of the first countries where these agencies were very successful. Now more than 4% of all Dutch employees works through employment agencies, compared to an average for the European market of less than 1%. The top six agencies are: Randstad, Start, Vedior, Adecco, Content and Manpower. Since January 1, 1999, all employment agencies work in keeping with Dutch employment law, which includes, among others, Flexibility and Certainty Act (Wet Flexibiliteit & Zekerheid). As many of you will not have moved to the Netherlands on an expat contract, the rules that apply to those employed directly by a Dutch employer or by an employment agency can be of great importance to you. For this reason, we include an overview of the main issues contained in this law:

PROBATION PERIOD

Type of Contract	Maximum Duration of probation
'Phase 1' contract (max. 26 weeks)	No probation period; either party can terminate the contract on a day-to-day basis.
Contract for less than 2 years	Maximum of 1 month
Permanent contract	Maximum of 2 months

The probation period must always be confirmed in writing in your employment contract. During this probation period, employees can typically be dismissed or resign with immediate effect.

CHAIN CONTRACTS

When you have successfully completed your first 26 weeks with an agency, you then have the possibility of receiving a contract for a definite period of time. If there have been more than three such fixed period employment contracts (a 'chain') between an employer and an employee, the employee may be awarded a permanent contract. This means that, should the employer wish to fire this employee, he will have to either ask permission from the Center for Work and Income (CWI) or have the courts dissolve the contract (see more about this further on). The employer, how-ever, is not obligated to award this permanent contract so that, due to the economic slump, they are not being awarded as readily as before. Depending on the contract end date terms, your contract could end automatically and, if you have not negotiated your permanent contract, you could then end up unemployed.

Three separate contracts with one employer within three years is permitted. If the period between two contracts exceeds three months, the 'chain' is broken and the counting starts again. However, if the intervals do not exceed three months, then the last employment contract is deemed to be a contract for an indefinite period of time.

It is important to know that, if you change agencies, your contract history connected to your current function/agency client must be honored.

MINIMUM/MAXIMUM DURATION CONTRACT

If you work on call and are not certain about the number of hours that you are working on a weekly or on a monthly basis, then you must always be paid out at least three hours a week even if you only worked, for example, two hours.

TERMINATING AN EMPLOYMENT CONTRACT

The Netherlands has a unique dual system of dismissal. If an employer wishes to terminate an employment agreement for an indefinite period of time, he has two options. His first option is to obtain prior approval from the CWI (Center for Work and Income), before serving the notice of termination. The purpose of this procedure is to avoid unreasonable or socially unjustifiable dismissals. Alternatively an employer may at any time request the sub-district sector of the District Court to dissolve the employment contract. The request for the dissolution must be based on important reasons, for instance bad performance or redundancy. Without the prior approval of the CWI or the dissolution of the District Court, the employment relationship – as a general rule – cannot be terminated unilaterally. It should be noted, though, that employment can be terminated by mutual consent, for urgent reasons (e.g. theft), or when the agreed fixed period of time has lapsed.

When dismissing an employee, it is not important whether Dutch law or the law of another country applies. If the employment agreement is governed by the national law of another country, the employee can still invoke the protection of the Dutch law if the employment relationship can be considered part of the socio-economic market in the Netherlands.

NOTICE PERIOD

When terminating an employment contract, an employer must apply the following notice periods (these do not apply when the employment contract is dissolved by the courts):

Length of employment period	Notice period
0 – 5 years	1 month
5 – 10 years	2 months
10 – 15 years	3 months
> 15 years	4 months

The above notice periods are only applicable to contracts for an indefinite period of time. In the case of other contract forms, such as a contract of temporary employment (a so-called 'temp' contract) – which is valid up to a maximum of 26 weeks – termination is/can be with immediate effect.

For an employee, the notice period is always one month, unless employer and employee, either in the employment contract or in a separate written agreement, agree upon a different notice period. Whereby it should be noted, that any personally agreed-upon notice period for the employee is doubled for the employer (i.e. if an employee agrees to a two-month notice period at the beginning of their contract, the employer must agree to give four months' termination notice to said employee).

SEVERANCE PAYMENT

There are no statutory rules on severance payment and the court judges the necessity for compensation in each individual case, based on the probably deliberately vague standard of 'reasonableness'.

Severance payment can be granted either as a lump sum, or as a periodically paid supplement to the unemployment benefit (for more on this benefit, see page 68) or lower wages in the next job. In the case of collective dismissals or highly paid individuals, the payment is usually in the form of a lump sum.

EGALITARIANISM

If you were to hear or read an interview with a Dutch captain of industry, you might be surprised to hear him (or her) downplay any central role he might have played in the company's success. He would declare himself a team player and would praise the creativity that is found throughout the company. He would accentuate the fact that all involved carried out the task as a team and that he would have of course accomplished nothing were it not for the energetic input and output of all of them. He would not sell himself as the genius with all the ideas but would describe himself as the coordinator, even if all involved realized deep in their hearts that, without his leadership, the stock values of the company would have long since plummeted. This all has to do with the great appreciation that the Dutch have for egalitarianism, and their general resistance to being told what to do without any preliminary discussion. And of course, their undeniable need to seek compromise whenever possible. But that's not all. The ingrained inclination to respect another person will not allow them to give out orders and commands. The modern Dutchman likes to 'recognize himself' (his input) – as he puts it – in any decision made. In other words, he expects to be involved in the decision-making. If ministers or CEOs choose to keep a low profile, then this is purely a matter of strategy and tact.

Foreigners who work with Dutch companies – either as a customer or as an employee – are often confused by this egalitarianism. They are amazed at the informality between those who occupy the various rungs on the corporate ladder. Secretaries are on a first-name basis with their bosses. There is little evidence of hierarchy. Even the managers' offices are soberly decorated and visitors are given a modest welcome. It is perfectly normal for the company CEO to stand in line for lunch with the other employees in the company cafeteria – with the visitor right next to him. This does not mean that this visitor is not an honored one, and it gives no indication whatsoever of whether this visit is appreciated. This will only become evident from the meetings themselves and the agreements reached.

COMPROMISE – OVERLEG

Those who work in the Netherlands are often under the impression that a lot of time is wasted on discussions and that these discussions all lead to nothing. There are often meetings, commonly named *overleg* (consultation, or deliberation), with documents, an agenda and a chairman. All those present have their say, after which their remarks are discussed. And all this can be done quite eloquently. At the end, everyone pulls out their agenda (calendar), to schedule the next meeting.

He who decides to skip an *overleg* because he has something more urgent to attend to, will soon learn that this is not a wise decision – even if his colleagues were to admit readily that there is much too much *overleg* going on. The interacting that takes place during such a meeting is very important for the general progress. He who does not appear is saying that he does not think that the subject is sufficiently important or, even worse, that he apparently does not take his colleagues seriously. Furthermore, he runs the risk of missing some of the essential information that may become evident during the meeting.

Those who are present during *overleg* show an interest in the problems of their colleagues. They supply suggestions, rather than amendments or commands, and thus declare themselves 'co-responsible'. The Dutch, in their final conclusions, like to use such metaphors as: 'we are all in one line'. Or even: 'our noses are pointing in the same direction again'. Ambitious beginners can also obtain useful information during an *overleg*: for instance, on what the pecking order is within the company.

As the Dutch only consider an idea to be partly theirs if they have been able to exercise influence on it and have been allowed to join the thinking process, it is advisable to take this into account when making plans. If you present a sharply chiseled decision, you will find that everyone has something to say about it and has questions to ask. This is why the Dutch will not be quick to present something as the only, the correct and the true solution. The advantage to this approach is that such an overleg will often lead to genuinely valuable suggestions for improvement on certain aspects of a plan. As a result, the plan will be a joint approach and you will be able to count on everyone's cooperation.

This time-consuming and seemingly useless process of *overleg* helps colleagues become a team. The amount of time that is lost around the table is more than made up for in efficiency and input once everyone goes back to work. Statistics clearly show this. Dutch employees are among the world's leaders when it comes to work productivity.

HARMONIOUS RELATIONSHIPS

You will find this attitude not only on a smaller scale, but also on a larger scale. Dutch business life is generally characterized by harmonious relationships. This is evident from the works council that companies are obligated to have by law and that is elected from and by the employees. Though this council does not have a lot of authority and can not do much more than advise the management, management has the obligation to consult it in many cases, such as reorganizations or large investment plans. The relationship between employer organizations and unions are also very harmonious, thus employees seldom go on strike in the Netherlands. The worst that could happen is that, in the case of wage negotiations, one of the parties involved leaves the negotiation table. Then, after a small concession has been made, the *overleg* will simply resume.

A few years ago, the courts introduced a calculation formula, known as the cantonal court formula (*kantonrechtersformule*), according to which the employee is awarded one, one-and-a-half or two months' salary per year of employment, depending on his age. Up till now, dismissed employees received this severance payment over and above their unemployment benefit (which they received provided their dismissal was involuntary); however, there is now a legislative proposal aimed at reducing the benefit by the amount of the severance pay. For more (hot-off-the-press) information, you can consult www.ontslag-krijgen.nl ('being fired').

WORKING THROUGH AN EMPLOYMENT AGENCY

Not all employment agencies are a member of a Union for Temporary Workers, as membership is not obligatory. However, all agencies must conform to the legally binding aspects of the CAO. There are two main Temporary Workers unions; the ABU and NBBU. These unions are governed by their own collective labor agreement (CAO), in which various regulations are given on (but not limited to) such subjects as:

*   statutory number of vacation days
*   holiday allowance
*   national holidays
*   salary statement specifications
*   working overtime
*   illness/sick pay
*   the 'Phase system' and 'Chain system'.

Please note that as per July 21, 2003, new laws have been imposed and all agencies must abide by the CAO, with the exception of articles 33 (pension), 34 (schooling) and 35 (facilities for employees). The current CAO is valid (declared generally applicable) until April 3, 2005, and the unions are re-negotiating certain articles, which could be incorporated after this date. These rulings will only become legally binding if and when the government passes them.

MULTILINGUAL JOBS

When looking for employment in the Netherlands whereby you can work in your native language, you can either register with various specialized employment agencies (a listing of these can be found at the end of this chapter) or you can apply directly to companies where the business language is your native language. The job market for foreign staff is not limited to the international call and shared service centers, but encompasses a wide spectrum of professions including, but not limited to: administration, secretarial, IT, finance, marketing, support staff, sales, logistics, middle and senior management, etc.

After the UK, Germany and France, the most 'multilingual' jobs are to be found in international call and shared service centers located in the Netherlands. There are over 150 multilingual call and shared service centers in the country, most of which are located in the Randstad region (The Hague, Rotterdam, Amsterdam). However, you will find more and more pan-European centers in Maastricht, Arnhem and other cities. Within these organizations, English is usually the business language.

Most Dutch people speak more than one foreign language, however, the international centers and companies have a preference for native speakers. This having been said, please do read the paragraph on *Protection Labor Market*, further on.

LANGUAGE

It is still pretty common for foreigners to live and work in the Netherlands for years without having to learn the language, however, we cannot emphasize enough the importance of learning Dutch; this will not only be beneficial within the work place but also during your day-to-day endeavors in the Netherlands. Far too many foreigners do not make the effort to even learn the basics, but the Dutch always appreciate and respect those who make the effort to learn their language. Dutch is not the easiest language to learn, and it can be very difficult for those in the Randstad to have the opportunity to practice their Dutch language skills, as the helpful Dutch will almost invariably switch to English once they detect an accent. But, please persevere; the effort will pay off in the end, especially for those who plan on staying in the Netherlands for a longer period of time.

Those of you coming to Holland from outside the EU will be obligated to follow the integration program, which includes learning the language.

PROTECTION LABOR MARKET

When applying for a work permit, beware of the stringent legal protection of the Dutch labor market, making it very difficult for non-EU/EEA/Swiss nationals to receive such a permit (you can read more about this on page 113) to work here. Being a native speaker will not longer automatically qualify you, if the Dutch authorities are of the opinion that your prospective employer should be able to find a Dutch/EU/EEA/Swiss employee who can also speak your language.

Please also note that when faced with the choice, the employer, who will be the one applying for your work permit, might well choose an employee who does not need a work permit over you (if you do need one) – as the application process is an expensive and time-consuming one.

SALARIES

In general, an expat may be surprised at the salaries of the Netherlands compared to those in their country of origin. Salaries are always commensurate with the general cost of living and pay parity is generally only reached at very senior management levels. For instance, in Belgium, France and Germany, wages generally are considerably higher. However, you will find that, in fact, the net wages are comparable as most expenses and some allowances are exempt of tax.

An average administrative position earns between € 1,150 and € 2,050 gross per month. A secretarial position earns between € 1,400 and € 2,800 gross per month, depending on age, job specification, experience, qualifications, and language skills. A statutory holiday allowance (minimum of 8% of a gross annual salary) is awarded to each individual pro-rated to the number of months worked. The holiday allowance is usually paid in the month of May.

But how much do you get in hand? Below, we have given an approximate indication:

Gross monthly salary	rate 2 (for most employees)*
€ 1,475	€ 1,175 in hand
€ 1,675	€ 1,275
€ 1,875	€ 1,400
€ 2,075	€ 1,500
€ 2,275	€ 1,600

€ 2,475	€ 1,700
€ 2,675	€ 1,900
€ 2,825	€ 1,975

* these amounts are approximates (not including and, if applicable travel allowance, union deductions, pension deduction, etc.)

(COMPULSORY) HEALTH INSURANCE

It is crucial to know that the rules on medical insurance in the Netherlands are extremely complicated so that it is in your interest to seek professional advice. However, we will give you a summary: If you are employed in the Netherlands and your gross annual salary does not exceed the so-called 'ceiling amount' (*ziekenfondsgrens*) of € 33,000, you are covered by the Health Insurance Act (*Ziekenfonds*). (See more on page 123.) If this is the case for you, you must register with a *Ziekenfonds* insurance company (most companies offer both *Ziekenfonds* and private coverage). A percentage of your wages will be deducted at source, while you will owe a further fixed contribution. We highly recommend that you contact your employer/agency to ensure that you are paying the correct contributions. The calculation model is not simply based on salary, but also on other allowances that could tip your salary above the 'ceiling', so it is not advisable to attempt this calculation yourself. Once your gross annual salary exceeds € 33,000, you must take out private insurance (*particuliere ziektekostenverzekering*). Please be aware that, though employers are not obligated to do this, most offer a collective insurance package to their employees and contribute the so-called 'employer's portion' to the premium. If you are in the country and not covered by the *Ziekenfonds* (due to your salary level or the fact that you are claiming benefits), you are obligated to have private medical insurance for yourself and family members.

Note: you must inform your employer of the name of your (*Ziekenfonds*) insurance company and your registration number at the start of your employment.

HOW TO FIND A JOB

Despite the possible language barrier, the Dutch employment market offers foreigners sufficient career opportunities. On the other hand, due to the virtual standstill of the economy during the year 2004, the demand for labor is still diminishing. The unemployment rate, still on the rise at the start of this year (2005), is above 6% now. Whereas the average job search took 2-3 months in 2001-2002, it now takes more than five months.

Because the Dutch economy is very internationally oriented, the ability to speak English – fluently – is an important requirement when looking for a good job. However, this is primarily the case for commercial companies and less so for certain sectors, such as the health sector, non-profit organizations and non-governmental organizations. Remember also that it is not easy to find a part-time job of fewer than four days a week.

THE FIRST STEP

There are four ways to find a job:
* through ads in the printed press and on the Internet (both on jobsites and on the websites of the employers)
* through employment and recruitment agencies

* by means of an open application with an employer
* by networking.

In principle, you should try all four and not limit yourself to one of these.

NEWSPAPERS

The best newspapers for English-language ads are:
* De *Telegraaf*, Saturday edition, for commercial and administrative/clerical jobs
* Het *Financieele Dagblad*, Thursday edition, for financial and bank positions
* *Algemeen Dagblad*, Saturday edition, for administrative/clerical and technical positions
* *Volkskrant*, Saturday edition, for positions in the non-profit and health sectors
* Your regional daily newspaper, Saturday edition, for administrative/clerical and secretarial positions
* The weekly magazine *Intermediair* for positions for those with a higher education.

EMPLOYMENT AND RECRUITMENT AGENCIES

For those who do not have sufficient (job-specific) work experience, *uitzendbureaus* (employment or temp agencies) are a good first step, but be clear about the type of job you do and do not want. If you have more than three years (specific) work experience, then you should also approach the specialized recruitment agencies, but ask in advance whether or not a command of the Dutch language is a requirement.

At the moment, there are a lot of job seekers out there, so keep in mind that the employment agencies are getting a lot of calls from a lot of candidates. Consequently, these agencies are *only* interested in candidates who fit the profiles for the vacancies they have. Keep this in mind when composing your cv: they will want to see it first, before deciding whether or not to meet you in person. If there is no fit, you will be wasting not only your time, but also theirs.

Beware that agencies are normally not interested in candidates who need a work permit to work in the Netherlands. If you need a work permit your best chance is through contacting companies directly and not through an agency (you can read more about when you need a work permit and the complicated legal rules around obtaining one on page 113).

OPEN APPLICATIONS

Open applications are also a good way of finding a job, though possibly not the quickest. Employers often appreciate the attention they receive and the clear willingness to take the initiative that you thus demonstrate. You should of course orient yourself on the organizational structure, the department and the positions. Do not be vague about what you want and what you have to offer. Furthermore, it is always advisable to address a specific person in your application, preferably the manager of the department for which you want to work or the human resource manager who is responsible for recruitment.

NETWORKING

Networking can also help you find a suitable job. It is important to follow a certain strategy in doing this. To start with, you should make an overview of your network (on paper) and consciously set

about expanding upon it. The most important thing to keep in mind is that you clearly and concisely communicate what you are looking for and what you have to offer to every person you meet. Good networkers express themselves clearly and concisely. Find out whether there is an organization of professionals within your profession in the Netherlands that you can join. A good place to start networking is with network-club.com; this club meets once every three months with a whole evening dedicated to networking in the Netherlands.

TIPS FOR WRITING YOUR RESUME

First of all: a resume is called a 'curriculum vitae' (or cv) in Europe. In the Netherlands, employers prefer a concise cv (one page) that has been tailor-made to the position within the organization. Always start with your work experience, unless you have just graduated and do not yet have any work experience. Arrange your experience chronologically, starting with the most recent experience. Pay special attention to the job titles of the positions you held: is the job title the same in the Netherlands as in the country you are from? Do not forget to have your diplomas evaluated by IDW (www.idw.nl, see the end of the chapter) so that your employer knows what the comparable Dutch diploma is. Also make clear if you have lived/worked/studied in more than one country as today's employers are specifically looking for employees who have international experience. Last but not least, clearly specify your language abilities.

TIPS FOR WRITING A COVER LETTER

Always send a cover letter along with your cv, in which you state why you are applying for this position. It goes without saying that it is important to know about the organization to which you are applying and in your cover letter it is always a good idea to include one or two sentences on what you expect to contribute to the company. Employers appreciate it when you try to place yourself in their customers' shoes and try to anticipate their wishes.

BE FLEXIBLE

Aside from showing your knowledge and abilities, it is important to be flexible, particularly when it comes to the type of employer that you want to work for. You will be missing opportunities if you insist on focusing on certain sectors (industries); many expats want to work in Consumer Goods (such as personal care products or sports shoes) and overlook the business to business-sectors (such as chemicals, engineering or energy). You should take into account that the competition is great in the consumer goods sectors and the number of job openings limited, as these companies are not expanding quickly, certainly not compared to certain business to business-sectors.

And of course, do not forget: don't choose an employer, choose your boss.

FINDING A JOB VIA THE INTERNET
A Fast Growing Use

One of the more interesting uses for the Internet is in the area of posting jobs and searching and applying for jobs. The Internet does not charge by the line and allows employers to reach potential employees the world round without having to take out expensive ads in dozens of newspapers. Companies can simply place a one-line reference to their website in newspapers and magazines and job seekers will know where to find them.

Advantages for Job Seekers

The advantages are plentiful. Job seekers can apply to jobs all across the world, without having to find a way to buy a local newspaper (say, you live in Brussels and are considering looking for a job in Hong Kong). Once you have found a company you are interested in, all you have to do is visit its Internet site to find out more about it; you no longer have to go to the library or ask the company to send you some information in advance. However, keep in mind that, as it is so easy to send your cv via the Internet, employers receive a shipload of cvs from all over the world. Consequently, they sometimes doubt the seriousness of the jobseekers, while many cvs may be of the dime-a-dozen variety (see more about setting up your cv further on, under *Key Words*). A good idea would be for you to make an initial or follow-up phone call to your prospective employer.

Advantages for Employers

The advantages for employers are also many: job applications that come in by e-mail, can be sorted by experience, interest or geographic area, allowing them to cut down considerably on the amount of time spent reading whether a particular application is of relevance to the department in question. (However, keep in mind that this depends on your prospective employer's degree of organization; if they do not have a good system for sorting out cvs, your cv might still get lost in the fray.) Thanks to electronic advertising and job applications (the advertisement goes on line immediately, responses are received just as quickly), the time spent filling a position can be cut in half.

Key Words

There are a number of issues you should keep in mind. Firstly, precisely because information on your potential employer is so easy to find via the Internet, the employer expects you to know more about the company once you come in for a job interview. Another is that you should not only work on composing a presentable letter, but you should also focus on using key words. You are looking for a job in Off-Shore Construction, you are applying for their position in Hong Kong, you have five years experience in Airport Sites, you speak three languages, including Cantonese. Now that your potential employer is likely to sort your letter according to the key words, make sure you don't express an interest for their position in 'Hog Kong' or a job in 'Constriction' – your application will simply never be picked up. To avoid this, make use of the 'spell-checker', but don't forget to use your own, ever-critical, eye. As mentioned earlier, thanks to the discovery of the convenience of Internet job applications, employers probably receive dozens of applications a day, causing them to doubt the seriousness of the applicants. So make sure you distinguish yourself through your

cv and cover letter: keep it concise and to-the-point, making it clear that you are applying for *this* job with *this* company (and why) – and what you have to offer them.

E-mailing Your Resume/cv

A word of advice for those sending their resume via electronic mail: do not include your letter as a separate attachment, but (also) make it part of the e-mail message. Attachments are not always easy to open and they may contain viruses that would cause the computer to reject them, and photos (may) take a lot of time to download.

E-LANCERS

The Internet and e-mail have increased the possibilities of working from your own home (or wherever you are) immeasurably and have led to a new phenomenon: e-lancing. E-lancing makes it possible to work and still be there for your family, to take on that one essential job when on vacation and, in certain countries, being a self-employed e-lancer allows you to benefit from great reductions for tax purposes, allowing you to convert a considerably higher amount of your gross income into net income. This is certainly the case for the Netherlands (see more on setting up your own business on page 72).

INTERNET ADDRESSES

If you've decided to give the Internet a try, you will find a few useful addresses at the end of the chapter.

SOFI-NUMBER

Everyone who is employed legally has a 'social-fiscal' number (sofi-nummer) for tax purposes, which you can obtain at the local tax office. This number is necessary for your employer to pay your salary and to ensure that contributions for your benefits are properly credited. You will also need a sofi-number when you register with temporary job agencies. To obtain a sofi-number, you must first go to the city offices and register with the population department (*Bevolkingsregister*). Once registered with the population department, you can ask them for the form stating your registration (*uittreksel*), which you need in order to get a sofi-number. Take the registration form and your passport (or EU/European identity card) to the tax office (*Belastingdienst*) to get your number. Only 18 tax offices are authorized to issue the sofi-number, so check up front what the nearest tax office is where you can get your number and keep in mind that you will probably have to make an appointment to show up in person. If you are a non-EU/EEA/Swiss national, you will also need your work permit and residence permit. If you are an EU/EEA/Swiss national, you will only have to bring along your passport in which the Aliens Department of the Police has noted that you are allowed to live/work here.

If you do not yet live in the Netherlands, you can submit a written request for a sofi-number with the tax office in Heerlen, however, keep in mind that the policy on issuing a sofi-number in this situation is not yet clear-cut – so that it is not guaranteed that you will get one.

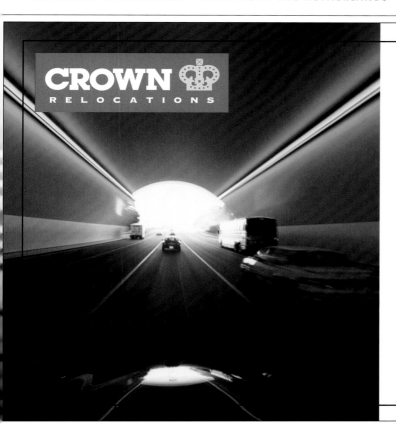

SOCIAL SECURITY

TO WHOM IS IT APPLICABLE

Those who are posted to the Netherlands to work are in principle subject to the Dutch social security system. This legislation is also important for their partners and/or other members of their families, unless they are exempt under EC Regulation 1408/71 or a bilateral treaty (both of which you will read about further on). There are two kinds of compulsory social insurance schemes in the Netherlands; one is applicable to the population in general and one to employees.

NATIONAL INSURANCE SCHEMES

In principle the national insurance schemes (*volksverzekeringen*) cover all persons living or working in the Netherlands. The schemes are as follows:

General Old Age Pensions Act (AOW)

Those who are covered by the AOW are entitled to an old age pension upon reaching the age of 65. The pension is accrued between the ages of 15 and 65 and each year the beneficiary is insured, he accrues 2% of the maximum benefit.

General Surviving Relatives Act (ANW)

Those who are covered by the General Surviving Relatives Act (ANW) are entitled to a widow's, widower's or 'dependent children'-benefit. The deceased spouse, partner or parent must have been insured under the ANW at the date of his or her death.

The amount paid out on the basis of the benefit is a percentage of the minimum wage – however, the actual benefit can be less since the ANW survivor's benefit is income-dependent.

Exceptional Medical Expenses Act (AWBZ)

The AWBZ makes a provision for treatment and nursing in recognized institutions and nursing homes. In addition, it provides coverage for the supply of artificial appliances, however, it does not generally provide for facilities that are covered by the Health Insurance Act (ZFW) or private health insurance.

Child Benefit Act (AKW)

In principle, this benefit (*Kinderbijslag*) is for children under the age of 18. The amount of the allowance depends on the age of the child. For children born before January 1, 1995, other rules apply when determining the amount due.

CONTRIBUTIONS (Payable to Tax Department)

Contributions for the national insurance schemes are levied on income up to € 30,357 per year, together with the income tax. The percentages are:

	employer	employee
AOW	-	17.90%
ANW	-	1.25%
AKW	-	-
AWBZ	-	13.45%
Total	-	32.60%

EMPLOYEE INSURANCE SCHEMES

In principle, anyone employed in the Netherlands is compulsorily insured under the employee insurance schemes (*werknemersverzekeringen*). If the total of any of the first three benefits and any other family income is less than the statutory social minimum income, the recipient is entitled to apply to the Social Security Institution for a supplement under the Supplemental Benefits Act (*Toeslagenwet*).

The schemes are as follows:

Sickness Benefits Act (ZW)/WULBZ

Pursuant to the WULBZ (*Wet Uitbreiding Loondoorbetaling bij Ziekte* – Continuation of Wage Payments during Sickness Act, which was introduced to partly replace the ZW), an employer is obligated to continue paying 70% (up to a maximum of € 114 gross per day) of the employee's salary during the first 104 weeks of sickness, provided the employee has a contract governed by the Dutch civil code. Depending on the employer, this payment is capped or can even be 100% of the employee's salary.

The Sickness Benefits Act (ZW) will only continue to exist as a 'safety net' for employees who do not – or no longer – have an employer, for example temporary workers and those who have taken out a voluntary ZW-insurance. Sick pay is usually 70% of the daily pay and is paid until the employee has been on sick leave for a maximum of 104 weeks.

Female employees are given leave of at least 16 weeks in the event of pregnancy, during which period sick pay is also paid out (you can read more about this on page 184). The benefit is then 100% of the salary, up to a maximum amount.

Disability Insurance Act (WAO)

The WAO entitles employees under the age of 65 to a benefit if they are still at least 15% unfit for work after 104 weeks of disability. The amount of the benefit depends on the degree of disability, the last wage earned and the age at which the disability occurred. The maximum benefit is the same as under the Sickness Benefits Act. How long the benefits are paid depends on the total years of insurance, income and age. It is also possible to take out additional private insurance.

Persons who are partially disabled and also partially unemployed may under certain circumstances be entitled to an additional benefit.

Unemployment Insurance Act (WW)

The WW insures employees against the financial consequences of unemployment. There are two requirements that must be met for a person to be entitled to a WW-benefit:

- he/she must have been employed for a period of at least 26 weeks over the 39 weeks immediately prior to becoming unemployed; and
- he/she must have received wages over 52 days or more in at least four of the five calendar years prior to the year in which he/she became unemployed.

If only the first requirement is met, the employee will receive a WW-benefit set at 70% of the minimum wage for a period of six months (or 70% of the daily wage if this is less than the minimum wage). If both requirements are met, he/she will receive a salary-related WW-benefit of 70% of the last-earned wage (with a maxi-

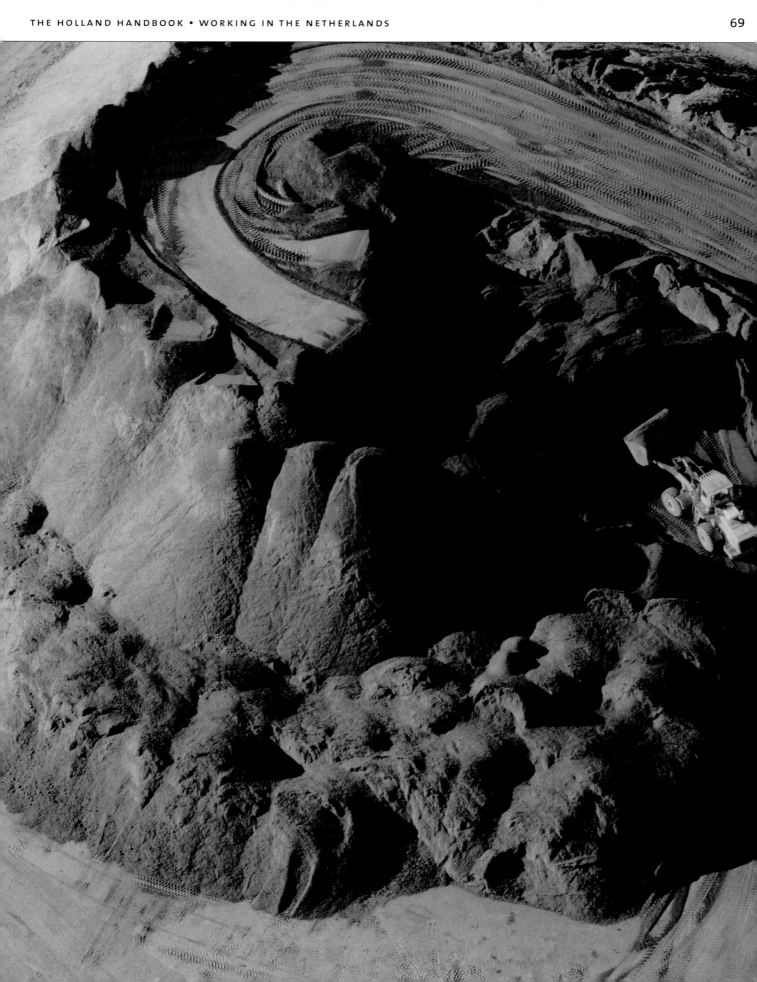

The Netherlands is one of the world's most prosperous countries.
A politically and economically stable member of the European Union,
the country ranks high in all-important standard-of-living indicators.

Almere Greater Amsterdam Area

Situated in the Greater Amsterdam Area, (within a 45-minute drive to Amsterdam Airport Schiphol) Almere is a new town with a current population of 172,000. Almere offers a variety of high quality industrial estates and office locations. Thousands of businesses, both large and small, have already established their companies in fast-growing, dynamic Almere.

Why?
Because this easily accessible and strategically situated town offers many advantages for the businesses established here. Furthermore, Almere is the leading city in The Netherlands in IT facilities such as broadband infrastructure to make the business climate even more complete.

Staff at Almere's Department of Economic Affairs think and act like entrepreneurs. Fast and professional and with your wishes in mind, they will work with you to establish the basis for your business in Almere. Almere gives you the space you need, in every respect. For more information please contact:

City of Almere
Department of Economic Affairs
P.O. Box 200, 1300 AE Almere
Telephone +31 36 548 48 00
Fax +31 36 539 99 20
e-mail: business@almere.nl
www.almere.nl/business

City of Almere

Almere: a city that works like a business, is a good place for a business

mum of € 167) gross per day. The duration of the salary-related benefit depends on the employee's employment record.

Health Insurance Act (ZFW)
Those who are covered by the ZFW are entitled to medical, paramedical and dental care and many other forms of treatment and provisions. Employees with an agreed fixed wage that does not exceed € 33,000 are compulsorily insured under the Health Insurance Act. In addition to paying a percentage of their wage as a contribution, they also pay a fixed nominal contribution.

CONTRIBUTIONS (Payable to Social Security Institution)

	employer	employee
WAO	5.60%	-
WW	2.45%	5.85%
ZFW	6.75%	1.45%

Except for the contributions payable under the Health Insurance Act, contributions for the employee insurance schemes are levied on wages and salaries up to € 30,357 per year, separately from income tax.

SELF-EMPLOYED PERSONS INSURANCE SCHEMES
For self-employed persons, there are the following insurance schemes:

Compulsory Health Insurance Act (ZFW)
Self-employed persons who earn an income below a certain level are compulsorily insured for the Compulsory Health Insurance Act. These are self-employed persons whose average taxable income was less than € 21,050 annually over the three to five years preceding the calendar year in question. They pay a contribution of 8.45% of their taxable income and in addition to this, they pay a fixed amount of contribution.

Self-Employed Persons Disability Act (WAZ)
This Act has been abolished as of August 1, 2004. There are a number of transitional rules for those self-employed persons who were already receiving this benefit or who were already pregnant before this date. Self-employed persons are now expected to arrange their own insurance (also if they become pregnant after above date). Should an insurance company refuse them – due to the extent of the risk – or impose certain restrictions, then so-called alternative insurance is available. You can read more about his on page 124.

CONTRIBUTIONS (Payable to Tax Department)
The contributions for the ZFW are levied by the tax department, together with the income tax.

SOCIAL INSURANCES

ANOTHER EU MEMBER STATE

Dutch Social Security
An employee who works in the Netherlands is, in principle, subject to the Dutch social security legislation, unless he has been posted from another EU or EEA (European Economic Area) member state, Switzerland or a state with which the Netherlands has entered into an agreement on social security. In the following sections this exception will be discussed in more detail.

Continued Social Security
Under Regulation (EC) No. 1408/71 of the European Community, a person who is employed by a foreign company in an EU member state and temporarily posted by this company to the Netherlands may remain covered by the social security legislation of the member state from which he is being sent, provided the following conditions are satisfied:
- the employee is covered by the social security schemes of the member state from which he is being sent
- the employee remains in the employment of the company in the other member state
- the anticipated duration of the duties for which the employee is posted abroad does not exceed 12 months. If the duration of the posting is likely to exceed the 12-month limit due to unforeseen circumstances, the legislation of the first member state may continue to apply for a further maximum period of 12 months. A request for such an extension must be submitted on time
- the employee is not sent to replace another person who has completed his maximum term of posting
- the Dutch company to which the person is temporarily posted will not subsequently post him to work for another company
- the employer usually (in the case of agencies) or substantially (in the case of other types of companies) carries out work on the territory of the sending state
- for third country nationals: they legally reside in the EU and have moved within the EU.

If the above conditions are satisfied, the social security legislation of the first member state will remain applicable and the employee will be exempted from the payment of social security contributions in the Netherlands.

Exceptions
The Regulation contains certain exceptions (article 17) that can be invoked in those cases in which it is in the interest of the employee to deviate from the above rules, for instance, when it is already clear beforehand that the duration of the posting will exceed 12 months. In the event of such a request, the two member states concerned will conduct negotiations and, if the request is granted, will reach an agreement. Requests to continue the applicability of the foreign social security legislation under these provisions are generally granted when the anticipated duration of the posting does not exceed five years. Extensions beyond the five-year period are only very exceptionally allowed.

Certificate
If, under the Regulation, the person posted abroad indeed remains insured in the state from which he is being sent, a certificate to this effect may be requested. Depending on the situation, either of two certificates (known as E 101 and E 102) will be required. The certificate can be produced in order to make clear in which country contributions have to be paid.
In order to receive medical care (ZFW or AWBZ) in the Netherlands, in addition to the form E 101, additional forms from the competent

institution abroad are needed, stating that the person is indeed insured and entitled to medical care.

ANOTHER TREATY MEMBER STATE

Social Security Treaty

If a person is posted from abroad to the Netherlands and the Netherlands has entered into a social security treaty with that other country, the applicable legislation will be determined in accordance with the rules of the treaty. It should first be determined whether the person is covered by the scope of the treaty. For this to be the case, it is generally required that the employee is a national of one of the treaty states and/or was insured in one of the states before being posted abroad.

Temporary Posting

If the posting is temporary, most treaties allow the continuation of the application of the legislation of the country from which the employee has been posted.

Conditions

The conditions that must be satisfied may vary slightly from one treaty to another, but will generally comprise the following:
- before being posted abroad, the employee was insured according to the social security legislation of the country from which he is being posted
- the employment with the company in the country from which the person is posted is continued.

Period

The period during which the posting is allowed to continue varies from 12 months to an unlimited period (depending on the treaty) and extension is sometimes possible (also depending on the treaty).

Certificate

It is advisable to apply for a certificate stating which legislation is applicable. In some treaty member states, such an application is one of the conditions for posting an employee abroad.

General Rule

If the conditions are not satisfied, the general rule of the relevant treaty takes effect. In all treaties, the general rule is that the Dutch legislation is applicable if the duties are carried out in the Netherlands. Nearly all treaties prevent the simultaneous applicability of the legislation of two countries.

A NON-TREATY MEMBER STATE

Exemption not Possible

If a person is posted from a country with which the Netherlands has not entered into a social security treaty, it is – in general – not possible to obtain an exemption from the Dutch social insurances. As there is no applicable treaty, it is possible that the employee will have to participate in the social security systems of both countries. This may result both in double liability to pay contributions and double entitlement to benefits.

Period Shorter than Six Months

If a non-resident carries out work in the Netherlands which lasts less than six months, he will under certain conditions not be under compulsory insurance for the employee insurance schemes. However, if his income earned in the Netherlands is subject to wage tax here, and the duties are in fact carried out in the Netherlands, he will nevertheless be under compulsory insurance for the national insurance schemes.

STARTING YOUR OWN COMPANY

Maybe you came to the Netherlands for the purpose of starting up your own company. Or maybe you came here with your spouse/partner – who was sent here by his or her employer – and are looking to start up your own source of income. In other words, you are considering setting up (your own) business in the Netherlands. What are some of the things you have to think of? And who can help you answer the many questions you will have? What diplomas do you need?
There are various organizations that you can turn to for help.

CHAMBERS OF COMMERCE

There are more than 20 regional Chambers of Commerce (*Kamers van Koophandel*) in the Netherlands. One of their main tasks is to register (practically) all companies based in Holland, whether they are of Dutch origin or foreign. Public and private limited companies, cooperative societies and mutual guarantee associations are obligated to register with the Chamber of Commerce of the district in which they are established, even if they do not carry out a business. Private persons who work on a free-lance basis are not obligated to register. The purpose of this registration is to enable third parties to find information on a company – such as who is liable, who can make binding commitments; in other words, the legal structure of a company. The system has been proven to be reliable, transparent and up-to-date.
The Chamber of Commerce is a public institution and the information desk can provide you with information on how to start a business, which diplomas you need for your specific line of business, how to write a business plan to be able to finance your ideas and what plans your municipality has within the area in which you want to establish your firm.

IMK

Another institution you can turn to for information is the *Instituut voor Midden- en Kleinbedrijf* (Institute for Small and Medium-Sized Companies). The IMK has prepared a manual covering the specifics for those who want to start up a business and offers starter courses. You will find its address and telephone number at the end of the chapter.

OTHER INSTITUTIONS

Other institutions that can offer you advice are banks and the national tax office. Both have information desks for people who plan to start their own business and can provide you with the needed information. And last, but not least, all major cities have a business desk in the town hall.

SETTING UP AN ESTABLISHMENT

The Dutch policy of free enterprise entails that there are no specific restrictions for foreign companies who wish to start a business in the Netherlands, nor are there restrictions on the ownership of real estate or on the remission of capital and profits abroad.

There are various ways in which foreign companies can set up a permanent establishment in the Netherlands. The Dutch legal system provides a framework with various options, which are described in this section.

- branch office
- *eenmanszaak*: a one-man business
- *maatschap*: partnership – form involving more than one person, usually used by accountants, doctors, etc.
- *vennootschap onder firma* (Vof): general or commercial partnership – form involving more than one person, under a common name, each severally liable
- *commanditaire vennootschap* (cv): limited partnership with managing and 'silent' partners
- *besloten vennootschap* (BV): private company with limited liability
- *naamloze vennootschap* (NV): (public) corporation.

BRANCH OFFICE

A foreign company does not require any prior approval from the Dutch authorities for the establishment of a branch office in the Netherlands. The foreign company has to file various details (i.e. name, trade name, objects, manager) and documents (i.e. articles of association) pertaining to the foreign company and the branch office. The local manager of the branch office does not have to be of Dutch nationality.

PARTNERSHIP

Under Dutch law it is possible to set up a partnership with two or more partners: the general partnership ('Vof' or vennootschap onder firma) and the limited partnership ('cv' or commanditaire vennootschap). The basic difference between these two forms of partnership is the partners' liabilities. A limited partnership has one or more managing partners (beherende vennoten) and one or more 'silent' partners (commanditaire vennoten). The liability of the 'silent' partners is limited to the amount of their capital contributions. Each partner in a general partnership is, in addition to the partnership itself, severally liable for the obligations of the company. Under Dutch law a partnership is similar to a business under single proprietorship, except that there are two or more owners.

COMPANIES WITH LIMITED LIABILITY

In the Netherlands, corporate law defines two different types of companies with limited liability: the NB (*naamloze vennootschap*), which is a public company with limited liability, and the BV (*besloten vennootschap*), which is a private company with limited liability.

The main differences between the two types of companies are:
- the shares in the NV can be either in bearer or in registered form; the shares in the BV are in registered form only
- the minimum issued and paid up capital of the NV is € 45,000; at present the BV's minimum capital amounts to € 18,000
- the Articles of Association of a BV must include restrictions for the transfer of its shares; such restrictions are optional for the NV
- the legal limitations regarding the company's purchase of shares in its own capital and regarding financial assistance by the company are stricter for an NV than for a BV
- the BV form is particularly suitable for a wholly-owned subsidiary, joint venture companies and family businesses. The NV is suitable for larger companies whose shares may be listed.

Ask your accountant, legal or financial advisor or the Chamber of Commerce about the legal and fiscal consequences of the above forms.

TAXES SELF-EMPLOYED PERSONS

If you run your own business you can be held liable for the following:
- wage tax
- income tax
- national insurance schemes
- employee insurance schemes
- VAT (value added tax)

Self-employed persons who have only themselves to think of owe income tax, VAT and, if their income is below a certain level, contributions for the Compulsory Health Insurance Scheme. You can read more about the national and employee insurance schemes (including the Compulsory Health Insurance Scheme) on page 68.

VAT

Those who deliver services and goods in the Netherlands are obligated to charge their customers VAT (*Belasting Toegevoegde Waarde* or BTW), which they subsequently pay to the tax authori-

ties. They owe this, no matter whether they (aim to) make a profit or not, the moment an invoice is sent out. For the delivery of goods and services outside the Netherlands, other rules apply.

The amount due should be reported on the *Aangifte omzet-belasting*, or Turnover Tax Return, on a regular basis (monthly, quarterly or yearly). However, the amount of VAT that you have paid to others, who deliver their goods and services to you, can be deducted from the amount of VAT you owe. Those whose 'VAT income' does not exceed a certain amount enjoy a full or limited exemption from paying the amount due to the tax authorities.

FINANCIAL AID AND DEDUCTIONS

The national tax office can tell you about the Tante Agaath-regulation, a scheme that makes it fiscally attractive for private persons to lend money to those who are setting up a business. Of course, you can approach a bank and see what they can do to help you, too.

When it comes to income tax, entrepreneurs enjoy an additional deduction over and above the levy rebate that every taxpayer has a right to every year. To this purpose you must prove that you spent at least 1,225 hours over the past tax year working for your own business (if your spouse works for the same company there are additional rules and possible deductions). Those who are starting up a new business (*startende ondernemers*) have a further deduction over the first few years.

DIPLOMAS

Depending on the type of business you want to start, there are a few different types of diplomas that you need. The most important of these is the AOV (*Algemene Ondernemers Vaardigheden*) or General Business Skills diploma – as you need it for virtually whatever type of business you want to start. You can ask at the Chamber of Commerce as to what type of diploma you will need and how or where you can obtain them. If you have an MBA, then you have met this requirement and do not need this diploma. Your diploma from home can be evaluated by Nuffic (see the end of the chapter), to see whether it qualifies.

FREE-LANCING

There are two ways you can go about free-lancing; either as a self-employed person or through an employment agency. In the first case, you can read about some of the rules that apply to you in this chapter; in the latter case, you are treated as an employee of the employment agency for tax purposes (you can read more about working for an employment agency in section A of this chapter).

PERMITS AND SOFI-NUMBER

Everyone who wants to work in the Netherlands needs a work and a residence permit as well as a sofi-number, see page 66 (for sofi-number) and page 113 (for permits).

REFERENCES

DUTCH SOCIAL SECURITY

MINISTRY OF SOCIAL AFFAIRS AND EMPLOYMENT (*Ministerie van Sociale Zaken en Werkgelegenheid*)
Anna van Hannoverstraat 4,
P.O. Box 90801, 2509 LV The Hague
Tel.: 070 333 44 44
Internet www.employment.gov.nl

TAXES

NATIONAL TAX OFFICE
Central Internet: www.belastingdienst.nl
National Tax Information, tel.: 0800 05 43

INTERNATIONAL TAX OFFICE HEERLEN
Postal address: P.O. Box 2865, 6401 DJ Heerlen
Visiting address: Kloosterweg 22,
6412 CN Heerlen (by appointment only)
Tel.: 045 560 31 11 or 0800 05 43 (National telephone number)
Internet: www.belastingdienst.nl/buitenland

NATIONAL TAX OFFICE STARTERSDESK
in the major offices:
Amsterdam, tel.: 020 687 65 00
The Hague, tel.: 070 330 40 86
Rotterdam, tel.: 010 290 53 28
Utrecht, tel.: 030 275 26 86
General tel. number for entrepreneurs:
0800 04 43
Central website: www.belastingdienst.nl

MAJOR REGIONAL CHAMBERS OF COMMERCE

AMSTERDAM CHAMBER OF COMMERCE
Kamer van Koophandel en Fabrieken voor Amsterdam
De Ruyterkade 5, 1013 AA Amsterdam
Tel.: 020 531 40 00
Fax: 020 531 47 99
Team International Trade Information
Tel.: 020 531 44 39
E-mail: post@amsterdam.kvk.nl
Internet: www.amsterdam.kvk.nl

ROTTERDAM CHAMBER OF COMMERCE
Kamer van Koophandel Rotterdam
Blaak 40, 3000 AL Rotterdam
Tel.: 010 402 77 77
Fax: 010 414 57 54
E-mail: post@rotterdam.kvk.nl
Internet: www.rotterdam.kvk.nl

THE HAGUE CHAMBER OF COMMERCE
Kamer van Koophandel Haaglanden
Koningskade 30, 2596 AA The Hague
Tel.: 070 328 71 00
Fax: 070 326 20 10
E-mail: info@denhaag.kvk.nl
Internet: www.denhaag.kvk.nl

UTRECHT CHAMBER OF COMMERCE
Kamer van Koophandel Utrecht
Kroonstraat 50, 3511 RC Utrecht
Tel.: 030 236 32 11
Fax: 030 231 28 04
E-mail: post@utrecht.kvk.nl
Internet: www.utrecht.kvk.nl

For other Regional Offices Contact:

ASSOCIATION OF CHAMBERS OF COMMERCE
VVK, *Vereniging van Kamers van Koophandel en Fabrieken in Nederland*
Watermolenlaan 1, 3447 GT Woerden
Tel.: 0348 426 911
Fax: 0348 426 216
National website: www.kvk.nl

INTERNATIONAL CHAMBERS OF COMMERCE

AMERICAN CHAMBER OF COMMERCE IN THE NETHERLANDS
Scheveningseweg 58,
2517 KW The Hague
Tel.: 070 365 98 08
Internet: www.amcham.nl

BELGISCH-LUXEMBURGSE KAMER VAN KOOPHANDEL VOOR NEDERLAND
Groenmarkt 17, 3311 BD Dordrecht
Tel: 078 635 19 90
Internet: www.beluned.nl

JAPANESE CHAMBER OF COMMERCE
World Trade Center 8-9,
Strawinskylaan 935,
1077 XX Amsterdam
Tel.: 020 662 14 57
Internet: www.jcc-holland.nl

NETHERLANDS BRITISH CHAMBER OF COMMERCE
Nieuwezijds Voorburgwal 328,
1012 RW Amsterdam
Tel.: 020 421 70 40
Internet: www.nbcc.co.uk

NETHERLANDS CANADIAN CHAMBER OF COMMERCE
Nieuwe Uitleg 26, 2514 BR The Hague
Tel.: 070 363 48 91
Internet: www.netherlandscanada.nl

CHAMBER OF COMMERCE NETHERLANDS ISRAËL
Bankrashof 3, 1183 NP Amstelveen
Tel: 020 503 80 63
Internet: www.kvkni.nl

NETHERLANDS GERMAN CHAMBER OF COMMERCE
Nassauplein 30, 2585 EC The Hague
Tel.: 070 311 41 36
Internet: www.dnhk.nl

NETHERLANDS FRANCE CHAMBER OF COMMERCE
Wibautstraat 129, 1091 GL Amsterdam
Tel: 020 562 82 00
Internet: www.cfci.nl

NETHERLANDS SOUTH AFRICAN CHAMBER OF COMMERCE
Bezuidenhoutseweg 181, 2594 AH The Hague
Tel: 070 347 07 81
Internet: www.sanec.nl

MAJOR BANKS IN THE NETHERLANDS

DE NEDERLANDSCHE BANK (Dutch Central Bank): www.dnb.nl/english
ABN AMRO Bank: www.abnamro.com
ING BANK: www.inggroup.com
FORTIS BANK: www.fortis.com
POSTBANK: www.postbank.nl
RABOBANK: www.rabobank.nl
SNS BANK: www.snsbank.nl

BUSINESS CLUBS/CENTERS

The Amsterdam American Business Club
Tel.: 020 520 75 34, internet: www.aabc.nl
The Hague American Business Club
Tel.: 070 314 15 29
The Hague International Network (THIN)
Tel.: 070 306 22 11
The Rotterdam American Business Club
Tel.: 06 418 243 57, internet: www.rabc.nl
The International Business Network
Tel.: 070 322 80 50
Club of Amsterdam
Internet: www.clubofamsterdam.com
Commercial Anglo Dutch Society

REFERENCES

Tel.: 0546 82 43 44
Australian Business in Europe
Tel.: 020 671 70 17
Asia House (various Asian Business Clubs)
Tel.: 020 676 66 86
Eastern Europe Trade Club
Tel.: 020 523 66 47
Irish Industrial Development Authority
Tel.: 020 679 86 66
Irish Trade Board
Tel.: 020 676 31 41
Italian Institute for foreign Trade
Tel.: 020 644 23 51
Australian Business in Europe
Tel.: 020 671 70 17
Euro Business Center Maastricht
Tel.: 043 356 63 00, internet:
www.eurobusinesscenter.nl
LIOF Business Hosting Limburg
Tel.: 043 280 280, internet:
www.liofbusinesshosting.nl
World Trade Center Business Club
Tel.: 020 575 30 47, internet:
www.wtcamsterdam.nl
World Trade Center Amsterdam
Tel.: 020 757 91 11, internet:
www.wtcamsterdam.nl
World Trade Center Amsterdam Airport
Tel.: 020 446 63 33, internet:
www.wtcschiphol.nl
World Trade Center Rotterdam
Tel.: 010 405 50 16, internet:
www.wtcrotterdam.nl

NETWORK CLUBS

NETWORK-CLUB.COM: a business club
dedicated to facilitating business by
providing a platform for members to
establish, strengthen, and utilize personal
business relationships. Their membership
represents a wide variety of people
representing companies from all vertical
markets and includes over 3,500 members
worldwide.
Internet www.network-club.com

**KEA KIWI EXPAT ASSOCIATION - NEW
ZEALAND** Expat Network in the Netherlands
this New Zealand business-networking
group has almost 300 members. KEA is a
global networking organization, with over
9,000 members worldwide in 65 countries
Tel.: Grant King 020 671 70 17
Internet: www.kiwiexpat.org.nz

**WOMEN'S INTERNATIONAL NETWORK
(WIN)**: the international networking association for professional women in the Netherlands. WIN is an affiliate of the European
Professional Women's Network. Internet:
www.womensinternational.net

DEVELOPMENT FOUNDATIONS

**AMSTERDAM FOREIGN INVESTMENT
OFFICE (AFIO)**
Weesperstraat 89, Metropool Building 4th
floor, 1018 VN Amsterdam
P.O. Box 2133, 1000 CC Amsterdam
Tel.: 020 552 35 36
E-mail: afio@ez.amsterdam.nl
Internet: www.afio.amsterdam.nl

CITY OF ALMERE
Department of Economic Affairs, Business
Counter
P.O. Box 200, 1300 AE Almere
Tel.: 036 548 46 00
E-mail: business@almere.nl
Internet: www.businessinalmere.nl

AMSTERDAM AIRPORT AREA
P.O. Box 75700, 1118 ZT Schiphol Airport
Tel.: 020 405 47 77
E-mail: info@aaarea.nl
Internet: www.aaarea.nl

**WEST-HOLLAND FOREIGN INVESTMENT
AGENCY, WFIA**
Koninginnegracht 14e, 2514 AA The Hague
P.O. Box 16067, 2500 BB The Hague
Tel.: 070 311 55 55. Internet: www.wfia.nl

THE MUNICIPALITY OF THE HAGUE
The Hague Hospitality Center
City Hall, Spui 70, Rooms B01.13 and B01.14
(1st floor), The Hague, tel.: 070 353 50 37
The International Corner
City Hall, Spui 70, Atrium (gemeentelijk
ContactCentrum), The Hague,
tel: 070 353 30 00
Internet: www.thehague.nl and
www.denhaag.nl

ONTWIKKELINGSBEDRIJF ROTTERDAM
Galvanistraat 15, 3029 AD Rotterdam
P.O. Box 6575, 3002 AN Rotterdam
Tel.: 010 489 69 44
Internet:www.obr.rotterdam.nl

**BRABANTSE ONTWIKKELINGS
MAATSCHAPPIJ**
P.O. Box 3240, 5003 DE Tilburg
Tel.: 013 463 44 00
Internet: www.bom.nl

**ONTWIKKELINGS MAATSCHAPPIJ
OOST NEDERLAND NV**
P.O. Box 5215, 6802 EE Arnhem
Tel.: 026 384 42 22
P.O. Box 5518, 7500 GM Enschede
Tel.: 053 484 96 49
Internet: www.oostnv.nl

**LIMBURGSE ONTWIKKELINGS
MAATSCHAPPIJ (LIOF)**
P.O. Box 1310, 6201 BH Maastricht
Tel.: 043 328 02 80
Internet: www.liof.com

TRADE AND INVESTMENT ORGANIZATIONS

**NFIA, NETHERLANDS FOREIGN
INVESTMENT AGENCY**
Bezuidenhoutseweg 16a, 2594 AV The Hague
P.O. Box 20101, 2500 EC The Hague
Tel.: 070 379 88 18
Internet: www.nfia.nl

**EVD, AGENCY FOR INTERNATIONAL
BUSINESS AND COOPERATION**
Bezuidenhoutseweg 181, 2594 AH The Hague
P.O. Box 20105, 2500 EC The Hague
Tel.: 070 379 88 11
Internet: www.hollandtrade.com

**NCH, NETHERLANDS COUNCIL FOR TRADE
PROMOTION**
Holland Trade House, Bezuidenhoutseweg 181
P.O. Box 10, 2501 CA The Hague
Tel.: 070 344 15 44
Internet: www.handelsbevordering.nl

TRADE FAIRS

EXPAT FAIR
Europe's largest (yearly) trade fair in Nieuwegein (Utrecht) for inpats, expats and international companies and organizations
Internet: www.expatinfo.nl

TO HAVE YOUR DIPLOMAS EVALUATED

IDW
x.o. Box 7338
2701 AH Zoetermeer
Tel.: 079 321 79 30
Internet: www.idw.nl

EMPLOYMENT AND RECRUITMENT AGENCIES FOR NON-DUTCH NATIONALS

Adams´ Multilingual Recruitment
Tel.: 020 330 41 88
Internet: www.adamsrecruit.nl

Blue Lynx Employment
The Hague, tel.: 070 311 78 22
Amsterdam (Schiphol), tel.: 020 406 91 80
Rotterdam, tel.: 010 205 21 20
Internet: www.bluelynx.nl

English Language Jobs
Tel.: 020 441 84 77
Internet: www.englishlanguagejobs.com

Kelly Services
Tel.: 030 280 66 00
Internet: www.dutchisnotrequired.nl

Projob International
Tel.: 020 573 83 83. Internet: www.projob.nl

Undutchables Recruitment Agency
Headoffice, tel.: 020 345 51 04
Amsterdam, tel.: 020 623 13 00
Amstelveen, tel.: 020 445 97 38
Rotterdam, tel.: 010 404 66 50
Utrecht, tel.: 030 238 22 28
Eindhoven, tel.: 040 237 33 95
Internet: www.undutchables.nl

Unique Multilingual Services
The Hague, tel.: 070 311 78 00
Amsterdam, tel.: 020 570 20 94
Rotterdam, tel.: 010 503 29 00
Utrecht, tel.: 030 232 63 40
Internet: www.uniquemls.com

JOB SEARCHING WEBSITES

FINDING A JOB IN THE NETHERLANDS
www.careera.nl
www.englishlanguagejobs.com
www.expatica.com/jobs
www.intermediar.nl
www.jobnews.nl
www.jobpilot.nl
www.jobtrack.nl
www.monsterboard.nl
www.nationalevacaturebank.nl
www.stepstone.nl
www.totaljobs.nl
www.vacature.overzicht.nl
www.werk.net

INTERNATIONAL JOBS
www.americasjobbank.com
www.careerbuilder.com
www.careermag.com
www.cooljobs.com
www.erc.org
www.escapeartist.com
www.futurestep.com
www.joblinks.f2s.com/index_eng.htm
www.megajobs.nl
www.michaelpage.nl
www.monster.com
www.newscientistjobs.com
www.overseasjobs.com
www.stepstone.com
www.wetfeet.com

FOR E-LANCERS
www.aquent.com
www.guru.com
www.mbafreeagents.com
www.monster.com
www.nolo.com

DUAL CAREER SERVICE

C&G CAREER SERVICES
Edisonstraat 24, 2811 EM Reeuwijk
Tel.: 0182 300 745
E-mail: mail@cg-services.com
Internet: www.cg-services.com

RECOMMENDED READING

EMPLOYMENT IN THE NETHERLANDS
Published by Loyens & Loeff
Conditions of employment, tax and social security aspects
Available on request by e-mail:
info@loyensloeff.com
Internet: www.loyensloeff.com

WORKING IN THE NETHERLANDS
Published by ACCESS
The Real Story on Career Options in the Netherlands
A step by step guide to finding employment in the Netherlands, including legal concerns, permits, tax numbers, diploma evaluations, cv to Dutch standards, helpful agencies, self-employment, professional clubs, volunteering etc.
Internet: www.access-nl.org
ISBN 90 74109 22 5

DEALING WITH THE DUTCH – 3RD EDITION
By Jacob Vossestein
Published by KIT Publishers
The cultural context of business and work in the Netherlands
Internet: www.kit.nl/publishers
ISBN 90 6832 565 5

NETWORK YOUR WAY TO SUCCESS
By Charles D.A. Ruffolo, MPA with Shirley Agudo
Charles Ruffolo´s guide to the power of networking
Internet: www.network-club.com
ISBN 90 8082361 9

HANDLING HOLLAND
By Janet Inglis
Published by XPat Media
A manual for international women in the Netherlands
Internet: www.xpat.nl -
www.hollandbooks.nl
ISBN 90 5594 232 4

LEGAL ASPECTS OF DOING BUSINESS IN THE NETHERLANDS
Edited by Tom Claassens
Published by Loyens & Loeff
For entrepeneurs and their legal service providers who are or about to be engaged in business operations in the Netherlands
Available on request by e-mail:
info@loyensloeff.com
Internet: www.loyensloeff.com

EXPAT TOOLKIT
By Ruud Blaakman, Rina Driece, Stephanie Dijkstra
Published by Kluwer
A guide to the Dutch workplace
Internet: www.managementboek.nl
ISBN 90 14 08395 5

A CAREER IN YOUR SUITCASE
By Joanna Parfitt
Published by Summertime Publishing
This book became a favorite with expatriate women around the world. It containes chapters on working from home, networking, working with computers, skills assessment and checklists.
Internet: www.career-in-your-suitcase.com
ISBN 0 9529453 0 4

One of the most favored locations to set up a European operation is the Netherlands. The annual survey of the Economist Intelligence Unit (EIU) ranks the Netherlands as number 2 in the list of best places worldwide in terms of business climate. Compared to other European cities, A1 office space in the Netherlands still has much lower lease prices, while the already high-quality facilities are still improving. Cost of living in general in the Netherlands is very attractive in comparison to other main cities in the world.

WHERE TO LOCATE

The western part of the Netherlands has the highest density in terms of population. The four largest cities (Amsterdam, Rotterdam, The Hague and Utrecht), also referred to as the 'Randstad', are located in this part of the country. In general, the largest number of foreign and/or multilingual (near native) people are to be found here. Reason for many international offices over the years to locate their offices here, with a strong preference for Amsterdam – the close vicinity of Amsterdam Schiphol Airport being one of the reasons. However, the Rotterdam port, an excellent business location for European-focused companies; The Hague, with its government offices; and Utrecht, being the center of the whole Dutch infrastructure, all have their own unique characteristics that are appealing to many Dutch and international companies.
Interesting alternative locations are Heerlen and Maastricht in the southeastern part of the country (province of Limburg), Groningen in the north and Almere, a new town steaming up to be the 5th city in the Netherlands soon, 30 kilometers away from Amsterdam.

FINANCIAL ASPECTS

For new, modern office space (good location/average quality) the annual rent per m^2 currently ranges from approximately € 160 to € 200 in the Randstad area and € 120 to € 160 in the other regions. In Table 1 an overview is given of the fixed annual expenses per m^2 (in euros excluding VAT) for an office facility of 2,500 m^2 including 25 parking places, in the Randstad area.

Annual costs office space (in euros excluding 19% VAT)	From	To
Rent per m^2	170	200
Parking per place (1 per 100 m^2)	500	1000
Service costs per m^2	20	30
Electricity (individual) per m^2	5	10
Cleaning (individual) per m^2	15	20
Security per m^2	5	10
Miscellaneous per m^2	5	10
Total annual costs per m^2	225	290

WAREHOUSE SPACE

Warehouse space can be found all across the country. However, most of the premises are concentrated around the logistical centers such as the harbors of Amsterdam and Rotterdam, Schiphol Airport and around the big cities. The annual rent per m^2 currently ranges from approximately € 50 to € 80 per m^2.

FIT-OUT

It is difficult to give ballpark figures for the investments related to the fit-out of an office facility. The investment level will differ, depending on the basic quality of the building, the specific requirements and the requested exposure. In Table 2 some global investment figures are given (in euros excluding VAT) for an office facility of 2,500 m^2, offering space to 125 people.

Investments fit-out office space (in euros excluding 19% VAT)	From	To
Fit-out per m^2	150	200
Alterations technical installations per m^2	75	150
ICT (excl. computers/av/etc.) per m^2	50	75
Furniture per m^2	150	200
One time costs (fees/contingencies) per m^2	100	100
Unforeseen	50	50
Total investment per m^2	575	725

Big business

Small business

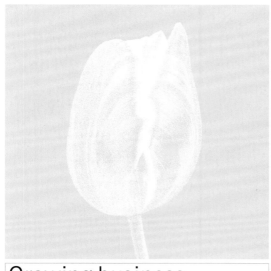

Growing business

Your business

Best for business

Looking for a location in Europe?
Call the Amsterdam Foreign Investment Office today
at +31 20 552 35 36 **or go to** www.afio.amsterdam.nl

I amsterdam ®

■ TRADING TRADITION ■ IT INFRASTRUCTURE ■ CONNECTED TO THE WORLD ■ FINANCIAL CITY ■ LOGISTICS HUB ■
■ SMART WORKFORCE ■ KNOWLEDGE NETWORK ■ QUALITY OF LIFE ■ CIVIC CO-OPERATION ■

Before buying or renting a house or apartment in the Netherlands, there are several things you should consider. This chapter offers you practical tips and useful information such as where to buy or rent, selecting an agent and negotiating the deal. This chapter also points out some of the consequences of your choice in terms of property taxes, waste collection taxes, sewerage taxes, etc., and the taxes or exemptions thereof surrounding importing your household goods.

A Place to Live

CONTRIBUTING AUTHORS: RINA DRIECE, PAUL LENOS, DENNIS VAN RIET,
LUYDERT SMIT AND ANNETTE DE VREEDE

RENT OR BUY

PRACTICAL TIPS AND INFORMATION

Around the turn of the millennium, the housing situation in the Netherlands became increasingly tight and sales prices doubled (and in some cases even tripled!) over a period of five years. Though the upward driving forces on the housing market have quieted down somewhat, the prices remain hovering around their high point – with all the necessary consequences, and without the promise of being able to sell a recently bought house again at a profit.

This not only affects the buying market but also the rental market. In the rental market it is important that the price and the quality of a property are in the right balance.

In the buying market, owners are sometimes forced to sell their properties because of their financial situation, whereby, because of the high mortgage, there is not much room for negotiation on the asking/selling price.

The rental market is different compared to some years ago. At this moment there are more houses available on the market – which makes it easier to find a nice rental, at a reasonable price. Furthermore, it must be said that, though the rental prices in the Netherlands are high compared to some other parts of Europe, they still are below those of other European capitals such as London or Paris.

FINDING A HOUSE

There is a considerable variety of properties to choose from, although much depends on the area where you want to live, the living space needed and your budget. There is a good choice of rental properties in the so-called Randstad area (Amsterdam, The Hague, Rotterdam and Utrecht) in the western part of the country. Due to the circumstances mentioned above, it is currently easier to find a good, reasonably priced house to rent or buy in downtown Amsterdam, as well as in other historic cities, such as The Hague, Haarlem and Leiden, where a larger range of properties is available.

One can find a house for sale or for rent via advertisements in the newspapers, on notice boards at the women's clubs, international schools or churches, or by driving around and looking out for the signs saying *Te Koop* (for sale) or sometimes *Te Huur* (for rent). However, it is advisable to contact an agent. Most expatriates have never lived in the Netherlands and are therefore not familiar with the price ranges, local contracts, laws and customs. Using an agent, even though this is more expensive, will help you get a good impression of the living area, speed up the search for suitable accommodation, as well as get a better deal on the property.

Another advantage to using an agent is that they have access to a computerized multiple-listing system which keeps them completely up-to-date on properties available in their district.

THE AGENT

If you have chosen to rent a property there are several rental organizations available. In The Hague and surrounding areas most available rental accommodation is put on the market by real es-tate agents, such as the members of the *Nederlandse Vereniging van Makelaars* (NVM, or Dutch Association of Real Estate Agents) or of *Vereniging Bemiddeling Onroerend Goed* (VBO – Association of Real Estate Intermediaries). There are also other large cooperating real estate agents that have rental properties (i.e. ERA *Makelaars, Garantie Makelaars*).

You can usually find the right agent to suit your needs through word-of-mouth, via the Human Resource Department of the company, via a Relocation Agency or via advertisements in expat journals. Basically every agent has the same information available through the multiple listing system, but much depends on how well the agent uses this information and how he goes about selecting the right properties according to the specifications of the lessee or buyer. Therefore, it is important that you feel you can trust your agent. It is practical and saves time and effort to use only one agent. If you are not satisfied, if you feel you are not seeing the right properties or that your agent does not understand your needs, get another agent.

TO BUY OR TO RENT

Of course, there are a lot of benefits when buying a house. Apart from the fact that you own real estate of which the price may increase again, there is the advantage of tax relief on the mortgage interest – it is fully tax deductible. In addition, some of the costs related to the financing of the house are also tax deductible. This means that some of the notary's fees, the closing commission, and the fee for the appraisal of the house are all tax deductible. Hence, if you are in the highest tax bracket of 52%, the net costs are 48%. Although at first sight it might seem an attractive option to buy a house, it is a decision that needs serious and careful consideration. A disadvantage when buying real estate in the Netherlands is that you have to pay approximately 11% of the purchase price as one-time buyers' expenses. These expenses consist of real estate tax (6%), estate agent fees, notary's fees, 1% commission for the bank, etc. In addition to this, home owners must add the so-called deemed rental value (*eigenwoningforfait* – you can read more about this on page 87) to their taxable income and pay taxes over this.

As a result, the break-even point between rent or buy usually occurs after thee years, assuming – and that's a big if – that housing prices remain constant. Bearing in mind that expatriates usually stay in the Netherlands for a maximum of four to five years, this is an important issue to keep in mind. This risk makes buying a medium to long-term decision.

Of course, if you rent a house, you circumvent a lot of the problems and risks, but you also miss out on the possible benefits. And don't forget: rent – though reasonable compared to other European countries – can be high in the Netherlands. You can read more about the tax consequences of renting, or having your rental costs reimbursed by your employer, on page 87.

CHECKLIST OF IMPORTANT ITEMS

If you decide to rent or to buy, make a checklist of items which are important to you and your family and which will influence the location and style of the property. Discuss these with your agent. For example:
- proximity to work and the children's school
- public transportation and school bus routes
- location of shopping centers
- type of neighborhood
- type of house: period or modern
- when renting: is it fully furnished – *gemeubileerd* (all furniture, fixtures and kitchen appliances provided).

AREAS

Most expatriates live in the Randstad, in the area between Amsterdam, The Hague, Rotterdam and Utrecht. There are also many pleasant residential areas near Amsterdam such as Amstelveen, Aerdenhout, Bloemendaal and Heemstede; in 't Gooi (between Amsterdam and Utrecht) which includes Bussum, Hilversum, Naarden, Huizen and Laren; near The Hague around Wassenaar, Voorschoten and Oegstgeest; or in the residential areas of Rotterdam such as Kralingen and Hillegersberg. Of course there are many more smaller villages where pleasant housing can be found.

THE ACTUAL HOUSE-HUNTING

It is advisable to make sure the agent is well informed of your specific wishes prior to the actual house-hunting in order for him to select a list of properties that meet your requirements. The agent can also help you become acquainted with the different terms and conditions of contracts and procedures, and check if the specifications you have given are in line with price ranges and the kind of housing available. On the basis of your specific requirements, a selection from the available market supply will be made and a tour of inspection of those residences will be organized. If necessary, more tours will follow until a suitable house is found.

NEGOTIATIONS

Prices quoted in the listings for sales and rentals are usually negotiable. In close consultation with the agent, price and conditions will be negotiated with the agent representing the owner.
These negotiations can consist of several rounds of verbal bidding and counter-bidding.

YOU HAVE DECIDED TO RENT

The Rental Contract

Many rental contracts have been especially designed to meet the needs of expatriates, and include an English translation. A rental contract usually includes the following items:
- rent: the rent is payable one month in advance
- a deposit: one month deposit/bank guarantee is customary; however, some owners demand a 2 or 3-month deposit
- an annual adjustment of the rent, based on increases in the cost of living, as determined by the Central Bureau of Statistics (CBS). This has averaged 1 to 2% over the last years
- user's costs, which are usually not included in the rent, i.e. utilities, municipal levies and garden maintenance
- the so-called diplomatic clause, which gives you the option of terminating the contract by giving two full calendar months' notice if you are transferred abroad
- the brokerage fee, usually one month rent, excl. 19% VAT
- a clause on minor repairs, irrespective of the cause: the lessee pays € 110 excl. VAT per case. All costs of larger repairs, external or internal, which are not due to any fault of the lessee, will be borne by the owner
- real estate tax, the user's part (for more information, see page 93)
- a clause stating that the lessee is responsible for the yearly cleaning of the central heating system, water boilers, chimneys, gutters and draining pipes
- the obligation to return the property in the same condition, normal wear and tear excepted, at the end of the rental period.

Few people have bought a house of which they thought: 'Yup, precisely the way I wanted it,' and left everything the way it was. On the other hand, few people are as notorious for clearing out all but the outside walls and rebuilding from scratch as the Dutch are. Likely, you are somewhere in the middle.

CONTRACTOR – AANNEMER
Should you wish to redo your house (change a wall or two, put in a new bathroom or kitchen, build a fireplace), the person you are looking for is a contractor. Contractors can be found in the Yellow Pages under the name *aannemers*. There you will find probably at least 100 to choose from – which does not make the choice much easier. A safe bet would be to opt for a contractor who is listed with BouwNed. Those listed with BouwNed must meet strict requirements, allowing them to carry the NVOB-label (www.nvob.nl). Otherwise, ask around and see whom others recommend. Be sure to invite a few *aannemers*, as prices can vary considerably, not to mention compatibility: chances are, these people will be running around your house for weeks, if not months.

OVERSEEING THE PROJECT
The *aannemer* could be a one-man operation or a company (*bouwbedrijf*) ranging in size from two people to several hundred skilled employees. They are responsible for purchasing all the necessary supplies (*bouw-materialen*) and overseeing the installation of the project, making sure that all of the skilled personnel (an *aannemer* has qualified plumbers, electricians, carpenters, etc. on his payroll) complete their portions of the project at the right moment in the process. They also make sure that the materials used are up to code and meet current safety requirements.

PAPERWORK
All necessary paperwork can also be handled by your *aannemer*. It is best to leave the requesting of building permits and the execution of building plans and blueprints in his hands. Not only does he have ample experience in dealing with the bureaucracy

inherent in securing permission, it tends to go much faster than if you attempt to do it yourself.

MONUMENTS
An important matter in this context is the question of whether your house is on the monumentenlijst (list of monuments). Houses that are protected under *Monumentenzorg* (Monuments Care) are subject to strict regulations and restrictions regarding maintenance, and any changes have to be approved by a commission from the Association for the Preservation of Monuments. Even seemingly straightforward matters such as the color of paint used often needs approval. It can take months of waiting for approvals, and in the meantime you are prohibited from making any changes. Your *aannemer* likely knows the best way to approach obtaining permission for any changes you wish to make – and how long it will take. He will also be able to give you a fair idea of what you will be allowed to do.

WORKING 'BLACK'
In order to have a guarantee on your work it is best to work *wit met een bonnetje* ('white with a receipt'). Some tradesmen will work *zwart* ('black'); that is, without a receipt, whereby you do not pay the 19% VAT (BTW) and thus may receive a discount on the rates – however, this is illegal and constitutes tax fraud. In addition, you forfeit your right to any claims due to shoddy workmanship or the incompletion of the project. Nor will insurance companies cover claims resulting from damages incurred by leaking pipes, electrical fires and the likes. Furthermore, you have no receipt of proof regarding the services rendered and materials used.

HANDYMAN
Sometimes people will hire in a handyman (*klusjesman*) who works at the going rate of around € 20 per hour. Once again, you can probably find a handyman who works 'black' (*zwartwerken*), but if he does, he will not be insured, and any liability claims that could arise from accidents (like his falling off your roof while working) will not be covered and a settlement will not be possible.

A NEW INTERIOR
Though the *aannemer* carries out the project, you yourself will have to select the kitchen cabinets, bathtub, closets, tiles, curtains, carpeting, faucets, paints colors, etc. If you want, you can do this with the help of an interior decorator (see the Yellow Pages, under *binnenhuisarchitectuur* or *interieurontwerpers*). To do it yourself, look under *woninginrichting* (decorating your home) for carpeting, curtains, but also beds and furniture (see page 154 for more on these), *keukens* for kitchens, *sanitaire artikelen* for bathrooms, *verf en lak* for paint. Often, your *aannemer* will have reached an agreement with a local bathroom, kitchen or tile specialist regarding deliveries and quality, so maybe you want to wait and see who he recommends – though you are not obligated to go by his recommendations alone.

GARDEN
If you want to do your own garden, you will find what you need at a garden center – to be found in the Yellow Pages under *tuincentra* (for plants and other necessities) or *tuinartikelen* (for garden furniture, sheds, ponds, lighting). If you want to enlist the help of a professional, look under *tuinaanleg en - onderhoud* (garden design and maintenance).

HIDDEN DEFECTS

If it turns out, after you have purchased the house, that there are a number of things that are not in order, you will have to ask yourself whether these are 'hidden defects' – in connection with who is to be held liable. In principle, you buy a house 'as it is'; this means, including all visible and invisible (as opposed to 'hidden') defects. The premise is that you, the new owner, are responsible. However, there are situations in which the former owner can be held liable (see further on).

OBLIGATIONS REALTOR
Your realtor has an obligation to inform you of known defects to the house. For instance, wooden constructions could be infected with wood rot, mold or fungus growth. Or there could be an oil tank in the back yard, or pests; causing you to run up a hefty bill for extermination.

REPORTING A DEFECT
In either a rental or purchase property, any hidden defect will need to be reported within a reasonable time frame from the date of purchase. It is best to ask your real estate agent or housing agency what term they apply. For a purchased property, you will have to report any defect or problems to the estate agent who sold you the property and he will negotiate on your behalf with the seller.

RESPONSIBILITIES ON PURCHASED PROPERTY
For the former owner to be held liable, the following conditions must be met:
- the defect must have been there at the time of the sale and you must be able to prove this
- you, the buyer, must have inspected the new home. If you could have detected the defect during this inspection, but didn't, then this is your responsibility. Some defects occur after the inspection, but before the transfer – these are for the liability of the seller
- the seller has an obligation to inform you of the defects that he is aware of if they are not easy to detect in the case of a normal inspection, or if the extent of the defects is not sufficiently clear – even if they would not influence a normal use of the house
- the defect must hinder a 'normal' use of (part of) the house – or, at the very least, the house must have the qualities that you could expect based on the sales contract.

Another important factor is the age of the house. The older it is, there more you can be expected to have anticipated certain problems.

If you compare points 3 and 4, they would appear to contradict each other. It is clear that there is a gray area there somewhere, so be sure to obtain expert advice in the case of problems. And keep in mind, while looking at a house, that if anything looks fishy (or rickety); ask, take notes, point it out...

PROBLEMS IN THE NEIGHBORHOOD
The seller also has the duty to report beforehand (*mededelingsplicht*) any knowledge of contaminated ground in the neighborhood, or problems in the area, such as wood rot of foundation poles under the houses. The buyer has a buyer's responsibility to also check to see if there are problems in the area, or if there are any pre-existing building reports (*bouwkundige keuringen*).

RESPONSIBILITIES ON RENTALS
A general rule of thumb is that anything that is structural is the responsibility of the party letting out the property (*verhuurder*). The best recourse is to be very clear beforehand as to the division of the responsibilities. If you discover problems after you have moved in, you will need to contact the landlord (and/or the housing agency) to make your complaint. Hopefully something can be done to solve the problem right away, however, sometimes this is not the case. You may wind up having to pay for the repairman or the exterminator yourself, and then attempt to be reimbursed.

INSURANCE
Depending on your realtor, it is possible, in cooperation your real estate agent, to take out a (maximum) three-year insurance against hidden mechanical and construction defects. If you request this, the house will be inspected and any defects noted will not be covered by the insurance – as they will obviously not constitute hidden defects. Any areas not inspected will also not be covered by the insurance.

LEGAL AID
If it turns out that you were not adequately informed, you may have to go to court and let the judge decide about compensation to repair the damages. Being as how proving conclusively whether or not one can presume that the selling party knowingly withheld vital information can be a rather 'gray area', you may need the services of a lawyer if a timely agreement to remedy the situation cannot be reached (see page 125 for more on legal aid).

CHECKING IN

When the agreements have been signed, and the rent and deposit are paid to the account of the agent, the lessee will be handed the keys to the property. Ideally, the lessee will be checked in by the owner or his representative, assisted by his own agent. A checklist will be filled out regarding the condition of the house, the furniture, fixtures and fittings belonging to the house, the condition of the exterior/garden, and there will be a check of the inventory. The house should be thoroughly cleaned, including the inside of kitchen and bathroom cabinets. The inspection report as well as the inventory list must be signed by lessee and lessor.
For more on hidden defects, see page 85.

CHECKING OUT/RETURN OF THE DEPOSIT

Preferably on the last day of the lease period a check-out is done with all parties concerned. The inventory and condition of the lease property are checked with the checklist made when checking in. If the state of the property is found satisfactory and all bills in connection with the property have been paid, the deposit will be paid back within three months after the check-out date. If necessary, the costs of bringing the rental property back in the required state will be deducted from the deposit in accordance with the bills provided by the lessor.

YOU HAVE DECIDED TO BUY

Points to Watch for When Buying a House

1. General: When you decide to buy a house, it is doubly advisable to engage an agent, as there are more complicated matters involved than when renting a house. For instance, you need expert advice on matters such as the fluctuation of prices in certain areas, environmental laws, the construction of a house, hidden defects (see page 85), and problems arising when you buy property on leasehold rather than free-hold.

2. Fixtures and fittings: When you start negotiating, you should bear in mind that the purchase price excludes furniture, carpets, curtains, light fixtures and sometimes kitchen appliances. You must reach a clear agreement with the seller on which goods are included in the purchase.

3. Deposit: The deposit on the house is generally 10% of the purchase price – to be paid by the buyer a few days after the deal has been made. This deposit is to be paid to a notary and can be replaced by a bank guarantee issued by a Dutch banking institution.

4. Additional Costs: The purchase transaction will cost you an approximately additional 11%. This amount represents a government transfer tax of 6%, land registry expenses, the notary's fees, and the real estate agent's commission.

5. Resolutive Conditions: If you need to obtain a mortgage to finance the purchase, any purchase agreement should be made subject to financing. If necessary, other resolutive conditions should be part of the agreement, such as being able to obtain a permit to occupy the real estate.

Purchase Deed and Transfer of Ownership

The verbal agreement is set down in writing in the purchase deed. A penalty clause is usually included in case the seller or the buyer does not meet his obligations. After being signed by all the parties, the purchase deed is sent to the civil-law notary who will deal with the conveyancing. After the agreement has been signed, the buyer (but not the seller) is given three days to think the matter over. During those three days the buyer can cancel the deal with- out any repercussions and without having to state any reason.
The choice of the notary is usually the buyer's. Upon receipt of the purchase deed, the notary inspects the public registers of the Land Registry regarding mortgages and/or attachments with which the property may be encumbered.
The transfer of ownership will take place at the civil-law notary's office by means of a deed of transfer to be drawn up by the notary and to be signed by the seller, the buyer and the notary. The notary will first send you a draft of this deed of transfer together with a statement showing the payment due in order to complete the purchase. This statement includes the purchase price, the transfer tax, the Land Registry fees, notarial fees, commission on a possible mortgage loan, real estate agent's fees, etc. If there is a mortgage loan, you will receive a draft of the mortgage deed. Your agent will also receive these documents and check them.
The day before the transfer, the agent will check with you to see whether the house has been vacated as agreed. It is the task of the

notary to take care of the financial settlement of the transaction and to ensure that the deed of transfer is entered in the public registers (Land Registry). The transfer then becomes official. Later you will receive a copy of this deed from the notary – this is your proof of ownership. During six months after deed has been entered in the Land Registry, you enjoy a further six months' protection against 'bad news' from the side of the seller; bankruptcy, seizure of the house or a higher bid by someone else.

THE TAX CONSEQUENCES OF RENTING OR BUYING A HOUSE

When moving to a new country, just about the first question you are faced with is; where am I going to live? This decision is, predictably, largely influenced by the decision: am I going to buy a house or am I going to rent one? Many of the issues involved in this choice have been discussed in the preceding paragraphs. However, one important question remains: what are the tax consequences of your decision? This is a complex matter, and I have given a short overview of the topics that will play a role when making your choice.

In some parts, reference will be made to the tax paragraph which you can find in the chapter on *Legal, Tax and Financial Matters*.

BUYING A HOUSE

Mortgage Expenses Deductible
The most important reason to buy real estate – instead of renting it – is most probably the fact that interest paid on a mortgage is fully deductible when you use the house as your principal place of residence. Aside from the interest, the one-time expenses related to the mortgage (for example, notary fee, registration fee, bank fee and appraisal fee) as well as ground rent are also deductible.

If you decide to take out a higher mortgage than required to finance the purchase of the house itself or for its reconstruction, the related part of the mortgage interest will *not* be deductible. Other expenses related to the house (such as insurance premiums) are never deductible.

New rules apply regarding the deductibility of mortgage interest if you sell a house and buy a new one. As the rules are too complicated to summarize for the purpose of this book, you are advised to consult a specialist should you find yourself in this situation.

What Type of Mortgage?
You should seek proper advice on the type of mortgage that is suitable in your situation, particularly in view of the limited period of time during which you may need the mortgage. Do not forget to inform the bank if you are benefiting from the 30%-ruling. If the mortgage is linked to a capital insurance, you may be faced with additional tax consequences. Be sure to get expert advice! More on mortgages on page 91.

Deemed Rental Value and woz-Value
Those who own a house and use it as their principal place of residence have to report a certain amount – related to the home ownership – on their income tax return. This amount is a percentage of the value of the house, called the *eigenwoningforfait*. The value on which the *eigenwoningforfait* is based, also known as the woz-value, is the official value of the house and is determined by the municipality. This value is valid for a period of four years (a new period will go into effect in 2005). Every owner receives a so-called *woz-beschikking* (woz-decision, see page 94), 'confirming' the value of the house. The general applicable rate of the *eigenwoningforfait* will be 0.6% as of 2005 – calculated using the woz-value of January 1, 2005, as a basis – to a maximum of € 8,750.

The balance of the deemed rental value and the interest should be deducted from the income of the partner to whom the income from the house is allocated. Partners can choose from whose income the balance is deducted, in any ratio they wish.

If your partner does not live in the Netherlands, then you can generally deduct only your own share in the mortgage. It would be a good idea for both of you to look into whether choosing to be treated as a resident taxpayer would be beneficial in your situation.

Preliminary Tax Refund
You can receive a tax refund on the mortgage interest deduction every month by requesting a preliminary negative tax bill with the tax authorities. This is done by means of a special form. The tax authorities will then deposit the refund directly into your bank account.

Real Estate Owned Abroad

If you are a *resident* taxpayer, you cannot deduct the negative income from real estate that is located outside the Netherlands as it is not your principal place of residence. If you are a *non-resident* taxpayer living abroad in your principal place of residence, you can choose to be treated as a resident taxpayer. In that case, you can deduct the mortgage interest (reduced with the deemed rental value) from your Netherlands taxable income. However, be aware of further – possibly negative – consequences of this choice.

You Don't Live Here, But Own Real Estate Here

House Not Rented Out

You will have to pay tax on a deemed benefit arising from the ownership of the real estate (a fixed assumed yield) in box 3. This 'benefit' is set at 4% of the (woz less the debt (the mortgage). The tax rate is 30%. Mortgage interest will no longer be deductible. Each partner has to report his or her own share. There are special rules for expatriates who leave the Netherlands only temporarily.

House Rented Out

The benefit is taxed in box 3, as explained above. The actual rental income is not taxed.

RENTING A HOUSE

Renting a house in the Netherlands is expensive, especially if you need to rent in the western part of the country of close to international schools. There is no tax facility for renting a house whatsoever. With any luck, your employer will choose to compensate you for the housing costs. But in that case, be aware of the tax consequences!

Free Housing Taxable

If you are a resident of the Netherlands (resident taxpayer or partial non-resident taxpayer), any compensation provided by your employer constitutes taxable income. Whether you will have to pay the tax yourself depends on your contract; is it net or gross?

If you are a 'real' non-resident taxpayer, you may benefit from an exemption during a period of two years, under certain conditions.

Special Treatment Under 30%-Ruling

Residents: If you are a resident of the Netherlands (also if you are a partial non-resident taxpayer), in principle the full benefit resulting from the fact that your employer is providing you with housing is a taxable benefit.

If you benefit from the 30%-ruling, special rules apply. A part of the rent may be qualified as an 'extraterritorial expense' (you can read more about this on page 110). That part of the rent can be compensated free of tax (thus reducing the amount of the fixed 30%-allowance!)

Non-Residents: If you are a non-resident of the Netherlands, any compensation of double housing expenses is regarded as compensation for extraterritorial expenses: tax-free, but resulting in a reduction of the 30%-allowance.

Mortgage Issues: The recommended mortgage depends on your special tax position and whether you are likely to move again, see the following paragraphs.

Cross-Border Support

Doing business effectively can present a challenge, especially if you operate in more than one country. When you face questions in this regard, look to KPMG for tailored and innovative solutions. KPMG in the Netherlands provides a full-service approach in assurance, international human resources, tax, and law.

Rely on KPMG for your cross-border support.

Your KPMG contacts are:

Assurance and international investment support:
Elbert Waller,
tel: + 31(0)20 656 7009
email: waller.elbert@kpmg.nl

International Human Resources
Mortgages:
Luydert Smit,
tel: + 31 (0)20 656 1880
email: smit.luydert@kpmg.nl

Tax:
Robert van der Jagt,
tel: + 31 (0)20 656 1356
email: vanderjagt.robert@kpmg.nl

understanding @

TAKING OUT A MORTGAGE

If you have decided to buy a house, you are faced with the question of what is the most appropriate type of mortgage. In this article we provide a brief explanation of the relevant types of mortgages that are available in the Netherlands. We will also make some recommendations as to which types are best suited to the expatriate's specific tax status.

THE RELEVANT TYPES OF MORTGAGES

Usually a mortgage has a duration of twenty or thirty years. Five categories can be distinguished. Below each of these forms will be briefly discussed. Special attention will be given to the tax consequences and the life insurances.

Mortgage with Linear Redemption

The most important characteristic of this mortgage is that the loan is repaid yearly in equal installments (i.e. linear). As a result of the repayments, the amount of interest payable diminishes every year. Since the interest expenditure decreases steadily, this mortgage is best suited for borrowers who cannot fully benefit from the tax relief on the interest payments.

The insurance that best matches this mortgage is a life insurance policy for an insured amount that decreases annually (i.e. also linear). This is calculated in such a way that the insured amount is always sufficient to cover the unredeemed part of the mortgage loan.

Annuity Mortgage

The chief characteristic of an annuity mortgage is that the yearly total of redemption and interest payments remains the same throughout its duration. Although the total remains the same, the mix of interest and redemption of course changes over the years. Owing to this balance between interest and redemption, the redemption is not on a linear basis.

In the first years, the amount paid by the borrower consists mainly of interest payments. Hence there is a large tax relief in the initial years. Consequently, an annuity mortgage is ideal for people who wish to have a large tax relief in the early years and expect to have a sufficiently high income in later years to be able to make the redemption payments that do not qualify for tax relief.

The insurance is a life policy with a non-proportional decrease in the amount insured which is in line with the redemptions made.

Endowment Mortgage (Levenhypotheek)

With an endowment mortgage, no repayments are made during the term of the mortgage. Instead, the whole loan is redeemed in a single lump sum at the end of the term. The redemption is financed by means of a with-profits endowment policy that matures on the expiry date of the mortgage.

The endowment policy is used to generate capital. Usually, a part of this capital is guaranteed at the end of the term and the remainder is made dependent on the investment return.

If the borrower dies before the expiration of the mortgage, a separate life insurance policy will pay out a lump sum. This may be based on the capital insured under the endowment policy. It can be equal to either the amount saved under the endowment policy or some other criterion, depending on the borrower's wishes.

Special Endowment Mortgage (Spaarhypotheek)

This is a variation on the Endowment Mortgage. It too provides for a lump-sum redemption of the mortgage loan at the end of the term. The distinguishing feature is that the interest rate on the loan is exactly the same as the rate of return on the investment under the endowment policy. This means that at the end of the term, the capital saved exactly matches the principal of the mortgage loan. There is neither an upside nor a downside potential.

A Special Endowment Mortgage is therefore a no-risk mortgage and is ideally suited for those of limited financial means. A potential disadvantage when compared to the ordinary endowment mortgage is that the loan, endowment and life insurance are inseparably linked. This reduces the investment flexibility.

If the borrower dies before the mortgage term expires, the amount paid under the life insurance policy exactly matches the amount of the mortgage loan.

Redemption-Free Mortgage

Here, no redemptions take place during the term of the mortgage. It is usually part of an ordinary Endowment Mortgage. We will not go into this mortgage any further here.

DUTCH TAX ISSUES FOR EXPATRIATES

In essence, a mortgage is a tax-driven product. Hence, to determine the most appropriate type of mortgage for you, it is necessary first to consider your tax status. In the Netherlands, the two major tax issues with which an expatriate is faced are the 30%-ruling and the choice between resident (*binnenlands belastingplichtige*) and partial non-resident tax status (*partieel buitenlands belastingplichtige*). You can read more about his on page 106.

The 30%-Ruling

Simply put, the 30%-ruling allows an employer to grant an employee a tax-free allowance of up to 30% of his total remuneration. The result of the 30%-ruling is a higher net salary. You should keep in mind that, if the 30%-ruling is applicable to you, this means you might be in a lower tax bracket – as a result of which your net savings thanks to your tax relief on the interest rate payable may be lower.

When applying for the 30%-ruling, the employee may choose to have resident or partial non-resident tax status, see the following paragraph (and page 110).

Partial Non-Resident Tax Status

Expatriates who are partial non-residents owe taxes on income derived from certain sources specifically stated in Dutch income tax legislation.

Partial non-residents are entitled to tax deductions insofar as they relate to specific income sources, alimony payments and mortgage interest payments for their principal place of residence. A final important observation regarding partial non-residents is that, contrary to resident taxpayers, net wealth (i.e. assets minus liabilities, taxed at 1.2%.) is not taxed. Hence, the ideal mortgage for a partial non-resident takes advantage of the fact that the interest payments on the mortgage are tax deductible and that the investment income is not taxed.

The corresponding mortgage is discussed further on.

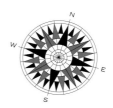

Resident Tax Status

Unless an expatriate chooses the partial non-resident tax status, he is viewed as a resident for Dutch tax purposes. He is then taxed just as any ordinary Dutch citizen. Resident taxpayers (as well as partial non-resident taxpayers) are only entitled to mortgage interest relief on the principal place of residence. The value of every other residence is subject to wealth tax (over, in principle, the fair market value of the property minus the mortgage loan – at a rate of 1.2%).

EXPATRIATES: WHAT MORTGAGES ARE APPROPRIATE?

The recommended mortgage depends on your special tax position and whether you are likely to move again.

The ordinary and the Special Endowment Mortgage are not appropriate for a number of reasons. The first reason has to do with the likely duration of your stay. If you leave within, say, seven years and upon leaving decide to surrender the endowment policy, you may receive back only the total of premiums paid. The reason why there will be hardly any investment return is that insurance companies write off all policy costs during the first years of the insurance. Hence, if you surrender within this write-off period, the investment return will only be marginal. Moreover, if the policy is surrendered prior to its minimum legal duration of fifteen years and there is an investment return, this return may be subject to income tax.

The second reason regards the possibility of continuing the endowment policy if you move to another country. If that is what you want to do, you risk an exit tax, imposed over the value of the policy calculated at the time of leaving the Netherlands.

Since you can always opt for the Endowment Mortgage once your stay is likely to become long-term, we advise you to take out an Endowment Mortgage at that moment. Until such moment, another type is more appropriate.

YOU ARE A RESIDENT TAXPAYER

If you benefit from the 30%-ruling, this will mean that you have a high net salary. This will enable you to make repayments. At the same time, income from wealth (e.g. dividends and interest received) is, in the new tax regime effective as of January 1, 2001, no longer taxed under the progressive income tax rate. Instead, net wealth is taxed at 1.2%. For that reason, pending special circumstances, repaying the loan will usually not be tax efficient.

YOU ARE A PARTIAL NON-RESIDENT TAXPAYER

In this case you need to find a mortgage which allows you to benefit from the tax-deductibility of the interest payments while at the same time allowing you to benefit from the tax-exempt investment income (since there is no 'wealth/Box 3' tax for partial non-resident taxpayers). A special type of mortgage can be found, allowing you to fully benefit from these advantages: a redemption-free mortgage combined with a compulsory savings scheme. Since there are no repayments, you benefit to the full from the tax deductibility of the interest payments.

Since the investment income on the savings scheme is not taxed, you can use this to generate capital with which all or part of the mortgage can be repaid once your partial non-resident tax status ceases to apply. Because the savings are not taxed, it is better to save than to make repayments: the after-tax effect of the repayments will usually be lower than the tax-free effect of the savings.

It follows that it is advisable to borrow as much as possible provided that it can be demonstrated that the funds are used for the acquisition of the immovable property in the Netherlands. Finally, as partial non-resident taxpayers benefit from the 30%-ruling; here too this allows you to make savings.

US TAXPAYERS

Special provisions apply to US taxpayers; these are not discussed here, but can be discussed with your tax advisor.

LOCAL TAXES

The aim of local taxes is to improve the taxpayers' surroundings, such as maintaining the streets, canals and city gardens, but also in the form of an extra contribution to education. And then there are the fun things, such as sports and recreational activities, art and culture.

Local taxes are levied and collected by the municipality or other government organizations. The majority of the total amount collected is levied through municipal property tax (*Onroerend Zaak Belasting – OZB*), waste collection taxes, sewerage charges, water control authority assessments and the pollution levy.

MUNICIPAL PROPERTY TAX

Municipal property tax (OZB) is divided into two parts: a user's part (for instance for those who rent the property) and an owner's part. If you are both user and owner, you pay both. When determining the amount due, the WOZ-value must first be determined. The municipality employs its own valuation surveyors to do this. This value is then applicable during the next four years and forms the basis for, among others, calculating the OZB. The WOZ-value is also used a basis for determining the deemed rental value for income tax purposes (see page 87).

Initially, in 2003, the government expressed its intention to abolish the user's part of the OZB as of January 1, 2005. As a consequence, the municipalities stand to lose an important source of income, which the government plans to compensate them for by means of general payment. It is not at all sure what the abolishment of the OZB will mean for our wallets – though clearly it will not be to everyone's advantage! As it stands now, this abolishment has been delayed until January 1, 2006.

WASTE COLLECTION TAXES

This tax is levied to cover the costs of collecting and processing household waste. This includes the emptying of the glass, paper and clothing containers that can be found in Dutch towns and cities. Processing waste is an expensive business. Environmental laws are becoming stricter and separating waste is a costly affair.

SEWERAGE CHARGES

These taxes are meant to cover the costs of maintaining the municipal sewage system. Everyone who makes use of this system, owes sewerage taxes. Only owners of immovable property have to pay it.

WATER BOARD ASSESSMENTS

This is money spent for keeping the water level in, among others, rivers, canals, ditches and streams at a certain level and ensuring a certain quality of the surface water. During the wet seasons, the water systems are drained. During the dry seasons, if necessary and possible, more water is brought in. Thus the water boards play an important role in this wet country. Your water board assessment helps to pay for these services. (See more on the water boards on page 29).

POLLUTION LEVY

The higher water control corporation, or *Hoogheemraadschap*, collects the pollution levy from all households. This levy is used for maintaining or improving the quality of surface water, while sewage treatment plants are used for cleaning waste water.

A COUNTRY OF TAXES

The Netherlands is truly a country of taxes. In order to guarantee or, where necessary, improve our enjoyment, local taxes are expected to continue to rise during the coming years. As they are levied locally, there are great differences in the amounts due be-tween municipalities. However, fortunately, there is the *Con-sumenten-bond* (Consumers Association), a Dutch organization that looks into and informs us on issues of importance to consumers. Among others, they investigate the local tax situation every year, to help ensure that these differences do not become too great.

DOG TAX

A very special tax is dog tax. Initially, the dog tax was a tax for companies that used dogs to pull carts. Now it is more of an environmental tax and is used to cover the costs of setting aside places for the dogs to run and play, and to clean up after them. It also covers the cost of a dog badge and anyone who owns a dog must pay this tax.

PAPER SERVICES

Also, we owe tax for the 'paper services' provided by municipalities. Some examples are:
- marriage license
- registration papers
- driver's license
- passport
- residence permit
- parking permit (in the larger cities).

Though municipalities are not allowed to make a profit on these services; they can pass on the costs in their entirety.

DENT

All these levies, added up together, can come to a considerable – and sometimes unexpected – amount and can put quite a dent in your vacation savings! So be sure to reserve at least € 3,000 for these taxes.

EXEMPTION FROM CUSTOMS DUTIES

If you transfer goods from a non EU-country to an EU-Member State (such as the Netherlands), you are subject to customs duties: VAT and other special taxes. The taxation incurred upon import can mean a great financial burden if you regularly change your place of residence for work or for other purposes. A special exemption can provide relief in these circumstances if you meet certain conditions.

EXTENT OF EXEMPTION

All EU-Member States provide an exemption if the imported goods form part of your household (personal) effects and they are transported as part of your change of fixed address. The exemption includes an exemption for VAT, customs duties, special taxes and other charges upon importation. Usually the removal company will ensure that you make use of the exemption and will take care of administrative obligations.

PERSONAL EFFECTS

These are effects such as clothing, furniture, linen, kitchen equipment, audio equipment, etc. Cars, (motor) bikes, pleasure yachts and pleasure aircraft are also deemed to be personal goods. Cars will not be included in the exemption if they are company cars or cars paid for by an employer.

CONDITIONS

There are certain conditions that must be met, in order for an application for an exemption to be considered:
- your usual place of residence must be transferred to an EU-Member State (in this case, the Netherlands)

- your usual place of residence must have been in a non-EU Member State for at least twelve months
- the goods to be transferred must have been in your personal possession, and must have been in your use during the last six months. In exceptional cases the authorities may grant an exception to this requirement
- before moving to the Netherlands, you must apply for a permit in the Netherlands
- with the exemption request, you should submit a signed list of household effects and other goods to be moved
- you should fulfill the usual customs requirements upon importation
- the goods must be imported within twelve months of your actual change of residency. The importation may take place in separate transports but in each case there must be a direct link between the change of residency and importation of goods
- you must use the goods for the same purpose in the Netherlands.

DETERMINING RESIDENCY

As mentioned above, the exemption can be requested if you change your place of permanent/usual residence from a non EU-country to the Netherlands and it will only be granted if you have been a resident of the non EU-country for at least twelve months preceding the move. Residency is presumed if you spent at least 185 days of the calendar year in a particular country due to personal and professional ties. It is up to you, when applying for the exemption, to prove the twelve-month residency in the non EU-country. If you can be deemed to have been resident in more than one country, the country where your personal ties (family and/or social commitments) are, will prevail.

MOVING FROM AN EU-MEMBER STATE TO THE NETHERLANDS

If you import goods from another member state, you will have already paid EU VAT and the exemption will therefore not be of any use. This is different, however, for cars. (For more information, see page 146).

REVOCATION OF THE EXEMPTION

After the permit has been granted and you have imported the goods, the exemption will be revoked if you lend, hire or sell any household effects, including the car, to another party within twelve months. Therefore, if anyone borrows your car, even for a short while, during your first twelve months in the EU, you will be liable for tax immediately. This condition is in effect for twelve months starting on the date when the customs authorities accept the customs declaration.

LARGE SAVINGS ON DUTIES

The exemption for household effects, when you move your permanent place of residence to the Netherlands, is subject to a number of strict conditions but when applied provides worthwhile savings on duties upon importation.

REFERENCES

GENERAL

MINISTRY OF HOUSING, SPATIAL PLANNING AND THE ENVIRONMENT
(Ministerie van Volkshuisvesting, Ruimtelijke Ordening en Milieubeheer)
Rijnstraat 8, P.O. Box 20951,
2500 EZ The Hague
Tel.: 070 339 50 50
Internet:www.vrom.nl/international

ORGANIZATIONS

NEDERLANDSE VERENIGING VAN MAKELAARS, NVM
Dutch Association of Real Estate Brokers
Fakkelstede 1, P.O.Box 2222,
3430 DC Nieuwegein
Tel.: 030 608 51 85
Internet: www.nvm.nl

DUTCH HOUSING ASSOCIATION
Vereniging Eigen Huis
Displayweg 1, P.O.Box 735,
3800 AS Amersfoort
Tel.: 033 450 77 52
Internet: www.eigenhuis.nl

STICHTING EIGEN HUIS AMSTERDAM
Orionstraat 6, 1033 EV Amsterdam
Tel.: 020 631 32 57

VERENIGING BEMIDDELING ONROEREND GOED (VBO)
Organization of Negotiating Agents for Properties
Internet: www.vbo.nl

CBS, CENTRAAL BUREAU VOOR DE STATISTIEK
Prinses Beatrixlaan 428, 2273 XZ Voorburg
Tel.: 070 337 38 00
Internet: www.cbs.nl

CONSUMENTENBOND
P.O. Box 1000, 2500 BA The Hague
Tel.: 070 445 45 45
Internet: www.consumentenbond.nl

KNB, KONINKLIJKE NOTARIËLE BEROEPSORGANISATIE
Spui 184, P.O. Box 16020, 2500 BA The Hague
Tel.: 070 330 71 11
Internet: www.notaris.nl

DUTCH CUSTOMS, DOUANE NEDERLAND
Service desk: 0800 0143
Internet: www.douane.nl

RECOMMENDED READING

HOUSING IN HOLLAND
Compiled by RMS, edited by Connie Moser
Published by xPat Media
A book especially developed in order to guide the English-speaking foreigner through the process involved in renting or purchasing a house in Holland.
Internet www.xpat.nl
www.hollandbooks.nl
ISBN 90 5594 252 9

WEBSITES

HOUSE HUNTING SITES
www.123huren.nl: for those who would rather rent than buy
www.digimmo.nl: to check on the price developments in respective areas, all transactions that are listed in the kadaster (city registry)
www.eigenhuis.nl: Vereniging Eigen Huis, association of homeowners
www.expatshousing.com: housing site for expats
www.funda.nl: site of the NVM Dutch Makelaars vereniging covering 60% of the housing market in the Netherlands.
www.huislijn.nl: website of the LMV Makelaars
www.huisnl.com: houses, building lots, company sites in the Netherlands
www.huisplein.nl: website of the VBO
www.huistekoop.nl: house for sale
www.inform.nl/woningbv/index.htm: list of all Woningbouwverenigingen or Housing Associations
www.kadaster.nl: land registry information in English
www.koophuis.nl: house for sale portal
www.lmv.nl: Landelijke Makelaars Vereniging (National Association of Real Estate Agents)
www.makelaars.net: Real Estate Brokers (Makelaars) portal
www.makelaars-nederland.nl: Real Estate Brokers (Makelaars) portal
www.mva-makelaars.nl: Makelaars Vereniging Amsterdam:
www.tvnsite.nl: temporary rentals for residential accommodation and housing management
www.vveplaza.nl: purchase of apartments
www.woninggids.nl: website of the Era estate agents
www.woningtransfer.nl: house-for-rent portal

HOUSING AGENCIES
Direct Wonen: www.directwonen.nl
Barrington Reals Estate: www.barrington.nl
Burger van Leeuwen: www.bvl-residential.nl
Dutchhousing Centre: www.dutchhousing.nl
Estata Makelaars: www.estata.nl
Holland Home Beheer & Verhuur: www.holland-home.nl
Gis Apartments: www.gis-apartments.nl
Haagen & Partners: www.haagen-partners.nl
Hakkenbroek Housing Company: www.hakkenbroekhousing.nl
Housingonline: www.housingonline.nl
Kimmel & Co: www.kimmel.nl
Makelaars Associatie: www.makass.nl
Nelisse Makelaars: www.Nelisse.nl
Van Paaschen Makelaardij: www.vanpaaschen.nl
Perfect Housing: www.perfecthousing.nl
Plink Adviesgroep: www.Plink.nl
Relocation Advisers: www.relocationadvisers.nl
Rots-Vast Groep: www.rotsvast.nl
Stoit Groep: www.stoit.nl
Welp Makelaardij: www.welpmakelaardij.nl

For more Housing Agencies see:
www.makelaars.net

TEMPORARY RESIDENCE
Ambassade Arena Aparthotel: www.aaahotel.nl
Egelshoek: www.egelshoek.nl
Hotel Business Suites: www.htel.nl
Rien vd Broeke Village: www.village.nl
Vesteda: www.vesteda.nl

BUILDING MARKETS – *BOUWMARKTEN*
Gamma: www.Gamma.com
Hubo: www.hubo.nl
Karwei: www.karwei.nl
Praxis: www.Praxis.nl

SAFETY
www.politie.nl: general police website
www.brandweer.nl: fire departments in the Netherlands
www.ecosa.org: European Consumer Safety Association
www.safewithin.com
www.babysafe.com/tips.htm
www.safekids.org

This chapter covers all of the legal, tax and financial information you may need during your stay in the Netherlands such as money matters; where much of your hard-earned money goes (the tax man); obtaining permits; getting married in the Netherlands and its legal consequences; what to do when you want a divorce; the rules of inheritance; insurances you need to consider; where to go for legal assistance, and much more.

Legal, Tax and
Financial Matters

CONTRIBUTING AUTHORS: RUUD BLAAKMAN, RINA DRIECE, NATHALIE IDSINGA, MARIKE MAAS, ANTON STEIJN,
GEESKE TUINSTRA AND ANNELIES VERHOEFF

MONEY MATTERS

THE EURO

Since January 2002, the monetary unit of the Netherlands has been the euro (or €), replacing 700 years of the guilder. The euro is also the currency in Austria, Belgium, Germany, Finland, France, Ireland, Italy, Luxembourg, Portugal and Spain – and though ten new countries joined the EU in May 2004, this does not automatically mean they have 'acquired' the euro. In order to do this they must meet certain economic criteria – which will be judged at some point in the future.

All EMU countries that have introduced the euro have the same bank notes and coins. These coins have two faces: the common euro face and a national face – though these coins look different, they can be used in any of the countries that have introduced the euro. There are seven bank notes: 5, 10, 20, 50, 100, 200 and 500 euros, and eight coins: 1 and 2 euros and 1, 2, 5, 10, 20 and 50 eurocents.

If you still have guilder notes and coins, De Nederlandsche Bank will accept coins until January 1, 2007, and bank notes until January 1, 2032.

NUMBER PUNCTUATION

The Dutch way of punctuating numbers and decimals is exactly opposite to the English way, so that € 25,25 is 25 euros and 25 eurocents, and € 10.000 is ten thousand euros. Round figures are written with a comma and a dash: e.g. 15 euros is € 15,-.

CHANGING MONEY

The introduction of the euro has made it easier to travel throughout Europe: you can go from country to country and use the same currency. However, for all other currencies the issue of exchange rates is still an important one.

The exchange rate (*wisselkoers*) is fixed every day and will be posted wherever you change money. The rate does not vary from one bank to the next, although the charges for changing money may differ. The most common place to change money is a bank (such as ABN-Amro, Fortis Bank, ING or Rabobank), a post office (Postbank), or a GWK exchange office. You will find GWK offices at railway stations, the airport, and places where there are many tourists. If you can show an international student card at a GWK exchange office, you will be charged less.

In very heavily touristed areas you may see other types of exchange offices, but their charges could be more, so it is best to wait until you see a bank or GWK office. There is no informal market for currency. Anyone who approaches you on the street with an offer to change money will be a thief or con artist rather than a money-changer.

OPENING YOUR ACCOUNT

To manage your day-to-day finances, you will need a current account. You can open this account either at a commercial bank, where it is called a *privérekening*, or at the post office (Postbank), where it is called a *girorekening*.

To open an account at a commercial bank you must visit the bank in person, bringing along proof of identification (passport or driver's license – though not all banks accept the latter!) and of your sofinumber. Most banks also like to see some type of proof of a regular income (such as a pay slip).

While opening the account, you also arrange your bank card (see further on). Some banks offer a choice of cards, depending on whether you plan to use it abroad or not, other banks offer 'only' one type of card. These cards allow you to withdraw up to several thousand euros a day at the bank or in the stores. For the use of these cards you pay a nominal annual fee. An account at a commercial bank is functional the same day that (or the day after) you open it. You can determine yourself whether you wish to receive your statements on a weekly, bi-weekly or monthly basis. With some banks, if you want to be able to overdraw your account ('go into the red'), you must bring proof of a source of regular income, so that you can determine together with the bank employee to what amount you can do this.

To open an account at the Postbank, you visit the post office and bring along proof of identification (passport) and of your sofi-number. Just as in any other bank, various types of accounts are available at the Postbank, as are various types of bank cards. A Postbank account is functional within two days.

All banks check with the BKR, whether you are 'creditworthy'; here they keep records of your credit card and bank history. If the BKR issues a negative advice, the bank can refuse you.

Current accounts pay no interest, but you are charged interest if you overdraw from them: i.e., if you 'go into the red'. Various other types of savings accounts are available for other purposes.

PAYING IN CASH

Paying in cash is common, and sometimes required under surprising circumstances. Furniture and other large household items, for example, are often paid for in cash, either as you leave the store (in which case you can use your bank card and pin), or which you give to the delivery man in exchange for a receipt when these items are delivered to your house. Though so-called 'ambulant' pin machines exist, allowing you to use your bank card for payments at your front door, not many delivery companies or persons have one (yet).

In shops, clerks sometimes have trouble making change and will ask you for coins. During the last few years of the guilder, the use of the single cent was unceremoniously abolished and prices got rounded off to the nearest five cents. With the introduction of the euro, came the introduction of not only the one cent-coin but also the two cent-coin, much to the annoyance of shopkeepers and customers. Starting towards the end of last year, it has become common use again to round prices off. Unfortunately, you cannot know yet where to expect this. Some stores return your change to the last cent, others expect you to know that they don't do that anymore, leaving you with an expectant upturned palm after having handed over two euros for a € 1.99 item.

CASH DISPENSERS
(OR AUTOMATED TELLER MACHINES, ATMS)

You will find a *geldautomaat* or cash dispenser at every bank and post office, and in railway stations and other public places where people are spending money. (At the post office the sign says *giro-maat*.) Dispensers will accept almost every kind of card, nowadays. You must find a match among the symbols on the dispenser and on your card.

To use a cash dispenser, you insert your card in the slot, and in most cases are given the option to select a language; Dutch, English, French or German. You type in your *pincode*, indicate that you want to withdraw money, select the amount, confirm it, and wait first for your card and then for your money. If a dispenser is not working it will say *buiten dienst*. If you type in the wrong *pincode* more than twice, the machine will swallow your card and you will have to go to the bank for a new one.

PAYING IN STORES

Paying with a bank card (the words are *pin, pinpas, pinnen* or *chippen*) is increasingly common and may even have become the most popular way of paying – after all, most stores (even stores where you buy large amounts of large objects, such as furniture or other household goods) still do not accept credit cards.

Shops have a link to the bank system, and the amount due is deducted immediately from your account. You or the clerk pass your card through a reader that looks like an oversized calculator and you type in your own secret four-digit personal identification

number (*PIN*, or *pincode*) – unless you are using a *chipknip* or *chippas*, which requires no pincode. The bank reports whether or not your balance will cover the amount; you verify the amount by pressing ja ('yes'), and the transaction is complete. For more information on the various bank and chip cards, read on.

BANK CARDS

When you open your account the bank will offer you options regarding plastic cards. The basic card, which the Postbank calls *giropas* and the regular banks call *bankpas* or *europas*, is used for making cash withdrawals from cash dispensers and for paying for things in stores using a *pinautomaat*. If you choose to have one – and we strongly recommend that you do, unless you want to have wads of cash in your wallet – you will receive notice in the mail that you can collect your card. This you can go collect at the bank or post office (for your Postbank card), along with some proof of identity (driver's license or passport). A few days later the bank or Postbank will send you your secret pincode by mail, which you must always enter in the card reader in order to activate the card when you make a purchase. You are supposed to memorize this so that a thief can never steal your card and find out your number at the same time. If you forget the number, you have to get a new card. If you want, you can change your *pincode* into any other four-digit combination you like, at the bank.

Your basic card will have various symbols on it, indicating its various functions. One symbol matches the one on eurocheques, for example, which means you have to show the card when you pay by eurocheque. Another symbol matches the one on pin automates, and others match symbols on cash dispensers. Most bank cards also work in other countries (and for other currencies). The bank or post office clerk can tell you which ones.

Some banks offer variations on this basic card, which give it extra functions. They will tell you about these possibilities.

When you open your account and apply for your basic plastic card, you and the clerk will decide on how deeply negative your account may go before your card will refuse to work.

CHIPKNIP/CHIPPAS

In order to overcome shop owners' objections against paying small amounts with your *bankpas*, the *chipknip* (or *chippas* for the Postbank) was introduced. This can be either a separate card (always the case for the Postbank cards), or your regular bank card with this added feature, that you 'load' at the bank (there is usually a machine next to the ATM-machine [automated teller machine] that looks just like it and says *chipknip*). Here you insert your card, the machine asks if you want to know your *saldo* (the amount still on the card) or whether you want to *opladen* (add money to it). If you want to add more money to the card, you choose *opladen*. Then you fill in the amount (maximum € 500 to € 1,000, depending on your bank and the amount on your bank account) and confirm it. If there is not enough, the machine will say *saldo niet toereikend*, after which you can try again for a new (lower) amount. It will be immediately deducted from your bank account. See earlier on how you can make payments with your *chipknip*. However, remember that if the amount that is still on your card is not enough to cover what you want to pay, then the machine in the store will also say *saldo niet toereikend*. You will then have to find another way to pay for your purchases – or re-load your card first.

You have probably already guessed the disadvantage of these cards: they require no pincode, as a result of which anybody who finds your (lost) *chipknip* can make payments with it (at least until he has used up the *saldo* on it).

CREDIT CARDS

A credit card is a separate card. In the Netherlands, the commercial banks and the Postbank mostly have an arrangement with either MasterCard or VISA. The money you spend with your Dutch credit card will be deducted directly from your account or you will receive an invoice from the credit card company.

The main difference between your basic bank card and a credit card is that your basic card will refuse to make a transaction if your balance is insufficient, whereas a credit card will always work unless it has been blocked – following theft, for example. This is why banks will give their clients credit cards only after they have known them a while, and have been able to determine, for instance, if the client has a regular source of income – and why the use of a credit card costs more.

Paying by credit card is less common in shops – especially smaller shops and supermarkets – mainly because the shops must pay a percentage of each sale to the credit-card company. Restaurants, hotels and department stores generally accept all major cards, however. Look at the window beside the door to see which cards they will take.

CHEQUES

Cheques are becoming less common as a way of paying for things in the Netherlands. The regular banks offer their clients *eurocheques*, and the Postbank offers *postcheques*, or *girobetaalkaarten*. Because these are guaranteed (i.e., the person to whom you write out a cheque gets his money whether you have the money in your account or not), clients are given only a limited number of cheques at a time. The banks are encouraging people to use the pin system instead. *Eurocheques* are useful when you travel in Europe because you can write them out in any currency and cash them at any bank. However, now that the euro (which is used in the EU countries) and the bank card (which allows you to withdraw money from ATMs virtually across the world) have been introduced, cheques have become less indispensable when traveling.

BANK TRANSFERS

Bills are generally paid by bank transfer, also known as the giro system. When bills are sent, they usually have a yellow *acceptgirokaart* attached to them. You fill in your own account number on it, sign your name, and send it to your own bank, which deducts the money from your account. Some banks provide you with postage-free envelopes for sending in the transfer forms.

Your bank will also provide you with forms for paying bills that do not have an *acceptgirokaart* attached. If it is a regular bank, these are called *overschrijvingsformulieren*; the Postbank calls them *overschrijvingskaarten*. On these you fill in the amount, the account number and the city of the recipient, indicate what the payment is for (where the form says *betreft*, *betalingskenmerk*, or *mededelingen*), and place your signature where it says *handtekening*.

For bills that you have to pay on a regular basis, such as your monthly rent, you can go to the bank or Postbank and fill in a form known as a *machtiging*. This gives the bank permission to transfer a certain amount from your account on a certain date. This will continue until you tell them to cancel a payment or to stop altogether. If you buy something by mail, the order form will sometimes include such a *machtiging* for a one-time payment. Your signature and account number are all the seller needs to get his money.

You can pay bills at the Postbank even if you do not have an account. Either present the clerk with the *acceptgirokaart* you received with the invoice, or ask the clerk for a transfer form. You then pay the amount in cash, plus a fee for the service. The date of payment at the Postbank is considered the date of payment and receipt of the money.

If you receive an *acceptgiro* in the mail, you can also pay it making use of your Internet or electronic banking options (see the following paragraphs). All you have to do is fill in the receiver's bank account number and the *betalingskenmerk* in the correct space and carry out all the other required steps.

PAYING ON THE INTERNET
Now that we do more and more virtual shopping on the Internet, we need a virtual purse. In this virtual purse, we of course find our credit card, but there are also alternatives. The two best known ways of paying make use of your e-mail address and are called Way2Pay and PayPal. For more information, visit their websites.

ELECTRONIC BANKING
All Dutch banks offer you the software that allows you to make payments from the comfort of your own home: electronic banking. Almost all banks offer this software in English – when you contact your bank, make sure to indicate that you would like to receive the English version. Most of these programs also have simple labeling options that allow you to keep itemized track of your spending habits.

INTERNET BANKING
More popular than electronic banking is Internet banking. It allows you to contact the bank via the Internet and – by means of an entry code – recall the amount on your bank account and carry out any payments. Furthermore, you can access an overview of your insurances and investments, and place orders for the buying and selling of shares, options, etc. Another advantage of this type of banking is that it is accessible from abroad. Contact your bank for what else they offer through Internet banking.

When you participate in an Internet savings 'plan', then you save money on an account that you can only access via the Internet. The amount of interest you receive on this account is relatively high, as the margins can be kept low, due to the fact that you are the one managing the account and executing the moves.

MOBILE BANKING
Mobile banking (m-banking) allows you to access your bank services by means of your mobile phone (or handheld computer or laptop). You can find out how much money is on your account, make payments and look up your receipts and payments. Not only that, but you can also find out what the state of your investments are, inform yourself of the latest financial news, the stock market and place orders on the Dutch and American stock markets. Among the banks that offer mobile banking are ABN-Amro, Rabobank, the Postbank and SNS.

The mobile banking market is a fluid and quickly developing one. We therefore suggest you check the bank's various websites on what they have to offer and who they are working with. Another player on this market is www.mobile2pay.nl, which offers you mobile banking services regardless of your bank (provided it is a Dutch bank) or your mobile phone service provider. Mobile2pay can be used anywhere where you cannot make use of your bank card (for instance when Internet-shopping or shopping from the comfort of the back seat of your car) and is currently also being introduced as a payment method in shops and restaurants across the country.

BANKING HOURS
Regular banks are open Monday through Friday, generally from 9 A.M. to 4 P.M. Many also open for a while on the one evening of the week that shops in the neighborhood stay open. This is usually a Thursday or a Friday. Post offices (Postbank) are generally open Monday through Friday from 9 A.M. to 5 P.M. Some main post offices will open for a few hours on Saturday mornings. In all cases, you will find the opening hours posted by the door.

TAXES

For purposes of application of the tax laws, it is very important to know whether you are a resident of the Netherlands or not. If so, you are regarded as a 'resident taxpayer'; if not, as a 'non-resident taxpayer'. Non-residents can choose to be treated as resident taxpayers, upon request. There is also a fourth option: if you are benefiting from the 30%-ruling, you may opt to be treated as a partial non-resident taxpayer. As it would – not surprisingly – require at least one book to tell you about the tax treatment of these four categories, we have picked out a handful of subjects that could be of interest to you, as an expatriate. These have been divided into the following headings: Income Tax, Wage Tax, and the 30%-Ruling.

INCOME TAX

ARE YOU A RESIDENT?
Under Dutch law, the question of a person's residence is determined 'according to the circumstances'. This is a question of facts, and in case law – among others – the following circumstances have been considered relevant when deciding on this issue:
- the place where you have your home
- the place where your family (partner) resides
- the place where you work
- the length of your stay in the Netherlands
- other personal ties with the Netherlands, such as (club) memberships, bank accounts, etc.

From the above list it can be deduced that the existence of a lasting relationship of a personal nature with the Netherlands is regarded as a very important factor when deciding whether or not you are a resident of the Netherlands.

THE NETHERLANDS TAX SYSTEM
There are different categories of income, each of which is treated differently for tax purposes, and these are the following:

BOX 1: INCOME FROM WORK AND HOME

This box includes, among others, income from employment, pensions, social security benefits, business income, periodic payments (e.g. alimony received), income from home ownership (*eigenwoningforfait*, if the house is your principal place of residence, see page 87) – less deductibles, for example expenses for child care, mortgage interest (again, if the house is your principal place of residence), alimony paid, child support, etc., etc.

The amount of tax due is calculated on the taxable income according to the progressive tax rates. The tax rates vary from 1.8% to 52%.

BOX 2: INCOME FROM SUBSTANTIAL SHAREHOLDING

If you own (possibly together with your partner) at least 5% of the shares in a Netherlands company (BV or NV), this income is taxed at 25%.

BOX 3: TAXABLE INCOME FROM SAVINGS AND INVESTMENTS

A notional income from investments is taxed, instead of the actual income. 30% is levied on 4% of the assets – after the deduction of debts and a personal allowance – the effective tax rate therefore being 1.2%.

PARTNER RULE

Dutch law contains the option for two people who are not married to choose to become 'partners'. They are then, for tax purposes, to be treated as if they were married. Spouses are automatically 'partners'. The status of 'partners' allows you to allocate income or deductibles in the way that allows you the greatest benefit from them.

LEVY REBATES

Instead of personal allowances, Dutch tax law contains levy rebates; rebates on tax and on the so-called general insurance contributions. Various levy rebates are available, depending on your personal circumstances. 'Partners' (see above) who do not work may also claim the (general) levy rebate; all they have to do is submit a request with the tax authorities for its application.

FOUR TAXPAYER OPTIONS

RESIDENT TAXPAYERS

If you are a resident taxpayer, you owe income tax on your entire, worldwide, income. In principle it makes no difference where in the world you earn your income (thus you may end up owing double taxes; see further on). The main sources of income that constitute taxable income are: business income, employment income, income in the form of periodic benefits (whether in cash or in kind) and notional investment income.

NON-RESIDENT TAXPAYERS

If you are a non-resident taxpayer, you are only liable to pay income tax on your income from certain sources in the Netherlands, resulting in a limited tax liability. The main sources of income that determine a non-resident taxpayer's income are: Dutch business income, employment income, income from real estate in the Netherlands and income in the form of periodic benefits (whether in cash or in kind) and a substantial shareholding in a Netherlands company. Employment income that you earn on working days that you physically spend outside the Netherlands is not taxable.

'REAL' NON-RESIDENTS CAN CHOOSE TO BE TREATED AS RESIDENT TAXPAYERS

This option is attractive if you are a non-resident earning your income in the Netherlands and would like to benefit from the available deductibles. Beware, however, of any negative consequences of this choice, especially if you change your mind within eight years of making it.

PARTIAL NON-RESIDENT TAXPAYERS

You only have the option of being treated as a partial non-resident taxpayer if you benefit from the so-called 30%-ruling (which will be discussed further on). When making use of this option, you are a resident of the Netherlands for income (and deductibles) in box, 1, but you are treated – upon your request – as a non-resident in boxes 2 and 3. This option gives you the best tax position you can have in the Netherlands.

TAX REFUND

In order to realize the tax benefit from deductibles (such as your mortgage interest) at an earlier point in time than through the final income tax bill, you can request the tax inspector to pay the tax refund in advance during the current year through a negative preliminary tax bill. The tax refund is then transferred directly by the tax office to you bank account, on a monthly basis.

DOUBLE TAXATION

RESIDENT TAXPAYERS

As a resident of the Netherlands, you have to pay tax on your worldwide income, as a consequence of which you may be faced with double taxation. After all, income earned abroad will often also be subject to taxation there. This situation is covered by the tax treaties that the Netherlands has entered into with many countries. In most of these treaties, income from employment in the Netherlands is tax-exempt in the Netherlands, provided all the following conditions are satisfied:

- you are present in the Netherlands for a period or periods not exceeding in the aggregate 183 days in any 12-month period or in a tax year, and
- the remuneration is paid by or on behalf of an employer who is not a resident of the Netherlands, and
- the remuneration is not borne by a permanent establishment or permanent representative of the employer in the Netherlands.

If the cumulative conditions summarized above are not met, your income will be taxable in the Netherlands. In that case, your country of residence will be expected to grant a relief for double taxation – at least, if there is a tax treaty between the two countries. For countries with which the Netherlands has not entered into a tax treaty, there is a unilateral arrangement. This will often mean that income earned abroad is exempt from taxation in the Netherlands, although it will be taken into account for the pur-pose of calculating the (progressive) tax rate applicable to your further income, which is then taxed in keeping with the 'normal' rules.

NON-RESIDENT TAXPAYERS

As a non-resident taxpayer, you generally owe tax in your country of residence on income earned in the Netherlands, as a consequence of which you may be faced with double taxation. This situation is also covered in tax treaties.

Internet Banking for expats.

www.abnamro.nl/english

US TAXPAYERS

If you are a US citizen benefiting from the 30%-ruling and you opt for the status of partial non-resident taxpayer, you owe tax in the Netherlands over income earned on working days physically spent in the Netherlands only. Therefore, if you spend a lot of time traveling outside the Netherlands, this could clearly be to your advantage.

A lower tax credit may, of course, have a negative impact on your US tax liability, but this will very likely be outweighed by the benefit.

This rule does not apply to statutory directors.

WAGE TAX

PAYROLL DEDUCTION

The term 'wage' is interpreted very widely and comprises cash benefits, benefits in kind, and also entitlements (such as pensions, which you can read about further on). In general, your employer is required to deduct the wage tax due from your wages and pay if to the Tax Office. The amount thus deducted can later on be credited with the income tax due. In some cases, no tax bill is imposed and thus the payroll deduction is the final tax due. If you are working for a non-Netherlands employer who does not have a permanent establishment, a deemed permanent establishment or a permanent representative in the Netherlands and is not registered to withhold wage tax, there is no wage tax liability. In that case, you are required to file an income tax return.

COST ALLOWANCES

The Netherlands wage tax law provides the following cost allowances for both resident and non-resident taxpayers:

- cost allowances: allowances for all kinds of expenses, the (non) taxability of which is determined by the business or personal nature of the expenses; the same applies to income in kind. Business expenses cannot be deducted on your personal income tax return
- 30%-ruling: under certain conditions, if you are an employee and have come to the Netherlands from abroad, extra expenses called 'extraterritorial expenses' can be reimbursed tax-free, either for the amount of the actual expenses or on a notional basis, being 30% of a certain basis. The latter can be done if the Tax Office has issued an official approval (the actual 30%-ruling).

PENSION

The term 'pension' has been strictly defined for tax purposes. A pension scheme that complies with this definition is a 'qualifying pension scheme'. If your pension scheme is indeed a qualifying pension scheme, your contributions are deductible and your employer's contributions are tax-exempt. The related benefits you will receive are subject to tax at the time of payment. However, if a pension scheme does not 'qualify', your contributions are not deductible nor are your employer's contributions tax-exempt.

The continuation of a non-Netherlands pension scheme requires particular attention, since it will often not satisfy the Dutch criteria. In order for your pension scheme to be considered a qualifying pension scheme, your employer will have to request the approval of the Dutch tax authorities. If it is approved, the pen-

TAX ISSUES FOR US CITIZENS

Living abroad creates complex tax issues that often confuse expatriates. The following is a brief overview of the main issues affecting US citizens or Green Card holders living in the Netherlands. The first item to note is that, if you are a US citizen or Green Card holder, you are still required to file a US tax return. There are, however, several provisions in the tax code and the tax treaty that act to reduce your tax liability. Another thing to keep in mind is that your tax return can, and may have to be, extended beyond the original filing deadline.

EXCLUSIONS FROM TAX

The first of these provisions is the foreign earned income exclusion under which you can exempt up to $ 80,000 per year. To qualify for this exclusion, you must meet one of two tests – the Physical Presence Test (PPT) or the Bona Fide Residence test (BFR). To qualify for PPT, you must be out of the country for 330 days out of a 365-day period – which can span two tax years. To qualify for BFR you must be living outside the US from January 1 to December 31 of the same calendar year. Another exclusion available to expatriates is the qualified housing exclusion, under which you can deduct a portion of your housing costs such as rent, certain utilities, and other expenses associated with maintaining a home in the Netherlands.

FOREIGN TAX CREDITS

Another strategy for reducing your US tax liability involves the use of foreign tax credits. Foreign tax credits may be taken whether you qualify for the abovementioned exclusions or not. Dutch income taxes paid on income that is not already excluded can be used as a credit towards your US taxes.

TAX TREATY

As mentioned above, the US has a tax treaty with the Netherlands that may exclude your income from either US or Dutch taxation. Generally, a person on a short business trip to the Netherlands will not have to pay Dutch taxes. Numerous requirements are set forth by the treaty, so caution should be used before applying this broad statement.

FILING EXTENSION

All Americans are familiar with the April 15 filing deadline. However, if you are living in the Netherlands on April 15, you are automatically granted an extension to June 15. For a variety of reasons, your US tax return may be further delayed and can be extended up to January 30 of the following year. The tax implications of a foreign assignment may seem confusing. The most important things to keep in mind are that there are provisions set up to avoid paying double tax on the same income and that good record keeping is very important.

If your career takes you abroad, does your insurance stay behind?

Contact Gouda Insurance to find out more about a comprehensive insurance package for working and living abroad.

Are you planning to work and live abroad? If so you will have to leave many familiar things behind. Maybe your insurance will be one of these. Gouda Insurance is a world leading specialist in dealing with tailor made insurance solutions for expatriates. Gouda Insurance can help you find an insurance package suited to your needs and adapted to the country in which you will temporarily stay. Worldwide.

Gouda Insurance offers a comprehensive package including Medical Expenses, Continuous Travel, Household Contents, Personal Liability, Personal Accident and an extensive Gouda Service Package for emergency assistance. And Gouda Insurance keeps it simple: one entire package, one policy number and one contact person.

Please visit www.expatriatesinsurance.com or contact your local insurance agent. Otherwise feel free to call us at +31 182 544 916 or send us an e-mail at expatriates@goudse.com and we'll be happy to help you.

Gouda
insurance

sion contributions that you pay will be deductible and your employer's contributions will not constitute taxable income. If you continue to contribute to a non-Netherlands pension scheme with a non-recognized foreign insurance company, you may receive a socalled 'protective tax bill'. This tax bill will only be 'cashed' if, according to Dutch law, improper use is made of the pension insurance.

COMPANY CAR

The 'benefit' that you enjoy from the private use of a company car is taxable as income from employment (to be reported on your income tax return only!) whether you are a resident or a non-resident taxpayer. It could prove worthwhile to keep a daily log of your private and business kilometers if you drive fewer than 500 kilometers per your for private purposes.

The 30%-ruling is not applicable. As of 2006, the benefit will have to be reported through the payroll administration; in that case, the 30%-ruling will be applicable.

30%-RULING

30%-RULING / EXTRATERRITORIAL EXPENSES

The 30%-ruling is a tax facility that has been created for employees who have been posted from or recruited outside the Netherlands to work in the Netherlands. You do not need to be a resident of the Netherlands and you do not have to (physically) carry out work in the Netherlands. The ruling can be found in the Wage Tax Act. The effect of this facility is that your employer can pay you a tax-free allowance of up to 30% of your wage for so-called 'extraterritorial expenses', as a result of which the effective rate of wage tax is reduced.

THE CONDITIONS FOR THE 30%-RULING

Whether you satisfy the conditions for the 30%-ruling or not depends on the circumstances at the start of your employment in the Netherlands as an 'extraterritorial employee'. These conditions are:

- *Posted or recruited from abroad*: you must have been posted to the Netherlands from another country or recruited abroad. Dutch nationals coming in from abroad may also qualify.
- *Netherlands payroll*: for the ruling to apply, there must be a Netherlands withholding entity. This means that your employer must deduct wage tax (and general insurance contributions, if applicable) from any wages paid out to you (in principle including any salary earned abroad) and pay this to the Dutch tax authorities. A non-Netherlands employer can also act as a Netherlands withholding entity.
- *Specific expertise/scarcity*: you must have 'a specific expertise which is not or scarcely available on the Dutch labor market'. Your employer has to demonstrate that a person with the required education, work experience (at least 2.5 years), expertise, etc. could only be found abroad. If a work permit is required and the permit is indeed issued, the condition of scarcity is implicitly met; the specific expertise, however, still has to be demonstrated. If you have been employed in the Netherlands on a job rotation basis and have worked at least 2.5 years within the same group of companies outside the Netherlands

at a middle or higher level, your employer does not have to demonstrate the scarce specific skills.

- *Request by both employee and employer*: you and your employer must jointly file a request. The application must be filed with the Tax Office for Non-Residents in Heerlen within four months after the start of your employment.

CHANGING EMPLOYERS

If you are benefiting from the 30%-ruling and you switch employers, you will still be able to benefit from the 30%-ruling in your employment (if a new employer is found within three months and the other conditions are satisfied) though only for the number of months left of the maximum of ten years. The request must be filed within four months of the change.

MAXIMUM PERIOD TEN YEARS

In principle, the ruling applies for a maximum period of ten years. At some point in time after five years have passed, your employer will have to demonstrate to the satisfaction of the tax authorities that an extended stay in the Netherlands is required because of the continued lack of the specific expertise on the Dutch labor market, in order to ensure that the 30%-ruling will continue to apply during the rest of the period.

EMPLOYMENT AGREEMENT

You may not simply split the gross salary for tax calculation purposes into a taxable part and a tax-free allowance. Your employment contract (or an addendum to it) should clearly indicate a reduced gross salary (reduced, since a 30% allowance should be paid out of the budget your employer has available for you), any further taxable or tax-free benefits, as well as the fixed 30%-allowance to be paid on top of salary and benefits. The Ministry of Finance has provided an approved draft that can serve as an addendum to the contract.

EXTRATERRITORIAL EXPENSES, NO 30%-RULING

If you do not qualify for the 30%-ruling, for whatever reason, your employer can reimburse you for the extraterritorial expenses actually incurred, without any tax consequences. In this situation, you have to deliver proof of the actual expenses.

CONSEQUENCES FOR WAGE TAX PURPOSES
BASIS FOR TAXATION

Your taxable wage, after having determined the tax-free 30%-allowance, is assessed according to the normal legal wage tax rules, in the same way as they apply to all employees in the Netherlands. This means that your employer may provide tax-exempt allowances for certain expenses in addition to the 30%-allowance. On the other hand, certain allowances for expenses that qualify as extraterritorial will reduce the level of the net 30%-allowance or will be taxable.

SCHOOL FEES INTERNATIONAL SCHOOLS

Your employer may pay a tax-free allowance for the school fees of children attending an international (primary or secondary) school or pay them directly. School fees that you pay yourself are not tax-deductible. Dutch schools with an international stream do not automatically qualify as international schools for purposes of the 30%-ruling.

SPECIAL RULES FOR WORK PERMITS

TEMPORARY WORK
In the case of temporary work, a work permit can be issued for a maximum period of 24 weeks. The work must then be carried out by a non-Dutch national who has not had a legal residence permit in connection with carrying out work during a period of 28 weeks preceding the issuing of the work permit. The work permit, it follows, cannot be extended. These permits are usually issued for seasonal work.

INCIDENTAL WORK/FOUR WEEKS
A work permit is not required for employees who have their principal place of residence outside the Netherlands and who come to carry out the following 'incidental work' or during a very short period:
- the assembling or fixing of equipment and machinery or the installing
- or adjustment of software, as well as the giving of instructions on its use the conducting of business meetings or the entering into of contracts.

INTER-COMPANY TRANSFER WITHIN A GROUP OF COMPANIES
For a work permit to be granted in the case of an inter-company transfer, proof must be delivered of the fact that the employee fills a high management position or highly qualified position and has that specific specialist knowledge that is essential for the company. Furthermore, the employment conditions must be in keeping with the function requirements that are applicable in the Netherlands. The company in question must be a large, independent company or group of companies whose aim it is to make a profit. It must also have an establishment in the Netherlands and an annual turnover of at least € 50 million. The salary of the employee must be at least € 50,000. For small companies and non-profit organizations special rules apply.

GUEST LECTURER
Work permits are not required for those who come as guest lecturers to universities, universities of professional education (*hogeschool* or HBO), institutions for higher international education, or research institutions that are connected to or operate in the area of a university, university of professional education, or institution for international education – under the condition that the lecturer has his principal place of residence outside the Netherlands and comes here for work every now and then or for no longer than four weeks within a three-month period.
Pursuant to the new rules on 'knowledge migrants', special rules also apply to those working on a Ph.D., and postdoctoral university professors who are younger than 30 years of age. (see page 115)

TRAINEES
There are special rules for employees of an international group of companies that have a university or higher professional (HBO) education.
In the case of traineeships, the employer must submit a program, showing the need for placing the employee in the Netherlands. Furthermore, in connection with the fact that the trainee is apparently not being sent to the Netherlands to fulfill a permanent position, the period of traineeship must be shorter than three years.

It is very important to comply with the rules given in the Act on Employment for Foreigners (WAV) and Aliens Act (Vw), as recent changes in the law may have as their consequence that if an employer has been convicted of illegal employment or does not comply with the arrangements made with the IND, he might not be able to arrange a residence permit for knowledge migrants or a work permit for his employees in the future. This could present great problems if the company is dependent on personnel that is brought in from abroad.

STUDENTS
RESIDENCE PERMIT
If you are planning on coming to the Netherlands to study, and your stay in the Netherlands will exceed three months, you will need an authorization temporary stay (MVV) in order to enter the country. If it will be shorter than three months, you will need a 'short stay visa' (visum kort verblijf). You apply for an MVV or short stay visa at the Dutch embassy or consulate in your home country. Your university (host institution) can also request an MVV for you, making use of the accelerated procedure of the IND (Immigration and Naturalization Services). If they do this, they must sign a guarantee on your behalf – and it depends on your host institution whether they are willing to do this. It is definitely worth your time to find out whether they are and what the requirements are.
Within three days, you must register with the municipality you are planning to stay in. If you are planning on staying longer than three months, you must, at the same time, apply for a residence permit; the MVV just allows you to enter the country.
Students that are nationals of EU/EEA member states, Switzerland, Monaco, Canada, the US, Japan, Australia and New Zealand do not need a an authorization temporary stay (MVV); EU-nationals do not even need a residence permit, however, in some cases, having the latter can greatly simplify matters when dealing with the authorities.

REQUIREMENTS EDUCATION

To be granted a residence permit for study purposes, you must follow a study at a recognized school or university (of professional education). It is not enough just to be taking Dutch language lessons. However, there is one exception to this. If you have met all the requirements for admission to a regular university program and you need only to pass the language proficiency test, you can obtain a special permit that allows you to stay one year to study Dutch (one year from the date you entered the country).

Many educational institutes offer a year-long 'familiarization and language' course (called a *schakeljaar*, or link-year), created specifically for students from non-European, non-Western countries who come to the Netherlands to follow an education at HBO or university level. You can read more about this in chapter 8.

WORK PERMIT

If you are a non-EU/EEA/Swiss student and want to follow an internship or do a work placement in the Netherlands, you need, aside from above documents, an employment permit (*tewerkstellingsvergunning*), to be requested by your employer. As a student you are allowed to work for a maximum of ten hours a week or full-time during the months of June, July and August. Your employer must apply for the work permit at least five weeks prior to your internship or work placement and should obtain it from the CWI (Center for Work and Income) after convincing them that all conditions have been met. He or she must also hand over the registration with the university (of professional education). Also to you, the Aliens Employment Act could apply, the purpose of which is to ensure that permanent residents of the EU/EEA/Switzerland are considered first for jobs. If you have any doubts about your status, ask your employer about it or contact the CWI. You risk being put out of the country if you are working illegally (without a permit if you should have one) and/or 'black' (your employer is not paying tax or social insurance premiums for you).

PROOF OF IDENTITY

As of January 1, 2005, you must, at all times, carry proof of identity on you - or risk a fine of € 50 (€ 25, if you are between the ages of 14 and 16). Valid proof of identity is: a passport, a valid (Dutch or European) identity card or a driver's license. Members of the police force or other persons of authority can ask you to show any of these documents.

IMPACT ON SOCIAL SECURITY AND PENSIONABLE BASE

Employee insurance contributions and pension rights may be accrued on your contractual (lower) gross salary only! In order to avoid a pension gap, ask your employer or seek expert advice; a solution is available.

PARTIAL NON-RESIDENT TAXPAYERS

If you have been granted the 30%-ruling, then you may choose to be treated as a partial non-resident taxpayer on your personal income tax return (see page 106).

PERMITS

SHORT STAY

If your stay in the Netherlands will not exceed three months, then most likely you will not need a visa to enter the Netherlands. In most cases a valid passport will be sufficient. You should check with the Dutch Embassy or Consulate in your home country whether or not a visa is needed. If you do, this type of visa is a *visum kort verblijf*, or short stay visa.

LONGER STAY

If you will be staying longer than three months, then you might need one of the following permits:

- Authorization temporary stay (*Machtiging tot Voorlopig Verblijf*, or MVV)
- Residence permit (*Verblijfsvergunning*)
- Work permit (*Tewerkstellingsvergunning*)

RESIDENCE PERMIT

EU/EEA AND SWISS NATIONALS

If you are a national of any of the European Union (EU) or European Economic Area (EEA) member states or Switzerland, you will not need an authorization temporary stay prior to traveling to the Netherlands.

Formally, EU/EEA and Swiss nationals also do not need a residence permit; however, you will not be entitled to certain social benefits if you do not have a residence permit, nor can you register with the municipal register. It is therefore always advisable to apply for a residence permit with the Immigrations Office or local town hall in your local place of residence. The competent authority and procedure might differ, depending on where you live. The Immigration and Naturalization Service (IND) will process all residence permit applications.

Although EU/EEA/Swiss nationals will be entitled to reside and work in the Netherlands without any kind of permit, they will only be entitled to a residence permit if they have a monthly income that exceeds the minimum wage and that will last for at least another year.

NON EU/EEA/SWISS NATIONALS

You are exempted from the authorization temporary stay requirement if you are from the United States, Canada, Japan, Australia or New Zealand. In all other cases, you need an authorization temporary stay prior to traveling to the Netherlands as well as to be able to apply for a residence permit upon arrival.

As of December 1998 you can no longer apply for a residence permit if you entered the Netherlands without making use of this entry visa.

PROCEDURE

You can apply for an authorization temporary stay (MVV) with the Dutch Embassy or Consulate in your home country/country of legal residence or your prospective employer can seek information with the IND in the Netherlands as to whether there is any objection against issuing one. If there is indeed no such objection, the IND will send an MVV-approval to the Dutch embassy in your home country/country of legal residence. An MVV must also be requested for your accompanying family members. Processing time is approximately four weeks, if you intend to work in the Netherlands and have already submitted a work permit with the IND. If you file your applications simultaneously, the same processing time will apply to your family members. If their applications are filed later, however, processing time for them may take up to six months. As soon as the Dutch authorities have given approval to issue the authorizations temporary stay, you can collect them at the Dutch Embassy or Consulate in your home country/country of legal residence.

Once the MVV has been granted by the Dutch Embassy or Consulate, you may travel to the Netherlands.

REGISTERING WITH THE MUNICIPALITY

Within three days of arrival, you have to report with the municipality (stadhuis or gemeentehuis) to apply for a residence permit and to have yourself entered in the municipal register (bevolkingsregister). Please keep in mind that both procedures (requesting a residence permit and registering with the municipality) can only be executed when suitable housing has been arranged.

REQUIRED DOCUMENTS

The documents that you have to submit when registering and/or applying for a residence permit are, among others:
- a legalized certified copy of your birth certificate (also your spouse's or partner's)
- a legalized marriage license if applicable
- if either you or your partner were previously married, a copy of the legalized divorce decree.

Whatever else you need depends on your circumstances and country of origin. Other documents, such as a passport, work permit and proof of insurance will be required at some later point, check with the IND what these are.

WORK PERMIT

EU/EEA/SWISS NATIONALS

In principle, if you are a national of an EU/EEA member state or of Switzerland, you may work in the Netherlands without a work permit.

NON EU/EEA/SWISS NATIONALS

If you are a non EU/EEA/Swiss national and wish to work in the Netherlands, even for only one day, you must obtain a work permit, unless you are a so-called 'knowledge worker' (or highly skilled employee) in which case you only need a residence permit (see further on). This can only be obtained if you are applying for a visa/authorization temporary stay or residence permit at the same time.

Your prospective employer has to submit an application for your work permit with the Center for Work and Income (CWI) in Zoetermeer. According to the Act on Employment for Foreigners (Wet Arbeid Vreemdelingen, or WAV) anyone hierarchically in a position to give you work instructions is seen as your employer. Whether or not there is an employment contract is not relevant. The CWI in Zoetermeer makes the final decision on this matter.

REQUIREMENTS

In general, the CWI only issues work permits if the employer has been able to convince them that there are no qualified individuals available on the EU/EEA labor market. The employer should therefore submit proof that he has done everything in his capacity to find individuals on the EU/EEA labor market (i.e. by submitting copies of advertisements, statements from recruitment agencies, postings on the Internet, etc.). Several months prior to filing the work permit application, the vacancy must be reported with the local CWI (Center for Work and Income). If this condition is not met, a work permit will not be issued. Furthermore, the permit may be granted under the condition that the employer provide retraining opportunities for EU/EEA nationals seeking jobs, insofar as this can reasonably be requested of him.

An easier way to obtain a work permit is on the basis of a so-called inter-company transfer, see Special Rules for Work Permits, on page 112.

PROCESSING TIME

Theoretically, the processing time for a work permit is five weeks after a complete application – together with the answers to possible additional questions raised by the CWI – have been submitted. During the application process, you will not be allowed to work in the Netherlands. Companies risk high penalties, and their directors even prison, if they break the law.

PERIOD OF VALIDITY

You will be issued a work permit for the duration of the employment as mentioned in the employment contract – with a maximum of three years. If it has been issued for a period shorter than three years, you cannot automatically extend it if you need to stay longer; you will have to apply for a new work permit – but this can only be done after your employer has fulfilled all relevant conditions (advertising, etc.). If you have had a residence permit and work permit for a continuous period of three years, then you are entitled to a residence permit without restrictions – and a work permit will no longer be needed. A work permit is not transferable to another employer or to another position.

REFUSAL

A reason to refuse an employment permit is if there is a suspicion that the vacancy will not be filled by people from EU/EEA-countries who are seeking work because the terms and conditions of employment or the working conditions in the business concerned do not comply with the collective labor agreement or the law.

WHO DOES WHAT

You need to take care of the residence permit application whereas your employer is responsible for the work permit application. If an authorization temporary stay is required, either you or your employer are involved in the process. Also for knowledge workers (see the following paragraphs), the involvement of the employer is required.

It is advisable to coordinate all permits from one point, for example the employer, who can deal with all the paperwork involved.

NEW: KNOWLEDGE WORKERS/MIGRANTS

As of January 1, 2005, a new policy for allowing knowledge workers (or knowledge migrants) into the Netherlands is being phased in. The aim of the policy is to simplify the entry of knowledge workers from outside the EU/EEA into the Netherlands in order to improve the position of the Netherlands as a knowledge economy and make the Netherlands more attractive as a work location for knowledge workers.

To this end, the work permit requirement for knowledge workers will be abolished and replaced by a residence permit under the restriction of 'knowledge worker'.

DURATION PERMIT

This permit will be issued for a maximum period of five years if the knowledge worker has an indefinite employment contract. If it is a fixed-term contract, the permit will be issued for the duration of the contract.

IND

The Dutch immigration service (IND) will have sole responsibility for implementing the procedures for entry to the Netherlands/ the Dutch employment market.

DEFINITION

Knowledge workers are defined as contracted employees earning a minimum gross income of € 45,000 per annum, to be indexed annually. The annual income includes salary withholding tax, employee and social security contributions, and the holiday allowance, but excludes supplements, bonuses and payments in kind (e.g. company car). Employer charges are also not taken into account.

Since this income requirement is a considerable obstacle for young migrant workers, a lower threshold applies to them; persons under the age of 30 who earn a minimum of € 33,000 gross per annum can also qualify as knowledge workers.

STUDENTS

Foreign students are not considered knowledge workers. Only once they have completed their studies and found a job under the applicable conditions within three months will they become eligible for a residence permit as a knowledge worker.

CHANGE OF EMPLOYER

Knowledge workers are allowed to change employers while their residence permit is still valid. The IND will test the change to a new employer against the applicable conditions.

If a knowledge worker is dismissed, a reasonable term of three months will be granted to find another position that satisfies the conditions.

Should the knowledge worker accept a position that does not satisfy the wage requirement, the work permit requirement will apply.

PARTNERS AND CHILDREN

Partners and children of knowledge workers will initially be granted a residence permit for one year, after which they can obtain a permit for five years. Partners of knowledge workers can apply for a work permit without having to go through the labor market assessment (see page 114, under Requirements).

PRACTICAL ISSUES

Companies can enter into a standard contract with the IND, which can be found on www.ind.nl. Once the IND has authorized the company to make use of the new regulation, the company will get entry codes to access the application forms that can be found on the IND website, allowing the IND to process applications within two weeks.

ACCELERATED MVV-PROCEDURE

The consequence of the new scheme is that all employers are eligible for using the accelerated MVV-procedure for knowledge workers. A decision on such a request will basically be made within two weeks.

Part of the procedure requires that the identity of the knowledge worker and his/her relatives be confirmed on the basis of a passport. Marriage certificates and birth certificates of children will still have to be authenticated to show the family ties. The authentication requirements that apply to so-called problem countries will also be abolished.

MARRIAGE

THE CEREMONY

JA, IK WIL – MARRIAGE DUTCH STYLE

Imagine this scenario: you spent months arranging your wedding; you've stood up in church and declared 'I do'; you've celebrated with your nearest and dearest; only to discover down the track that your wedding was as valid as Mick Jagger and Jerry Hall's Bali nuptials. In the Netherlands a church service alone does not satisfy the legal requirements for the state of marriage. A civil service is all that is deemed legally valid. This is actually the case in many countries, the difference being that in some other countries churches are licensed to register marriages. If you want a church wedding in the Netherlands you will also have to undergo a separate civil service.

CIVIL WEDDING

For most people the term 'civil' conjures up images of a hurried, impersonal service held in an ugly municipal building with couples queuing up for the privilege. In the Netherlands it doesn't need to be like this as there is a great variety of interesting locations available for a civil wedding. The municipality of The Hague alone offers six possible locations, whilst nearby Voorburg offers a

further three. Couples are not restricted to marrying within their own municipality (*gemeente*). They could consider any of the following options: a windmill in Leidschendam; the Rotterdam Zoo; the Huygensmuseum Hofwijck, Voorburg; a castle in the countryside; the Commandeurskamer at the Bataviawerf in Lelystad; or the trouwzaal of an historic *stadhuis* such as those in The Hague, Delft, Gouda or Middelburg.

ONDERTROUW

The first step in organizing a wedding is a visit to the local *gemeente* (municipality) for the *ondertrouw*. This can be done a maximum of one year or a minimum of two weeks in advance of the wedding date. In the English language there is not a simple, one-word translation for *ondertrouw*. It can best be described as 'reading of the banns', or 'notice of intent to marry'. If marrying in an area outside of your *gemeente* then you will need to use your (or your intended's) local *gemeente* for the *ondertrouw*, and book the wedding arrangements separately with the *gemeente* of that region. There is a small administrative fee required for the *ondertrouw*, and you need to produce passports (identity cards), birth certificates, witness forms (see next paragraph for more on witnesses), proof of single status and evidence of your Dutch residency. Documents from overseas require the appropriate *apostille* stamp (see International Certificate for an explanation of the *apostille* stamp). If a foreigner is marrying a Dutch national or a resident of the Netherlands then the *vreemdelingendienst* (Aliens Department) must issue a declaration (called M46), stating that they do not object to the marriage – which it sends directly to the municipality. An M46 is not required for EU-citizens. If neither of you lives in the Netherlands, then you can register for *ondertrouw* in The Hague. Two foreign nationals may marry in the Netherlands only if one of them has residency in this country.

If you wish to obtain a registered partnership (see further on, under *A Few Issues*), then you must also register for this in advance (minimum 14 days, maximum 1 year). If you have permanent residence permit, then you can show this, instead of obtaining an M46. All required documents may not be older than six months.

WITNESSES

At least two witnesses or a maximum of four witnesses must sign the marriage certificate. Witnesses can be of any nationality, and you need to provide copies of their passports to the *gemeente* where you are marrying. This is one document you don't need to have stamped with an apostille!

INTERNATIONAL CERTIFICATE

A foreigner marrying in the Netherlands may pay a small sum extra to have an international marriage certificate issued. This certificate is valid in ten languages so it should save many people the cost of having the certificate officially translated for use in another country. However, if the certificate is needed for official use in a country outside the Netherlands then it will need to be endorsed by the Dutch authorities with an apostille stamp. An apostille stamp is simply an internationally recognized certification of authenticity and is required by all countries on official documents issued outside their own.

AGE, SAME SEX, REGISTERED PARTNERSHIP

Eighteen is the minimum legal age for marriage, although a pregnant female may marry at sixteen providing she has proof from her gynecologist and permission from her parents/guardians. Same-sex marriages are also possible (since April 1, 2001).

Since 1998, it is also possible for two people of the same or the opposite sex to undergo a similar arrangement to marriage, known as a registered partnership. A registered partnership or marriage between two persons of the same sex affords nearly all the same rights as marriage and differs only in regards to children and adoption. It is not legally recognized outside of the Netherlands.

A registered partnership can be converted into a marriage and vice versa.

WEEKDAY WEDDINGS

Many foreigners are surprised by the fact that Dutch weddings often take place on weekdays. This may have something to do with the costs involved. A free civil service wedding is possible, but it is usually only available between 9 – 10 A.M. on a Monday or Wednesday morning. It probably won't be conducted within an atmospheric *trouwzaal*, but in a small room at the *gemeentehuis*. Despite the fact that the service is free it will still set you back some money as you are required to purchase a *registratieboekje* (a booklet in which your marriage is registered), and pay for witnesses if you can't provide your own.

The costs for a civil wedding service range quite dramatically, starting from around € 40 and going up to around € 850, depending on the time and location chosen. Generally speaking Monday to Thursday between 9 A.M. and 4 P.M. is the cheapest time to marry. After 4 P.M weekdays and weekends the costs can increase substantially. The cost for marrying on a Saturday is approximately three times as much as mid-week wedding, making it very attractive to marry on a Friday. For example it would cost approximately € 292 to marry at the town hall of Leidschendam on a weekday before 5 P.M., € 559 to marry after 5 P.M., and an exorbitant € 842 to get married on a Sunday. For further information regarding times available for weddings, and the relevant costs involved, consult the *Huwelijksdata Gids*, available from local *gemeentehuizen*.

A ROOF OVER YOUR HEAD

If you have always dreamed of an outdoor setting for your wedding, and you are brave enough to try such a thing in the Netherlands, then you need to be aware that for a marriage to be legal it has to take place with a roof above your heads. In effect this means that you could have the ceremony conducted outdoors, but you would need to move inside for the signing of the registrar.

LAST NAMES

Once married, the couple has a number of choices regarding their last names. In the Netherlands it is possible for the husband to choose his wife's surname after marriage, and vice versa. It is also possible to choose to use your surname followed by your spouse's surname, or the reverse, your spouse's surname followed by your surname. Alternately both husband and wife may choose to keep their own surnames.

RING FINGERS

If you are used to surreptitiously checking out a person's marital status by the sight of a wedding band on the ring finger of the left hand, be aware that in the Netherlands a wedding ring may be worn on the ring finger of either hand. During a civil wedding service the couple will place rings on their right hands. For a church wedding the tradition in this country is that Catholics wear their wedding ring on the left hand, whilst Protestants wear it on the right hand.

DUTCH LAW ON MATRIMONIAL PROPERTY

GENERAL COMMUNITY PROPERTY

The Dutch legal system determines that if you get married under Dutch law without having made a marriage contract, in principle all property and debts that either of you had before the marriage, become joint property and joint debts once you are married. The same applies to property and debts that you acquire during your marriage. This legal system is called general community property.

MARRIAGE CONTRACT

You can deviate from the legal system before or after entering into marriage by means of a marriage contract. The marriage contract has to be set up by a civil law notary and the deed containing the marriage contract has to be entered in the public matrimonial property register at the Dutch court. This is to ensure that anyone can find out whether you have a marriage contract and what clauses it contains. The contract can help avoid that debts, incurred by you or your spouse, can be recovered from the other.

REGISTERED PARTNERSHIP

Whereas two people of the same sex originally could not enter into marriage, since 1998 they can become registered as common law partners. The consequences of such a registered partnership are (apart from children) exactly the same as the consequences of an ordinary marriage, such as general community property in case a partnership contract is absent and alimony in case of divorce. The registered partnership is available for people of the same sex as well as for people of different sexes. As of 2001, marriage is also available for people of the same sex.

FUTURE CHANGES IN THE LAW

Currently a bill is being proposed that slightly restricts the general community property, as a consequence of which inheritances and gifts, as well as assets and debts that a spouse had before the marriage, do not form part of the general community property.
At the moment, these assets/debts, inheritances and gifts *do* form part of the general community property. As far as the inheritances and gifts, this is not the case if the testator or donator has stipulated otherwise.

THE LAW ABROAD AND INTERNATIONAL PRIVATE LAW

Every country has its own rules on matrimonial property. International private law determines which legislation is applicable to a marriage with international aspects – for instance in the case you and your spouse were married abroad or do not have the same nationality. Every country has its own rules on international private law and the authorities of a country always apply the country's own rules of international private law. This can lead to different, conflicting results. International treaties are meant to avoid such conflicting results. Regarding the law on matrimonial property, the Dutch authorities apply the rules of the Hague Matrimonial Treaty 1978.

THE HAGUE MATRIMONIAL PROPERTY TREATY 1978

At the moment, the Netherlands, France and Luxembourg are party to the treaty of 1978, which, with certain exceptions, is only applicable to you if you entered into marriage on or after September 1, 1992. The premise of the treaty is that if you have not stated a particular choice of law in a marriage contract, the law of the country in which you both settle directly after entering into marriage is applicable. If you and your spouse have the same nationality, there are some exceptions to aforementioned premise. The Treaty does not apply to registered partners and it is not yet clear whether is applies to same-sex marriages.

EMIGRATION, IMMIGRATION OR NATURALIZATION

The treaty has determined that during the marriage, due to emigration, immigration or naturalization, the originally applicable law on matrimonial property may be replaced by the law on matrimonial property of a different country. This is only the case if you entered into marriage on or after September 1, 1992 and did not explicitly state a choice of law in your marriage contract. The replacement of the applicable law can have great consequences for, for instance, the extent and the division of the matrimonial property in the case you get divorced or either one of you dies.

MOVING TO THE NETHERLANDS

If you got married on or after September 1, 1992, lived abroad at the time of the marriage and subsequently moved to the Netherlands, the matrimonial property system changes after ten years. Ten years after you moved to the Netherlands, if you do not have a marriage contract, you become married according to the Dutch system of general community property. If you are both of Dutch nationality at the time of the move, then the Dutch law of matrimonial property becomes applicable as of the moment you settle in the Netherlands.
The change in system of matrimonial property also takes place if you married on or after September 1, 1992 and both subsequently acquired Dutch nationality while living in the Netherlands. As of the moment you acquire Dutch nationality, the Dutch legal system is applicable to your matrimonial property regime – unless you have explicitly chosen another applicable law.

CHOOSING AN APPLICABLE LAW

By stipulating which law is to apply, you leave no doubt as to which law of matrimonial property is applicable. Making such a choice is of particular importance in cases where the marriage has international aspects. A choice of law helps to avoid that – due to emigration, immigration or naturalization – a different law becomes applicable. However, beware of the fact that a choice made in the Netherlands does not always have the desired effect in a country that is not a party to the Hague Matrimonial Property Treaty 1978. In such a situation it is best to seek advice on this matter in both countries.

MAKING THE MATRIMONIAL PROPERTY REGIME KNOWN

Third parties, such as creditors, are not always bound by your matrimonial property regime. By entering your choice of law in the Dutch matrimonial property register (which should be done by a Dutch notary public), you can effectuate that the rules of your marriage system are binding for, for instance, creditors in the Netherlands. If you do not have your system of matrimonial property registered in the Dutch matrimonial property register,

then a creditor may assume that you have been married according to the Dutch legal system (which would be general community property) unless he knew or could have known to the contrary. However, both you and your creditor had to have been living in the Netherlands at the time the debt was incurred.

DIVORCE

Dutch law distinguishes between a divorce by mutual request and a divorce upon request of one of the spouses. The proceedings are started by means of a (unilateral or joint) petition.

COMPETENCE OF THE COURTS
In the Netherlands you can file a petition for a divorce before the District Court of the district in which you and/or your spouse lives. If both of you have Dutch nationality, the Dutch courts are competent. If one of you has been living in the Netherlands for a period of 12 months or more, or if one of you is Dutch and has been living here for a period of six months or more, then the Dutch courts are also competent. In all other cases, the Dutch courts are not competent and you cannot file for divorce in the Netherlands.

APPLICABLE LAW
The fact that the Dutch courts are competent does not mean that

they must apply Dutch law. The rules are as follows:
- if both of you have the same nationality, the law of that country is applicable
- if you do not both have the same nationality, but reside in the same country, the law of that country is applicable
- if you do not have the same nationality and do not reside in the same country, Dutch law is applicable.
- Dutch law can be made applicable, if you make the choice together, or if one of you makes that choice and the other does not contradict it.

RECOGNITION
Whether or not the ruling of the Dutch court will be recognized abroad depends on whether or not your country is a party to the treaty that the Netherlands has entered into on this matter, the Treaty on the Recognition of Divorces.

UNILATERAL PETITION
Should you be the one filing the unilateral petition, the petition should contain a request on how you would like the four consequences of the divorce (which you will find below) to be arranged. Your spouse can lodge a statement of defense, containing his/her wishes regarding the consequences.
In a hearing, the court will allow itself to be further informed on these matters and will determine on which date, in the future, it

will rule on this matter. If you or your spouse do not agree with the final ruling, you or your spouse can bring an appeal before the Court of Appeals.

JOINT PETITION

If both of you have come to an agreement regarding the four consequences of divorce, you can have these drawn up in a settlement. This settlement can be drawn up by two lawyers, if each of you has a lawyer, or by one lawyer, who is then the 'divorce mediator'.

MEDIATION

The purpose of a divorce mediator is to have both of you arrange the consequences of the divorce together, thus promoting the acceptation and durability of the agreement. The idea is that the discussion with the mediator provides you with better insight into the underlying emotional problems, allowing you to better describe your differences and see the merits of the various solutions that the mediator suggests. The settlement is submitted before the court along with the petition and the court rules in keeping with this settlement.

In the case of divorce, there are several reasonably diverse areas that the mediator should be able to advise you on, such as custody, alimony, and the division of marital property. If he cannot advise you on all these matters, he will be able to refer you to a specialist who can.

THE FOUR CONSEQUENCES OF DIVORCE

There are four areas in which a divorce has consequences and for which the court, or the two of you, must find a solution. These are:

1. CHILDREN

Custody. In principle both of you retain custody of the child(ren). This is only different if you both agree, or one of you is of the opinion, that it is in the interest of the children that only one of you has custody. In that case you or your spouse should submit a request before the court to rule on this matter when ruling on the divorce.

Child support and care. The amount of child support due will be determined, depending on your (joint) income and based on the actual costs that the children represent. It is based on the thought that the children should be allowed to maintain the same 'standard of living' after the divorce. To determine the amount of financial support that is needed to achieve this, the court looks at the actual 'costs' that are related to the children and what the net family income was before the divorce. Alimony for children is due until the children become financially independent (they have a job or receive a benefit) or reach the age of 21. As of their 18th birthday, the alimony is to be paid out directly to the children.

You can find more information on the financial aspects of divorce in the brochure *Geldwijzer Alimentatie* (Money Guide for Alimony), which you can order from NIBUD (you will find the address at the end of the chapter). This booklet can help you make an overview of the needs of the children, including the costs of maintenance.

When both of you are to share an equal part in the raising and maintaining of the children, then one of you will receive the Child Benefit (*Kinderbijslag* – see page 186) while the other will be granted a deduction for exceptional expenses (to qualify for this, a certain minimum amount of child support must be paid to the other parent). The parent whose address is the one where the child is registered at the municipality is the parent who receives the Child Benefit; the other is granted the deduction.

Visitation rights. If the two of you share custody, you can request the court to determine the visitation rights. If one of you has custody, the other can submit this request.

2. 'PARTNER' ALIMONY

The court will determine whether and to what degree you will have to support each other financially. In doing this, the court takes the following into account:

a. The needs of the one who has the right to alimony
Say, you are the one who will be receiving alimony. To determine your minimum needs, the court will take into account the legal minimum income for those who are unemployed plus other, unavoidable, living expenses. However, your actual financial capacity will also be taken into account as well as the standard of living that you were accustomed to during the marriage.

b. Financial capacity of the other spouse
Having determined your needs, the court determines the amount that your husband/wife can contribute, taking into account his/her income. He/she gets to keep an amount that is equal to the legal minimum income and other, unavoidable, living expenses, such as:
- the costs related to having living space, insofar as these exceed the rent subsidy, and insofar as they can be considered reasonable
- the premium for a medical expenses insurance
- interest related to debts incurred during the marriage
- visitation expenses
- redecoration expenses, to a certain maximum amount if he/she left the marital home.

60% of the difference between the income and the costs mentioned above is available for alimony, after deduction of the alimony for the children, if there are any. If the receiving spouse moves in together with another person, he/she loses the right to partner alimony.

Alimony paid to former spouses is entirely deductible, the former spouse, however, owes the related income tax.

Alimony is due over a maximum period of twelve years, however, the spouses can agree to a different period.

3. DIVISION OF THE MARITAL PROPERTY

The ruling of the court on the divorce should contain rules on how the marital property should be divided (taking into account the fact that your marriage is governed by the Dutch rules on community property or that you have a pre or postnuptial agreement, see page 118). Legally, that which is part of the communal property should be divided equally among you, including the debts; however, you can agree otherwise.

4. PENSION RIGHTS

In the case of divorce, each of you has a right to a portion of the amount of old age pension accrued by the other during the period of marriage. You can agree otherwise, allowing it to stay entirely with the person who built it up, or agreeing to a different division.

DUTCH INHERITANCE LAW

SUCCESSION BY WILL
In the Netherlands you can determine who your heirs are in a will (succession by will). If the will is absent, then the law determines who your heirs are (succession by law/intestate succession). If you make a will in the Netherlands, according to Dutch law, it should be done by means of a deed made up by a Dutch public notary.

SUCCESSION BY LAW
As of January 2003, the Dutch law regulating intestate succession has changed. The law defines four groups of heirs. Only blood relatives, spouses or registered partners are entitled to the inheritance. The (grand)children and spouse or registered partner form the first group of heirs, each inheriting an equal share. The brothers, sisters (and their children) and parents form the second group of heirs. Grandparents and great-grandparents finally form the third and fourth group. If there are no relatives within the first, second or third group respectively, then the relatives within the next group are eligible.

ALLOCATION BY LAW
If the spouse or registered partner, together with one or more children of the deceased, is the heir, then, by intestate succession, the spouse or registered partner will get all assets and debts of the deceased. The children will only have a monetary claim on the spouse or registered partner to the amount of their share, claimable at the time the spouse or registered partner dies or goes bankrupt. Should the spouse or registered partner remarry, the children are entitled to claim the proprietary rights of assets derived from the inheritance, to avoid that these assets end up with the stepfamily. The spouse or registered partner may retain the usufruct of these assets.
This allocation by law can be set aside in a will so that, for instance, the children also take part in the proprietary rights and liabilities as of the day of the devolution of the estate, instead of just having the monetary claim.

STATUTORY CLAIMS
Children always have a right to a fixed, minimum value of the estate of their parents, also referred to as the statutory claim. Even if, for example, a parent states in a will that a child is not to inherit anything, the child can make this monetary claim on the joint heirs anyway. The statutory claim amounts to half of the value of the portion which the child would have inherited had it not been disinherited. In a will, the parent can state that the statutory claim is not claimable until his or her spouse, registered partner or partner with whom the parent has a cohabitation agreement, dies.
If the spouse or registered partner is disinherited, he or she can claim the usufruct of the family dwelling and furniture and even of other assets, insofar as he or she is in need of this.

FOREIGN INHERITANCE LAW AND INTERNATIONAL PRIVATE LAW
Every country has its own rules on inheritance law. International private law determines which legislation is applicable to an estate that has a certain international nature – for instance the deceased did not have Dutch nationality or was not residing in the Netherlands at the time of his death. Every country has its own rules on international private law and the authorities of a country always apply the country's own rules of international private law. This can lead to different, conflicting results. International treaties are meant to avoid such conflicting results. Regarding inheritance law, the Dutch authorities apply the rules of the Hague Inheritance Treaty 1989.

THE HAGUE INHERITANCE TREATY 1989
According to the treaty of 1989, Dutch inheritance law is applicable if:
- the deceased was living in the Netherlands at the time of his death and was of Dutch nationality, or
- the deceased was living in the Netherlands at the time of his death and was not of Dutch nationality, but had been living in the Netherlands for more than five years before he/she died, or
- the deceased explicitly stipulated, in his or her will, that Dutch inheritance law was applicable.

CHOOSING AN APPLICABLE LAW
By stipulating which law is to apply, you leave no doubt as to which law is applicable to the inheritance. Making such a choice is of particular importance in cases where the inheritance has international aspects. A choice of law helps avoid that – due to emigration, immigration or naturalization – a different law becomes applicable to the inheritance. However, though you might have explicitly made such a choice, it is not always recognized in other countries, especially regarding real estate outside the Netherlands. In such a situation it is best to seek advice on this matter in both countries.

SETTLEMENT OF THE INHERITANCE AND INTERNATIONAL PRIVATE LAW
The Dutch Inheritance Conflict Act determines that the settlement of an inheritance (for example: how should the heirs accept or refuse an inheritance, what powers does the executor of a will have) is governed by Dutch law, if the deceased was residing in the Netherlands at the time of his death.

TAXES IN THE CASE OF DEATH
NATIONALITY NOT IMPORTANT
If you are a resident of the Netherlands when you die, then, in all likelihood, taxes will be due in the Netherlands. It does not matter what your nationality is: the entire estate of non-Dutch nationals who die while living in the Netherlands is (also) subject to taxation here.

FACTUAL SITUATION
To determine whether you were living in the Netherlands, the factual situation is taken into account. If you had a house in the Netherlands and a family that also lived in the Netherlands for Dutch tax purposes, then you will most probably be deemed to

have been a resident of the Netherlands (resident tax liability). Also if you benefited from the so-called 30%-ruling, but opted for the status of 'partial non-resident taxpayer' (see page 106) you are still deemed to have been a resident taxpayer for inheritance tax purposes. In other words, the 30%-ruling has no bearing on this.

DOUBLE TAXATION

As not every country applies the same taxation principle as the Netherlands, your passing away while living in the Netherlands can lead to double taxation. Some countries apply the principle of nationality of the deceased instead of the principle of residence. Furthermore, most countries levy inheritance tax on any portion of the estate located in the country (for instance immovable property). As a consequence of the various taxation principles, double taxation may arise. To avoid this, the Netherlands has entered into tax treaties with a number of countries. In the situation in which there is no treaty, a national ruling aimed at the avoidance of double taxation can be invoked. However, this is no guarantee that double taxation will be completely avoided.

EXEMPTIONS

The inheritance law contains a few exemptions. The most important ones are:
- the spouse has an exemption of € 496,324. Subject to certain criteria the live-in partner can qualify for this exemption too
- children have an age-related exemption. This runs from an amount of € 97,589 for a child of the age of 0 to € 8,483 for a child of the age of 23. For older children, there is an exemption of € 8,483 if they do not inherit more than € 25,448. They cannot invoke this exemption if they receive more
- parents have an exemption of € 42,413
- grandparents and grandchildren have an exemption of € 8,483 (if the inheritance exceeds this amount, they owe tax over the entire amount)
- other relatives (including brothers and sisters) and third parties have an exemption of € 1,839 (if the inheritance exceeds this amount, they owe tax over the entire amount)
- certain recognized institutions have a fiscal exemption of € 8,483 per inheritance (if the inheritance exceeds this amount, they owe 11% tax over the entire amount)

These exemptions are subject, however, to certain deductions, such as for pensions.

RATES

Inheritances that exceed the exemption are subject to various rates. The rates in inheritance law are 'double progressive'. This means that the higher the value of the inheritance, the higher the rate; and the greater the (family) distance to the deceased relative, the higher the rate. Inheritances between parents and their children are subject to a rate between 5 and 27%. If there is no family relationship or only a distant one (nieces/nephews, cousins), the rates are between 41 and 68%, depending on the value of the inheritance. The same categories apply to spouses/ partners: spouses and registered partners pay a rate between 5 and 27%, partners that do not meet the legal requirements are subject to a rate between 41 and 68%.

LAW ON MATRIMONIAL PROPERTY

As you could read earlier in the sub-chapter on marriage, the main rule in Dutch matrimonial law is that if you get married you do this in general community property. In other countries this is often the exception and, in many cases, you will have drawn up a marriage contract in accordance with your (foreign) law. You should be aware of the fact that, should you pass away in the Netherlands, the law on matrimonial property can have several unexpected fiscal consequences. For instance, you may have included a survivorship clause or a settlement clause in your marriage contract, the aim of which is to avoid inheritance tax. However, you should take into account that it might not have the intended fiscal consequences as long as you are living in the Netherlands: the law contains what are referred to as 'fictions', pursuant to which taxes can be levied after all. 'Fictions' allow certain situations that might otherwise not be covered by a law to fall under its scope anyway.

TRANSFER TAX

Even if the deceased and the heirs were living outside the Netherlands at the time of death, there is still such a thing as transfer tax. The criterion used for the tax is whether the goods had a strong connection to the Netherlands. The most important items on which transfer tax can be levied are:
1. a Dutch company that has a permanent establishment in the Netherlands
2. the following assets belonging to a non-Dutch company:
   - real estate situated in the Netherlands, after deduction of the mortgage debts
   - the direct right to profits that a company owner has, without the benefit of shares, regarding profits or losses of this company which is established in the Netherlands, after deduction of any debts the company may have incurred
   - shares in a company that primarily owns real estate.

There are no exemptions to the transfer tax. The rates are the same as the rates for inheritance tax.

WHAT TYPE OF INSURANCE IS AVAILABLE

It is possible that you have not even thought about insurance at this stage. Insurance is, however, of the utmost importance for a safe and healthy stay abroad. You can fall off your Dutch bicycle, have appendicitis, or have your house broken into. It is, therefore, advisable to arrange your insurance if possible before you leave or immediately upon your arrival in the Netherlands. What exactly do you have to insure yourself against? Here is an overview of a few of the standard insurances available in the Netherlands, either through private insurance companies, banks, your employer, or the state. Whereby it is worth knowing that some insurance companies offer you the possibility to put together your own insurance package with all the insurance you need.

When arranging your insurance it is useful to know that the greater part of insurances in the Netherlands are arranged through an insurance broker. You can find more information on brokers' associations and the Dutch insurance situation on the websites listed at the end of the chapter.

MEDICAL

Having good insurance for medical expenses is very important. To cover your medical expenses, you are either covered by a social health insurance, called the *Ziekenfonds* or you can take out private insurance. If you are not sure if you are covered or if your cover meets your needs, contact either the *Ziekenfonds*, an insurance broker or a direct writer to make sure that you are well covered. Keep in mind that the *Ziekenfonds* is not allowed to exclude you on the basis of pre-existing conditions, but that private insurance companies are. However, if you are having difficulties taking out a private health insurance based on your health situation, all private insurance companies have a Standard Package Policy (*Standaard Pakket Polis*) that will cover anyone.

ZIEKENFONDS

Employees with an agreed fixed wage that is below a certain level, are compulsorily insured under the *Ziekenfonds* (Health Insurance Fund), as are those who receive welfare, unemployment or disability benefits. The wage level for the year 2005 has been fixed at € 33,000 a year. If your income exceeds this level you have to take out private insurance. The date to keep in mind for this is November 1 of each year: if are covered by the *Ziekenfonds* and your income exceeded € 33,000 by November 1, 2004, you will have to make sure you arrange private insurance as of January 1, 2005.

The *Ziekenfonds* covers the following: visits to your family doctor (*huisarts*), specialists, physical therapy, home care after birth, hospitalization, most prescription drugs and medical equipment (though not all). Most dental treatments are not covered by the *Ziekenfonds*, though you can take out an additional insurance to cover these costs.

PRIVATE INSURANCE

If your income lies above the Ziekenfonds level, you will have to take out private insurance – often your or your partner's/spouse's employer will have a company insurance plan with a private insurance company. Depending on your insurance company or the company's insurance plan, private insurance can cover almost anything you like, at the level of cover that you wish, with the deductibles you choose, and you will pay a premium accordingly. Every Dutch private medical insurance not only allows you to be treated in a Dutch hospital, but also gives you access to treatment in other EU/EEA countries, covered up to the maximum payable for the same treatment in the Netherlands.

INSURANCES FOR EXPATS?

Only a few Dutch insurance companies are specialized in expatriates and can offer tailor-made products. These insurance companies not only cover medical expenses in the country of residence but, for instance, also offer coverage (not subject to a maximum) should you be staying in your home country for the holidays – be this a country inside or outside the EU. Often they work together with a 24-hour 'assistance center': in case of serious illness, an accident or death abroad, they can help you or your relatives 24 hours a day. They will issue a guarantee or, in those instances where such a guarantee is not accepted, arrange payment, subject to the terms and conditions of the chosen coverage, of any required hospital admittance charges. They also take care of emergency evacuation and repatriation, pre-trip referral information and allow you to obtain medical advice from a medical practitioner if you are unable to obtain advice from a medical practitioner locally. Some insurance companies cover the organization and reimbursement of transportation in connection with the death or serious illness of a family member in the home country, or in the event that you should be in mortal danger, organize and reimburse the transportation of family members to your country of residence.

LEGAL CONTRIBUTIONS

Do be aware that if you take out private health insurance in the Netherlands you will have to pay legal contributions in addition to the insurance premium. The amount of these legal contributions, called 'MOOZ/WTZ', is announced each year by the Dutch government (since 1987). For example, the annual MOOZ/WTZ contribution for 2005 for those between the ages of 20 and 64 amounts to € 534.

CHILDBIRTH

If you have Ziekenfonds or basic private insurance, pregnancy and childbirth costs are covered. However, you should keep in mind that, in the Netherlands, a 'normal' childbirth takes place in the home, with the help of a midwife. In this scenario, during the pregnancy, you visit a midwife with increasing frequency up to and including delivery; this is covered by either type of insurance. The costs of a hospital delivery are not covered by the *Ziekenfonds* or your basic private insurance, unless your midwife, *huisarts* or *specialist* has determined that, for health and safety reasons, the baby should be delivered in the hospital. This is called a *bevalling op medische indicatie* and is covered by either type of insurance. In actual fact, it should be noted that approximately 30% of deliveries take place at home.

STUDENTS

Students will often find that their host institution has made sure that they are insured – as everyone is required by law to have health insurance – though you should verify this, of course. Special arrangements for students are available.

SELF-EMPLOYED PERSONS

Illness

What about if you have set up your own company? Do you have to take out private insurance, or are you covered by social insurance in the case of illness? That depends, actually, on your income (see the preceding paragraphs). If, on November 1, 2004, your income was below € 21,050, then you are under compulsory health insurance (*Ziekenfonds*) coverage. If your income is above that level, you have to take out private insurance.

Disability

Until 2004, the Netherlands had the Self-Employed Persons Disability Act (WAZ), according to which those who had been disabled for work for more than 52 weeks, or those who were pregnant and gave birth, received a benefit. This Act was abolished as of August of that year, creating a potential insurance problem for you if you are self-employed and considered a high-risk client, as the insurance company you approach may charge a higher premium or refuse to insure you at all. For this reason, the cabinet has requested that private insurance companies offer a so-called alternative insurance, that sets no medical limitations. To make use of this possibility, you must request this disability insurance within three months of starting your own company.

If you become disabled for work, you start receiving a payment from your insurance company after 104 weeks of illness. These payments will last five years if you become sick within five years of taking out the insurance; if you become sick after five years of self-employment, you will receive your payments till you reach the pensionable age (65).

You should investigate your options well as to whether you want to take out this insurance or the insurance with the higher premium/exclusions as the latter may, in fact, turn out to be more attractive, despite its drawbacks. And you may simply opt not to insure yourself at all; this particular insurance is not obligatory.

Pregnancy

The abolishment of the WAZ also means that if you are pregnant and self-employed, you no longer can rely on this Act to pay out during the so-called pregnancy leave, being the period of 16 weeks surrounding the birth (for more on this, see page 184). You will now either just have to manage somehow, or take out private insurance. Be sure to check whether the insurance company will pay; some do not pay out anything if you become pregnant within two years of taking out the insurance. This is another issue that is on the cabinet's agenda for rectification.

HOUSE

You've finally settled for that beautiful house in the center of Amsterdam or out in the woods. Just putting your key in the lock makes you feel happy. Now you want it insured!

A house insurance generally covers the financial consequences of fire, breaking and entry, as well as such unexpected events as storm, fire, lightning, theft, vandalism, explosions and more.

HOUSEHOLD CONTENTS

And how about that beautiful, expensive couch, or your antique dining room, or Dutch painting? A household contents insurance covers virtually everything you have in your house against fire, theft, water damage, storms and more. For possessions that are especially valuable, such as jewelry, antique musical instruments or your stamp collection, you can take out additional insurance for Valuable Possessions.

TRAVEL

You've finally booked that wonderful trip to Singapore, but you are worried about whether your luggage will come back in one piece, or that you might be pickpocketed, or lose your camera! Or maybe you've decided to go skiing instead, but are worried about what type of costs you might incur if you fall and break a leg. In that case, you might want to contribute to your peace of mind (and what else are vacations for?) by taking out travel insurance. You might find it economically more interesting, even, to take out year-round travel insurance; it often only costs little more than the insurance for a three-week vacation.

CAR

Driving around in the Netherlands can be risky business. Though the Netherlands is considered one of the safest countries when it comes to driving, the Dutch are not the gentlest of people behind the steering wheel. Particularly tail-gating and claiming the right of way (which they have when coming from the right, unless indicated otherwise) can lead to some hair-raising situations. In short, if you own a car here, you will want to take out car insurance. Furthermore, car owners are obligated by law to have minimum liability coverage. If you take out car insurance, this will automatically include minimum liability insurance (which can be extended upon for a fee). You can also opt to include legal aid insurance, if you do not already have a general one.

ACCIDENT

This insurance covers any type of accident (not only those on the road), such as falling off the stepladder, or dislocating your arm playing rugby. Those who take out this insurance are paid a lump sum if something goes wrong, to cover any large expenses that may be the consequence of the accident. You can take out individual or family insurance.

PASSENGER

Other drivers claiming their right of way can be particularly unnerving for passengers. Should anything happen to one of your passengers, this is most often not covered by your regular car insurance and therefore it is advisable to take out this additional insurance. It covers not only the situation in which you are 'rolling', but also when you are at the side of the road because your car has broken down, or when you are filling your gas tank. You will probably have two choices: a 'damages' insurance and an 'accidents to passengers' insurance. The former pays out damages, including a certain amount of emotional damages, the latter pays out a fixed amount in the case of death or permanent disability.

LIABILITY FOR PRIVATE PERSONS

Say, the little apples of your eye have decided to play soccer in the front yard after all and have kicked the soccer ball not through your window, but your neighbor's. Or that you drop a can of paint on the car parked next to yours. To cover the expenses related to any of these accidents, you can take out liability insurance for private persons, which will then cover the bills. You can take out individual or family insurance.

DISABILITY

The days that you could count on the government to guarantee you a lifestyle as the one you were used to before you became disabled for work are over.

The government has had to introduce a few changes in its spending pattern too and nowadays you might do better to take out additional private disability insurance. Thus you can be sure that, should something happen to you, you can keep up the comfortable lifestyle you were accustomed to – and not only you but also your family. There is, however, a possibility that your employer has taken care of additional arrangements. Please ask your employer about this before taking out your own additional insurance.

LEGAL AID

You might end up having to deal with the situation in which a person you have held liable will not pay, or your kitchen has not been delivered, or your boss is not sticking to that which you agreed to in your employment contract. This can be very hard and quite time-consuming, especially in another culture, language and legal system – and is hardly something you can do without legal aid. To this end, you can take out legal aid insurance, which will not only provide you with the aid you need, but will also cover your legal aid expenses. Family members are often auto-matically included in this insurance.

MOTOR AND 'SCOOTER'

Maybe you want to go touring around the country and actually feel the wind in your face. Then you might choose to buy a motorcycle or a moped. For these types of vehicles there is a separate insurance, called the Motor and Scooter Insurance. Also for motorcycles and mopeds, you can take out additional Passenger Insurance.

BICYCLE

One of the thriving black markets in the Netherlands is that of stolen bicycles. After a few months of watching those happy Dutch cyclists, you may succumb to the temptation of buying one of those environment-friendly contraptions yourself, only to have it stolen! Or damaged. It's a good thing you can take out bicycle insurance.

LEGAL PROBLEMS

Legal problems are always on the lure: for example, your rental agreement could be canceled, you could be fired, or your landlord could refuse to make needed repairs. You could have problems with the tax authorities or with receiving your benefits. Repairs to your washing machine were not done properly. Your divorce is pending or, following an accident, your damages have not been reimbursed. In other words, since there are many kinds of legal problems, chances are that you might have one or two of your own.

You might want some legal advice as well, before making an important decision. For example, before accepting a job, borrowing money or renting a house. In all such cases, it is good to know where you can go for legal advice.

ADVICE

All legal aid agencies offer advice. These include legal aid societies, trade unions, lawyers and municipal social service counselors.

LEGAL PROCEEDINGS

CIVIL LAW

There is no obligation to have legal representation before the subdistrict sector of the District Court. Cases involving amounts lower than € 5,000, labor law cases and cases involving rent law are to be brought before the subdistrict sector of the District Court and therefore do not require representation by a lawyer.

You can choose between representing yourself, or letting yourself be represented by a person with legal training, such as a process-server.

In all other situations, legal representation is mandatory before the District Court (with the exception of administrative law-cases), the Court of Appeals and the Netherlands Supreme Court. If you have not arranged it, the magistrates will not accept the case.

ADMINISTRATIVE LAW

Administrative law applies to governmental decisions, for example, relating to building permits or benefit payments. A lawyer is not required for administrative law issues. Also here, you may represent yourself. For more complex matters, however, it would be wise to consult an expert – for example, a lawyer.

CRIMINAL LAW

In principle, criminal law does not require legal representation. You, as a defendant, may defend yourself. If you are taken into custody, you are automatically assigned a lawyer. However, you are free to change lawyers if you wish. If you face criminal charges but are not in custody, you can consult a lawyer.

FEES

There are no flat rates for the services of lawyers. The rates change not only from one law office to the other but also according to the type of case. Therefore, it is worth the trouble to inquire at several law offices about their (hourly) rates for the type of case, and about the time the lawyer expects to dedicate to the case.

FINANCIAL ASSISTANCE

For many people, legal fees can be a problem. If you wish to start or are facing legal proceedings but cannot pay for them (completely), you can request government-financed legal aid (called *toevoeging*). If it is granted – and this depends, among others, on your income and financial means – the government will pay part of your legal fees. *Toevoeging* is only granted to help cover what you owe your lawyer and not related expenses, such as court registry fees, extract fees, process server expenses, etc.

If your income is high or you have sufficient financial means and do not qualify for government-financed legal aid, you must pay the legal fees yourself. You can, however, take out legal aid insurance to help pay for lawyers' fees. There may be a first risk clause.

INTERPRETERS

The Dutch courts make use of interpreters in the case of (criminal) law proceedings, police hearings and for asylum seekers. If the court requests the assistance of an interpreter, the costs are carried either by the state or by the party who is ordered to pay the costs in a civil case. If you need the use of a translator/interpreter, ask your legal aid agency where you can find one and what the costs will be. Beware that price and quality are not always consistent.

WHERE TO OBTAIN LEGAL AID ASSISTANCE

LEGAL AID SOCIETIES (Buro voor Rechtshulp)

There are legal aid societies in over forty municipalities in the Netherlands. Should you need assistance, call your municipality to find out if there is one where you live. Lawyers representing legal aid societies can provide you with information, legal advice and assistance with legal proceedings. They specialize in matters relating to labor, job dismissal, benefits, rent and residence permits ('Alien Affairs'). You are eligible for aid from legal aid societies if you have a low or average income (see above, under *Fees*). If your income is too high you must bear the costs of legal aid yourself. The income limits in question are fixed and are regularly adjusted (for more information, visit www.bureaurechtshulp.nl). Legal aid societies hold free consultation hours, during which you have half an hour to discuss your matter. During the first such consultation, the society's lawyer will make an individual case appraisal to see where to go from there.

JURIDISCH LOKET – Legal Counter

Recently, the Second Chamber approved a new plan for legal aid, which will lead to the abolition of the legal aid societies. The tasks of the legal aid societies were twofold; on the one hand they answered legal questions and on the other hand, they provided legal aid. From now on, the Legal Counter will stick to answering legal questions after which, if you wish, they will make an appointment for you with a lawyer – or, though the set-up for this is still in the make, a mediator (see further on). Free legal consultation will still be available for very elementary issues that can be dealt with in less than an hour. If an issue appears not to be a legal one, the Counter can refer you to the correct organization for further assistance.

The legal aid societies will transfer their legal aid function to either existing or new legal offices, who will continue to provide subsidized legal aid.

The first Legal Counters opened somewhere halfway 2004 and the plan is for a total of approximately 30 to open over the course of 2005.

LAWYERS

For legal assistance, most people choose to consult a lawyer, whether they are seeking advice or starting legal proceedings. As stated above, you are required under civil law to do this in law courts (except before the subdistrict sector of the district court), the Court of Appeals and the Supreme Court. Though you are not required to, but might want to, you can also consult a lawyer in other cases (before a subdistrict's court, for criminal cases or for those cases involving administrative law). It is usually wise to seek representation by a lawyer, especially if the other party already has.

The First Consultation

Certain lawyers offer free introductory consultations. The first consultation lasts about thirty minutes during which the lawyer will examine your case and recommend any steps you should take. If you want, you can ask in advance whether the lawyer charges for the first consultation.

There are Lawyers and Lawyers

Lawyers often specialize in certain types of cases or legal areas. Legal aid societies/Legal Counters can sometimes recommend a particular lawyer to you, depending on your case. You can also approach the Netherlands Bar Association for more information. This is an organization to which all lawyers in the Netherlands belong. If that fails to prove helpful, and you find you are still in need of advice, you can seek help from legal offices.

MEDIATORS

The option of mediation first noticeably entered the 'conflict scene' in divorce cases, but is now rapidly gaining popularity in other legal areas as well. It is, of course, an attractive approach as it is likely to save you both time and money – and produce a solution that is a true compromise reached by the parties involved, rather than one that is chosen for you by an emotionally distant judge.

Also once a case has gone to court, it is not too late to enlist the help of a mediator: either you and the other party together can decide to go to a mediator or, either before or during the court hearings, the judge (or a so-called 'referral secretary') can refer you to one. Note: as mediation is still in a relatively early stage in the Netherlands, not all courts can refer you to a mediator yet!

FEES

No cure, no pay does not apply if you enlist the help of a mediator: you will owe his or her fees and the reimbursement of any expenses he/she may have incurred. Rest assured, this will always be considerably less than what you would end up paying in legal fees if you went to court. In principle, both parties carry an equal share in the expenses, but you may choose to divide the costs differently. In many cases, a mediator can also request *toevoeging* for you, allowing your mediation expenses to be subsidized.

MUNICIPAL COUNCILORS

Many municipalities have municipal councilors (ask at your *gemeentehuis* whether this is the case where you live). These councilors can answer many questions issues regarding social and societal interests. You can also ask them legal questions, particularly on the subject of living, social security, taxes and certain financial issues. Their advice is free of charge.

PROCESS-SERVERS

Also process-servers offer legal aid, particularly, of course, when it comes to collecting your debts, but also with financial questions. As mentioned earlier, there where you are not required to have yourself represented by a lawyer in civil cases, you can request the assistance of a process-server.

UNIONS

All unions have a legal department that you can consult for information and advice if you are a member. They offer assistance in labor law cases and social security cases – all free of charge, if you are a member.

LEGAL ADVICE CENTERS

Anyone can go to a Legal Advice Center, for information and advice. They are usually manned by volunteers, mostly law students.

OTHER ORGANIZATIONS

There are a number of organizations you can turn to for advice and aid as well, if you are a member. Some of the more useful ones are:
- the Consumers Association (*Consumentenbond*): this association offers advice on consumer issues, such as the renting or buying of products and/or services. Though they do not offer legal-procedural aid, they can mediate in conflicts with manufacturers or those who provide services.
- ANWB: members of the ANWB are given free legal advice on issues regarding transportation, recreation and tourism. You do not have to be a member if you need legal advice following a serious traffic accident. The ANWB offers its members full legal aid in the case of accidents abroad that do not involve your own vehicle (skiing, hiking, bus or air travel incidents). If you have the *reis- en kredietbrief* you also receive legal aid in accidents abroad involving your own vehicle.
- Vereniging Eigen Huis (Homeowners' Association): Vereniging Eigen Huis offers its members advice on issues involving home ownership, such as financing, building and legal matters.

If you have taken out legal aid insurance, the organizations that provide the insurance often also offer legal aid.

REFERENCES

MONEY

EURO INTERNET FOR THE NETHERLANDS:
www.euro.nl
**DE NEDERLANDSCHE BANK (DUTCH
CENTRAL BANK):** www.dnb.nl/english
EUROPEAN CENTRAL BANK: www.ecb.int
EUROPEAN INTERNET:
www.europa.eu.int/euro/

MAJOR BANKS IN THE NETHERLANDS

DE NEDERLANDSCHE BANK (Dutch
Central Bank): www.dnb.nl/english
ABN.Amro Bank: www.abnamro.nl
or www.abnamro.com
ING BANK: www.inggroup.com
FORTIS BANK: www.fortis.com
POSTBANK: www.postbank.nl
RABOBANK: www.rabobank.nl or
www.rabobank.com
ROBECO ADVIES: www.robeco.com
SNS BANK: www.sns.nl
STAAL BANKIERS: www.staalbankiers.nl
CENE BANK: www.cenebankiers.nl

For a complete listing of the banks and
financial institutions in the Netherlands
(and Europe) go to the start page:
http://banken.pagina.nl

TAXES

NATIONAL TAX OFFICE
Central Internet: www.belastingdienst.nl
National Tax Information, tel.: 0800 05 43

INTERNATIONAL TAX OFFICE HEERLEN
Postal address: P.O. Box 2865, 6401 DJ Heerlen
Visiting address: Kloosterweg 22, 6412 CN
Heerlen (by appointment only)
Tel.: 045 560 31 11 or 0800 05 43 (National
telephone number)
Internet: www.belastingdienst.nl/buiten-
land

TAXATION IN THE NETHERLANDS
Published by the Ministry of Finance, this
guide (in English) gives a good overview of
taxation in the Netherlands.
Internet: www.minfin.nl

IMMIGRATION/PERMITS

GENERAL: www.immigratiedienst.nl

**IMMIGRATION AND NATURALIZATION
SERVICE** (Immigratie en Naturalisatie
Dienst, IND)
Dr. H. Colijnlaan 341, P.O. Box 5800,
2280 HV Rijswijk
Tel.: 0900 123 45 61
Internet: www.ind.nl

MINISTRY OF FOREIGN AFFAIRS
(*Ministerie van Buitenlandse Zaken*)
Bezuidenhoutseweg 67, P.O. Box 20061,
2500 EB The Hague
Tel.: 070 348 64 86
Internet: www.minbuza.nl/english

PERMITS FOUNDATION: an international
corporate initiative to promote the improvement of work permit regulations for the
spouses of expatriate employees.
Internet: www.permitsfoundation.com

WORK PERMITS:
www.workpermit.com/netherlands

LEGAL INFORMATION

MINISTRY OF JUSTICE (*Ministerie van Justitie*)
Schedeldoekshaven 100, P.O. Box 20301,
2500 EH The Hague
Tel.: 070 370 78 11
Internet: www.justitie.nl

EMBASSY SERVICES:
www.ambassadediensten.nl

DUTCH CUSTOMS (*Douane*):
www.douane.nl

**INSTITUTE FOR INTERNATIONAL PRIVATE
AND PUBLIC INTERNATIONAL LAW**
Commercial Arbitrage
T.M.C. Asser Instituut
R.J. Schimmelpennincklaan 20-22,
2517 JN The Hague
Tel.: 070 342 03 00
Internet: www.asser.nl

ROYAL DUTCH NOTARIES, KNB,
Koninklijke Notariële Beroepsorganisatie
Spui 184, 2511 BW The Hague

Tel.: 070 3307111
Internet: www.notaris.nl

THE NOTARY HELPLINE
(Notaristelefoon): 0900 346 93 93

RVR,
Raden voor Rechtsbijstand:
www.rechtshulp.nl

NETHERLANDS BAR ASSOCIATION
Nederlandse Orde van Advocaten
Neuhuyskade 94, 2596 XM The Hague
P.O. Box 30 851, 2500 GW The Hague
Tel.: 070 335 35 35
Internet: www.advocatenorde.nl,
www.alleadvocaten.nl

**VERENIGING VAN PERSONEN-
EN FAMILIERECHT ADVOCATEN**
An association of family lawyers.
P.O. Box 65707, 2506 EA The Hague
Tel. : 070 427 12 63
Internet: www.vpfa.nl

CONSUMENTENBOND
P.O. Box 1000, 2500 BA The Hague
Tel.: 070 445 45 45
Internet: www.consumentenbond.nl

DUTCH HOUSING ASSOCIATION
Vereniging Eigen Huis
P.O. Box 734, 3800 AS Amersfoort
Tel.: 033 450 77 50
Internet: www.eigenhuis.nl

CHILD CARE AND PROTECTION BOARD
Raad voor de Kinderbescherming
St. Jacobsstraat 61, 3511 BP Utrecht
Tel.: 030 888 27 00
Internet: www.kinderbescherming.nl

NEDERLANDS MEDIATION INSTITUUT
www.nmi-mediation.nl and specifically
for divorce mediation:
www.vas-scheidingsbemiddeling.nl

THE ROYAL DUTCH TOURING CLUB (ANWB)
Wassenaarseweg 220, 2596 EC The Hague
Legal Assistance, tel.: 070 314 77 88
Specially for victims of traffic accidents,
tel.: 070 314 77 66 (also for non-members)
Internet: www.anwb.nl

EMBASSIES BY COUNTRY

AUSTRALIA
Carnegielaan 4, 2517 KH The Hague
Tel.: 070 310 82 00
Internet: www.australian-embassy.nl

BELGIUM
Alexanderveld 97, 2585 DB The Hague
Tel.: 070 312 34 56
Internet: www.diplobel.org

BRAZIL
Mauritskade 19, 2514 HD The Hague
Tel.: 070 302 39 59
Internet: www.brazilianembassy.nl

CANADA
Sophialaan 7, 2514 JP The Hague
Tel.: 070 311 16 00
Internet: www.Canada.nl

CHINA
Willem Lodewijklaan 10, 2517 JT The Hague
Tel.: 070 306 50 61
Internet: www.chinaembassy.nl

DENMARK
Koninginnegracht 30, 2514 AB The Hague
Tel.: 070 302 59 59
Internet: www.danishembassy.nl

FINLAND
Groot Hertoginnelaan 16, 2517 EG The Hague
Tel.: 070 346 97 54

FRANCE
Smidsplein 1, 2514 BT The Hague
Tel.: 070 312 58 00
Internet: www.ambafrance.nl

GERMANY
Groot Hertoginnelaan 18 - 20,
2517 EG The Hague
Tel.: 070 342 06 00
Internet: www.duitse-ambassade.nl

GREECE
Amaliastraat 1, 2514 JC The Hague
Tel.: 070 363 87 00

INDIA
Buitenrustweg 2, 2517 KD The Hague
Tel.: 070 346 97 71
Internet: www.indianembassy.nl

INDONESIA
Tobias Asserlaan 8, 2517 KC The Hague
Tel.: 070 310 81 00
Internet: www.indonesia.nl

IRELAND
Dr. Kuyperstraat 9, 2514 BA The Hague
Tel.: 070 363 09 93

ISRAEL
Buitenhof 47, 2513 AH The Hague
Tel.: 070 376 05 00
Internet: www.israel.nl

ITALY
Alexanderstraat 12, 2514 JL The Hague
Tel.: 070 302 10 30
Internet: www.italy.nl

JAPAN
Tobias Asserlaan 2, 2517 KC The Hague
Tel.: 070 346 95 44
Internet: www.nl.emb-japan.go.jp

NEW ZEALAND
Carnegielaan 10, 4th floor,
2517 KH The Hague
Tel.: 070 346 93 24
Internet: www.mft.govt.nz

NORWAY
Lange Vijverberg 11, 2513 AC The Hague
Tel.: 070 311 76 11
Internet: www.noorwegen.nl

PAKISTAN
Amaliastraat 8, 2517 JC The Hague
Tel.: 070 364 89 48
Internet: www.embassyofpakistan.com

RUSSIAN FEDERATION
A. Bickerweg 2, 2517 JP The Hague
Tel.: 070 345 13 00
Internet: www.netherlands.mid.ru

SAUDI ARABIA
Alexanderstraat 19, 2514 JM The Hague
Tel.: 070 361 43 91

SOUTH AFRICA
Wassenaarseweg 40, 2596 CJ The Hague
Tel.: 070 392 45 01
Internet: www.zuidafrika.nl

SPAIN
Lange Voorhout 50, 2514 EG The Hague
Tel.: 070 302 49 99
Internet: www.claboral.nl

SWEDEN
Burg. Van Karnebeeklaan 6a,
2585 DB The Hague
TEL.: 070 412 02 00
Internet:http://www.swedenembnl.org
www.swedenabroad.com/thehague

UNITED KINGDOM
Lange Voorhout 10, 2514 ED The Hague
Tel.: 070 427 04 27
Internet: www.britain.nl

UNITED STATES OF AMERICA
Lange Voorhout 102, 2514 EJ The Hague
Tel.: 070 310 92 09
Internet: www.usemb.nl

INSURANCE

**NEDERLANDSE VERENIGING VAN
ASSURANTIEADVISEURS:**
www.nva.nl
VERBOND VAN VERZEKERAARS:
www.verzekeraars.org
**VERENIGING VAN ONAFHANKELIJKE
FINANCIËLE EN ASSURANTIEADVISEURS:**
www.nbva.nl
GOUDA INTERNATIONAL INSURANCE:
www.expatriatesinsurance.com
INTERGLOBAL: www.interglobalpmi.com
**BUPA WORLDWIDE HEALTH AND
CARE ORGANIZATION:**www.bupa.com
OOM VERZEKERINGEN:
www.oominsurances.com

Getting around in the Netherlands is quite simple, the road networks are good and the public transportation, including airports, is excellent. All you need to know is how the system works. This chapter points out some of the idiosyncrasies of Dutch drivers, the public transportation system, how to get a Dutch driver's license, the system of vehicle approval, whether or not you should buy a car here, the fact that you have to pay road tax, the Dutch automobile association and last but definitely not least, the Dutch airports.

Getting Around

BY STEPHANIE DIJKSTRA AND TOON DE RUITER

THE SPIDER IN THE INTERNATIONAL WEB

In some ways, the Netherlands is like the spider in the web of Europe. Rotterdam, the largest seaport in the world, is the place where millions of goods enter and leave Europe; the International Court of Justice is in The Hague; Amsterdam is one of the diamond capitals of the world; there are excellent international universities in the various cities of the Netherlands; world-renowned museums can be found here; unique exhibitions are arranged here; and cultural events lure tens of thousands visitors to the country every year. A lot of international business is negotiated in this little country, facilitated by the fact that almost everyone here speaks at least one other language – mostly English. For this reason, millions of people enter and travel around the country, either on business, on vacation or to set up home here.

All this requires a lot of traveling and could not be achieved without an excellent infrastructure: Schiphol is the fourth largest airport in Europe, the Thalys-train takes you from Amsterdam to Paris in a mere four hours, the Betuwe train-line is being set up to transport goods to the east (particularly Germany) and the roads promise a comfortable cruise to your destination.

AIR TRAVEL

SCHIPHOL

As mentioned before, Schiphol is the fourth largest airport in Europe, through which approximately 42 million passengers and 1.5 million tons of freight pass per year. Aside from its logistic uses, it is also a prime business location, with a World Trade Center, a number of hotels, recreational activities, over 500 companies

that employ almost 55,000 people, and, of course, its booming duty-free shopping business. (Though there is no longer such a thing as duty-free shopping in Europe, this is being maintained artificially, whereby the airport contributes approximately 40 million euros a year to keep the products cheap.)

SECURITY

Those who are departing from Amsterdam are advised to arrive three hours in advance in connection with the added security measures after September 11, 2001.

TRAVELING BY TRAIN FROM SCHIPHOL

Amsterdam is 15 minutes away (those who are in transit and have some time to kill, make a quick visit to Amsterdam!), Rotterdam and Utrecht 45 minutes; Brussels two hours; Cologne three; and Paris four – and a train station is located right underneath the Arrivals Hall, allowing you to catch the various Intercity and high speed-lines to these destinations.

REGIONAL AIRPORTS

The Netherlands boasts many regional airports, such as Eindhoven, Groningen, Maastricht, Rotterdam, Enschede and Lelystad, which offer both direct flights abroad, as well as flights to Schiphol airport. The advantages of making use of one of these airports are not hard to think of: often they are closer to your home or office; they are easily accessible by car, taxi or bus; parking is cheap; the walking distances are short; check-in times are brief; and there are special services for business travelers. If you use them as a start-out point from which to go to Schiphol, there are additional advantages: check-in time is considerably less time-consuming at the regional airports and most often you do not have to check in again at Schiphol, making total check-in and transfer times short as your luggage is automatically labeled onward. Often there are special through-connection fares for those who wish to make use of this opportunity.

TRAIN TRAVEL

The Netherlands has a dense railway network that offers frequent service, as well as the quickest way to travel between city centers. The carriages are modern and clean and, although many Dutch people complain about delays, the trains usually run on time. (Everything is relative!)

HIGH-SPEED TRAVEL
As mentioned above, you can travel by high-speed train (the Thalys or the TGV) from Amsterdam, Schiphol, The Hague or Rotterdam to Belgium and – final destination – Paris. This is really only a worthwhile option if you intend to travel all the way to Paris as, within the Netherlands and largely also within Belgium, the train still travels at regular speeds through the densely populated areas. In other words, have no illusion that by taking the high-speed train you will be traveling from Amsterdam to Rotterdam in 15 minutes.

However, we would like to point out that you may only travel on a high-speed train if you have bought a special ticket and made a reservation. If you inadvertently step on the Thalys in The Hague to go visit you friend in Rotterdam and you are caught, you can find yourself paying a hefty fine!

OPTIONS
On the train you have a choice of carriages: smoking (*roken*) or non-smoking (*niet roken*), and first or second class, which is indicated with a large 1 or 2 painted on the outside. First class costs about 50% more and gives you a slightly larger seat in a compartment that is less likely to be full.

TICKETS
Regular tickets are either one-way (*enkele reis*) or return (*retour*). You buy your ticket at a ticket window or at a yellow ticket machine, which you will find either in the main hall of the station or on the platform. The ticket machine – which, at many stations, is starting to replace ticket windows altogether – takes either cash, bank card or *chipknip / chippas*. Tickets are valid only on the day you buy them, unless you ask specifically for a ticket with a different date or no date. In that case, you must have the date stamped on the ticket before you get into the train on the day you travel. You do this either at the ticket window or in one of the yellow automats.

PASSES
There is a wide variety of passes and special tickets that can save you money. Which type you choose depends on the kind of traveling you will do – frequent or infrequent, long distances or short, alone or in a group, during rush hour or not, and your age. The clerks at the ticket windows can advise you and will be especially helpful if you choose a time of day when they are not busy. Also one-day passes are available, which can be used for traveling by bus, tram, metro or train.

INSPECTORS
You will often travel in the train without anyone ever looking at your ticket. If the conductor catches you without a ticket, however, you will have to buy one from him or her at a higher rate. In the larger cities, the railway is trying to reduce the number of people who hang around the stations. For this reason you might be asked to show your ticket on the platform. It is therefore wise to keep it handy until you have left the station.

TIMETABLES AND INFORMATION
You can buy the complete railway timetable at the station and at most bookstores. A much abbreviated version that lists only the major so-called Intercity trains is also available. If you have access to a computer, you can also buy the entire timetable on disc. All text is in Dutch, but you will catch on quickly.
You can also call the general number for information about public transportation: 0900 9292.

SMOKING
As of January 1, 2004, you are no longer allowed to smoke on trains – not even on the balconies. The same applies to Belgian and Benelux trains. This ban also applies to all areas you might be in while waiting for, walking to, or leaving, your train; halls, stairs, flyovers, elevators and covered platforms – though restau-

rants and cafeterias will continue having 'smoking/non smoking' areas. Covered platforms will have a designated smokers' area, indicated by a pillar with an ashtray as well as a 'smoking' sign and the words *rookzone*. You are still allowed to smoke on open-air platforms, but not in their closed waiting areas.

Only on international trains, as the situation differs per country, will the division 'smokers' vs. 'non-smokers' be maintained.

ONCE YOU GET THERE

Once you arrive at your destination, you have a few options on how to get where you are going. These you find in the following paragraphs.

TAXI SERVICES

Say you want to visit your long-lost cousin in the remote, but picturesque village of Cothen. You find out that you can take a train to Zeist – which you courageously do – but what do you do once you get there? Cothen would constitute a brisk, say, two hour walk from there.

Or perhaps you've agreed to meet your friends in Amsterdam, and need to get from Central Station to the Rijksmuseum within half an hour?

- There are about 16 million bicycles in Holland, making that approximately one for every inhabitant
- About 1.3 million new bicycles are sold every year.
- There are 3,277 bicycle shops in Holland
- There are 19,100 kilometers of bicycle paths and lanes, and 116,500 kilometers of paved roads (including 2,235 kilometers of expressways)
- There are 5,046 kilometers of waterways navigable for ships of 50 tons)
- There are 2,808 kilometers of standard gauge railways
- Almost 15% of the Dutch households have two or more cars, while less than one family in ten does not have a car
- Holland is the fourth safest country to drive in. Only the UK, Sweden and Norway have lower numbers of fatalities.

TIP   If a stranger offers to sell you a bicycle for less than € 25, don't buy it. It's probably stolen, and you too are violating the law if you take possession of it.

TAXIS

You cannot hail taxis on the street in the Netherlands as you can in many parts of the world. You must either telephone (look in the Yellow Pages or the telephone book under *Taxi*), or go to a taxi-stand where taxis wait. All major railway stations have a taxi-stand. Hotels and restaurants are always happy to call a taxi for you if you ask.

All regular Dutch taxis use meters and all charge roughly the same rates. When you start, the meter will already show a balance of several euros. This ensures the driver a minimum fare. Only for very long distances is it sometimes possible to negotiate a fare in advance. Otherwise you pay what the meter indicates. It is customary to give taxi drivers a tip, which usually means increasing the amount up to a round figure.

TRAIN-TAXIS

If you are visiting your long-lost cousin in remote Cothen, the trip by bus from the train station in Zeist to this little town could take up to an hour. An attractive (cheap) alternative would be to take the train taxi. These special taxis are available at more than half of the country's railway stations. In general, only the largest cities and smallest towns do not have train-taxis (ask at the railway station for the free booklet that lists them).

You buy train-taxi tickets when you buy your train ticket (also from the yellow automats), or upon arrival at your destination (you must buy it in the train station; you cannot step in the taxi and then buy the ticket!). One trip costs € 4 for one person, no matter where you are going within the local area. The difference with regular taxis is that you will probably not be alone in the taxi. A train-taxi takes several passengers at once and follows a logical route to drop them off, so you may have to wait before a train-taxi departs and you might take the roundabout way to Cothen, but at least you will be very comfortable and won't be lurching back and forth at every bus stop!

To go back to the station, you telephone the national (0900 *TREIN-TAXI*) or local train-taxi number and arrange a time to be picked up. The number is in the booklet listing the train-taxis. Again, the fare is only € 4. Contrary to the situation upon arrival at your destination by train, you can buy a one-way train-taxi ticket with the driver for your return to the train station – for the slightly increased price of € 5.

PUBLIC TRANSPORTATION TAXIS (REGIOTAXI)

The Dutch public transportation company Connexxion also offers a taxi service around Leiden and in the province of the North Holland that is particularly convenient (but not exclusively) for

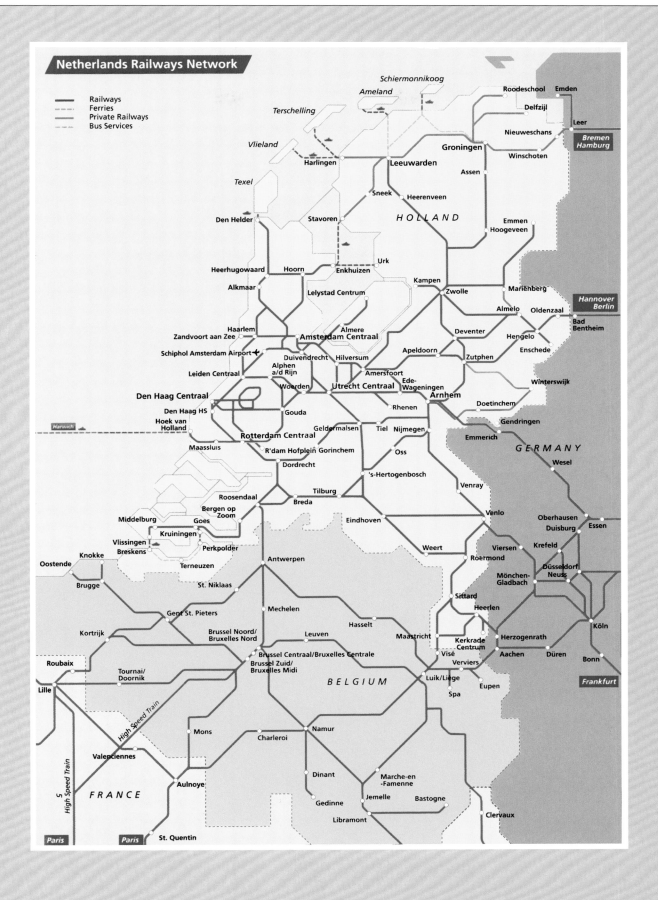

Netherlands Railways Network

elderly and handicapped persons. For other areas of the Netherlands, there is the Regiotaxi. For more information and rates, visit www.connexxion.nl and click on *taxivervoer*, under *connexxion vervoer*. These regional taxis only ride, as the name suggests, within their particular region and offer cheaper fares as they combine passengers where possible. Their greatest advantage is that they take you from door to door. To order a taxi, call 0900 8415.

SCHIPHOL AIRPORT TAXI

And last, but not least, there is the Schiphol Travel Taxi to take you to and from the airport, saving you the hassle of arranging long-term parking, dragging your luggage to the connecting bus and worrying about your car while away. Visit www.schipholtravel-taxi.nl for more information.

BUSES AND TRAMS

If you are looking to make your way through the larger cities, or from one town to the next, the Dutch transportation companies provide frequent services on buses and trams. Amsterdam and Rotterdam also have subways (called the metro). Rural communities are linked by bus.

THE INTERLINER

Initially, the Interliner-bus line was created to bring passengers there where trains don't go. It has since expanded to cover approximately 25 intermediate distances. Though formerly linked with the NS (train travel), this is no longer the case (visit www. connexxion.nl to find out where you can catch one of the various bus lines, which operate under a variety of names). The advantage of the Interliner is that it avoids busy areas, has the right of way at traffic lights and is allowed to use special lanes. Its stops have been strategically placed closed to other public transportation connection points (buses, trains and taxis) as well as easily accessible parking areas. For those who come there by bicycle, there are bicycle racks.

Similar to the trains, the Interliner offers its own Interliner taxi service (€ 4.50) at the stop you get out at, which you share with other passengers. It will take you to any destination in the area surrounding the Interliner-stop, but – at regular taxi rates – can also take you to a further destination. Ask your driver to order the taxi at least 30 minutes in advance, or have one pick you up at your home by dialing 0900 8415 (they are not available in The Hague, Amsterdam or Rotterdam or at Schiphol Airport).

To pay for your trip with the Interliner, you buy either an Interliner-ticket, or, under circumstances, you can use a train ticket (that is explicitly valid also on an Interliner bus, while there is no parallel train trajectory, etc. etc. – in short, a rather complex set of rules applies). Visit the website to see which passes can be used and for an overview of the rates-system.

FIGURING IT OUT

As soon as you can, get the public transportation map of your area, which sometimes is accompanied by schedules (*dienstregeling openbaar vervoer*). In the larger cities, the local transportation companies have their own windows at the railway stations. Otherwise try either the VVV tourist office or the municipal offices (*gemeentehuis, stadhuis or stadskantoor*).

Also in the larger cities, you will find a map of the city – dotted and lined with the bus, tram and subway (metro) lines – at many of the tramstops, allowing you to figure out just where you can go and how to get there (and how many 'strips' this will cost you – see the next paragraph).

THE STRIP TICKET – STRIPPENKAART

You can use the same ticket in all of the buses, trams and subways throughout the country. It is called a *strippenkaart*, or strip ticket. You can buy one that has two or three strips from the bus or tram driver, but the tickets with 15 or 45 strips that you buy in advance are much cheaper. You can buy these more economical tickets at all railway stations and post offices and at many bookstores and cigarette shops.

The entire country has been divided into public transportation zones, and the fare you pay depends on the number of zones you travel through. A small city will be a single zone, but to get from one end of a larger city to the other end may take you through three or four zones. You can see these zones on the transportation map.

A stamp on a strip cancels that strip and all those above it. A journey will cost you one strip plus the number of zones you will travel through.

If the driver is stamping strip tickets as people enter, you must tell him either your destination or the number of zones. In the tram, you may have to stamp your ticket yourself in the yellow automat near the door. Sometimes there are yellow automats for canceling strips on the platform; you can then stamp your own ticket before you enter the tram or bus. The stamp indicates the zone in which the ticket was stamped and the time. It remains valid for one hour, or somewhat longer in the case of multiple zones.

If you have made a mistake and canceled too many strips, tell the driver and he or she will put a sticker over the incorrect stamp.

Information Number

For information about public transportation anywhere in the country you can telephone 0900 9292. You will first get a recorded message in Dutch, but if you wait, a live person will come on the line who can also speak English, French or German. Else, you can visit www.ns.nl to plan your trip, which also has an English-language section (just click on *English*). The number for information about international buses and trains is 0900 9296.

PASSES

If you will be using the buses and trams four days a week or more, it might be more economical for you to buy a monthly pass. Ask about this at the same place you bought your public transportation map.

INSPECTORS

When you enter a bus you generally show the driver your pass or have him stamp your *strippenkaart*. In the tram, however, you will generally stamp your *strippenkaart* yourself.

A team of inspectors can suddenly appear in the bus or tram, and if you are caught traveling without a valid ticket (stamped *strippenkaart*) you risk a fine.

ONE-DAY PASSES

You can buy one-day passes: either for the bus/tram /metro, the train or a combination thereof. Passes are available at reduced prices for children, senior citizens, and dogs(!). During the summer months, the bus companies sell a special one-day pass for tourists. Have the information service (0900 9292) help you plan a route.

GREENWHEELS SHARE CAR

On 20-plus locations in the Netherlands, you can take out a 'subscription' on a Greenwheels Share (rental) car in, among others, Amsterdam, The Hague, Rotterdam and Utrecht. You can take a monthly subscription for yourself or a shared subscription for up to three drivers. Gas is included in the rent. If you have any of the following types of passes – *Voordeelurenkaart* (off-peak traveling), NS/OV (train/public transportation) or ov-student pass – the subscription is reduced by 50%. Visit www.greenwheels.nl.

PUBLIC TRANSPORTATION BICYCLE

One final way to get to your destination once you have arrived somewhere by train is by Public Transportation Bicycle. To rent one of these, you pay € 2.75 per 20 hours, to a maximum of € 33 per month. You can request a public transportation bicycle pass (OV-fietspas) or have your rail pass registered, either of which you can then use to pick up a bike. Payments are done after the fact, by means of an automatic payment (*automatische incasso*). Bicycles are available in approximately 60 different towns/cities in the Netherlands, and at various locations within the bigger cities of Amsterdam, The Hague and Rotterdam.

Approximately 100 train stations also offer the possibility of renting a bicycle, on a non-public transportation basis; the costs for this are € 5.40-7.30, plus a deposit, ranging from € 30-145 (the latter for a tandem!).

WATER TRANSPORTATION

If there is one thing that we have in abundance in the Netherlands, it's water. So it would be only fair to expect a public water transportation net – which there is. There are the 'fast-flying ferries' between Amsterdam and IJmuiden; there is the fast ferry between Rotterdam and Dordrecht (via Krimpen a/d IJssel, Ridderkerk and Alblasserdam); you can take a ferry across the North Sea Canal (which connects Amsterdam and the North Sea); there is the waterbus in Dordrecht and there is a watertaxi/ *maastaxi* in Rotterdam. The former three are very convenient for commuters. The water and *maastaxi* in Rotterdam offer a much-needed connection between the two city-shores.

There are also plenty of non-public transportation and very picturesque ferries across the many rivers and canals of the Netherlands. Sometimes it could be well worth your while (it could save you time as well as stress!) to get off the highway, out of the traffic jam and take an inland road to a ferry across the river.

DRIVING YOUR CAR

Remember the bumper sticker: 'If you don't like my driving, get off of the sidewalk'? Well, sometimes partaking of the road system here feels that way too. All of a sudden, you are supposed to know that any car coming from the right has the right of way, unless specifically indicated otherwise. This means not only developing rightview paranoia, but also rearview paranoia; if you do not take your right of way, you are almost sure to incur the wrath (if not front bumper) of the car behind you. It is also important to know that the window of opportunity for taking your right of way is about a second-and-a-half, after which you might as well settle for letting the other car go first – in other words, there is lots of potential for upsetting at least one other person!

Also, slowing down to see if this is the street you want to enter – or parking space you wish to take – is almost certain to guarantee an irritated passing by (either left or right, depending on where there is more space) so that it is best to check before making your definite turn. Since we're on the subject of checking, be sure, before making any turn, that there are no bicycles going straight ahead as they have the right of way over you (even if you 'are' the car).

Other, guaranteed, sources of irritation to Dutch drivers are: lingering in the left-hand lane on the highway if you are only planning on exceeding the speed limit by 10 kilometers, taking more than two seconds to get your car rolling once the light turns green – and driving an obviously very expensive car (but that is a whole other issue).

Having said all these deliciously unkind things about the Dutch drivers, fairness requires us to point out that the Netherlands is statistically one of the safest countries in the world to drive in!

OWNING A CAR

Once you plan on owning a car, keep the following in mind. You must:

- have a valid driver's license (see *Driver's License*)
- know the rules of the road (you will find a few further on)
- arrange a periodic check-up of the car (Vehicle Approval – APK, see further on)
- have the registration certificate of the car transferred to your name (see the next paragraph)
- take out car and liability insurance (more on insurances in chapter 4)
- pay road tax (see *Road Tax*).

THE VEHICLE REGISTRATION CERTIFICATE

When you own a car, three important documents will come with it, called *deel I*, *deel II* and *deel III* (parts 1, 2 and 3) – which, together, constitute the *kentekenbewijs* (vehicle registration certificate). *Deel I* contains all the technical information on your car, such as brand, type and number. Whoever is driving the car must always carry this with him. *Deel II* contains the name and address of the owner of the car and is your proof of ownership. You must not buy a car from someone who cannot produce this document and you cannot sell your car without it. Ownership is transferred, making use of this document, at the post office. If you buy a new car, or a used car from a dealer, they take care of this formality for you. It is best not to keep this document in the car. *Deel I* is used to register your car when it is given its annual general technical test (APK, see further on). *Deel III* is used as proof of ownership for cars sold before 1996. Newer cars no longer have a *deel III*.

VEHICLE TAX – BPM

BPM is a vehicle tax that is due by the first person to register a car or motorcycle in his name in the Netherlands. If you buy a car in the Netherlands, the official car importer takes care of it (the tax is included in the price). If you bring your car/motorcycle in from abroad, convert a non-passenger car into a passenger car, or drive a car/motorcycle with foreign license plates in the Netherlands, then you have to take care of it yourself.

Approval RDW

To register your car for the BPM, you must have your car approved by the RDW (see page 142). To this purpose, you visit an RDW-vehicle approval center (call 0900 0739 to find the one nearest you), bringing:
- the vehicle
- proof of identity (driver's license or passport)
- proof of origin of the vehicle (such as the vehicle registration certificate)
- a declaration of conformity, if the vehicle does not have European type approval
- the certificate of conformity, if it does have European type approval.

Once the vehicle is approved, you will receive a BPM-form.

Registration

With this form, you go to the BPM-department of the Tax Authorities. Here they will determine how much BPM you owe. Once you have paid this, the RDW will send you your vehicle registration documents (*kentekenbewijs*), and the car will have been registered in your name.

You also must contend with import duties and VAT, see page 146 on possible exemptions from these and the BPM.

RULES OF THE ROAD

Here, in summary, are a few main traffic rules for cars:
- traffic coming from the right has the right of way (unless you are driving on a priority road, indicated by an orange diamond for you and 'shark's teeth' for the incoming roads)
- cars turning off a road must give priority to cyclists and pedestrians who are continuing straight ahead on it
- traffic entering a roundabout (traffic circle) has right of way unless indicated otherwise

- the speed limits, unless otherwise marked, are 50 kilometers an hour in cities and towns, 80 on secondary roads, and 100 or 120 on the motorways
- children over the age of 12 may sit in the front seat
- when crossing railroad tracks: as the bells start ringing and the lights start flashing, get off. You may only proceed across the tracks once the lights have stopped flashing
- seat belts are mandatory.

A CHILD IN THE CAR

For children who sit in the front of the car, car seats – including armrests and head support – or booster seats are mandatory for children until the age of 12, unless they are taller than 1 meter 50 – in which case, they must, of course, use seat belts. However, you should not place a child in the front seat if your car has an air bag. Grown-ups may not sit in the front with a child on their lap.

In the back seat, between the ages of 3 and 12, children should make use of at least a seat belt and booster seat (or car seat) if they are not yet 1 meter 50 tall (in which case they should use a seat belt). Interestingly enough, there are no *legal* requirements for transporting a child under the age of 3 in the car (the rule is: *if* there is a car seat, you *must* use it; but if there isn't, you do not have to use the seat belt). The Dutch law leaves the responsibility for transporting children of this age up to the driver – and who, in their right mind, is going to leave a two-year-old crawling around on the back seat?

For babies, there are special carrier seats available that you may place in the passenger seat next to you (provided there is no air bag), or else on the back seat. These carrier seats can be taken out (no need to wake up baby when you reach your destination!) and placed on a stroller under-carriage. These take babies up to 13 kg (be sure and check this, as the older ones went to 10 kg).

Approved car seats (according to the European standards) have an orange ECE-sticker on them. If the sticker says 03-44, they are technically very safe. 02-44 means they are sufficiently safe. Stickers that start with 00 or 01 do not meet the current safety standards anymore. The sticker also indicates the weight category for which the seat has been created.

USING A MOBILE PHONE

Effective March 30, 2002, the Netherlands has new legislation regarding the use of cell phones in cars. Drivers/riders of motorized vehicles, mopeds and vehicles for people with disabilities may no longer call or receive calls without an aid, such as a headset or car kit. Sending and receiving SMS, e-mail and WAP messages is no longer allowed. You may not even hold your cell phone in your hand, not even in a traffic jam. If you need to talk, you must stop your vehicle.

This legislation does not apply to cyclists, horse riders and driving instructors in passenger seats. Nor does it apply to the use of equipment such as radiophones in cabs and 27 MC communication equipment.

Violation of this prohibition carries an € 140 fine. In addition, your cell phone may be confiscated. The cost of a 'hands free car kit' is less than the fine, so it is a smart move to purchase a plug-in car kit with loudspeaker and microphone if you need to communicate while driving your car.

Traffic and Safety

On average, there are three fatalities due to traffic accidents in the Netherlands per day. This amounts to an annual total of more than 1,000 – in a country that houses a little over 16 million people. However lamentable this may sound, compared to France for instance – 9,000 victims and 60 million inhabitants – the Netherlands scores alright within Europe. Though the Dutch are considered to be relatively tranquil drivers, the Verenigde Veiligheids Organisatie 3vo (United Safety Organization) is not satisfied and wants to reduce the number of fatalities to 750 by the year 2010. It aims to do this by having the government introduce two new rules: the first reducing the maximum speed limit, both within and outside city limits – and the second being: no more alcohol whatsoever. Though three fatalities a day may not sound too shocking, there are still an additional 100,000 persons who are injured in traffic every year – sometimes permanently.

MOST FREQUENTLY ASKED QUESTIONS FOR THE 3VO:
WHAT IS THE PERMITTED BLOOD ALCOHOL LEVEL?
The law says 0.5 promille is the limit for all drivers. This does not translate into a fixed number of glasses of a particular type of alcohol – it depends on weight, age, sex, stomach content, etc. For drivers on a learner's permit (which was introduced on March 30, 2002) it has been proposed to make this 0.2 promille over the first five years. The limit is not only for the drivers of cars, but also of (motor)cycles and mopeds!

MAY I USE A MOBILE PHONE IN THE CAR?
Not while driving or even standing still in front of a red light. See page 139.

SHOULD MY CHILD USE A BICYCLE HELMET?
Though they are not obligatory, there is no doubt that they can help avoid serious head injury, if worn correctly (which also means using the right size). There are many bicycle riders in the Netherlands and every year, there are 26 fatal accidents involving children; 14,000 children end up in the hospital and 23,000 have to see a doctor due to biking accidents.

WHERE SHOULD MOPEDS/SCOOTERS RIDE?
As of December 1999, mopeds ride in the regular car lanes within city limits. Outside city limits, they tend to stick to the bicycle lanes. For further information, we refer you to the road signs and their explanation.
Scooters and motorized bicycles (*snorfiets*) may make use of bicycle lanes. Helmets are not required. The drivers must have passed a theoretical traffic exam and must have taken out insurance.

WHAT ABOUT CAR LIGHTS?
During the day, if you cannot see clearly, and after dark, you use regular headlights. In the case of fog, snow or rain, you may use your fog lights front and back.

For more information, visit: www.3vo.nl.

SPEED LIMIT

Maximum speed limit

End maximum speed limit zone

Maximum speed limit on electronic sign

Advised speed limit

End advised speed limit

CLOSED

Closed in both directions

One way only, no entry

One way

Priority road

End of priority road

Priority intersection

Entry permitted

Limited to vehicles with 2 wheels

Closed to all vehicles

Closed to mopeds

Closed to bicycles

Priority intersection incoming road from the left

Priority intersection incoming road from the right

Give way

Stop!, give way

Traffic circle / roundabout

Signs indicating direction of traffic

No parking

No stopping

RIGHT OF WAY

DIRECTION

PARKING AND STANDING STILL

PARKING AND STANDING STILL

No bicycles and mopeds parking

Parking

Taxi stand

Immediate loading and unloading of goods

Permit parking only

Parking for carpoolers

City limits

End of city limits

ALLOWED AND NOT ALLOWED

No passing

End no passing zone

Oncoming traffic must get off road. Traffic moving in this direction has right of way

No U-turns

End of all indicated directions

End of all directions given on electronic signals

WARNING

Bad road conditions

Right-hand curve ahead

Left-hand curve ahead

S-curve

Dangerous intersection

Traffic circle / roundabout

Guarded railroad crossing

Unguarded railroad crossing

Tram crossing

Road works ahead

Road narrowing ahead

Slippery when wet

Children crossing

Pedestrian crossing

Pedestrians

Bicycles and moped

Quay or riverside

Oncoming traffic

Possible wind gusts

Traffic lights

Traffic jam

Bus / tram stop

RULES OF THE ROAD

Highway

End of highway

Motor vehicles only

End of motor vehicles only zone

Traffic under restrictions

End of traffic under restrictions zone

Sidewalk

End of sidewalk

Bicycle path

End of bicycle path

Bicycle / moped path

End of bicycle / moped path

SIGNS

Rest area, food, fuel

Route indicators (national and European)

Local signs

Signs for bicycles and mopeds

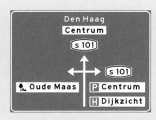
Directions within city limits

District directions within city limits (names)

District directions within city limits (numbers)

INFORMATION

Choose lane
Number of lanes

Dead end

TRAFFIC SIGNS

In general, blue signs tell you what is permitted, and red signs warn you of a restriction. A red circle indicates that something is forbidden, and a red triangle tells you something about the road conditions. A yellow or orange diamond indicates that you are on a road with priority (in which case, right does not have the right of way).

If you will be driving a car, you should know all the rules and signs. Copies of the Dutch traffic laws, translated into various languages, are available from the company Veka Best, see the phone number at the end of the chapter.

PARKING

Parking regulations vary from city to city, so you should ask someone else who drives in your area what they do about park- ing. A local map will have carparks marked with a blue symbol and a P. Carparks with controlled entry have various payment systems. Sometimes streets and carparks look as though you can park in them for free, but in fact there is a ticket dispenser (it will have a blue sign with a white P on it) nearby. Look for signs that say *betaald parkeren* (paid parking), and *parkeerautomaat*. During certain hours, which are posted on the dispenser, you must deposit enough coins to cover the period you will be parked. (In more and more dispensers – particularly in the big cities – you can pay with your *chipknip/chippas*.) You then place the ticket that comes out on the dashboard of your car so that the parking inspectors can read it.

Also beware, particularly in the inner cities, of signs saying *Parkeren voor vergunninghouders*. These are placed few and far apart, but usually indicate that the entire area, if not neighborhood, is reserved for car owners holding a parking permit. If you live in this area, you can get one of these permits at the *gemeentehuis* or the local *Dienst Parkeerzaken* (parking department). Prices vary per city. Sometimes you can 'park & pay' in these areas, this is indicated by one of those blue signs with a white P, with an automat underneath. Whether you can get a permit if you work in one of these areas, depends on the city's rules.

In some of the smaller towns, you will see blue lines painted along where you park. This means that you need to place a *parkeerschijf* (parking disc) on your dashboard, indicating your time of arrival. On signs along the street (usually at the beginning) you will see how long you may remain parked there (the sign will say, for instance, 'max. 30 min.' or 'max. 2 uur').

Parking violations are punished rather severely. Fines start at € 25, but what can make it expensive is that, in some places, the inspectors will attach a wheel clamp or tow away your car, thereby running up a fantastic bill for you.

THE RDW

If you own a car, you will soon find out about the *Rijksdienst voor Wegverkeer*, or RDW. The RDW is the Dutch Road Traffic and Transport Authority. A government-commissioned body, it produces the technical and administrative regulations that make Dutch road traffic and transport as safe and effective as possible. Its reliable and tamper-proof vehicle registration system enables the efficient administration of the country's vehicular details. It makes it possible to quickly locate the owners or holders of vehicles and to call their attention to tax, insurance and APK obligations (see the next paragraph), for instance. This driver accountability is also indispensable when following up traffic offenses.

Besides the vehicle registration system, the RDW also manages the Central Driver's License and Moped Certificate Register, and the exchange of Dutch driver's licenses for those issued outside the Netherlands.

VEHICLE APPROVAL – APK

Before a vehicle is allowed onto the Dutch roads, and at intervals during its use, the RDW (Vehicle Technology and Information Center) ensures that the vehicle meets environmental, safety and economic demands. This work includes providing vehicle type approvals, carrying out certain tests independently, and supervising the Dutch Algemene Periodieke Keuring, or APK (annual general technical test). This monitoring of vehicle technical standards helps to keep Dutch road use as safe, environmentally responsible and economically beneficial as possible. An APK is carried out annually once a car is older than three years and can be done by specialized centers, called *keuringsstations*, or by a local garage that has been recognized by the RDW. There is no fixed price for this test, and prices vary greatly. If you do not agree with the outcome of the test, you can submit a request for a renewed test with the RDW.

It is your responsibility to remember to have the APK done; the RDW will not remind you (beware that they have been known to carry out random tests and that you are obligated to cooperate!). As an extra service, your garage may send you a letter of reminder.

IF YOUR CAR BREAKS DOWN

For sixty years, the ANWB (see page 143) held the monopoly on offering road-side car-breakdown services. 2004 saw the introduction of a competitor to the market, Route Mobiel, which offers cheaper membership – while still providing help within 30 minutes, as well as assistance abroad. Approximately 65,000 members of the ANWB made the switch – however, on page 143 you can read what other services ANWB offers, before making your choice.

Countries on whose license you are allowed to drive in the Netherlands for a period of one year: Austria, Belgium, Cyprus, Czech Republic, Denmark, Estonia, Finland, France, Germany, Greece, Hungary, Iceland, Ireland, Italy, Latvia, Liechtenstein, Lithuania, Luxembourg, Malta, Norway, Poland, Portugal, Slovenia, Slovakia, Spain, Sweden, the United Kingdom (including Northern Ireland). On a license issued in any other country, you are allowed to drive during a period of 6 months.

THE ANWB

Almost all Dutch drivers are members of the ANWB, the Royal Dutch Touring Club. As befits this country of cyclists, the ANWB started – more than 100 years ago – as an organization for cyclists. Though they still offer, for instance, recreational maps to cyclists and hikers, they were clever enough to expand their services to include car drivers. Members of the ANWB are offered the following:

ROAD SERVICES – WEGENWACHT

The ANWB Road Services offer members of the ANWB 24-hour breakdown assistance on the Dutch roads (and for an extra fee: in your driveway!). Help usually arrives within 30 minutes, though this of course depends on road, traffic and weather conditions, as well as the number of breakdowns on the route. If the repair service cannot repair your vehicle on the spot, it offers free transportation of your vehicle and the passengers and even offers free accommodation. Furthermore, members making use of Road Services also have the option of the Replacement Car Service. With this service you are loaned a car if yours cannot be repaired within the hour.

SERVICES WHEN TRAVELING ABROAD

When traveling abroad, ANWB membership also offers you certain benefits. If you are a member, you can receive, for an extra fee, an International Letter of Credit and Assistance Booklet from the ANWB, with which you can request personal and legal assistance if you have a problem concerning your vehicle. This assistance includes advantages such as credit vouchers, the IRK credit card (an internationally recognized card) to give you access to cash in the case of an emergency, assistance from foreign road services organizations, and more.

LEGAL SERVICE

Every member of the ANWB has a right to legal assistance. When abroad, you are given help when returning to the Netherlands in case of an emergency or illness. Furthermore, the ANWB legal services department provides its members with advice and information by phone, including mediation should problems arise concerning travel insurance or in the case of an accident.

STORES AND PUBLICATIONS

Members of the ANWB are issued membership cards which offer them special discounts on books, maps, guides and other items sold at the special ANWB stores – including travel pouches, car seats for children and outdoor clothing. Furthermore, they receive a copy of ANWB's magazine *De Kampioen* in which tours, travel information and other travel-related topics are discussed.

GAS STATIONS

On February 14, 2003, the ANWB opened its first 'unmanned' gas station, offering a discount of at least 6% on the regular fuel prices. Holders of the ANWB – mobility card will enjoy an extra 1 cent-reduction. The plan is for the ANWB to open approximately 100 such gas stations in the Netherlands in the near future, making it a new major player on this market.

MEMBERSHIP CARD

Showing your ANWB-membership card will also provide you with a discount on fuel prices at 500 other gas stations across the country, as well as a discount on entrances fees to amusement parks and museums; on hotel and shop prices; and on fees for rental cars in approximately 50 countries.

For more information, you can contact the ANWB at: 0800 0503 or visit their website: www.anwb.nl.

KILOMETER CHART

	Amersfoort	Amsterdam	Apeldoorn	Arnhem	Assen	Breda	Den Haag (The Hague)	Den Helder	Eindhoven	Emmen	Enschede	Groningen	Haarlem	Heerenveen	Heerlen	's-Hertogenbosch	Leeuwarden	Lelystad	Maastricht	Middelburg	Nijmegen	Rotterdam	Tilburg	Utrecht	Venlo	Zwolle
Amersfoort	–	51	45	54	144	95	85	129	107	142	117	169	72	128	197	71	149	55	192	180	72	78	98	23	131	68
Amsterdam	51	–	87	112	186	121	60	80	133	184	159	178	19	127	224	97	138	56	218	204	128	85	121	47	188	110
Apeldoorn	45	87	–	32	119	140	130	166	130	117	74	144	108	103	220	94	132	60	214	225	50	123	121	68	124	43
Arnhem	54	112	32	–	143	120	121	186	98	141	96	168	119	126	189	63	155	89	183	206	18	113	90	69	93	66
Assen	144	186	119	143	–	239	229	175	240	46	119	27	207	82	330	204	85	139	325	325	161	222	232	167	235	81
Breda	95	121	140	120	239	–	74	195	67	237	212	265	128	217	158	62	214	146	152	94	116	47	35	79	122	163
Den Haag (The Hague)	85	60	130	121	229	74	–	130	136	227	201	232	63	181	227	106	190	110	221	152	136	33	104	62	191	153
Den Helder	129	80	166	186	175	195	130	–	207	189	236	152	73	101	297	171	90	104	297	273	204	154	198	121	261	164
Eindhoven	107	133	130	98	240	67	136	207	–	238	193	266	140	229	90	39	253	158	84	156	83	109	36	91	54	164
Emmen	142	184	117	141	46	237	227	189	238	–	95	57	205	90	328	202	95	137	323	323	159	220	230	165	233	79
Enschede	117	159	74	96	119	212	201	236	193	95	–	144	180	140	283	157	169	136	278	297	114	195	185	140	188	74
Groningen	169	178	144	168	27	265	232	152	266	57	144	–	199	59	356	230	62	126	351	350	186	248	257	193	260	107
Haarlem	72	19	108	119	207	128	63	73	140	205	180	199	–	148	230	104	138	77	225	206	135	87	132	54	195	131
Heerenveen	128	127	103	126	82	217	181	101	229	90	140	59	148	–	320	193	31	74	314	303	144	201	213	135	218	65
Heerlen	197	224	220	189	330	158	227	297	90	328	283	356	230	320	–	128	342	247	21	245	137	198	126	180	81	253
's-Hertogenbosch	71	97	94	63	204	62	106	171	39	202	157	230	104	193	128	–	217	115	123	152	47	78	30	55	93	128
Leeuwarden	149	138	132	155	85	241	190	90	253	95	169	62	138	31	342	217	–	98	338	326	174	214	244	158	247	94
Lelystad	55	56	60	89	139	146	110	104	158	137	136	126	77	74	247	115	98	–	243	232	106	130	142	64	185	63
Maastricht	192	218	214	183	325	152	221	292	84	323	278	351	225	314	21	123	338	243	–	241	133	194	121	176	77	249
Middelburg	180	204	225	206	325	94	152	273	156	323	297	350	206	303	245	152	326	232	241	–	193	124	123	165	210	249
Nijmegen	72	128	50	18	161	116	136	204	83	159	114	186	135	144	137	47	174	106	133	193	–	109	74	86	62	84
Rotterdam	78	85	123	113	222	47	33	154	109	220	195	248	87	201	198	78	214	130	194	124	109	–	76	55	163	146
Tilburg	98	121	121	90	232	35	104	198	36	230	185	257	132	213	126	30	244	142	121	123	74	76	–	85	91	156
Utrecht	23	47	68	69	167	79	62	121	91	165	140	193	54	135	180	55	158	64	176	165	86	55	85	–	146	91
Venlo	131	188	124	93	235	122	191	261	54	233	188	260	195	218	81	93	247	185	77	210	62	163	91	146	–	162
Zwolle	68	110	43	66	81	163	153	164	164	79	74	107	131	65	253	128	94	63	249	249	84	146	156	91	162	–

DRIVER'S LICENSE

As a rule, residents of the Netherlands are required to have a Dutch driver's license in order to drive a motor vehicle. You are a resident if you spend at least 185 days per calendar year in the Netherlands. There are, however, a number of exceptions to this rule. If you have a driver's license that has been issued in the countries listed on page 142 , you are entitled to drive in the Netherlands on your foreign license for a year after registering as a Dutch resident. If you want to use your driver's license for longer than a year, you must have it registered at the municipal offices. You can then use it for a period of ten years after the original issuance of the license. You can also opt to exchange it for a Dutch license.

If you have a driver's license that has been issued in any other country, you may drive in the Netherlands on your foreign license for a period of six months (185 days) after registering as a Dutch resident. As soon as this period expires, you have to take a driving test in the Netherlands to acquire a Dutch driver's license.

Special rules apply to those who have been accorded diplomatic or consular staff status, as well their families. Contact the RDW (Dutch Road Traffic and Transport Authority – for numbers, see the end of the chapter) or the Ministry of Foreign Affairs, Protocol Department, for more information. Special rules also apply to those who benefit from the 30%-ruling, see further on.

Furthermore, you must be at least 18 years of age to drive a car in the Netherlands.

EXCHANGING A FOREIGN DRIVER'S LICENSE

In certain cases you may trade in your foreign-issued driver's license for a Dutch license. This is only possible if you live in the Netherlands and possess valid residential status. Valid driver's licenses issued by the countries listed on page 142, as well as Monaco, Isle of Man, State of Jersey, and Switzerland can be traded in. Driver's licenses issued in the following countries can only be exchanged if they cover the categories listed here: Taiwan, B (passenger car); Israel, B (passenger car); Japan, IB (passenger cars and motorcycles larger than 400cc); Singapore, Class 2 (motorcycles larger than 400cc), Class 3 (passenger car), Andorra, B (license for passenger cars) and South Korea, second class ordinary license.

It is not possible to exchange a so-called international driver's license for a Dutch license, as it is merely considered to be translation of the national driver's license.

One condition for trading in a foreign-issued driver's license is that it must be valid when you submit your request. The driver's license must also have been issued within a one-year period during which the holder resided at least 185 days in the issuing country.

The 30%-Ruling

If you are benefiting from the 30% tax ruling, you and the other member(s) of your family can simply exchange your license, no matter where you are from. Ask for an exchange form for your foreign driver's license at your local municipal office.

The Procedure

In order to exchange your foreign driver's license, you must go to your local municipal office. There you request (and pay for) a document stating who you are and where you live (also referred to as the *uittreksel bevolkingsregister*), a health form (called *eigen verklaring*), and an exchange form. The health form should be filled in by you and a doctor who is not the family doctor. Once it has been completed, you should mail it and the *uittreksel bevolkingsregister* in a pre-printed envelope to the CBR (Centraal Bureau Rijvaardigheid – Central Road Aptitude Bureau). They will process this and send you a 'certificate of fitness' (see more about this certificate further on) in the mail, after which you can return to the municipal office, where you will submit:

- the original, valid foreign driver's license
- proof of identity
- the certificate of fitness
- two identical, recent passport photographs
- for non-EU/EEA citizens: a residence permit
- the exchange form, which has been partially been filled in by you and partially by a civil servant from the municipal office
- (if you are benefiting from the 30%-ruling:) a copy of a statement issued by the Tax Office in Heerlen proving that you or the other member(s) of your family are benefiting from the 30% tax-ruling.

As soon as the municipal fees have been paid, the municipal office will send the entire application to the RDW, who will evaluate the request and – if they grant it – send you a Dutch driver's license at your home address within two to three weeks. This means that you will leave the municipal office without a license, *without which you are not allowed to drive*. Be sure to make a photocopy of your license and the request should you need to drive during these weeks – which, however, you are strongly advised not to do as you will not be insured!

Return of Your Original Driver's License

The original driver's license will be returned to your country of origin, unless you are an EU citizen and benefiting from the 30%-ruling, in which case it will be sent to your address in the Netherlands. If you have a clearly demonstrable interest in having your foreign driver's license returned, you should submit a written request with your exchange application, enclosing any documents proving this interest, such as a letter from your employer stating that you need your foreign license. Other than the situation described at the start of this paragraph, subject to certain conditions, depending on your country of origin, your driver's license will be sent to your Dutch home address.

Verification

As so many different types of driver's licenses from various countries are submitted for exchange, the validity or authenticity of every document has to be verified. The Department of Road Transport may therefore ask you to have the validity and significance of certain information confirmed by the Consulate or Embassy of the country that issued the foreign driver's license. You may also be required to have the content of the foreign driver's license translated by an approved interpreter/translator. For Japanese, Taiwanese and Chinese licenses, this is obligatory.

RETAKING THE TEST

If your driver's license cannot be traded in, you will have to take a theory test and a road test at the Central Road Aptitude Bureau (*Centraal Bureau Rijvaardigheid*, or CBR). More information on this subject can be obtained from the Special Driving Test Office (*Bureau Nader Onderzoek Rijvaardigheidsbewijzen*, or BNOR).

CERTIFICATE OF FITNESS

In several instances, the Central Road Aptitude Bureau (CBR) requires a 'certificate of fitness' over and above the health form when applying for a driver's license. These instances are:

- when a Dutch license is first issued
- when trading in a license issued by certain countries
- when the application is made by diplomatic or consular staff or their families
- when certain medical issues are involved
- when you are older than 65.

For holders of a EU/EEA driver's license or a license issued in Norway, Liechtenstein or Iceland, there are separate reasons for needing a certificate of fitness pertaining in particular to:

- a shorter period of validity than usual (for medical reasons or otherwise)
- unrecognized limitations it may contain
- a remaining period of validity that is shorter than one year
- failure to have it registered
- the age of the driver (65/70 or older)

More information on the 'certificate of fitness' can be obtained from the CBR, your town hall, or the RDW

SHOULD YOU KEEP YOUR CAR?

When moving to another country there is always the question of what to do with your car. Should you keep your old car, buy a new one in the country you are leaving or buy a new one in the country you are going to? All these options have their own merits for tax purposes. And, when returning to your native country, the same questions arise.

In this article you will find a brief overview of some of the issues you should be aware of. This article is based on the premise that the Netherlands is your country of residence, however the same principles are applicable in every country of the European Union. In the Netherlands the taxes involved are the Value Added Tax (VAT/BTW, the *Bijzondere Verbruiksbelasting van Personenauto's* (BPM – see page 139) and import duties.

LEAVING THE NETHERLANDS

When leaving the Netherlands, the first question of importance is: am I going to another member state of the European Union, or am I leaving the European Union altogether.

Going to Another Member State

When you are going to another member state there are no special requirements for taking your old car with you. The Dutch authorities simply do not give any refund of the taxes paid on your car. If you are considering buying a new car though, you should be aware that the taxes levied on a new car in the Netherlands are extremely high. They can amount up to 45% of the list price. If the car is bought whilst living in the Netherlands, there won't be any refund of the taxes on the new car either. In view of the fact that there is hardly any country in the European Union that levies the same amount of taxes on new cars, it is therefore advisable to buy your new car in the country you are going to. Another option would be to buy it in the Netherlands when you are already living in the other country. In that case you might even be cheaper off altogether, because then you do not have to pay VAT/BTW and BPM in the Netherlands but only the taxes in the country you are then living in and the list prices here are relatively cheap. If you live in the United Kingdom, for instance, this could lead to a price difference of € 2,270) and more, and you will even have the steering wheel on the right-hand side (as this can easily be arranged here, too).

Mind you, when your car is less than six months or 6,000 km old, you will have to pay VAT in the member state you are going to. On the other hand, you can get a (partial) refund of the VAT/BTW paid when the car was delivered to you.

Leaving the European Union

When leaving the European Union altogether there also are no special requirements for taking your old car with you. The Dutch authorities still do not give any refund of the taxes paid on your car. When you buy a new car in the Netherlands and it is exported within 30 days, you can buy the car duty-free. In effect it is the same procedure as described before for buying a car in the Netherlands whilst living in another member state. It is very important that you can prove that the car actually left the European Union within 30 days. The tax authorities can demand that you produce evidence of the importation and the car duties paid – in your new country.

Of course the country you are moving to might levy import duties on your car. In general they will grant you an exemption if you have owned the car for more than six months. It is vital that you get detailed information on the applicable rules before you move.

RETURNING TO THE NETHERLANDS
From a European Union Member State

What has been said earlier about going to another member state when leaving the Netherlands, is also applicable *mutatis mutandis* when returning to the Netherlands.

From a Non-European Union Member State

If goods are imported into an EU-member state, customs duties are due. However, for your household effects – that includes cars – there can be an exemption from customs duties (see page 94). Some of the conditions to be met are that you must have lived in a non EU-member state for a period of at least twelve months and that you must have had the car in your possession for at least six months.

WHERE DO YOU LIVE?

The usual place of residence is the place where you normally live for at least 185 days of each calendar year for personal and professional reasons. If there are no professional reasons, evidence must be produced proving that personal commitments lead to close ties between yourself and your place of residence. If you are living in a country in order to carry out an assignment, the usual place of residence is the country where you have your personal commitments. Personal commitments mean family and/or social commitments, such as:
- the place of residence of your family, your children or other people with whom you have a personal relationship
- the place with which you have social ties (e.g. cultural activities societies, sports clubs, committees).

POSSESSION FOR A PERIOD OF SIX MONTHS

You must have had the car in your possession for at least six months and you must have used it in the non EU-member state from which you are moving. This condition is very important. If your employer has put a car at your disposal, the customs authorities are of the point of view that the car is not in your possession. The same applies in the case you have leased a car in the country from which you are moving. In these cases, the exemption of customs duties is not granted for your car.

CONDITIONS AFTER THE EXEMPTION IS GRANTED

After the customs authorities have granted an exemption and you have imported the car, you may not lend out, hire out or sell your car within a period of twelve months after the customs have accepted your customs declaration. If this condition is not met, you will be liable to pay taxes immediately and even be fined for misuse of the rules. Even if the car is stolen or badly damaged and the insurance company sells the wreckage, the exemption will be revoked. In those cases you will have to pay duties for a car you do not and could not own anymore!

TAKE CARE OF BUSINESS BEFORE YOU MOVE

There are plenty of possibilities for reducing the tax burden on your car when you are leaving or returning to a country. Because of the detailed rules concerning this issue, you should take care of business before you actually move. Preferably you should seek professional help at least six months before moving. That will give you the opportunity to use the rules to your advantage.

ROAD TAX

As mentioned earlier, if you own a car, delivery van or motorcycle in the Netherlands, you must pay road tax.

A delivery van is a vehicle with cargo space and also a maximum permitted loaded weight of 3,500 kg. Other regulations apply to vehicles with cargo space and a higher maximum permitted loaded weight. They are covered in a separate brochure entitled *Zware Bedrijfsauto's, Bussen en Opleggers* (*Heavy Commercial Vans, Buses, Trailers and Semitrailers*).

WHEN DO YOU HAVE TO PAY?

You have to pay road tax from the time your name is transferred to the vehicle registration certificate (*kentekenbewijs*, see page 139). Regardless of whether you are temporarily unable or unwilling to use your vehicle, you are always required to pay road tax. You pay for possession of a vehicle, even if it remains parked on private premises. (See further on, for suspension possibilities.)

DECLARATION AND PAYMENT

When you buy a vehicle, you must have your name transferred to the registration certificate, which you can do at any large post office. If you buy your car (either new or second-hand) via a garage, then, in most cases, they take care of this for you. Once your name is transferred to the registration certificate, this also serves as a road tax declaration. You must indicate whether you want to pay for each three-month period separately or for four consecutive periods at once. Soon afterwards, you will automatically be sent a bill and *giro* payment slip (*acceptgiro*) for the road tax for which you are liable (if, for some or other reason you don't, contact the Central Tax Office). Thereafter, the bills will always be posted to you automatically. The period for which you must pay road tax is stated on the bill, as is the due date. You can also arrange to have your bank pay the tax automatically, without your intervention, by means of a *machtiging*. You either arrange this via your bank, or sign a *machtigingsformulier* that you receive along with your first *acceptgiro*.

ROAD TAX RATES

The amount of road tax you pay depends on the following:
- the type of vehicle (i.e. passenger car, delivery van, motorcycle)
- for passenger cars and delivery vans: tare weight. This is stated on part of the registration certificate (under *massa ledig voertuig*)
- for passenger cars: the fuel used (gasoline, diesel, LPG or a combination of gasoline/LPG)
- the province in which you live
- whether your vehicle is equipped and intended to be powered primarily by an electric motor
- the age of your car; if it is 25 years or older, then you do not owe road tax.

You never have to pay additional road tax for a caravan (camper), collapsible caravan or static caravan, even if their maximum permitted loaded weight exceeds 750 kg.

You can always inquire at any large post office or the Tax Department offices of the Central Office for Motor Vehicle Taxes, if you want to know precisely how much road tax you have to pay for your vehicle.

TRAILERS

You also pay road tax for a trailer, if its permitted maximum weight exceeds 750 kg (which you will see on the RDW-registration form) *and* it has been attached to your car. You register separately for this tax – the form can be obtained at the tax offices.

VEHICLE MODIFICATIONS

You may have to pay more, or less, road tax if you modify your vehicle. For example if:
- modification of your vehicle results in a change in its tare weight. As a result, your vehicle may then fall under a different weight category
- you change the type of fuel you use in your passenger car. If you modify your vehicle in this way, you must have your registration certificate adjusted. For this, contact the RDW Centrum voor Voertuitechniek en Informatie (0900 0739). They will inform the Tax Department of the change
- vehicle conversions: for instance, from van to camper or to regular car.

If you have made these changes, you must have the vehicle inspected by the RDW and change the license plates (for which you also must contact the RDW). As of the next road tax period, you will owe the new amount. If you paid road tax for a full year in advance, you will receive an additional assessment or a reimbursement, depending on the situation.

MOVING WITHIN THE COUNTRY

If you move within the Netherlands, you register with your (new) municipality. They will pass on the new address to the tax authorities, who will send the bills to your new address.

SALE OF YOUR VEHICLE

When you sell your vehicle, you must pay road tax over the period during which it was sold, but you can be reimbursed. If you have yet to receive a bill for the tax, you will be sent one for a lesser amount. If you have already paid it, you will be reimbursed. Automatic payments will be stopped automatically.

You deliver proof of the sale of your vehicle by means of the *vrijwaringsbewijs* (warranty against liability), which you will either receive from the garage to which you sell it, or at the post office when the *kentekenbewijs* is transferred to the new owner.

GOING ABROAD TEMPORARILY

If you temporarily go abroad, you are still required to pay road tax on time for the duration of your absence, regardless of whether you take your vehicle with you (however, see following paragraph on *Suspension*). There are two ways to ensure that the road tax is paid on time. You can:
- pay the bill(s) for the duration of your stay abroad in advance. For this, contact the Central Office for Motor Vehicle Taxes
- authorize someone to pay the bill(s) for you
- arrange a *machtiging*, allowing the bank to make the periodic payments for you.

SUSPENSION

If you will not be using your vehicle for an extended period of time (for instance because you are going abroad), you can apply for suspension of the registration certificate at a large post office – for a fee. You will not owe road tax as of the date of suspension (provided the period of suspension lasts at least three months) and will automatically be reimbursed for amounts already paid. If you end the suspension before three months have passed, then you will owe road tax over the entire three month-period. Sus-pension is granted for a maximum period of one year, but can be extended after this period has passed. During the period of suspension you will not be allowed to drive your vehicle on a public highway and you must inform the Tax Office of its physical whereabouts during this period.

You can read more about this in the brochure entitled *Uw Auto of Motor en het Kentekenbewijs (Your Car or Motorcycle and the Registration Certificate)*, available, among others, at the post office.

YOUR VEHICLE LEAVES THE COUNTRY PERMANENTLY

If your vehicle leaves the country permanently, you must de-register it with the RDW. You will then automatically receive a road tax reimbursement for the period after which your car is no longer in the Netherlands. If you paid road tax for four consecutive periods at once, you will also receive a tax reimbursement for the periods that have not yet taken effect.

If your car has already left the country and you have not de-registered it with the RDW, then you must inform the Customs authorities of this (Douane, at 0455 74 30 31).

FREQUENT CHECKS

The Central Office for Motor Vehicle Taxes closely monitors the payment of road tax. Photographs, customs data and police information, such as fines and records, are also utilized. If it is discovered that you have not paid road tax, or have paid too little, you will receive an increased assessment.

THE BICYCLE

THE BEST WAY TO GET AROUND

If you really want to sample Dutch life, and get around quickly and easily, buy yourself a bicycle – one like those that people in the Netherlands use as a serious form of transport: a sturdy, no-nonsense bike, preferably not too expensive so that if it gets stolen you will not feel too bad. Fancy, 10-speed bicycles are relatively rare, and used only for recreational cycling.

A new bicycle, made by one of the better-known manufacturers and sold at a bicycle shop, costs between € 275 and € 475. A discount store will sell you a new, imported bike for as little as € 175, but you must examine it to make sure the quality is alright.

BUYING A SECOND-HAND BICYCLE

Most students (and foreign visitors) buy second-hand bicycles (*tweedehands fietsen* or *tweedehands rijwielen*). A reasonable one will cost you between € 75 and € 125. You can find them at second-hand bicycle shops, or at the bicycle parking facilities near railway stations. They will also be advertised in the small ads at the back of the local newspaper under *Rijwielen*, or on the notice board at the supermarket or anywhere students congregate. (A woman's bike is a *damesfiets* and a man's bike is a *herenfiets*. Dutch men are not embarrassed to ride on women's bicycles – and vice versa.)

Since the second-hand bicycle market is different in different towns, you should ask a local for advice. They may know of an especially good place, and, if you're lucky, may even help you to pick your bicycle and negotiate the price.

When you buy a bicycle, make sure that its lights work and that it has a sturdy lock (*slot*). Even better is to buy a chain and padlock so you can fasten your bicycle to something when you park it (secure parking for bicycles is available at most railway stations and in some city centers. Look for the signs to *rijwielstalling* or *fietsenstalling*).

RENTING A BICYCLE

You can also rent bicycles by the day from the parking facility at many railway stations, under payment of a deposit. It is wise to telephone in advance to make a reservation. Ask at the railway station for the free booklet. At certain places, such as the Veluwe National Park, bicycles are available, free of charge, to roam the beautiful woods at your leisure.

For more on renting a bicycle and on the Public Transportation Bicycle, see page 138.

TRAFFIC RULES FOR CYCLISTS

As a cyclist, you too must obey the traffic signs and rules, and stay in the bicycle lanes marked on the street. As a rule, cars that are turning across your path are supposed to stop for you, but it is wise to watch out. You should also signal with your arm if you are planning to turn. You can be fined for riding at night without lights, and for drunken cycling. Contrary to the situation in many countries, you may *not* ride your bicycle on the sidewalk.

BEING A PEDESTRIAN

Tourists have been known to take a seat in the window of a café at a busy Amsterdam intersection just to watch the show of Dutch traffic interaction. All pedestrians jaywalk, none of the bicycle riders pay any attention to the color of their traffic light, trams trundle along and stop within an inch of all cars' lives (be they Mercedes or Toyota), buses wheeze their asthmatic way through this all with an inch to spare, and cars ... well, cars take whatever space everyone else deigns to grant them.

In all this mess, being a pedestrian is by far the most convenient. Riding a bike is faster, but pedestrians can squeeze through, around or over any obstacle and, if it starts to rain, they can hop on a tram or bus and get out of there in nothing flat.

BLIND PEDESTRIANS

Luckily, this does not mean that those of us who cannot see had best stay home. In many cities and towns, there is a whole intricate system in place to help the blind navigate their way. For instance, the pedestrian lights produce a variety of ticking sounds, depending on whether they signal WALK or DON'T WALK. Also, hidden among the regular sidewalk tiles, are special ribbed or rubber tiles (also in place at railroad stations), indicating where the sidewalks end. And fellow-pedestrians, but also other road users, have an eye out for the special white sticks with red rims, used by the blind – and often take the time to lend a helping hand.

RULES

Jaywalking may be quicker, but, if you want to make sure you make it across in one piece, it's nice to know that cars must yield to pedestrians on zebra crossings (but don't be naïve; car drivers are not naturally inclined to yield to anyone who isn't at least half way across – they expect you to 'wait your turn'). Cars making a turn on a green light must yield to pedestrians going straight ahead on a zebra crossing. Don't expect them to wait till you have made it all the way across, though; just out of their way gives them plenty of room to proceed, as far as the Dutch drivers are concerned.

Also make sure that you don't mistake a bicycle path (*fietspad*) for a pedestrian path, they often look very much the same and at times run parallel. Generally speaking, the path closest to the road is the bicycle path.

Trams have priority over everyone, no matter where they are coming from.

REFERENCES

GENERAL

MINISTRY OF TRANSPORT, PUBLIC WORKS AND WATER MANAGEMENT: (*MINISTERIE VAN VERKEER EN WATERSTAAT*)
Plesmanweg 1 – 6, P.O. Box 20901,
2500 EX The Hague
Tel.: 070 351 61 71
Internet: www.minvenw.nl
DUTCH CUSTOMS (*DOUANE*):
www.douane.nl

TRAVEL

PUBLIC TRANSPORTATION (GENERAL),
prices, departure and arrival times, info tel.:
0900 92 92, internet: www.9292ov.nl
DUTCH RAILWAYS (*Nederlandse Spoorwegen*)
Prices, departure and arrival times:
www.ns.nl
TRAVEL PLANNER: www.ns.nl
International trains and prices,
info tel.: 0900 92 96
Brochure *Exploring Holland by Train* in
six languages: available at the main train
stations
TAXI COMPANIES: www.taxi.nl
THE INTERLINER: 0900 84 15
THALYS: www.thalys.com
SCHIPHOL AIRPORT FLIGHT INFORMATION:
www.schiphol.nl
STENA LINE: www.stenaline.com
P&O FERRIES: http://Poferries.com

DRIVER'S LICENSE

BUREAU NADER ONDERZOEK RIJVAARDIGHEIDSBEWIJZEN, BNOR (*SPECIAL DRIVING TEST OFFICE*)
Tel.: 070 413 03 00
Internet: www.rijbewijs.nl

CBR – DUTCH DRIVING TEST ORGANIZATION (*CENTRAAL BUREAU RIJVAARDIGHEIDSBEWIJZEN*)
P.C. Boutenslaan 1, P.O. Box 5301,
2280 HH Rijswijk
Tel.: 070 327 05 00
Internet: www.cbr.nl

GENERAL INFORMATION ON DRIVER'S LICENSES, TRADE-INS, AND REGISTRATION:
RDW (*NATIONAL TRAFFIC AUTHORITY*)

Vehicle technology and information center
Tel.: 0900 0739
Internet: www.rdw.nl/eng

DRIVER'S LICENSE INFORMATION FOR PERSONS HOLDING DIPLOMATIC OR CONSULAR STAFF STATUS:
Ministry of Foreign Affairs, Protocol
Department
Tel.: 070 348 64 86

MINISTRY OF TRANSPORT, PUBLIC WORKS AND WATER MANAGEMENT
P.O. Box 20901, 2500 EX The Hague
Tel.: 070 351 77 10
Internet: www.minvenw.nl

ROAD TAX

CENTRAL OFFICE FOR MOTOR VEHICLE TAXES (*CENTRAAL BUREAU MOTORRIJTUIGENBELASTING*)
Tel.: 0800 0749 on working days from
8 A.M. - 5 P.M.
Postal address: P.O. Box 9047,
7300 GJ Apeldoorn
Visiting address: J.F. Kennedylaan 8,
Apeldoorn
Internet: www.belastingdienst.nl

MINISTRY FOR TRANSPORT INDUSTRIES (*RIJKSDIENST VOOR HET WEGVERKEER*)
For questions about registration certificates
contact tel.: 0598 62 42 40 on weekdays from
8 A.M. - 5 P.M.
Postal address: P.O. Box 30 000,
9640 RA Veendam
Internet: www.rdw.nl

OTHER BROCHURES ON ROAD TAX:
Personenauto's en bestelauto's (Passenger cars and delivery vans)
Motoren (Motor cycles)
These brochures are available at large post offices, Tax Department (*Belastingdienst*) offices, and the Central Office for Motor Vehicle Taxes (*Centraal Bureau Motorrijtuigenbelasting*).

ORGANIZATIONS

THE ROYAL DUTCH TOURING CLUB (ANWB)
P.O. Box 93200, 2509 BA The Hague

Wassenaarseweg 220, 2596 EC The Hague
General information, tel.: 0800 0503
To become a member call tel.: 0800 0503
Legal assistance, tel.: 070 314 77 88
Road Traffic Victim Assistance, tel.: 070 314 77 66 (also for non-members)
Travel agency, tel.: 070 314 14 80
Traffic information, tel.: 0900 9622
Car advice line: tel.: 070 314 50 00
Roadside Assistance Service (Wegenwacht),
tel.: 0800 0888
Internet: www.anwb.nl
Route Planner: http://route.anwb.nl

CYCLING

CYCLING VACATIONS IN THE NETHERLANDS: www.tulipcycling.com
CYCLE TOURS (860 in the Netherlands and 275 in Belgium): www.fietsen.123.nl
CYCLING IN THE NETHERLANDS:
www.hsa.lr.tudelft.nl/~bvo/fiets/nlbybike.htm
CYCLING IN ROTTERDAM:
www.rotterdambycycle.nl

AIRPORTS

AMSTERDAM AIRPORT SCHIPHOL
Tel.: 0900 7244 7465
Internet: www.schiphol.nl

ROTTERDAM AIRPORT
Rotterdam Airportplein 60,
3045 AP Rotterdam
Tel.: 010 446 34 44
Internet: www.rotterdam-airport.nl

MAASTRICHT AACHEN AIRPORT
Vliegveldweg 17, 6191 SB Beek
Tel.: 0800 0143
Internet: www.maa.nl

EINDHOVEN AIRPORT
Luchthavenweg 25, 5657 EA Eindhoven
Tel.: 040 291 98 18
Internet: www.eindhovenairport.nl

GRONINGEN AIRPORT EELDE
Machlaan 14, 9761 TK Eelde
Tel.: 050 309 70 70
Internet: www.groningenairporteelde.nl

ENSCHEDE AIRPORT TWENTE
Vliegveldweg 333, 7524 PT Enschede
Tel.: 053 486 22 22
Internet: www.enschede-airport.nl

LELYSTAD AIRPORT
Tel.: 0320 284 775
Internet: www.lelystad-airport.nl

DUTCH AIRLINES

KLM ROYAL DUTCH AIRLINES
Koninklijke Luchtvaart Maatschappij N.V.
Schipholdijk 35 D 115, Luchthaven Schiphol
Tel.: 020 649 91 23
Internet: www.klm.nl

MARTINAIR HOLLAND
Havenmeesterweg 201, 1118 CD Schiphol
Tel.: 020 601 12 22
Internet: www.martinair.nl

TRANSAVIA AIRLINES
Westelijke Landweg 3,
1118 CR Luchthaven Schiphol
Tel.: 020 406 04 06
Internet: www.transavia.nl and
www.transavia.com (former Basiq Air)

FOREIGN AIRLINES

Air France, tel.: 020 654 57 20,
Aer Lingus, tel.   : 020 520 02 88,
internet: www.aerlingus.com
Air Canada, tel.   : 020 346 95 39,
internet: www.aircanada.nl
Air France, tel.: 020 654 57 20,
internet: www.airfrance.com
Alitalia, tel.: 0900 202 26 22,
internet: www.alitalia.nl
British Airways, tel.: 020 346 95 59,
internet: www.britishairways.com
Delta Airlines, tel.: 020 201 35 36,
internet: www.delta.com
Easyjet, tel. 023 568 48 80,
internet: www.easyjet.com
Iberia, tel.: 0900 202 11 64,
internet: www.iberia.com
Japan Airlines, tel.: 020 582 94 88,
internet: www.jal.co.jp
Lufthansa, tel.: 020 582 94 56,
internet: www.lufthansa.com
Northwest Airlines, tel.: 020 555 99 99,
internet: www.nwairlines.com

Qantas Airways, tel.: 023 569 82 82,
internet: www.qantas.com
Ryanair, internet: www.ryanair.com
SAS, tel.: 9000 746 37 27,
internet: www.scandinavian.net
Singapore Airlines, tel.: 020 548 88 88,
internet: www.singaporeair.com
US Airways, tel.: 020 201 35 50,
internet: www.usairways.com
Virgin Atlantic (US, Far East, S.Africa,
Caribbean, India, Australia, UK),
internet: www.virgin.com/atlantic
Virgin Express (European Cities),
internet: www.virgin.com/express

GENERAL TICKET INFO AND BOOKING

VLIEGWINKEL.NL: www.vliegwinkel.nl

AIRPORT HOTELS

AMSTERDAM SCHIPHOL AIRPORT HILTON
tel.: 020 710 40 00, internet: www.hilton.com
AIRPORT TERMINAL HOTEL MERCURE
tel.: 020 522 16 16, internet: www.mercure.nl
AMSTERDAM AIRPORT SHERATON HOTEL
tel.: 020 316 43 00, internet: www.sheraton.nl

HOTEL BOOKINGS

www.bookings.nl
www.expedia.nl
www.hotels.nl

Once you have solved the more pressing matters, there are many other things you will need to know about living in the Netherlands such as shopping hours and customs, household help, safety, pets, Dutch gardens and family life, (mobile) telephone, and Internet Service Providers – not necessarily in that order. You will find answers to such questions as 'Why do the Dutch leave their curtains open?', but also on how to get your telephone service started and whether the Netherlands is a safe country to live in. In this chapter, we have included material from the book *Food Shoppers' Guide to Holland* – if you would like to read more on shopping and food in the Netherlands, you can find information on this book at the end of the chapter.

TEL. 466259

Daily Life

CONTRIBUTING AUTHORS: STEPHANIE DIJKSTRA, CONNIE MOSER AND ADA HENNE KOENE

SHOPPING

OPENING HOURS

Shopping hours in the Netherlands for a long time were based on the idea that people who work in shops should be able to live according to much the same pattern as other people. Nearly all shops were therefore closed on Sundays and in the evening. This started to change during the 90s and in 1996 the government extended the number of hours shops are allowed to stay open. The pattern has therefore become much more variable.

In general, shops in the Netherlands are open Monday through Saturday from 9 A.M. to 6 P.M. But there are a growing number of exceptions to this rule. The following are the most common exceptions:

- most shops are closed on Monday mornings to enable shop-keepers to stock the shelves and do their administration
- small shops often close an hour or two early on Saturdays
- one evening each week, all shops in an area will either stay open until 9 P.M., or open again from 7 – 9 P.M. This is called *koopavond*, and whether it is Thursday or Friday depends on the town
- small shops might close at other times – at lunch-time, or on Wednesday afternoon, for example, when children are free from school
- the bigger supermarkets open an hour earlier and stay open a few hours longer in the evening to give people time to shop before or after work
- all stores in an area may decide to open their doors on certain Sundays

- in the big cities you might be able to find a small grocery shop that specializes in being open late in the evenings and on Sundays. This is called an *avondwinkel*, and its prices will be higher than prices elsewhere
- mini-markets carrying a small selection of goods can be found at some gas stations, larger train stations and at Schiphol airport.

THE OPEN-AIR MARKET

Once or twice a week, each town or district will have an open-air market, often in the central market square. This starts at about 8/9 A.M. or 1 P.M. and closes between 4 and 6 P.M. Here you can buy fruit and vegetables, fish, sweets, bakery products, fabric, clothing, bedding, cosmetics and many other items. Excellent bargains can be found, but you must have a critical eye for quality.

Especially in the big city markets, products are available from all across the world in stalls that cater to the tastes of customers from among others the Caribbean and Mediterranean regions.

Keep in mind that the rules regarding starting and finishing hours can be applied so strictly that a market salesman will refuse to sell you his goods 15 minutes before 'opening time', even though it is pouring rain and you have a cantankerous baby with you and chances are absolutely nil that you will return at any other point during the day.

APPLIANCES

The current used in the Netherlands is 220 volt, so – unless you are inclined to import a shipload of converters or are moving here from another 220-volt country – you are most likely going to be doing quite some household shopping when you move here.

The good news is that there are several chains for buying house-hold appliances. They usually sell all that you need in one place: refrigerators, washing machines, dryers, dishwashers, vacuum cleaners, toasters, coffee machines, deep-frying pans, televisions, video and DVD recorders, CD-players, radios, heaters – that sort of stuff. Prices among these chains can vary considerably, so have a good look around before you spend a whole lot of unnecessary euros. Check the Yellow Pages under *Huishoudelijke apparaten en artikelen*.

One tip is that little stores – that reek of exclusivity – in little towns filled with expats and other high-spenders are bound to have a nice little margin on top of the acquisition price. On the other hand, they are also more likely to have someone who is willing to come over and help you install it all. This is worth looking into and may even be worth that margin.

Another thought is that, as expats often move on to other countries with yet a different current, you could try the various international (women's) clubs and your (spouse's) employer's Intranet-bulletins for second-hand goods.

For buying a telephone, see further on, in *Being Connected*.

COMPUTERS AND SOFTWARE

Computers and software can be bought at computer chain stores, stores that specialize in smaller technology such as cameras, telephones and televisions or via the Internet. In the supermarkets and at book/magazine stores you can buy computer magazines (in Dutch) where several businesses advertise their ware, which can be ordered by telephone. Keep in mind that phone-ordered goods are often paid for, *in cash*, upon delivery.

FURNITURE, BEDS

Furniture can be bought in any number of places, from tiny, exclusive little shops to big well-known chains. The Netherlands has two names for its furniture conglomerates, being either *meubel-boulevards* or *woonboulevards* (furniture or living boulevards). Some are huge indoor malls with stores of all levels of exclusivity, some are geographic locations where a large collection of larger stores are all located. There are also *brocante*-stores (where they sell furniture and other more decorative items that do not yet quite deserve the name antique, but are already in the 'nostalgic'-category) as well as, of course, antique stores (see more about these in Chapter 10, under *For Antique Lovers Only*). In Chapter 8, under *Living On A Shoestring*, you will find more on low-budget spending.

Beds can be bought at either certain furniture chains or stores as well as in specialized stores.

BOOKS

With the exception of the bookstores in possibly the littler towns, they almost all carry a selection of English-language books. In the bigger cities, there are specialized English-language bookstores such as the American Book Center or Waterstone's – and then there are the large bookstores that carry not only English-language books, but also, for instance, French, German and Spanish.

A CLEAN HOME AND SELF

Detergents, floor polishers, carpet cleaners and the like can be bought both in supermarkets (again, prices can vary considerably, so if you have a tight budget shop around!), but also at the drug-store (*drogisterij*) – where you will also find drain de-cloggers, stain removers, mold remover and some of the more chemical products.

Soaps, shampoos, toothbrushes, toothpaste, shaving cream, hand cream and sanitary items can also be bought at supermarkets and *drogisterijen* – while at the latter you will also find make-up, homeopathic medicines, dietary supplements, bubble baths, some toys, travel kits, mosquito repellent and a range of massage oils, for starters.

Baby necessities can also be bought at either type of store, including food and formula.

SHOPPING ETIQUETTE

Take one or more shopping bags with you when you go to buy groceries. Even in the supermarket, you must pack your groceries yourself. Shops can generally give or sell you a plastic bag, but most people use their own heavier carry-all bags. You can buy these in supermarkets and department stores, at the market, and in shops that sell handbags and luggage. All supermarkets have shopping carts handy at the entrance but in most supermarkets, they are interlocked with chains and it takes a 50 cent-euro coin to unlock the connection. You get your coin back when you re-connect the cart. Payment can be made with cash but shops also accept PIN or bank debit cards and *chipknip/chippas* cards – which is like cash (see page 103).

GETTING SERVED

The Dutch do not queue, as you will soon notice. You must learn the art of gently but firmly pushing your way into the bus or train, for example. You must also learn the art of getting served in a shop. Look first to see if there is a system by which people take numbers from a small dispenser at the entrance. This makes it

- the Dutch consume an average of 7.7 kilograms of coffee per person per year. This makes the Dutch the fourth biggest coffee drinkers in the world, after Finland, Norway and Sweden.
- 91% of the population (15 years old and over) drinks coffee
- the Dutch drink an average of 84 liters of beer per person per year
- there are 1.2 million milk cows in the Netherlands. They produce 10.5 billion liters of milk
- over half of all the milk produced in the Netherlands is turned into cheese
- the Netherlands is the world's largest exporter of cheese, butter and powdered milk

easy; you need only watch for your number to come up. Otherwise you are expected to keep track of who was waiting before you and to speak up when it is your turn. A trick, used by many Dutch, is to enquire: 'Wie was het laatste' (who came in last?), this way, you only have to keep an eye on this person to know when your turn is. This takes practice (and patience).

BARGAINING
This is not customary. You are expected to pay the price that is marked, especially for new items. If you are buying something second-hand – at a flea market, for example – you can try making an offer. The answer will be an angry 'no', however, if you drop the price by more than about 25%.

EYE CONTACT AND GREETINGS
When Dutch people enter and leave a small shop, they generally greet the shopkeeper ('Goede dag' – good day – is always a friendly greeting). It is important in any case to acknowledge the shopkeeper's presence by at least establishing eye contact.

FOOD

The Netherlands is a former shipping and colonial power that had interests in Indonesia, South Africa and the Caribbean. Many people from these countries eventually came to live in the Netherlands. They were later joined by guest workers from the Mediterranean countries and by international businessmen and women and their families as the Netherlands became the hub of their business interests in Europe. Thus, the Netherlands is a truly international country and it is relatively easy to find supermarkets and delicatessen/gourmet food shops that cater to most culinary needs.

DUTCH WAY OF EATING
The Dutch usually only eat one hot meal a day; it can be served for lunch or dinner, but it is generally served as the evening meal. Breakfast may consist of fresh breads or open-faced sandwiches made of Dutch rusks (beschuit) and rolls, croissants and light or dark whole wheat bread topped with butter, jams or jellies, cheese,

sausages or cold cuts. Lunch is usually more of the same, but it might include a small cup of hot soup (this does not qualify as a hot meal), fruit, a *kroket* (croquettes – *kroketten* are shaped like a short hot dog, but made with a soft, meat-based filling, covered in bread crumbs and fried) or an *uitsmijter* (two fried eggs on a layer of ham, roast beef and/or cheese on two slices of bread). The meal is accompanied by milk, coffee or tea. There are coffee and/or tea breaks in the mornings and afternoons that are sacred in the Netherlands and the piping hot beverages are served with cookies – or pastries or cakes, if there is a special occasion. In the evening, there might be a *borrel* or drink consisting of the Dutch *jenever* (gin) and a snack such as *bitterballen* (little meatballs) before din-ner – though, again, this is most often saved for a special occasion. Dinner is heartier with a main vegetable, meat and a healthy ser-ving of the ubiquitous potato side dish like *patat frites* (French fries) or merely potatoes that are boiled or steamed. Sometimes, the vegetables and potatoes mashed together to create the tra-ditional Dutch *stamppot* dishes (see next paragraph), which are served with some delicious *rookworst* (smoked sausage) or *draad-jesvlees* (simmered beef). There is also some kind of dessert. It is usually yogurt that comes in all different tastes and *vla* (custard), fruit and sometimes cheese. To accompany the meals, the Dutch usually stick to water or milk or maybe soft drinks – wine is more often saved for special occasions.

When the Dutch eat out, they will eat the foods they don't cook at home, in other words, Indonesian, Italian, French, and Chinese, among others.

TYPICAL DUTCH FOODS

While the local cuisine is rich in variety due to the inclusion of many recipes that criss-cross international borders, there is a basic Dutch cuisine that is best described as 'home cooking'. It is the 'comfort food' that most Dutchmen crave when away from home for prolonged periods or after a summer of light meals.

If you were to ask a Dutchman to name one national dish, he would probably mention *erwtensoep* (pea soup). Next would come the *stamppot* dishes of *boerenkool met worst* (curly kale with sausage), *hachée* (beef and onion stew), *zuurkool met worst* (sauer-kraut with sausage) and *witlof met ham en kaas* (Belgian endives with ham and cheese sauce). In May and June, everyone eats *asperges met ham en eieren* (asparagus with ham and eggs).

INDONESIAN/CHINESE FOOD & SPICES

At last count, there were over 900 Chinese/Indonesian shops in the Netherlands. Thus it is safe to say that everyone in the Nether-lands eats Indonesian food in what has become known as the Indonesian *rijsttafel* where rice is the central dish with any number of side dishes. These may include three different types of rice, several fish, meat, poultry and vegetables dishes and condi-ments. The *rijsttafel* may be prepared at home, eaten at restau-rants or carried home from Indonesian or Chinese/Indonesian takeouts.

Since the 16th century, spices have had an important place in the Dutch kitchen cabinet. Most are available in the supermarkets. If you don't find what you are looking for there, almost all of the herbs and spices known to man are sold in Indonesian shops or *tokos*, and Chinese supermarkets.

ETHNIC SHOPS

Also in the big cities you will find shops specializing in foods and other products for specific ethnic groups, such as a *Turkse slager* (a *slager* is a butcher) or a *Turkse winkel*, where they sell products from Turkey and the eastern Mediterranean. At a *toko*, which you can find even in the smallest towns, you will find Indonesian food. You can buy meat that is *halal* at an *Islamitische slager*. In Amsterdam you can find kosher (Jewish) meat markets, and in both Amsterdam and Rotterdam there is a small Chinatown. And there are more possibilities: Moroccan, Japanese, Indian, etc. Also available in recent years are the Tex/Mex dishes popular in Ameri-ca and most supermarkets have a small Tex/Mex department.

If you are looking for something from a specific culinary/geo-graphic area, check the telephone book or the Yellow Pages.

SUPERMARKETS

Dutch supermarkets carry the basic groceries such as baking and cooking ingredients, dairy products including cheese, herbs and spices, bakery goods, some health foods, fruits and vegetables, meats, fish and poultry, baby foods, pet foods, along with daily house and kitchen supplies (such as detergent, toilet paper and cleaning supplies). The selection of frozen foods is proportionate to the capacity of the store; the larger the supermarket, the more goods there are on offer.

At the supermarkets you can browse at your leisure while getting acquainted with the local products and buy the basics to stock your pantry. If you feel shy or awkward about the language, con-tact can be kept to a minimum. The check-out system is relatively simple and not all that different from the systems in other coun-tries. However, there will come a time when you will overcome your fears and be lured by the sights and smells of the neighbor-hood specialty shops, or stalls at open markets.

ALCOHOL USE

SALES OF LIQUOR

From the age of 16 you may legally buy beer and wine. To buy liquor you must be 18 years of age. Alcoholic beverages are for sale at liquor stores and supermarkets. Supermarkets only sell beer, wine and alcoholic beverages with an alcohol percentage up to 12 to 13%. Bartenders, liquor dealers and cashiers must ask youngsters whom they sell alcohol to for proof of age, such as a passport or driver's license. After all, it is often difficult to estimate somebody's age. If either of these cannot be supplied, you may be refused alcohol.

DRINKING AND DRIVING

It is prohibited to drive if you are over the 0.54-blood alcohol level. Driving under the influence is a criminal offense and applies to driving a car and riding a motorcycle, scooter, moped or bicycle. You risk a fine running from € 190 to € 1,015, depending on your blood alcohol plus a possible ban on driving of up to almost a year and possible incarceration. In some cases, you may be required to take a three-day, € 500-course (to be paid by you), which, if you do not take it (from start to finish) could lead to the loss of you driver's license.

DRUG USE

For the record, trafficking in (importing or exporting), selling, producing and processing either hard or soft drugs are offenses in the Netherlands. The possession of soft drugs for personal use (up to 30 grams) is a summary, non-indictable offense.

COFFEE SHOPS

Coffee shops can sell soft drugs without being prosecuted, providing they observe strict rules. The aim of this policy is to prevent users of soft drugs from becoming marginalized or being exposed to more harmful drugs.

A coffee shop can best be described as a café, which does not sell alcoholic beverages (except in Amsterdam, where some do), and in which, under certain circumstances, soft drugs may be sold.

Although the sale of soft drugs is an offense, low priority is given to the prosecution of coffee shop owners, provided they sell small quantities only and meet the following conditions:

- no more than five grams per person may be sold in any one transaction
- the stock may not exceed 500 grams
- no hard drugs may be sold
- drugs may not be advertised
- the coffee shop must not cause any nuisance
- no drugs may be sold to persons under the age of 18, nor may minors be admitted onto the premises.

Municipalities may set up extra rules, for instance regarding the proximity to schools, the presence of informational material and the required physical presence of the proprietor. Agreements are made with the local police regarding routine checks and the mayor of a city has the authority to close coffee shops that do not meet these conditions.

For those of you who think coffee shops can only be found in the bigger cities: there are somewhere in the vicinity of 900 coffee shops, spread over 100-plus municipalities. Three-quarters of the cannabis sold is of the home-grown variety (referred to as 'nederwiet').

COFFEE SHOPS

If you want a cup of coffee and a piece of very

delicious Dutch apple pie, a 'Coffee Shop' is

not necessarily the place you want to be.

Coffee Shop is a Dutch euphemism for a soft-

drugs café. They can sell customers up to five

grams of cannabis for personal use. Unless

that is what you are looking for, you want to

go to a café, a snack bar, or cafeteria instead.

DAIRY PRODUCTS

Of all of the wonderful foodstuffs produced in the Netherlands, the Dutch are probably most proud of their milk and milk products. The ubiquitous purveyor of this life-sustaining substance, the Holstein Frisian cow, grazes everywhere. The Gouda and Edam cheeses are so well-known around the globe that wherever cheese is sold, Gouda and/or Edam are always present.

While the supermarkets offer a good selection of fresh and processed cheese, serious cheese lovers and connoisseurs shop at their local cheese specialist or *kaasspecialist*. He not only has the largest selection of cheeses, but he ages his Dutch cheeses naturally to obtain the optimum taste and perfection and his cheeses never hit the shelves until they are least two months old. And, since most Dutch cheeses are classified according to age, he keeps a watchful eye on the aging process. The cheese shops and supermarket cheese departments are also well-stocked with imported cheeses from among others France, Italy, Belgium and England.

Generally, the place to buy your milk and other dairy products is in the supermarket, however, you might also consider buying directly from the cheese farms and shops that sell fresh farmer's milk, buttermilk, eggs and cheese.

BAKERY – *BAKKERIJ*

The shops that probably delight foreign residents most are the bakeries (*bakkerijen*) that turn out those mouth-watering fresh breads, rolls, cookies and pastries and creamy bon-bons. At Christmas-time they have a full range of seasonal breads and cookies, then at Easter-time they outdo themselves with a stunning array of brilliant, foil-wrapped chocolate bunnies, bon-bons, marzipan animals and fruits and cakes decorated for the season.

The bakeries often also offer breads from France, Italy and the Middle East. Bread is baked fresh daily and is often still hot when you get it home.

THE FISH SHOP – *VISHANDEL*

Although not the great seafaring nation it once was, the Netherlands still retains its reputation for being a purveyor of fine seafood. The quality and quantity available here are excellent. Supermarkets may carry a small variety of fish and seafood but the seafood specialists in the shops called *vishandel* offer by far the largest selection. Not every village has one, so look in the larger towns for the best selection.

Much of what is on sale is cold water fish but occasionally you will see some excellent fish from the Mediterranean. In addition to the fish you buy to prepare yourself, the fishmonger will have some pre-fried haddock and codpieces, raw and pickled herring and some excellent prepared dishes such as fish salads, jambalaya and paella. The fishmonger will also cut or fillet your fish to your specifications.

THE CHICKEN OR POULTRY SPECIALIST – *POELIER*

While most supermarkets and butcher shops and some stalls at open markets carry whole chicken, chicken parts and eggs, there are some shops that specialize in all kinds of poultry and eggs and, in the late autumn and winter months, game birds and game. The signs outside their establishments either read *kip specialist* or *poelier – wild en gevogelte* (venison and fowl). Most of these shops have a selection of chicken and turkey parts, rolled roasts, ground

CONVERSIONS

LENGTH

AMERICAN	METRIC
0.03937 in	1 millimeter [mm]
0.3937 in	1 centimeter [cm]
39.37 in / 1094 yard	1 meter [m]
0.621 mi / 3281.5 ft	1 kilometer [km]

AMERICAN	METRIC
1 inch	2.54 cm
1 foot	0.3048 m
1 yard	0.9144 m
1 mile	1609 m

DRY MEASURES

AMERICAN/BRITISH	METRIC
1 ounce	30 grams
1/2 pound	225 grams
1 pound	450 grams
2.2 pounds	1 kilogram

AMERICAN	DUTCH
31/2 ounces	1 ons = 100 grams
1.1 pounds	5 ons = 500 gram= 1 pond
2.2 pounds	10 ons = 2 pond= 1 kg
1/2 cup + 1T	1 kopje
1T	1 eetlepel [el] = 15 gram
1/2 t	1 theelepel [tl] = een lepeltje

LIQUID MEASURES

AMERICAN	DUTCH
1 quart + 3T	1 liter
3T + 1t	1/2 deciliter [dl]
6T +1t	1 deciliter = 1/10 liter
1/2c + 2t	2 deciliter
3/4c + 2t	21/2 deciliter
11/3 c	3 deciliter

TEMPERATURE

Fahrenheit to Celcius
• Substract 32 and multiply by 5, then divide by 9
• Example: 68°F: 68-32=36, 36x5=180, 180/9=20°C

Celcius to Fahrenheit
• Multiply by 9, divide by 5 and add 32
• Example: 20°C: 20x9=180, 180/5=36, 36+32=68°F

OVEN TEMPERATURES

FAHRENHEIT	CELSIUS
300	150
325	165
350	180
375	190
400	205
425	220
450	230
475	245
500	260

chicken and turkey, and prepared foods such as chicken saté and grilled chicken, as well as (prepared) rice and vegetable dishes.

GREENGROCERY – *GROENTEBOER*

Dutch farmers provide this country with a stunning variety of fruits and vegetables. There is a large concentration of apple, pear and cherry orchards in the Betuwe region while vegetable gardens and greenhouses dot the landscape. To supplement these locally-grown products, fruits and vegetables are imported from as far as China.

Vegetables play a central role in the Dutch meal, so you can expect them to be fresh and tasty. Supermarkets all have a fruit and vegetable department but for the best selection and personal service, you might want to try the independent greengrocer known as *groenteboer* and his/her shop, called the *groentewinkel*. Many greengrocers offer prepared *rauwkost* (cut fruits or salad material ready for mixed salads), soups, stews and casseroles. In the late autumn and winter months they sell packets of pre-cut vegetables for the famous Dutch pea soup and *stamppot* dishes.

THE BUTCHER'S – *SLAGER*

Dutch farmers produce very fine beef, pork, lamb, veal and poultry. However, if you have been raised on succulent marbled steaks and roasts carved from grain-fed beef cattle, the local beef may be disappointing; it is lean – but it does have a fuller flavor than its grain-fed cousins. Thus, a good butcher is invaluable. You will find him behind the butcher counter in butcher shops and supermarkets. He is called a *slager* and his business is called a *slagerij*. Visit him on a quiet day and he will usually be willing to give advice on how to cook the Dutch meats. Notice the singular way he trims and presents his meats. Almost all fat and bones are removed from the beef and if you want the bones for soups and stews, you will have to pay extra.

A good, innovative butcher prepares the meats for barbecues, fondues and snacks and sells prepared salads and sauces as accompaniments. He might also have some delicatessen dishes such as quiches and savory meat pies. He most certainly offers some delicious locally-made sausages and cold cuts from all across Europe.

CHILDREN'S FOODS

Everything is in place for raising healthy babies in the Netherlands. Supermarkets, drug stores (*drogisterijen*) and pharmacies (*apotheken*) all carry baby foods in jars, vitamins and infant formulas. For weekend emergencies, at least one designated pharmacy stays open in each area on Saturdays, Sundays and evenings. The name of the appointed pharmacy is displayed on all other pharmacy doors. Your *huisarts* or the doctor at the *consultatiebureau* (Well-Baby Clinic) can also recommend foods for your baby and will refer you to a specialist if required.

HEALTH AND VEGETARIAN FOODS

The Dutch are very aware of the benefits of eating well and there are health food departments in every supermarket. There are also health food stores (*reformhuizen* or *reformwinkels*) in most cities. Theirs are natural products with no chemicals added and are made from organically grown or *biologische* materials. Many greengrocers also have prepared vegetarian foods and organically-grown or eco foods.

QUANTITIES TO BUY:

Food sold in bulk is advertised by the piece (per stuk) or by weight:
kilo = 1,000 grams = 2.2 pounds
pond = 500 grams = 1.1 pounds
ons = 100 grams = approx. 3.5 ounces

HOUSEHOLD HELP

Quite a few Dutch households make use of a household help/cleaning lady, most often referred to as *hulp in het huishouden* – literally 'household help' – or a *werkster*. Cleaning ladies are very hard to find and there are a few ways in which you can go about this: you can hang a little card on the notice board of your local supermarket or you can place an ad in the local newspaper. Most newspapers have an item called *Kleintjes*, which means 'little ones' that has been specifically created for short notices and ads. The card or ad should state: *hulp in het huishouden gezocht* and you might want to add the fact that it would be helpful if (he or) she spoke English – or some other common language. A third, and probably best, way to find household help is through friends, neighbors and other acquaintances, as this way you are more likely to find a reliable, dependable and honest one.

In all honesty, most (if not all) cleaning ladies 'work black' (*zwart werken*), meaning that no taxes or social insurance contributions are withheld on their wages. They are simply paid a per-hour price at the end of the day. This per-hour price is usually around € 8-12, plus sometimes their public transportation fare. Granted, this is not legal, but everyone does it and everyone knows it. On the other hand, in the bigger cities, regular cleaning companies (that earn their keep cleaning offices after-hours) offer an on-the-side service of *witte werksters*. This is not a race-inspired statement, but, rather, a tax statement: contrary to *werksters* who work 'black', they work 'white': taxes and social insurance contributions are withheld on their wages. Their hourly rate is consequently a bit higher. To find one of these companies, you can check the Yellow Pages under *Schoonmaakbedrijven*, and see if one of them offers *Huishoudelijk werk*. Or else just select one of the bigger looking companies and call and ask. Beware of the fact that they may have long waiting lists!

HIRING OUT YOUR HOUSEKEEPING

In today's world of fast movers and double-income couples, the home has become little more than a place to eat, sleep and entertain. The problem with this, however, is that food needs to be bought, clothes need to be washed and ironed, beds need to be cleaned, living rooms need to be decorated and menus need to be composed. Where does the current fast mover find the time to do that? They don't. And this has become a lucrative niche in the market for those who are willing to offer their home-making services, or, if you will, expertise. Currently, you can sit around the table with experts who can tell you exactly what someone like you should have in the living room to keep up with the Joneses – or to make your living room the envy of the Joneses. You can meet once a week with someone who will run through the menus of the week, including Thursday evening when your new colleague is coming to dinner with his wife – and to, of course, do the shopping. There are organizations who offer to come and inspect you kitchen, oil the necessary hinges, and make a report of what you should do to your kitchen to 'avoid unnecessary costs' in the future. You can hire someone to do your laundry, take your car to the garage for its annual tune-up, wait for the repair man to fix your dryer, let out your dog, stock your liquor cabinet, install your computer, take your kids to school, pick them up, select your vacation destination, make the bookings, etc. etc. etc. Currently, certain apartment complexes are offering this type of in-house services, such as the Montevideo and De Hoge Heren-complexes in Rotterdam. Other services available are offered by supermarkets themselves, who allow you to phone, or e-mail, in your needs and who deliver them at your door (try www.phicoop.nl or www.albert.nl). Furthermore, there is www.watnu.nl (meaning: Now What?), a website dedicated to helping you find someone if your dishwasher has broken down or your central heating is on the blink – but also if you lost your credit card, need a taxi or are looking for a doctor on night duty. And, of course, there are also employers who offer in-house dry-cleaning, a shopping service, shoe shiners, shirt ironers, hairdressers / barbers and more.

In short, if Mohammed can't come to the mountain, the mountain will come to him. If you don't have time to go to the stores, then the stores will come to you. And if you don't have the time to do your daily household chores, then ask around, surf around or check the Yellow Pages and you will probably find an organization that will gladly supply you with the necessary 'experts'.

A list of online 'grocery stores' can be found on standaard-pagina.nl/boodschappen.htm (no www) or www.nedshop.nl/levensmiddelen.html.

SAFETY

The Netherlands is a safe country to live in. Your children can safely ride their bikes to school (the impatience of the average Dutch driver presents far more of a threat here) and you can safely go out to dinner – even in the 'big' cities and even after dark. In the smaller towns, life is even safer.

Drug-related crime, murder and other forms of human aggression are at a low level here. But let's remain realistic: they do, of course, take place and you must always keep your eyes and senses (particularly your common sense) open. Do not go walking in deserted (woody) areas after dark. Do not use the cash dispenser, when the only other person around is a nervous, strung out-looking individual. When walking alone, search for well-lit areas. Keep your eye on your child. And no matter where you are, do not leave your mobile phone, computer or other obvious valuables behind in the car, where everyone can see them.

BEING IN THE BIG CITIES

It goes without saying that, as in any big city, you should keep your eye on your purse, bags, cameras and whatever else you might have on you. And that you should not wander alone into a dark alley-way. And that if you do not like the looks of certain characters hanging around the street you want to go into, you should walk down the next, if you can. And it also goes without saying that it is always better to have the look of a worldly-wise, undaunted cosmopolitan – rather than a frightened, hunted deer. It is human nature for con artists, thieves and other unpleasant folk to zero in on a person asking to be a victim. But that goes for Atlanta, Santiago, Seville and Singapore too.

A MYTH OR TWO

Now that we are talking about the big cities, this is a good opportunity to deal with a myth or two about the Netherlands. Yes, the government hands out drugs – for free – to so-called 'incurable' drug addicts. As you might know, the Dutch are big on helping the underdog, and assistance is given to drug addicts to promote their rehabilitation, to improve their physical and mental condition and to improve their social circumstances. However, when 'free' drugs are handed out, this is not so much to make life easier for the drug users, but rather to decrease crime in the streets. Instead of having desperate junkies roaming the streets, looking for someone to mug, the government has chosen to hand out drugs, which they do in fixed places in the big cities – away from the crowds, where the addicts know where to find them.

And yes, there are areas in the cities where prostitution is condoned. One of these areas, the so-called red-light district in Amsterdam, is famous for it. It might interest you to know that this can be considered one of the safest areas of Amsterdam: it is always well-lit, well-patrolled by the police and never deserted, as the prostitution industry is one that works 24 hours a day – particularly at night, of course. However, should you wish to visit the area, a day-time visit may be a better idea as this will reduce the risk of being targeted by the nevertheless ever-present pick-pockets or questionable characters with dubious intentions. If there is ever any problem, you can rest assured that there is nothing the police hasn't seen or dealt with – so don't hesitate to enlist their help.

REPORTING A CRIME

Should you become a victim of crime, locate the nearest police officer or police station to report it. The police will take your statement, and provide advice on canceling credit cards with helpful phone numbers and addresses. Be sure to give a description of the culprit and the location. In the Netherlands good citizens turn in found wallets or purses to the police. Thieves remove the cash, bank cards and credit cards and toss the rest.

Confirm the loss or theft in writing to your insurance company including a copy of the police report. It is always a good idea to have copies of your travel documents and/or important papers in case something unfortunate does happen.

LOCK YOUR DOOR

Streets are generally well-lit in the cities and towns in the Netherlands, so that you can safely let out your dog in the evening, run to the supermarket or walk to your friends' house a couple of streets away. When you leave the house, however, it is always best to lock the door, particularly if you live in a reasonably well-to-do neighborhood. There is always the chance that there is a certain individual out there, waiting for you to leave the house.

Make sure you have good locks on doors and windows. Double locks on doors, or dead bolts, can offer additional protection. A *dievenklauw* is a special lock that prevents entry. A locksmith can install these for you, or you can purchase locks yourself at a hardware or do-it-yourself store.

A SAFE HOME

Although it is customary for the Dutch to leave their curtains open so that you can see into their homes, it is generally not a good idea to show off too many possessions. Having expensive television, stereo and computer equipment out in full view might prove to be too tempting. Likewise leaving a pocketbook or wallet on the table, or jewelry you have removed from your person could pique the interest of a potential thief.

There are security systems companies (*beveiligingsbedrijven*) with security specialists who can install security systems for you. They can help you with alarm systems, video cameras, security fences, electronic eyes, movement detectors, security lighting, etc. In order to ascertain that you are dealing with a reputable agency for your security needs, look for the BORG *Certificaat* registration. Not only does this guarantee the reliability of their personnel and the quality of the work, it also is recognized by insurance companies, so that you may be entitled to discounts on your personal property and home owners' insurance (*inboedel* and *opstal verzekering*). The National *Centrum voor Preventie* publishes a list on their website. See www. ncpreventie.nl under NCP *erkende bedrijven* for a listing of those security companies who have this accreditation. Always ask if a company has this certification before doing business with them.

If you would prefer not to leave behind an empty house, but can't find anyone who'd be willing to watch over it for while, you could always try to find someone via a house-sitter organization. One such organization is the *Landelijke Oppas Centrale* (National House-Sitting Center), which you can find on www.holidaylink. com). House-sitters will even take care of your pets, if you want.

SECURITY SITUATION

Most local police departments have a program called *Veilig Wonen* and will send an expert to your house to do a thorough check of your current security situation. This service is free of charge as the intention is of course to prevent burglaries. The police expert will provide you with suggestions for improving your security measures.

If you are leaving for an extended period of time, you can let the police know that the house will be vacant and who has a key and access to the house.

FIRE PROTECTION

All homes should have smoke alarms, and they are easily installed. If you are renting, ask your landlord to do it. If he is unwilling, do it yourself. Smoke alarms can be bought at Do-It-Yourself/hardware stores such as Gamma, Karwei, Hubo, but also department stores. Small fire extinguishers can also be purchased at Do It Yourself/hardware stores, while fire blankets for kitchens and powder extinguishers are also avail-able.

OCCUPANT IDENTIFICATION CARD

Special red, white and blue identification cards should be filled in listing the names of all of the occupants of the house (including pets). In Dutch, these are called Meterkast *Identificatie Kaart*. This ID-card is then hung in your meter closet (*meterkast*) in the hallway. In the event of an emergency, or a fire, the police and fire department will first look here for any information on the inhabitants of the house. Cards are available at your local police bureau.

EMERGENCY!

Should you have an emergency and need the police, the fire department or an ambulance, the national number for all services in Holland is: **1-1-2**.

You should have a **1-1-2** sticker on your phone, and let all family members know this is the number to call if a serious emergency arises. The operator will send the services you need, or all three if required.

If there is a problem that does not constitute an emergency, 0900 8844 will connect you to your local police.

RECYCLING AND WASTE MANAGEMENT

In general the Netherlands is considered to be a very 'green' country; not just for its wide-open fields, but also for the mentality of the Dutch in protecting their environment. The vast majority of the population takes part in various recycling efforts. From the organic waste, which is collected separately, compost is made which is then reused in gardens and agriculture. Of the more than two million tons of paper collected, close to 90% is recycled and used for new products. More than 89% of all glass is recycled. There are many organizations working to maintain the welfare of the people and monitor issues such as living space, respect for nature, space and raw materials.

The Dutch Environmental Ministry VROM (Ministerie van Volkshuisvesting Ruimtelijk Ordening en Milieubeheer) works in close cooperation with international and domestic partners on improving the living environment of this country. Over 4,000 people are concerned with issues of living space, housing and environment. An additional task is to plan, conduct and supervise the building of projects in government housing, and to develop a sustainable environmental policy. There are numerous programs and activities for getting involved in helping to preserve and improve the environment.

To foreigners coming to live in the Netherlands, the rules and regulations may seem to be bewildering in their detail, so here is a basic guideline to the most common recycling practices.

1. *Recycling tax:* upon purchasing new electronic and household equipment, you will automatically be charged a recycling tax or removal tax known as *verwijderingsbijdrage*, regardless of whether you are handing in an old appliance or not. The assumption is that, for each new appliance purchased, the old one will have to be environmentally disposed of or recycled at some point in time. A list of tariffs is available from the store.

2. *Household waste:* outside of Amsterdam, households are usually furnished with two separate waste containers (green *groenbak* for garden, fruit and vegetable waste and gray *grijs container* for all remaining waste). These containers are emptied on alternating weeks. Pay attention – if you place the wrong container at the curbside it will not be emptied. In some cities the city provides a multi-purpose waste container, a so-called *duobak*. This is one container with a separation inside. The smaller part in the back is intended for 'green' waste, the larger part in the front for all other waste. If you feel the container(s) provided is/are not sufficient, you can always contact the city council for an additional one. This will entail an additional yearly contribution, as the additional waste also needs to be disposed of. Make sure you do not leave your containers on the street at the end of the day. You can be fined for not returning them to your home. There are also towns where glass and paper are also collected curbside, usually in wealthier suburban areas. Most households make use of regular garbage bags, too. These are picked up every week.

3. *Groenbak:* cat litter and used baby diapers are not considered organic waste for the *groenbak* and should be placed in the gray container. Milk packages, plastic bags, large pieces of wood and thick tree branches, the ashes from your fireplace, sand, dog and cat hair and the contents of your vacuum cleaner are also NOT to be placed in the green container. 'Green waste' is vegetable, fruit, and potato peels, leftover cooked food, fish and meat leftovers with bones (wrapped in newspaper in the summer months) nut shells and eggshells, hardened cooking fat, tea bags, coffee filters with coffee grains, small garden trimmings, mowed grass and leaves, weeds, flowers and houseplants, straw and *mest* from small animals such as hamsters and rabbits.

In some cities, due to the lack of space, there unfortunately is no separation of waste, other than what a private individual brings to the separate waste disposal stations and/or containers. Most towns publish a calendar, distributed around November (regarding the following year) to each household, of contact addresses for properly disposing of all types of wastes, as well as pick-up dates and locations for *chemokars* (chemical cars – see further on, under chemical waste). If you don't have one, you can request one from your *gemeentereinigingsdienst* (sanitation department).

4. *Refunds on bottles:* most glass soft drink bottles, the large acrylic plastic *euroflessen* and some small glass bottles or jars have a deposit that is paid upon buying them. The word *statie-geld* (deposit) and an amount will be listed on the label. Once you return these to the store for recycling (there are special bottle stations for these at most supermarkets), the deposit is returned to you by way of a *bonnetje* or paper receipt after you have placed the bottles into the bottle return machine. This receipt can be redeemed when you pay for your groceries or at the *klantenservice* (customer service).

5. *Glass:* all glass that does not have a deposit can be dropped in special containers which are usually placed at convenient locations throughout the town (such as in the supermarket parking area). There is often a symbol on the label showing a hand with a bottle and the word *glasbak*. These 'glass collectors' (*glasbakken*) are often, but not always, yellow. Some cities allow for the separation of white, green and brown glass. The containers will stipulate *bont* (white), *groen* (green), or *bruin* (brown). Since this effort was started, the Dutch have come to recycle more than 89% of their glass.

6. *Paper:* often placed near to the glass recycling containers you will find the blue paper collectors (*papierbakken*). Again, most of the paper in the Netherlands is recycled. You may recycle newspapers, magazines, junk mail, envelopes, paper packaging, and wrappers. No plastic please.

7. *Batteries:* most supermarkets and some stores and schools have special containers for collecting old batteries. Often these are located by the bottle recycling station at the grocery store or at the checkout counter of stores; the *batterijenbak* is usually red or blue. If none are available close by, you can ask at the supermarket or inquire with the city council on the nearest collection points (batteries can also be handed in with other chemical waste – see next point).

8. *Chemical waste* (paint and painting materials, toners, printer cartridges, oil, turpentine, nail polish and caustic cleaning agents, etc.): many cities have a special car (*chemokar*) that comes by every three months to collect chemical waste. You can check with the city council on collection dates and times or request the calendar listing all relevant contact information for the year. Alternatively, you can dispose of these materials, as other large pieces of rubbish (construction waste, car tires, etc.), with the waste separation and recycling station that is available in nearly every city and town.

9. *Medicines:* outdated prescriptions and any overdue non-prescription medicine can be handed in at most pharmacies for proper disposal. Pills, cough syrup, suppositories, antibiotic crèmes, etc. should all be disposed of via the pharmacy.

10. *Clothing:* some cities and towns have a large container for clothes and shoes, generally placed by local organizations, and most often located close to a shopping area. During the year there are often also special initiatives by schools or churches to collect clothes for specific charities. Apart from the Salvation Army (*Leger des Heils*) you can contact the following toll free

number to get information on addresses to hand in clothes: Stichting Kleding Inzameling Charitatieve Instellingen (KICI), tel.: 0800 022 80 90 or www. kici.nl.

11. *Large waste (grof vuil):* any furniture (if not recycled through second hand shops) and large household debris can be collected by special appointment through the city's waste collection department. Within certain volume limitations, this waste will be collected free of charge, but it has to comply with certain regulations, e.g. wooden parts have to be gathered and tied with rope. Anything outside city regulations is best brought to the municipal waste separation and recycling station (*Afvalscheidingsstation*) or, alternatively, one could order a private container to collect and dispose of all waste. This *puinbak* waste container (generally used during construction for large amounts of debris) can be ordered for a fee covering the delivery and removal. Contact your town hall and ask for *gemeentereiniging grof vuil.*

12. *Afvalscheidingsstation (waste separation and recycling station):* anything that is too large or specific (e.g. chemical waste) to be put in your regular waste container can be taken to a waste disposal station. For private individuals the rules here are pretty lax, as opposed to business disposal of waste, which usually comes at a price. You will usually be questioned upon entering the station as to what kind of waste you want to discard and will be directed to the right locations. There are, for instance, separate containers for wood, cardboard, tires, stones and construction rubbish and chemical waste.
It bears to be kept in mind that any soil and earth removed when redoing a garden is generally not accepted unless a special government inspection (at a price) has taken place to ensure that it is not polluted by contaminants such as oil, lead or chemicals.

13. *Computers, printers and scanners:* if you need to dispose of ICT equipment in working order you can contact ICT Netherlands, tel.: 0348 493 636, and ask about *grijsgoed* (gray goods) recycling. Another option is to donate your old computer equipment to Stichting Computer Bemiddeling Onderwijs, www. scbo.nl, where it will be used for educational purposes in schools. Another benefit: your contribution is tax deductible.

If you wish to become involved in a local environmental group you may check with your *gemeente*. There are 'eco-teams' in many neighborhoods who work to increase awareness of the necessity to recycle and to protect our milieu or environment. Some local projects are carried out.
For additional information on environmental policy and recycling contact VROM, the Ministry of Spatial Planning, Housing and En vironment (*Mininsterie van Volkshuisvesting, Ruimtelijk Ordening en Miliuebeheer* – www.vrom.nl).

PETS

DOG TAX
If you have been living in the Netherlands for a while, you have undoubtedly taken a slip over *hondenpoep* – dog poop. Rather

than enjoying the beautiful architecture of the Dutch cities, you find yourself staring at the sidewalks, navigating your way around the deposits of our furry friends. How can it be that this nation of clean, hygienic, well-educated people can live with sidewalks pockmarked with *hondenpoep*? If we had an answer, we'd tell you. There is, however, an ongoing campaign to have dog owners train their dogs to leave their mess in the gutters (watch out when stepping out of the car!) and, as you can read elsewhere in this book, dog owners pay taxes for their hounds. This tax used to be a 'corporate' tax, but is now levied on private dog owners, the proceeds of which are used to create areas within the cities and towns that can be considered public dog toilets. This is the only pet-related tax there is, so maybe there is some justice after all.

FAVORITE PETS
Furthermore, there is a whole array of other favorite pets: cats, canaries, parrots and fish, for instance. And for children; rabbits, guinea pigs and hamsters are very popular. In some gardens, you will find the occasional goat, miniature pony or pot-bellied swine and in some children's bedrooms; rats, snakes, spiders, turtles and the occasional bat.

PET CARE

Pets have a position in Dutch households that is very similar to that of the children. Some are served the best cut of the rarest beef, others are given the best chair, with the best view of the TV – and, naturally, access to the accompanying snacks. And the care provided is top-notch: the veterinary services (a vet is called a *dierenarts*) are excellent in the Netherlands, while there are animal hospitals, ambulances and even crematoriums. There are also dog-walking services (*honden uitlaat service*) for those who can't imagine life without Whoofy, but unfortunately have to spend the whole day in the office – an hour's drive away. The pet stores in the Netherlands offer a wonderful array of toys, cushions, cages, leashes, snacks, top-of-the-line food and... pets, of course.

FINDING A PET

If you want to buy a dog, however, it is always better to do this via a recognized breeder rather than through a pet store. Breeders can be found through the Raad van Beheer op Kynologische Gebied in Nederland, the phone number of which you will find at the end of the chapter. For any other type of animal (other than the household rodent type – for which the pet store (or the petting farm, called *kinderboerderij*, will do fine) – you can best ask the local vet where you can find one. If you are looking to save an unwanted cat or dog, there are kennels, called *dierenasiel*, where 'lost and found' or otherwise homeless animals are brought. These kennels are very well-run and most of the time have a good profile of the animals they are trying to place (often, they have to find a new home for the pets of families who have to go abroad, or one of whom is allergic to animals) and find it greatly rewarding to have found such a loving pet a new home.

RELOCATING YOUR PET

The family pet has relocation needs as well. Each year more than 750,000 animals are transported around the world. For admittance to the Netherlands, cats and dogs must have a health certificate in Dutch, English, French or German legalized by the Veterinary Service in the country of origin, stating a complete description of the animal (genus, age, breed, color, hair, marks), the name of the owner, and that a complete vaccination against rabies has taken place with the date, type of vaccine used, expiry date, batch number and manufacturer, which has taken place at least 30 days and not more than 3 months before entry into the Netherlands. Animals must be de-wormed and checked for ticks. Some countries have quarantine regulations. It is best to check with the Dutch Consulate well in advance what the requirements are so that you can make sure you meet them (see the website at the end of the chapter).

NEW RULES

As of July 3, 2004, there are new rules on the transportation of dogs, cats and ferrets (yes, ferrets...) in Europe; they must have a European-style passport, been given a rabies-vaccination and have identification (a chip). Rabbits, small rodents, birds, fish, amphibians and reptiles usually only need a declaration of health issued by a vet. For more information, visit the bilingual website of the KNMVD (Koninklijke Nederlandse Maatschappij voor Diergeneeskunde, or Royal Netherlands Veterinary Association) at www.knmvd.nl.

EXPERT ADVICE ON ANIMAL TRANSFER

A professional organization such as KLM Cargo, specialists in animal transfer, can inform you of all regulations, provide you with helpful travel tips for your pet and arrange suitable transport of your animal. Whether a house pet or a horse, they have the expertise to comfortably transport your animal. They also operate a 24 hour-a-day animal hotel at the Schiphol airport (their website and phone number can be found at the end of the chapter).

IDENTIFICATION AND REGISTRATION

In order to make identification and registration of pets easily accessible in case of loss or theft, identification microchips may be easily implanted by a veterinarian. Close to 5 million animals have already been registered in the system. Many animals travel with their owners and some get lost or separated from them. The site makes it possible to find information about the databank(s) where the lost animal is registered. See the paragraph on *New Rules*, regarding traveling with your pets.

ANIMAL BOARDING

Though you love your animals and have brought them all the way here, traveling back and forth may not be something you wish to subject them to on too regular a basis. Should you be leaving the country on vacation (or for work) you might wish them the same comfort and care that you hope to enjoy during your trip. Look in the Yellow Pages under *dierenpension* to find a list of 'animal hotels' (a *hondenpension* is specifically for dogs, a *kattenpension*

for cats). There is no surefire way to find out whether you can expect your family pet to be happy there – the best you can do is visit the place itself to discuss your (animal's) needs, check out the conditions and see whether you have a good feeling about the place and the owner in general. Maybe a trial run over a weekend will give you some peace of mind.

GARDENS AND CURTAINS

Ask the Belgians what they find typical of the homes of their Northern Neighbors and they will mention two things. One is their gardens, and the other is their curtains. In Belgium, family life is for the family: there are virtually no front yards (the garden is in the back) and huge, no-nonsense blinds go down as soon as the first lights go on inside the house.

Not so the Dutch. The Dutch are very proud of their gardens, be they postage stamp-size or park-size (particularly their front yards, as these are what everyone sees). They love a cozy (*gezellig*) neighborhood with flowers, flowering bushes, little rock gardens and – yes – the occasional garden gnome or even windmill. It is not without reason that Dutch flower bulbs are exported all across the world and that the hub of the world's flower industry is near Schiphol airport: the Netherlands is where the flowering heart of the world beats.

The neighborhoods in the Netherlands can look very prim and proper: there are special rules about not building too many differ-

ent types of houses in one street (this is of course different in the very expensive areas, where the houses are so far apart (if they are even visible) that no one really cares). So what you get is a row of well-kept, dime-a-dozen houses, with picture-perfect front yards and... uncurtained windows.

If you take an evening stroll after sunset, you get a chance to admire family life, Dutch style. Grandma and Grandpa are sitting behind a steaming cup of coffee, savoring their evening ration of one cookie. Or Mom and Pop are reading a magazine, with one of their teenage children surreptitiously eyeing the TV over his homework. Or the living room is empty and upstairs you see Mom dressing baby on the dressing table, while Pop is chasing their three-year-old from room to room. Later in the evening, Mom and Dad will settle down to their well-deserved cup of coffee – still to be admired through open curtains. Only once they go to bed, will the curtains downstairs be closed. For those of you who were wondering: bedroom curtains are always closed once the lights go on.

The Dutch do not feel self-conscious about what goes on behind their front door and feel comfortable with their curtains open. The rule of Dutch behavior is *doe maar gewoon, dan doe je gek genoeg* – act normal and you will be acting crazy enough. What this boils down to, basically, is modesty. Act modest, live modestly: do not buy expensive cars, do not have any airs, decorate your home simply, and don't do anything I wouldn't do. If you close your curtains, you probably have something to hide. And this is why many Dutch families leave their curtains open so that everyone can see for themselves: look, we are acting 'normal'.

THE MEDIA

THE PRINTED MEDIA

In the Netherlands, 11 independent companies publish 32 daily newspapers – 9 nation-wide and 23 regional – each with its own editorial staff and amounting to a daily total of 4 million. The five major newspapers in the Netherlands are *De Telegraaf* (circulation 782,000), *De Volkskrant* (329,000), the *Algemeen Dagblad* (303,000), *NRC Handelsblad* (269,000), and *Trouw* (122,000). Popular among those who are active in the business world is the *Financieele Dagblad* (56,000), which has economic news and stock market analyses – and an English-language section. These numbers do not include online subscriptions (you can find the websites at the end of the chapter). 75 households in 100 receive a daily newspaper; of the 4.15 million newspapers distributed per day (46% national, 54% regional newspapers), 90% goes to subscribers – giving the Netherlands the highest percentage of subscribers in the world. (Incidentally, approximately 25% of the subscribers share their newspaper – for instance, with their neighbors.) Over 2004, newspaper sales went down by 3.2% – to counter this, *De Telegraaf* came up with a special Sunday edition and the *Algemeen Dagblad* started to publish a special sports section. Both measures were successful in countering the threatening loss of sales.

Interesting news is that a number of regional newspapers (such as for Rotterdam, Utrecht, Dordrecht, The Hague, Amersfoort and Gouda) and the *Algemeen Dagblad* – published by either PCM or Wegenaar – might be merged into one, aimed at the provinces of South Holland and Utrecht and attaining an initial circulation of approximately 630,000. Whether, where and under what name this will take place will be announced sometime in 2005.

As mentioned above, there are also many regional newspapers, which can provide you with important information on what's going on in your region. If you want to know what is going on in your town, you can also take out a subscription to the local town paper. The Netherlands also has many magazines; for art lovers, computer fanatics, travelers, feminists, men, children, animal lovers, garden lovers and just about any other type of hobby. Do not despair, however, that you will have to wait until you speak Dutch before you can read about what is going on in the world, as sometimes even in the smallest towns you will find such magazines as *Newsweek, Time Magazine, The Economist, The Financial Times* as well as the newspapers *El País, The International Herald Tribune, USA Today* and more (such as German, Italian, Turkish, French magazines and newspapers, to name but a few). See http://kranten. pagina.nl for all newspapers online.

TELEVISION AND RADIO

Dutch television will also not present much of a problem as it is subtitled, leaving all foreign movies, series and other programs in their original language. The Netherlands has a plethora of television channels to choose from available through cable (often more than 30 channels) including British, Belgian, French, Spanish, German, Italian and Turkish television as well as CNN (news) and MTV (music) – but keep in mind that the cable package available depends on the area where you live.

The main Dutch broadcasting companies are: TROS (general) VARA (social-democratic), AVRO (general), NCRV (Protestant), KRO (Catholic), VPRO (progressive), BNN (general, young audience) and EO (evangelical Christian) who all work together in the NOS (Netherlands Broadcasting Corporation). The fact that these companies have a certain denomination does not mean that you will watch solely Catholic programs on the KRO, or social-democratic programs on the VARA: these denominations are to be considered from where the broadcasting company originated and dictate only a certain percentage of the types of program you will see (with the exception of the EO, whose character is most clearly noticeable in the type of programs it broadcasts). These eight broadcasting companies share broadcasting time on Nederland 1, 2 and 3, but there are more Dutch channels, such as Yorin, RTL 4, RTL 5, Net 5, SBS 6, and Veronica who mainly broadcast popular (often US-purchased) programs. For more viewing pleasure there is Discovery Channel, National Geographic, Animal Planet, MTV, TMF, The Box, TCM, CNN and EuroSport, as well as German, Belgian and British channels. Children's programming is available daily from 7 A.M. on several of the Dutch channels as well as on Nickelodeon, Ketnet/Canvas (Belgium) and on BBC 2. (For an overview of what's on, go to www.tvgids. nl). If thirty channels is not enough, or you cannot be connected to the cable lines because you bought a farm house way out in the middle of nowhere, then, of course, you can solve this problem by purchasing a satellite dish.

Furthermore, the Netherlands has five national radio stations and several regional ones, but the fun thing is, of course, that certainly when it comes to radio, you can listen to broadcasts from just about anywhere in the world. For an overview of program scheduling for over 180 European channels updated daily see: www. eurotv.com.

KIJKWIJZER

The NICAM or Netherlands Institute for the Classification of Audiovisual Media has developed the *kijkwijzer* (whose principle is *weet wat je ziet* or know what you see), a system using pictograms to rate the contents of films, videos, dvds, television programs and computer games. The picture symbols indicate violence, sex, fear, discrimination, drug and alcohol misuse, and rough language. Also shown are age limit recommendations of AL (all ages), MG6 (watch with children under 6), 12 (not younger) and 16 (not younger). Any media items with a 16 year-advice should not be rented to or sold to minors under 16, and movie theaters may refuse entrance to teenagers. For more information, visit www.kijkwijzer.nl and view the icons or pictograms.

BEING CONNECTED

STARTING YOUR TELEPHONE SERVICE

Initially, you will need to dial 0900 0244 (KPN Telecom's customer service) for more information – as the rules regarding starting a telephone service as a foreigner change regularly. You will hear a recording in Dutch, at the end of which you can dial a 1 (for private use), then 1 (for requesting a new line) and then 1 again (also for requesting a new line). This will connect you with an operator, who can help you in English, French or German. If there is no one immediately available, you will hear a recorded message asking you for *een ogenblik geduld, alstublieft* (one moment, please).

Here they will tell you that, if you are a non-Dutch national, you will need to go to a *Primafoon-winkel*, the official KPN Telecom (the Dutch telecom company) store, which you will find in the cities or the bigger towns (check your telephone book for their address). The employees in the *Primafoon* store should have sufficient command of the English language to help you. You will need to bring valid proof of identification (a passport), as well as approximately € 45 to pay a 'connection fee'. This amount will subsequently be deducted from your first phone bill.

To arrange payment of your bills, you can either sign a *machtiging* (see page 104, under *Bank Transfers*) or make use of an *acceptgirokaart* (again, see page 104).

SUBSCRIPTION

In the Netherlands, you are not only charged per telephone conversation (depending on the length of the call), but you also have to pay a 'subscription', the amount of which you will find on your bi-monthly telephone bill. If you also want ISDN, then the amount of the subscription will be higher. You will have to 'subscribe' for a minimum period of one year, even if you only want to subscribe for a shorter period of time.

CHEAPER RATES

Although efforts have been made to introduce competition in this market, KPN Telecom is still the main company providing fixed phone lines in the Netherlands. However, it no longer has a monopoly on the telephone lines; other companies have bought up the rights to a certain number of the KPN lines and offer cheaper rates (also when phoning abroad) if you make use of their lines. However, keep in mind that you will still have to pay a subscription to KPN and receive a bi-monthly bill for that. The good

news is that the existence of these companies has forced KPN to reduce their rates. You might want to compare the rates, before choosing to register with one of these companies. For more information, check out the Yellow Pages, under *Telecommunicatie-diensten* or *Telefoon-, Telex- en Faxservice.* You may see advertising for One.Tel, BudgetPhone, Tele2, NetSource, Ocean, Scarlet, Vocalis, Primus as well as cable based providers such as Essent-Kabelcom and UPC. For a complete overview of discount providers, also for mobile, see: www.spraakmakertele.com.

IP, WIFI, CABLE AND SKYPE

IP (Internet Protocol)-telephony is the making of a phone call over the Internet. Whereas on a regular phone line, the line is open and reserved entirely for this particular conversation, when talking over the Internet, this can simultaneously be transferred with other data, such as text, pictures, video and more.

In some places, it is already possible to make phone calls over the wireless WiFi-net, while retaining your own number and telephone. This way you can call anywhere in the Netherlands at local rates and in the rest of the world at very cheap rates.

Cheaper calling is also available for those making use of cable, see page 174 for more on this.

Relatively new on the telephony market is Skype, a VoIP (Voice over Internet Protocol) program that allows you to make free telephone calls to another Skype-user (also abroad), via your computer – or, for a small fee, to a fixed or mobile telephone (visit www.skype.com for more information or to simply download the software needed).

Privver

Privver is the digital mailbox offered by TPG post. Launched in December 2002, the Privver digital mailbox offers what some call the next generation of important mail delivery. Banks, utilities, KPN telephone, health insurers, petrol stations, cable companies, and a host of other companies will send their bills to your Privver-box (so nothing ever gets lost in the mail!). You receive notice of received mail by e-mail and with one click you can open, look at and pay your bills online. You determine which mail you wish to receive via Privver. The service is free. The senders pay the costs. For more information see www.privver.nl.

MOBILE TELEPHONES

The Netherlands has the highest number of mobile operators in Europe, and yet a population of just over 16 million. It would appear that this would be an advantage for the consumer, but instead it has become quite confusing due to the numerous special pro-motions and mobile telephone options. 2001 saw the first decrease in 20 years in the demand for mobile phones, a slump that the mobile phone market has still not managed to lift itself out of.

CHOOSING A MOBILE PHONE SERVICE

There are several criteria that are important to consider when choosing a mobile phone service. The time of day or night that you normally make telephone calls, the total number of minutes per month that you use, whether calls are made to fixed telephones or mobile phones, and the need for additional services such as voicemail, SMS messages, calling long distance and using the mobile phone when abroad. Depending on your needs, you will use one of the following two possibilities:

- subscription services with a contract, which includes a certain number of minutes that you can call. You receive a monthly bill (for the subscription and, if you have exceeded your contractual number of minutes, a fee for these minutes). Subscription services will charge an initial connection fee, but there are many special offers available for attracting new customers – so shop around
- a pre-pay service based on buying a card with call units and no subscription fee.

THE PRE-PAY HYPE

This is a popular choice among Dutch users, particularly young people. One reason is that the pre-pay phone allows users to pay for their calls in advance, and so avoid subscription fees and hefty bills. They are cheap, convenient and provide enough coverage for most Dutch users in the Netherlands.

Each pre-pay phone will only be suitable for that particular network, for example, if you buy a T-Mobile phone, you are restricted to using that phone and buying call units for the T-Mobile network. However, this need not stop you from calling overseas and receiving calls from overseas – see further on in *Free to Roam?*

Pre-pay cards are available in denominations of 10, 20, 25, 40, and 50 euros and can be bought at a variety of locations, such as certain supermarkets and drugstores, as well as the phone company-stores. For more on the various arrangements offered by the mobile phone companies, visit their websites, as they are continually subject to change.

BUYING A MOBILE PHONE

If you are buying a (subscription or pre-pay) mobile phone, you can do this at the larger department stores, electronic chains, brand stores or through non-brand telephone stores. It is always worth your while to shop around, as both the brand stores and the non-brand stores may offer certain reductions and other special promotions. Be sure to bring a copy of your passport and proof (such as a bank statement) of your most current address if you are planning on buying a mobile phone with a subscription.

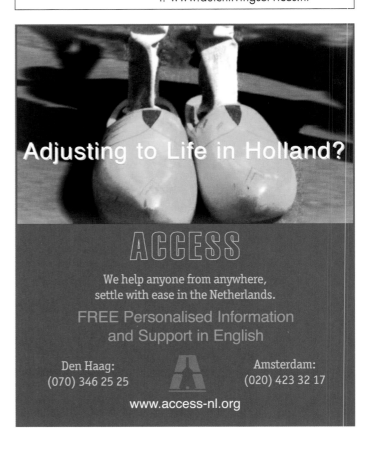

SWITCHING

Once you have chosen a particular mobile phone company for your phone with subscription, you are not stuck for life. You can switch companies and even keep your own phone number. Check with your company to see what the rules are (giving notice and over what period), if you are not yet sure which one to go for. The same goes for pre-pay phones, whereby you can also switch from pre-pay to subscription and vice versa. In most cases, the phone company that you are planning on switching to, arranges the switch. You wait for a message from them that they have completed the switch and they terminate your contract with your former provider.

FREE TO ROAM?

From the expat's perspective, it is perhaps important to be able to make and receive calls in other countries. Through international 'roaming' agreements, cellular operators allow foreign operators to use their networks so that they have broader international coverage. Mobile phone services are available in another region or country if there is a company that has a roaming agreement with the user's GSM network operator. Unsurprisingly, the cost of using a mobile for international and overseas calling is high.

As mentioned earlier, also pre-pay phones nowadays have roaming possibilities, the extension and cost of which depend on the telephone company.

Do keep in mind that not all mobile phones (and networks) are compatible. Other countries (such as the US, Canada and Latin American countries) use other networks, so that you cannot use your Dutch mobile phone there. Some mobile phone companies offer the possibility of placing the SIM card (containing your phone's memory, including your own phone number) of your Dutch mobile phone in a phone that will work in the other country – this can be done at the Rentcenter at Schiphol Airport or Rotterdam Airport (www. rentcenter.nl) or you can visit www. cellhire.com. Do keep in mind that you will have to deposit a considerable guarantee for this and that the phones rates will be steep; if you place a call within the US, you will first be calling back to the Netherlands and from there back again to the US.

SATELLITE MOBILES

There is one other possibility though for traveling telephone users: if your mobile phone provides you with satellite connection you are no longer dependent on GSM Network coverage and can call to and from the entire planet (as well as surf the Internet or send and receive e-mails). However, this is not exactly a cheap option – calling within western Europe can cost up to € 2 per minute, not to mention calling elsewhere in the world.

MOBILE PHONE TECHNOLOGIES

- GPRS (General Packet Radio Service) allows the mobile phone network to function more like the Internet, creating a form of mobile Internetting.
- UMTS – Universal Mobile Telephone Communication System – combines the PC and a GSM phone. It delivers pictures, graphics, video communications and other wide-band information as well as voice and data, directly to people on the move.

- WiFi (Wireless Fidelity) is a type of wireless network that, if you have a WiFi-card in your laptop, allows access to the Internet at great speeds and, on many locations, for free.
- WAP (Wireless Application Protocol) allows you to access information – such as stock market prices, traffic and information, tips for going out and more) – via your mobile phone. Your mobile phone must have WAP-capabilities in order to be able to do this.
- SMS stands for Short Messages Service and allows you to type short messages on the screen of your mobile phone and send them. You can also send SMS-messages and images from your home computer.
- E(mail) Messaging System allowing you to access your e-mail account in order to retrieve and send e-mail through your mobile phone.
- MMS, Multimedia Messaging Services, allows you to send text, sound, animations and in principle also photographs to other mobile phones or e-mail addresses.

As the technology and the offers of the various mobile telephone companies are continuously changing, we recommend that you visit the various mobile phone company websites to see what they have to offer.

MORE TECHNOLOGIES

xda has been put on the market by O2/Telfort and is a pocket pc, mobile phone and organizer in one. It allows mobile e-mailing, mobile working, mobile access to the Internet as well as access to Word-documents – making a separate PDA (Personal Digital Assistant) and mobile telephone unnecessary. It also allows you to listen to MP3 and WMA-music as well as enjoy streaming video and audio.

i-mode offers mobile Internet-like access to special i-mode sites (you can also create your own!) by mobile phone and has been brought on the market by KPN. With it, you can browse, send and receive e-mail and MMS and do mobile banking (even abroad, provided KPN has an international call agreement within this country). Some examples of i-mode site-categories are: news/weather, financial, transportation, sports, shopping, etc.

Live!, introduced by Vodafone, allows, in addition to the i-mode-type services, the possibility of taking pictures with a built-in camera, sending e-mails, and enjoying audio and video services, such as the news and video clips.

MOBILE PHONE USE IN THE CAR

Effective March 30, 2002, the Netherlands has new legislation regarding the use of cell phones in cars. You can read more about this on page 139.

OVERVIEW OF THE MOBILE PHONE OPERATORS

At the moment, there are five mobile networks that cover the entire country:
1. KPN Mobile: which offers Hi and Flexibel
2. Vodafone: which offers Vodafone Izi and Vizzavi
3. Telfort
4. T-Mobile
5. Orange.

Most consumers make use of the service providers of these network operators, however, there is also Debitel, where you can obtain an independent subscription while making use of the networks of either KPN, Vodafone or Telfort. Furthermore, there are Tele2-Mobiel, Hema, qick, AH, Call4Care and Transatel – all less-profiled companies that offer financially attractive pre-pay and/or subscription services.

New are the MVNOs; Mobile Virtual Network Operators, which allow companies to rent a network from a network operator, thereby creating their own – virtual – network.

WEBSITES

In past years, we provided you with an overview of the subscription and prepaid services and packages offered by the various mobile phone operators. However, since these are continually changing and so as not to give you potentially outdated information, we now refer you to their websites, which you will find at the end of the chapter. For more on their possible UMTS, GPRS, MMS-services as well as other options (xda, i-mode, Live!), see the preceding paragraphs as well as the websites.

INTERNET SERVICE PROVIDERS

ISPS IN THE NETHERLANDS

There are more than 100 Internet service providers active on the Dutch market and competition has been intensifying with the entry of the free access providers. These providers do not charge subscription fees for Internet access, so that the user can surf the Internet for the cost of a local phone call. But 'free' is not really completely free because the user still has to pay for the telephone costs. As if the competitive environment was not already fraught with activity, there are also cable companies offering Internet services such as Casema and UPC. Cable Internet services may work out to be more cost-effective because you do not have to pay a telephone charge, you do not have to call in to make a connection, and your telephone line is not blocked (if you still have only one).

Another option is to make use of ADSL (Asynchronous Double Switched Line), a high-speed permanent Internet connection that uses a regular phone connection, without the related telephone costs. Instead, you pay a fixed monthly subscription that covers both your telecom provider and your ISP.

CHOOSING AN ISP

Your choice of ISP will depend upon why you want the Internet. In this dynamic market, service offerings are constantly changing and so it is best to call up the ISPs on the numbers provided, and ask them to post you their latest subscription information packs – or check their websites.

SELECTION CRITERIA FOR THE EXPAT

The main selection criteria in choosing an ISP for the expat fall into five main categories: costs, e-mail, speed of access, language and connection costs when traveling abroad.

- *THE COST* of having an Internet service will typically involve the user paying a regular subscription fee to the ISP and a telephone connection charge to the telecoms group. The individual ISP rates vary. With regard to the telephone charge, the Internet user pays according to the length of time of connection. For example, KPN Telecom has a range of rates depending on use. With the introduction of ADSL (see above) you can now choose for a subscription package whereby, for a monthly fee, you have permanent telephone connection and an ISP. The disadvantage is that this is only available for Dutch ISPs, as opposed to global ISPs.

- *SPEED OF ACCESS* is an important factor for most Internet users. Most subscribers depend on dial-up access through an ordinary phone and it is not uncommon for residential users to experience considerable delays while trying to log on because the network lacks the capacity to meet demand. Most of the ISPs have an analogue speed of 33.6kbps or 56kbps. However, the subscriber can opt for an integrated services digital network (ISDN) line, usually at an additional charge. ISDN offers faster connection (typically 64kbps or 128kbps) and comes with four phone lines, so that you can still use the telephone while connected to the Internet. Even faster are cable connections and ADSL connections.

- *LANGUAGE* is another key feature to consider when making a choice of ISP. Basically, any ISP trying to implement a pan-European strategy will have to take into account the heterogeneity, of the European market, particularly when it comes to basic marketing and content and language of websites.

- *E-MAIL* services are provided by all of the ISPs shown and they all possess the technology to allow you to access your e-mail account from other computers connected to the Internet. This is handy because you can, for example, read your home e-mail messages at work. The limiting factor of these e-mail accounts is that if you change ISPs, your e-mail address becomes redundant.

- *POP3 E-MAIL ADDRESSES AND WEBMAIL.* A Pop3 e-mail box is an e-mail address with a unique login name and password. This type of e-mail usually allows a user to forward a message. What is the difference between Pop3 e-mail box and webmail? Pop3 e-mail box has the advantage that you can check, read and write your mail off-line while not connected. The disadvantage is that if you are abroad, you have to take your login name, password and server name with you. This is not necessary with webmail, whereby you can read the e-mails on your provider's Internet page and you only need your login name and your password. In both cases, you can prepare messages in a Word document and then send this as an attachment. Hotmail and Yahoo! are examples of webmail. They are accessed through the Web, and e-mail services are free and portable so you can keep the same address even if you change ISP. This means you can get an Internet connection service with your own ISP, but use the e-mail service of Yahoo!; you simply connect to the Internet through your ISP, and then go to the Yahoo website to obtain an e-mail account with them in minutes! Other options are news, games, and instant messenger service chat capabilities with web cam set-up allowing you to see the folks back home, and let them see you and how the kids are growing!

- *TRAVELING ABROAD FREQUENTLY* may necessitate an ISP *with an international presence* as this will allow the traveler to pay local call rates when roaming between different countries. If the ISP only has regional presence, it is more likely that to connect to the Internet from a different country, you will have to connect via the local country of the ISP which means paying international rates. If the ISP has a stronger international presence, then you can connect to the Internet via a local server in that particular region and pay local rates. There are also non-Dutch ISPs that offer such services, such as Compuserve, whose phone number you will find at the end of this chapter.

If you simply want to surf the Internet while abroad, you can do this from any computer with an Internet connection – the office, hotel, cybercafé and so on – and just pay the local rate. You only need to use your own Internet account while abroad (and thus also pay international rates) if you want to use your e-mail services. But even then, if you have a Web-based e-mail account such as Hotmail or Yahoo!, you do not have to log-in to your own account, any Internet connection will do.

ADDITIONAL SERVICES AND FEATURES

Helpdesks

This can actually be a critical factor. For some providers, you have to pay if you call their helpdesk and that includes the waiting time. You can also use their Internet site, if you still have access to the Internet, and you can send an e-mail, but then response time can be quite long. Also the quality of the information provided is sometimes questionable.

Homepages

Some providers offer their clients the possibility to have more than one e-mail address and to set up their own small home-pages. They also offer easy-to-make web pages assistance online.

Your Choice

Your own personal selection criteria will determine which ISPs meet your Internet requirements. The telephone numbers and websites of ISPs in the Netherlands are listed at the end of the chapter.

To find ADSL information, go to www.adslmetacrawler.com and make comparisons. For cable, phone and satellite options, go to www.internetten.nl for an overview and price comparisons.

CABLE TV

DENSELY CABLED

The Netherlands, along with Belgium, is the most densely-cabled country in the world. Approximately 97% of the six million TV households in the Netherlands has cable TV subscribers, and a further 100,000 homes are passed by cable. At an average of € 12-14 a month, access is so cheap that most people don't even know what they pay for it.

MAIN PLAYERS

Over the past twenty-five years, there has been steady consolidation from several cable TV companies and municipalities to a few main players, to the point where UPC Nederland, Essent Kabelcom, NV Casema and Multikabel account for 91 % of the market, covering key cities including Amsterdam, The Hague, Eindhoven and Utrecht.

While consumers may assume that this means they have no choice if they are not happy with their service and that they are at the whim of the cable companies, this is not the case; consumers are protected by heavy regulations on cable TV companies.

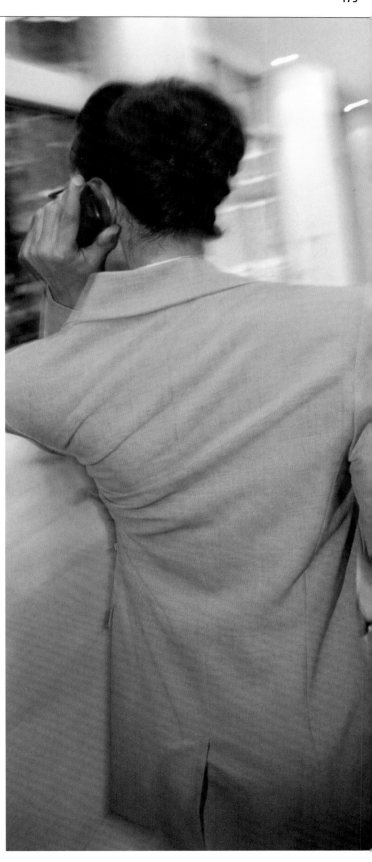

EXPANDED SERVICES

Since the main competitor to cable, satellite TV, came on the scene in the mid 1980s, the number of channels available to the cable TV subscriber has jumped from 20 to around 35. Significantly, however, the bandwidth (capacity and speed) of the new fiber-optic backbone networks that many cable companies have invested in over the last few years, means that they now can – and are – offering much more than this. Cable has ready-made interactive capabilities and expanded channel options (for instance, one cable company offers more than 60 channels) available through digital TV, as well as high-speed Internet and local and long-distance telephony. At least the four largest Dutch cable companies can offer digital TV and high-speed Internet services to their subscribers now and have considerably expanded services, including discounted telephony (Casema starts in 2005). Halfway 2004, KPN Telecom initiated discussions with the largest cable companies regarding the possibilities of renting their cable network, so that it can also offer telephone, Internet, radio and television services.

ALSO INCLUDED

In addition to channel options, all digital TV packages include an electronic program guide. Near-Video-On-Demand is also available. Fun for those who like to share their opinion: in the near future, you will be able to react to television programs on-the-spot, giving your opinion on a program or a current affair, or asking for more information on a particular subject. For sports fiends, there will be the option of choosing through which camera you watch the game or event.

All the cable companies currently offering digital services are busy implementing upgrades, including more theme and film channels. Check out the cable companies' websites, given at the end of the chapter, for their Internet and digital TV packages.

HIGH-SPEED CABLE INTERNET

At least the four big cable companies offer high-speed Internet services; Casema through its Wanadoo Internet service provider and UPC through the Internet service provider Chello. Also Multi-kabel offers Internet via cable, as does Essent Kabelcom (but only in the north, east and south areas of the Netherlands). All of them offer a variety of packages to choose from.

ADSL AND BROADBAND

The providers for ADSL high-speed Internet can be found at www. adslmetacrawler. nl.

The list of those offering high-speed capabilities is ever changing, so rather than list the ones that can be found at the time of typing this contribution, we recommend you visit this site. You simply type in your postal code, and are presented with a list of what is available in your area. If you are into (Internet) speed, check out www.breedband-start. nl, with great links to films, video and audio.

If you visit www.haalallesuitdekabel.nl (get everything from cable), you can also type in your postal code, and it will tell you what you can get out of your cable connection in your area.

CHEAPER PHONE CALLS

At least the four largest cable companies offer local and long-distance telephony services, presenting a considerable cost advantage over the incumbent KPN Telecom. While many European countries' local phone networks are still monopolized, fortunately for residents in the Netherlands, Dutch regulators have historically encouraged competition in the telecommunications industry, meaning that cable operators have been encouraged to offer competitive phone services – which they have.

FAST-MOVING INDUSTRY

This is a fast-moving industry and, as this book appears only once a year, we have found ourselves limited to describing the situation as it was in January 2005. To become more up-to-date, we advise you to call the cable net-companies or visit their websites, which you will find at the end of the chapter.

THREAT TO CABLE TV

A new technology has been introduced over the past years and by now covers most (if not all) of the Netherlands: *digitenne* (digitenna). Your TV receives its signals through a tiny antenna that is no longer than 17.5 cm. For € 8.95-26.90 (depending on the number of TVs you have) a month, subscribers will be able to watch 26 TV channels, which are digital, and listen to 17 radio channels. Not only does this make cable and satellite redundant, not a happy thought for those who have created a cable network, but Digitenne (a consortium between KPN, Nozema and the public and commercial broadcasting companies) is also considering offering Internet at some point.

The antenna can be placed on the TV or your windowsill and you need a smartcard to act as a decoder. By means of a so-called SCART-cable (which many of you already have) you transmit the signals to your TV. Also digital IDTVs will be introduced; TVs with a built-in receiver. You will be able to receive the signals anywhere across the country, should you wish to take your portable radio or TV on your boat or camping trip.

Not only will the sound and vision be of a much better quality; interactive TV will also be possible, allowing you to react to programs and to place orders. Teletext will be expanded upon, there will be an electronic TV Guide, a weather channel, games – and more is being dreamed up.

Digital subscriptions and receivers can be bought, among others, at TV stores.

THE ALTERNATIVE: SATELLITE TV

If you do not have cable (by choice or because you live in a remote area) or want to see channels not available through cable, you can opt for satellite TV. This involves finding an electronics store or other distributor who sells satellite dishes and arranging for its installation. Canal+ offers a digital satellite package for the Netherlands, including Nederland 1, 2 and 3, RTL 4 and 5, SBS 6, Net5, Yorin, V8, TMF and BVN TV, which you can receive by making use of a special decoder (if you have Digitenne, you can use the same decoder). For an additional charge, you can choose from several other packages (Basispakket, including Eurosport, Discovery Channel, etc.; Cinecinema; Canal+packet, and more).

Canal+ is also available through cable and Digitenne.

Visit www. \canalplus.nl.

LIBERALIZED UTILITIES

UTILITIES

As of July 1 2004, the utilities (gas and electricity) market has been liberalized. This means that as of this date you, the consumer, can 'buy' these utilities wherever you want to, provided the supplier has been issued a license by the government. You can find a list of licensed suppliers on www.dte.nl.

Before changing or choosing suppliers, be sure to shop around. Things to look for are:
- whether the quoted price includes tax and VAT (BTW)
- whether the price includes the 'transportation costs' of the energy or gas
- whether your meter has one or two positions: double position meters allow you to benefit from low-rate periods (such as nights)
- the period during which the quoted price/rate applies (they might offer you a low rate for the first six months, to attract you as a client, and then raise it substantially).

If your Dutch is somewhat up to par, you can find a price comparison on www.energieprijzen.nl.

Via this site, after comparing prices, you can also effectuate your change of supplier with their aid at no extra cost.

'GREEN' ENERGY

A hot topic is, of course, so-called green energy. There a number of issues that are looked at when defining green energy: noise pollution, the amount of space a facility occupies, the degree to which the existence of the facility (negatively) effects the (aesthetics) of the surroundings, the emission of acids (leading to acid rain), and particularly the emission of elements that contribute to the greenhouse effect. Quite a few suppliers in this country offer green energy. The site mentioned above www.energieprijzen.nl, also answers the question as to 'how green' the energy is that a company supplies.

REFERENCES

SAFETY

NATIONAL EMERGENCIE NUMBER: 112

TO CONTACT THE POLICE
EMERGENCIES: 112
Central National Police Information Number,
tel.: 0900 8844,
internet: www.politie.nl
For Amsterdam, tel.: 020 559 91 11
For Rotterdam, tel.: 0900 88 44
For The Hague, tel.: 070 310 49 11
For Utrecht, tel.: 030 239 71 11

TO CONTACT THE FIRE DEPARTMENT
EMERGENCIES: 112
General website: www.brandweer.nl
For Amsterdam, tel.: 020 621 21 21
For Rotterdam, tel.: 010 446 89 00
For The Hague, tel.: 070 359 15 91
For Utrecht, tel.: 030 286 78 78

AMBULANCE
EMERGENCIES: 112
For Amsterdam, tel.: 020 555 55 55
For Rotterdam, tel.: 010 433 33 00
For The Hague, tel.: 070 322 21 11
For Utrecht, tel.: 030 233 22 22

NEWS

MAIN DUTCH NEWSPAPERS

ALGEMEEN DAGBLAD: www.ad.nl
NRC HANDELSBLAD: www.nrc.nl
HET PAROOL: www.parool.nl
DE TELEGRAAF: www.detelegraaf.nl
DE VOLKSKRANT: www.volkskrant.nl
TROUW: www.trouw.nl

LOCAL NEWS IN ENGLISH

RADIO NETHERLANDS: News, radio, television and current affairs are all covered in English and radio is covered in several languages. Dutch newspapers can be accessed via 'nederlinks' on: www.rnw.nl

THE INTERNATIONAL HERALD TRIBUNE
Daily English language newspaper covering general world news.
Van Eeghenstraat 66, 1071 GK Amsterdam
tel.: 0800 022 5158 (customer services - toll free)

email: subs@iht.com
internet: www.iht.com

THE AMSTERDAM TIMES AND
THE HAGUE TIMES
Free English-language newspapers for readers in the area of Amsterdam and The Hague with each week regional news on politics, sports, economics, entertainment and real estate.
P.O. Box 96089, 1006 EB Amsterdam
Internet: www.theamsterdamtimes.nl

AMSTERDAM WEEKLY
Free cultural newspaper aimed at local Amsterdammers, both international residents and cosmopolitan Dutch.
De Ruyterkade 106, 1011 AB Amsterdam
Tel.: 020 522 5200
Internet: www.amsterdamweekly.nl

ONLINE NEWSPAPERS:
http://kranten.pagina.nl

GETTING CONNECTED

KPN TELECOM CUSTOMER SERVICE,
tel. : 0900 0244, internet: www.kpn.com
KPN INTERNATIONAL NETWORK,
internet: www.eurorings.kpn.com

TELEPHONE DIRECTORIES
Directory enquiries - inland, tel.: 0900 8008
Directory enquiries - international, tel.: 0900 8418
www.detelefoongids.com: telephone directory of KPN
www.nationaletelefoongids.nl: a quick on-line telephone book with links to telephone directories in other countries
www.goudengids.nl: Yellow Pages directory
www.faxgids.nl: directory for fax numbers

COMPARING TELEPHONE RATES
www.bellen.com: telephone rates, discount carriers
www.internetten.nl: internet providers cost comparisons
www.belwijzer.nl: mobile & fixed telephone costs
www.vakantiebellen.nl: costs within Europe mobile 'vacation' calls

DISCOUNT PROVIDERS
Bel1601: www.bel1601.nl

BudgetPhone: www.budgetphone.nl
Freetel.nl: www.freetel.nl
Pretium Telecom: www.pretium-telecom.nl
Scarlet: www.scarlet.nl
Tele2: www.tele2.nl
Vocalis: www.vocalis.nl

TO CALL THROUGH THE INTERNET
To call other people on their computers or regular phones: www.skype.com

MOBILE TELEPHONE SERVICE PROVIDERS

DEBITEL: www.debitel.nl
KPN MOBILE: www.kpn.com , tel.: 0800 0105
ORANGE: www.orange.nl
TELFORT: www.telfort.nl, tel.: 0800 444 4444
T-MOBILE: www.t-mobile.nl, tel.: 0800 7111
VODAFONE: www.vodafone.nl, tel.: 0800 0560

EXCHANGING YOUR MOBILE PHONE FOR OTHER COUNTRIES
Rentcenter Schiphol: 020 653 09 99,
internet: www.rentcenter.nl
Rentcenter Rotterdam: 010 262 33 01,
internet: www.rentcenter.nl

GENERAL INFORMATION ON INTERNET PROVIDERS
www.internetten.nl
http://provider.pagina.nl
www.adslmetacrawler.com: ADSL Information
www.breedbandstart.nl: Broadband Information

INTERNET PROVIDERS
12move: www.12move.nl
Bart: www.bart.nl
Chello: www.chello.nl
Compuserve: www.compuserve.nl
Demon: www.demon.nl
Freeler: www.freeler.nl
Het Net: www.hetnet.nl
Orange: www.orange.nl
Planet Internet: www.planet.nl
Quicknet: www.quicknet.nl
Speedlinq: www.speedlinq.nl
Studenten.net: www.studenten.net
Tiscali: www.tiscali.nl
Wanadoo: www.wanadoo.nl
XS4ALL: www.xs4all.nl
Zonnet: www.zonnet.nl

TELEVISION PROVIDERS/CABLE COMPANIES
Canal+: www.canalplus.nl
Casema: www.casema.nl
Chello: www.chello.nl
Essent Kabelcom: www.essent.nl,
www.essentkabel.com
UPC: www.upc.nl

UTILITIES
www.energieprijzen.nl: to compare energy
prizes

DUTCH POST
www.tpgpost.nl

DUTCH SEARCH ENGINES
www.altavista.nl
www.google.nl
www.ilse.nl
www.vindex.nl
www.zoeken.nl

PETS

TO REPORT LOST ANIMALS: 0900 4040456
EUROPEAN PET NETWORK:
www.europetnet.com

PET MOVING SERVICES
KLM Cargo: www.klmcargo.nl
International Animal Transport DTC:
www.dtciat.com
Air Pets Oceanic: www.airpets.com
Air Animal: www.airanimal.com

DISPOSAL OF USED GOODS

SALVATION ARMY (LEGER DES HEILS)
National Headquarters, tel.: 036 539 81 11
Amsterdam, tel.: 020 692 49 11
Rotterdam, tel.: 010 212 54 21
The Hague, tel. : 070 331 87 37

ONLINE GROCERIES

Albert Heijn, Etos, Gall & Gall, Deli XL:
www.albert.nl
Tomas Green's: www.forage.nl
Webwinkel Phicoop: www.phicoop.nl

ONLINE SHOPPING

www.neckermann.nl
www.wehkamp.nl
www.kijkshop.nl
www.ebay.nl

SELLING AND BUYING PORTALS

www.marktplaats.nl
www.viavia.nl

RECOMMENDED READING

FOOD SHOPPERS' GUIDE TO HOLLAND
By Ada Henne Koene
Published by Eburon
A comprehensive review of the finest food
products in the Dutch marketplace and a
very useful food dictionary.
Internet: www.eburon.nl
Information, tel.: 015 213 14 84
ISBN: 90 5166 777 9

DUTCH COOKING TODAY
Published by Inmerc
This book has typical Dutch dishes, honest
stews, juicy one-pan dishes, the best snacks,
the tastiest cakes and the yummiest
desserts. The book allows all – from lovers of
the *Hollandse Pot* (Dutch Pan) to admirers of
trendy cuisine – to become acquainted with
old and new dishes of the Netherlands.
Internet: www.zoekboeken.nl
ISBN 90 6611 207 7

DUTCH COOKING – THE NEW KITCHEN
Compiled by Manon Sikkel and Michiel
Klønhammer
Published by Gottmers Uitgevers Groep BV
This book contains a selection of delicious
Dutch recipes, from *poffertjes* (miniature
pancakes), to cheese soup, to *kroketten*
(croquettes), to 'the best recipe for apple
pie – even better than our grandmothers
made it!'
ISBN 90 230 1127 9

HOUSING IN HOLLAND
Compiled by RMS, edited by Connie Moser
Published by xPat Media
A book special developed in order to guide
the English speaking foreigner through the
process involved in renting or purchasing a

house in Holland.
Internet: www.xpat.nl / www.holland-books.nl
ISBN 90 5594 252 9

HANDLING HOLLAND
By Janet Inglis
Published by xPat Media
A manual for international women in the
Netherlands
Internet: www.xpat.nl
www.hollandbooks.nl
ISBN 90 5594 232 4

ONLINE BOOKSELLERS

www.abc.nl
www.amazon.co.uk
www.amazon.com
www.deslegte.nl
www.hollandbooks.nl
www.bol.com

ENGLISH LANGUAGE BOOKSTORES

THE AMERICAN BOOK CENTER
Kalverstraat 185
1012 XC Amsterdam
Tel.: 020 625 55 37
Internet: www.abc.nl

THE AMERICAN BOOK CENTER
Lange Poten 23
2511 CM The Hague
Tel.: 070 346 27 42
Internet: www.abc.nl

WATERSTONE'S BOOKSELLERS
Kalverstraat 152
1012 XE Amsterdam
Tel.: 020 638 38 21
Internet: www.waterstones.com

THE ENGLISH BOOK SHOP
Lauriersgracht 71
1016 RH Amsterdam
Tel.: 020 626 42 30
Internet: www.englishbookshop.nl

7

Children are a very important part of the expat population. The success of a placement abroad depends largely on whether the children (the family as a whole) manage to settle in in their new country. Luckily, the Netherlands is probably one of the smoothest countries to ease into. There are many international schools (see the end of chapter 8), almost everyone speaks English (a language also spoken by a large majority of the expats), general health and health care is excellent, and... there is a whole lot to do! Read on through this chapter to learn about day care, the Child Benefit, parental leave, birthday parties, Sinterklaas, shopping, general entertainment and a host of other subjects.

Kids

BY STEPHANIE DIJKSTRA AND LEE TOLMAN

DAY CARE

Although the Dutch government is keen on keeping women in the work force, the current demand for day care far outweighs availability. Waiting lists remain long, although official figures are unavailable, so we advise that you register early on (preferably as soon as you are pregnant) and still be prepared to wait anywhere between six and eighteen months before your child is placed.

Kinderopvang is the general term used in Dutch to cover childcare. In the following paragraphs you will find a brief description of the various options available to you as a (working) parent. Though every type of *opvang* has its own approach, it might be reassuring to know that every municipality has a legal obligation to ensure that minimum rules regarding the following are implemented: hygiene, safety, size of groups, sleeping space, toys, insurance and sick children (they must stay at home).

KINDERDAGVERBLIJF

Kinderdagverblijf is a cross between a day care center and nursery school and is available for children between the ages of 0 and 4 (infants as of six weeks). Approximately 320,000 children currently make use of the 3,700 day care centers in the country. Drop-off time is somewhere between 8 and 8:30 A.M., pick-up time between 5:30 and 6 P.M. You can place your child there for a number of mornings and/or afternoons a week (called *dagdelen*; day-portions) or for a full week, if necessary. Some of the *kinderdagverblijven* also have arrangements for older children (until the age of 12) for after-school hours and school holidays.

Finding a Kinderdagverblijf

A good start would be to visit the website www.kinderopvang.pagina.nl. This is a start engine which maintains a list of day care centers by province or type of day care. Many other relevant websites are also listed. Another site to check is www.kinderopvang.net. Just click on *ouders* (parents) then *adressenzoeker* (address finder). After clicking on either *postcode* (postal code) or *plaats* (place) and filling in the appropriate information, a list will pop up on your screen of day care centers or host parents in your neighborhood. The address of a specific center can then be found by clicking once again. *Stichting Kinderopvang Nederland* (SKON) also maintains a website (www.skon.nl) but can also be contacted by e-mail or phone (list at end of chapter).

You might have been told that employers arrange a day care spot for their employees, however, as of the beginning of this year, this is no longer the case. Subsidized *kinderopvang*, as it was arranged until now, has also ceased to exist – though there is a transitional arrangement through the year 2007. The new rules on day care can be found under *New Regulations*.

COST: fees vary from municipality to municipality, from one day care center to another and of course depending on whether you receive a subsidized spot. Expect to pay approximately € 280 per full day per month to € 1,000 for five full days per month.

New Regulations

As of January 1, 2005, a new law entered into force regarding *kinderopvang*, placing the full responsibility for arranging day care on parents. Until then, as mentioned above, many employers reserved a certain number of day care spots and arranged the related payments with the center. Now parents are expected to enter into their own contract with a day care center, pay for it and then recover a percentage of this from their employer.

The main idea is that each employer contributes one-sixth of the cost of the day care, so that if there are two working parents, you receive one-third. However, employers are not obligated to con-

tribute – and they can contribute less, but they can also contribute more. If the total contribution exceeds this fraction, the excess is taxable as wages in kind. If you receive less than one-third, you can seek (income-dependent) compensation from the government, to be requested via the tax authorities. This is called the 'missing employer's portion' and will be compensated at least until the year 2008 – at first for virtually all levels of income, and then gradually, by 2009, only for parents who earn a maximum of approximately € 45,000. You can also request (income-dependent) assistance from the government for the remaining two-thirds of the fee. The tax-deductible item for day care no longer exists. Keep in mind, also, that if your employer's contribution until now has been included in your employment contract, a company regulation or a collective labor agreement – and exceeds one-sixth – your employer cannot unilaterally change it downwards without consulting the relevant party/parties.

For certain categories of parents, such as those who are rejoining the labor market after a long period of time (combined with either a benefit or a registration with the Center for Work and Income), those receiving an artist's benefit, those following a familiarization course (*inburgeringscursus*) and a number of other categories, the municipality and/or the UWV (social security office) will contribute the one-third/one-sixth amount.

In order for you to qualify for a government contribution, the organization providing the *kinderopvang* must be registered as an acknowledged organization. It is not yet clear where this register will be maintained and how you can access it.

If your Dutch is any good, an excellent explanation of the whole situation can be found on www.kinderopvang.com or www. home. szw.nl.

PEUTERSPEELZALEN (TODDLER GROUPS)

Peuterspeelzalen are toddler groups for children age 2 – 4 and are typically open in the mornings although some municipalities now offer afternoon programs. Technically speaking, the *peuterspeelzaal* is not a day care facility but should be seen more as a pre-school, especially since opening hours are limited. Often, they are connected with (and on the same premises as) a primary school and allow an easy transition from the *speelzaal* to the school. There are approximately 15 children in a group and there are two teachers. Typically, children are accepted two or three fixed mornings per week. You will find *peuterspeelzalen* in the *Gemeentegids* – a guide published by your municipality with useful addresses – or in the telephone book.

COST: the cost of sending your child to a peuterspeelzaal may be income-indexed. Expect to pay anywhere from € 40 to € 120 per month for two mornings a week.

BUITENSCHOOLSE / NASCHOOLSE OPVANG (AFTER-SCHOOL DAY CARE)

Both the *buitenschoolse opvang* (BSO) as well as the *naschoolse opvang* provide day care during after school hours and holidays to children between the ages of 4 and 12. The BSO also offers an additional service during pre-school hours. These services are, as you can imagine, in great demand. Landelijk Informatiepunt BSO and SKON also provide information regarding this type of care (see the list at the end of chapter).

COST: the fee structure is much the same as for the *kinderdagverblijf* (see www.minvws.nl for specific details regarding the new rules on employer contributions).

In order for you to qualify for a government contribution, the organization providing the *buitenschoolse opvang* and *naschoolse opvang* must be registered as an acknowledged organization. It is not yet clear where this register will be maintained and how you can access it.

GASTOUDER (HOST PARENT)

A host parent usually has children of her own and cares for up to three children in her home. In some cases, the *gastouder* will come to your house. There appears to be a growing demand for this type of day care. Look in your local telephone book or *gemeentegids* (municipal guide) under *kinderopvang* to find a *gastouderbureau* in your neighborhood. *Gastouderbureaus* (host parent offices) are responsible for the registration of both prospective parents and *gastouders*. Word-of-mouth is also a good source of *gastouders*; plenty of excellent *gastouders* are not officially registered, but rely on the mommy network.

COST: the *gastouderbureau* maintains strict guidelines regarding fees and responsibilities. The cost of sending your child to a *gastouder* is usually income-indexed and currently ranges around € 2.75 to € 3.50 per hour. Sending your child to a *gastouder* is also covered by the new legislation regarding employer contributions as described on page 179. In order for you to qualify for a government contribution, the *gastouderbureau* must be registered as an acknowledged organization. It is not yet clear where this register will be maintained and how you can access it.

AU PAIR

Au pairs in Holland receive room and board and in exchange, their primary responsibility is child care. In addition, the au pair may be required to help with light housekeeping duties. In most cases, you select an au pair with the help of an intermediary or au pair organization. Their responsibilities include interviewing and selecting qualified host families and au pair candidates, making up contracts, helping with the visa process and assisting with adjustment difficulties.

COST: room and board amounts to approximately € 250 to € 320 per month, while the host family is also responsible for covering visa, permit and insurance expenses. Furthermore, you will pay the au pair organization a one-time interview, registration and placement fee. Some organizations also charge a monthly management fee, so be sure to check out several organizations (see list at the end of the chapter) before signing on the dotted line.

OPPAS (BABY SIT)

Planning a quiet evening out with your partner? A neighborhood high school or university student is probably your best bet. Although some communities maintain an *Oppascentrale* (central listing of local baby-sitters and telephone numbers – check your local telephone book), often the best way to locate a reliable sitter is through your local network or by word-of-mouth.

COST: depending on age, experience and geographic region, fees can range from € 2 to € 3.50 per hour. Other rates apply should you decide to employ a baby-sitter on a permanent basis in your home. In this case, an hourly fee of around € 3 to € 5 is paid for basic child-care responsibilities. Another fee schedule applies if housekeeping duties are also required (approximately € 6 to € 9 per hour).

LESS RUN-OF-THE-MILL OPTIONS

1. *Flexibel Kindercentrum (Flexible Child Center):* This is a type of child care center that is open 24 hours a day, 7 days a week, but receives no government grant. You will find them in the larger cities in the Netherlands. To find one, check your *gemeentegids*. The cost depends entirely on the center, but can amount to approximately € 11,500 per year for five days a week.

2. *Project:* This is an arrangement whereby a certified kindergarten/nursery school teacher comes to your (or someone else's) house and looks after a maximum of four children. For more information, you can call Stichting Scobi (tel.: 030 233 34 33) and Stichting Impuls (tel.: 020 610 96 76). Costs are approximately € 14 per hour, but more after 7 P.M. and on the weekends.

3. *Nanny:* Visit: www.nanny. nl for more information on nannies, housekeepers, care-takers and chauffeurs. Through this agency, a nanny costs between € 7.50 and € 9.50 an hour, or you can choose to have a so-called 'residing nanny' – cost between € 1,000 and 1,250 a month.

4. *International Women's Clubs:* Many international women's clubs have their own Moms and Tots Groups and will be happy to have you join the group. Although this is not, per se, a day care option, it is a great way to meet other parents and network. For a list of (women's) clubs, see page 247. ACCESS also maintains a list of non-Dutch day care options (toddler playgroups, pre-schools, international day care centers, etc.). You can find their number at the end of the chapter.

FERTILE STORKS

During the 17th century, there was no such thing as the sexual revolution. Babies and the conception thereof were shrouded in mystery. In order to answer such painful questions as 'Where do babies come from?' the Dutch came up with the following, absolutely plausible, explanation: babies were brought by the stork. If this failed to impress the children, other, equally plausible, explanations were available: babies were found among the beets, or they were found in wells or in hollow trees.

Why, of all birds, did the stork get to be the one to deliver this precious freight? In the Netherlands, storks were always considered harbingers of good luck. Therefore it was only logical that they would be the ones to bring proof of the fact that the mother was fertile, the marriage fruitful and the father a real man.

Nowadays, if you pass a front yard with a stork in it, you can be sure that this is the announcement of the birth of a new world citizen. The use of storks is also very popular on birth announcements.

PARTY TIME

Life is a party! Here are a few festivities in honor of children:

KRAAMBEZOEK
(Visiting the New-Born Child)

In the Netherlands, when a child is born, you send out announcements (called *geboortekaarten*, or birth cards) to just about anyone you know: 90-year-old aunts, colleagues you haven't seen in five years, uncles you never really liked, your best friend from nursery school. And they all respond! You might end up sending out 150 announcements – but beware! The Dutch interpret this is an invitation to come and admire the little tyke; so be sure you stock up on some *beschuit met muisjes* (rusks covered with sugared aniseeds – pink aniseeds for a girl and blue aniseeds for a boy) as your 90-year-old aunt, your colleagues, your uncle and your best friend from nursery school will be arriving shortly. This is why so many birth announcements contain the short sentence: *Moeder en kind rusten van 13.00 – 15.00 en ná 20.00 uur,* (Mother and child will be resting ...) or *Bezoek is welkom, maar bel even* (Visitors are welcome, but please call in advance).

Often the question is asked: 'How so rusks with aniseed?' – well; eating aniseeds will do the mother a lot of good as tradition has it that they stimulate her milk production. That explains why mommy is eating them, but what about everybody else?

VERJAARDAG (BIRTHDAY)

Kids' birthdays are, of course, Very Important Events. Luckily, the Dutch think so too. So, what do they do about them? On the day of the birthday, the birthday boy or girl gets to *trakteren* at school. This means that at some point in the morning, he or she hands out little items of food to his or her classmates. There are about 25 students per class; consequently this happens, on average, twice a month. For this reason, many teachers prefer that you bring something other than sweets, such as tangerines, cheese or *worst* (slices of sausage) on a toothpick, an apple or maybe even little bags of potato chips. Some parents put a lot of effort into making these packages look fun: they make bugs or boats or dolls by arranging the cheese, pickles or carrots just so.

Dutch children also get to give birthday parties, to which they invite a couple of their best friends from school and/or the neighborhood. Interestingly, kids often have *two* birthday parties: one with fun and games for the kids from school and the neighborhood and one for the extended family (including *their* kids). The latter is usually without organized fun and games and mostly involves the receiving of gifts, the eating of cake and cookies and putting up with aunts and uncles saying how much everybody has *grown* since the last time they saw them. What you organize for the former (more official) party more or less depends on your budget and your imagination (a visit from a clown, a treasure hunt, dressing up and making a movie, visiting a circus, visiting a puppet theater, you name it). Ask other parents about what is popular among the children in your child's age group.

If your kid is invited to a Dutch birthday party, the invitation will state when and where it is taking place and what to bring in terms of, for instance, a bathing suit or a dress-up costume. The Dutch are not into big expensive gifts: generally speaking something in the price range between € 4.50 and € 10 will suffice. If you bring something more expensive, they often feel embarrassed and possibly even a little annoyed (are you grandstanding them? Do you expect something similar in return?). And of course: do not forget to arrive ON TIME. This is Holland, remember?

SINTERKLAAS (SAINT NICHOLAS)

You will find more about Sinterklaas on page 48, however, he is definitely worth mentioning here as he is *the* children's friend in the Netherlands (or as one favorite song goes: '... every kid's best friend').

Sinterklaas has a few 'official' arrival points in the Netherlands where he arrives on his steamboat from Spain (loaded with gifts and populated by Zwarte Pieten or Black Petes, his helpers) around the middle of November. However, almost all cities and towns organize their own local *intocht* ('entrance'), whereby he makes his way down the shopping street in a little parade, accompanied by Zwarte Pieten, who hand out candies called *pepernoten, kruidnoten* and *schuimpjes*. Between his official arrival and December 5th (his birthday), he visits schools, *kinderdagverblijven*, companies, stores and hospitals – after which he returns to Spain.

Even though Sinterklaas is the Good Guy, his visit to school makes children *very nervous*. They are told that if they are not good (and Sinterklaas knows *everything*), Zwarte Piet will be asked to pack them up in a bag and take them back to Spain, where they will have to stay and work for a year. Even the bravest of children will hide behind mommy's skirts once a Zwarte Piet comes into sight. During this same period, children leave a shoe underneath the chimney every night with a little something for Sinterklaas, Zwarte Piet or even Sinterklaas's horse and sing a little song – hoping to encourage Sinterklaas to leave them a little gift, which they will find in their shoes in the morning. These gifts are just minor, preparatory, gifts; the real thing is on December 5th itself, on which day the family gets together (mostly in the evening) in happy anticipation of a visit from the great man himself. Usually, the parents leave a sack with gifts with the neighbors and ask them to bang on the window and deposit the sack by the front door, so that they can open the door and exclaim in surprise that Sinterklaas appears to have left a whole sack of goodies! Sometime, around the age of 7 or 8, children begin to realize that there is no real Sinterklaas or Zwarte Piet; however, both a healthy sense of self-preservation and a healthy sense of materialism keep them on their toes during the three weeks between his arrival and his departure. Once the entire family has outgrown the fantasy stage, a different type of festivity is arranged whereby, by means of a 'lottery', each member of the family draws another member to make a surprise gift (called a *surprise*, pronounced sirpreezuh) and compose a poem for. These are often very personal, home-made gifts and more often than not involve an element of teasing (particularly in the poems).

KERSTMIS (CHRISTMAS)

Does all this mean that there is no Christmas in the Netherlands? Not at all. Though the celebration of Christmas, as many know it, is based on the Dutch tradition of Sinterklaas (and is therefore really a 'repeat' just three weeks later), it is celebrated with just as much dedication and vigor, including gifts (though no *surprises* or poems). Living in a country where the sun sets just after 4 P.M. lends itself perfectly for Christmas lighting, Christmas trees and a general holiday atmosphere (including hopes for a white Christmas). Some Dutch purists limit the gift-giving to only Sinterklaas

and view Christmas as a season of togetherness, gratitude and a possible visit to midnight mass (which generally *ends* at midnight). It is often said that the Dutch do not appreciate, nor know how to prepare, good food, but it must be said that Christmas is a time of excellent eating, with venison, good wines and rich desserts and lots of friends and family to enjoy them.

As you know, it is very hard not to give presents to children when everyone else seems to be getting them, so, on the kiddie calendar, this is also a very important day.

LEGAL ISSUES

ZWANGERSCHAPSVERKLARING – 'STATEMENT OF PREGNANCY'

If you are pregnant, currently working and plan to do so following delivery, you will need to obtain a *zwangerschapsverklaring* from your midwife or gynaecologist. This document confirms your estimated due date and will be used to determine when you will be eligible for *zwangerschapsverlof* (pregnancy leave).

See more on the continued payment of wages during pregnancy leave in the next paragraph.

ZWANGERSCHAPSVERLOF – PREGNANCY LEAVE

In the Netherlands, women have the right to 16 weeks paid leave. This may be initiated between 4-6 weeks prior to the estimated due date. The law states that you may not work from 4 weeks before, until 6 weeks after, delivery. Should the baby arrive early, you still have a right to the full 16 weeks. If it is late, and you have used up the 6 weeks beforehand, you still have the right to a 10-week leave following the baby's birth. *When* you take up your leave should be determined together with your employer.

During pregnancy leave you receive 100% of your normal wages – either directly from the social security office or via your employer. Previously, if you were self-employed, then you were insured via the WAZ, allowing you to receive 100% of your monthly income over a period of four months. This law has been abolished and nothing has been created to replace it. Your only recourse is to take out private insurance – however, some insurance companies do not pay out in the case of pregnancy or childbirth that occurs within two years of taking out the insurance. The government is looking into what can be done about this.

If, prior to the start of your pregnancy leave, you are unable to work due to a pregnancy-related illness and must stay at home, then you have the right to 100% pay. If you are unable to *return* to work due to medical reasons secondary to pregnancy and/or delivery, then you have the right to up to 52 weeks of benefits at 100%.

Would you like to take more than the government stipulated 16-week leave? In order to do so you need to apply for a *vrijwillige ziektewetverzekering* (Voluntary Sickness Benefits Insurance) at your social security office within four weeks of stopping work.

YOUR RIGHTS AS A PREGNANT EMPLOYEE

You are not obligated to tell a prospective employer that you are pregnant, and if you do so, they may not turn you down for this reason. You *do* have an obligation to tell your existing employer that you are pregnant, however – at the latest three weeks before your pregnancy leave is due to start. You may not be fired during pregnancy or within 12 weeks following the birth of your child.

And only under very special conditions, for example in the case of bankruptcy, may your work be terminated. Should your contract end during pregnancy, you have the right to unemployment (WW) and sickness benefits.

During pregnancy, your employer has an obligation to protect your safety and health and you are eligible for certain additional rights. Discuss these with your employer. If you do not tell your employer that you are pregnant, you cannot exercise these rights. A few examples of your rights are the right to regular working and resting hours, extra breaks and a suitable, closed-off space to rest (and where you can lie down). You are under no obligation to work overtime or at night. These rights are applicable up until six months after delivery. You also have the right to other work or to other working hours if your current work is unsafe or hazardous to your health. If neither option is possible, you have the right to be exempted from work. There are also special regulations regarding nursing, hard physical labor, stress, chemicals, radiation, risk of infection, noise, extreme vibrations, extreme heat or cold, etc. Check the website of the Ministerie van Sociale Zaken en Werkgelegenheid (Ministry of Social Affairs and Employment) for details.

'DELIVERY LEAVE'

Daddies have a right to stand by their wife/partner while she gives birth, followed by two days 'delivery leave', which can be used up at any point, within four weeks after the birth of the child(ren). Under the banner of 'calamity leave' (though this hardly qualifies as such!), daddies may also take time off to register the birth of their child – not a full day, but for however much time is needed to do this.

REGISTRATION

Within three working days your baby has to be registered at the *gemeentehuis* (town hall). This must take place in the town hall in which your baby was born – not in your home town, if different. The father usually performs this task. If this is not possible, then it must be done by someone who was present at birth. He will need to take a passport, a certified copy of the marriage license and the certificate of birth supplied by the doctor, hospital or midwife. In order to avoid undue hassle, check with the *gemeentehuis* in question prior to registration what is needed, as requirements vary from one municipality to another. Also ask for an International Birth Certificate (for an additional fee) at this time. This document will come in handy when registering your baby with your embassy or consulate and when applying for a passport. Being born in the Netherlands does not give your baby the right to a Dutch passport – that is unless one, or both, of the parents is/are Dutch.

LEGALLY RECOGNIZING BABY

If you and your partner are not married, the father may choose to legally recognize the baby either prior to birth, at the time of registration at the town hall or at a later date. As the mother must also be present in most cases, by far the easiest method is before birth. This must take place in the town hall where you reside – not where you register the birth (unless of course this is one and the same). Check with your *gemeentehuis* or lawyer to verify which documents are necessary and what other requirements there are. If the mother is not Dutch, while the father is, the baby will only

acquire Dutch nationality automatically at birth, if it was legally recognized by the father prior to its birth.

Also, if only one – or neither – of you has Dutch nationality, then the civil servant of the municipality will have to check whether recognition is possible. Make sure you are well informed of the consequences of recognition for the baby's nationality, name and military duties (at a later age), as well as the father's obligation to support it.

KINDERBIJSLAG – CHILD BENEFIT

If you are living in the Netherlands and/or are employed and pay Dutch wage taxes, then you are entitled to *kinderbijslag*. This holds true not only for your own children, but also for either a step or foster child (in case of legal guardianship). Following registration of your child's birth, the *gemeentehuis* forwards your data to the Sociale Verzekeringsbank (the Social Insurance Bank). Within a few days you receive a registration form. Payment is made on a quarterly basis directly into your bank account up until your child is 18 years of age. The amount paid out is based on the age of your child and is currently set at € 176.62 for children between the ages of 0-6, € 214.46 for children between the ages of 6-12, with a more complicated set of rules for older children and children who do not live at home (see www.svb.nl).

OUDERSCHAPSVERLOF – PARENTAL LEAVE

The law stipulates that both working parents have the right to take a non-paid leave of absence to care for a child (adoption or foster child included). Leave may be taken either by both parents together or one after the other, at any time during the first eight years of the child's life. In the case of twins, leave is available for each child. To be eligible, you must have worked for your current employer for at least one year. The legal amount of time allotted is based on the number of hours per week worked, calculated over 13 weeks (36 hrs. per week x 13 weeks = 468 hrs.). There are two basic guidelines: the entire leave of absence must be taken within a period of 6 months after the start of the leave and the maximum number of hours a week off must not exceed 50% of your normal weekly total. As the rules are not always practical – for either the em-ployee or employer – other conditions may be agreed upon. The official request for *ouderschapsverlof* must be filed in writing with the employer at least two months in advance. In principle, you determine which hours you would like to work, but your employer can insist on a different division of hours, on 'serious grounds'. Although not required by law, some employers continue to pay up to 75% of wages during parental leave.

Check whether a collective labor agreement applies to you, in which there may be further, more beneficial, rules on parental leave.

BORSTVOEDING – BREAST-FEEDING

Employers must provide breast-feeding employees a quiet space in which to breast-feed or express – not the women's room! If this is not feasible, then the employer must allow the employee find an appropriate spot or to go to the baby in order to do this. Feeding /expressing time is considered work time and a maximum of one quarter of normal working hours may be used for this purpose, up until the child is nine months old. Discuss the various options with your employer prior to initiating pregnancy leave.

ZORGVERLOF – CARE LEAVE

By law, a full-time employee has the right to take a maximum of 10 days paid leave per 12 months in order to care for a sick child, partner or parent (if you work 36 hours a week, you have a right to 72 hours, with 32 hours you have a right to 64 hours, and so on). This leave does not have to be taken up in one go. The employer is obligated to continue to pay at least 70% of your wages during this period.

CALAMITY LEAVE

Calamity leave has been created for unforeseen situations in which you have to act immediately and personally, for instance, to find a baby sit for your suddenly sick child, to find a plumber if the water pipes have burst, in the case of sudden death in the family or, as mentioned above, to register the birth of your newborn child. In principle, this leave is granted for a couple of hours, though it could extend to a couple of days, during which period your employer is to continue 100% payment of your salary.

Under circumstances, calamity leave could become care leave.

LAST WILL AND TESTAMENT

Preparing a will is probably one of the most important steps you will take to ensure the future well-being of your newborn. Although not common knowledge, not all foreign wills are valid in the Netherlands. This depends, among others, on your country of origin (what are the requirements for a valid will there?), how the will has been drawn up and whether the Netherlands has entered into a treaty on the matter with your country.

If something were to happen to both parents, the courts will appoint a guardian; most often the person mentioned in the will. If the will states nothing on this matter, a relative in the country of origin will appointed. In order to guarantee that the *voogdij* (guardianship) of your child is given to someone of your choosing, it would be best to have a testament drawn up by a Dutch *notaris* (notary) – to be on the safe side. Check the Yellow Pages or get a referral from a friend for the name of a notary in your area.

VACATION

According to Dutch law, all children as of the age of 5 are *leerplichtig* and must attend school (unless they are sick). Exceptions may be made for parents who are required to work during standard school holidays and vacations, generally up to a maximum of 10 days. Extraordinary family situations such as special birthdays, anniversaries, illness or death are other exceptions. Dutch schools are very strict in this matter and a formal request in writing is required prior to taking your child out of school. International schools may have their own set of regulations – so when in doubt, ask!

SHOPPING

BABY FOOD AND FORMULA

Baby food (*babyvoeding*) can be purchased in all supermarkets and in most *drogisterijen* (drug stores) and *apotheken* (pharmacies). You can also find formula (*opvolgmelk*, treated milk for babies) in these stores, however, the very specialized types of formula for babies with allergies (soy-based products) you will find

at the *apotheek*. Also health food stores (reformhuizen or reform-winkels) carry their own baby foods and formula.
You will be advised as to what kind of formula to try by the *Consultatiebureau* (see page 222).

BABY CARE PRODUCTS
(Popular) baby care products – baby shampoos, soaps, crèmes, etc. – can be found at the *drogist* (drugstore), while a smaller selection is available in the grocery stores. Brand name and own label diapers are available at the drogist and the supermarket.

CLOTHES
Clothes for babies and children can be found in the larger department stores, certain brand stores and, of course, stores specializing in baby and children's items (which you can find in the Yellow Pages under *Babyartikelen*). Virtually every main shopping street in every little town has a store that carries a large variety of children's clothing. Children's shoes can be bought at almost any shoe store. At the end of the chapter you will find a list of shops.

MATERNITY CLOTHES
Maternity clothes are called *positiekleding* or *zwangerschapskleding*. Many department stores carry maternity clothes, as do the specialty shops listed at the end of the chapter. You can also purchase very stylish 'large clothes' at an Extra Size (*grote maten*) woman's shop or in the XL larger sizes sections of most clothing stores. Many second-hand clothing shops (*tweedehands winkels*) have a selection of maternity clothes, too. *Zwangerschapszwempakken* (swim suits) can best be purchased at a specialty shop.

FURNITURE
There are large chains of stores as well as smaller shops, all across the Netherlands, that specialize in baby furniture. Here you can also find cribs, strollers, car seats, high chairs, lamps, bottles, baths, clothes, toys, the works. Check the Yellow Pages under *Baby-artikelen* and check out the list at the end of the chapter.

TOYS & GAMES
Speelgoedwinkels are toy stores carrying a wide selection of toys and games – which can also be found in department stores and even in a few of the household chains. Second-hand children's shops carry playthings as well as children's books. Often they will have a message board for posting larger items for sale such as carriages, cribs, furniture, etc. Furthermore, there are wonderful toy stores all across the country that do not belong to any chain and that sell some of the more old-fashioned variety of (wooden) toys.

FUN THINGS TO DO

EXTRA-CURRICULAR ACTIVITIES

Some of you may be used to extra-curricular activities arranged by the school – unfortunately, Dutch schools do not arrange many activities (on the other side, tuition is free if you send your child to a local school, so this may have something to do with it). But this does not mean that your child has to twiddle his or her thumbs all day, once school is out. In almost all municipalities you will find an organization that arranges and houses all sorts of activities, such as carpentry, painting, music, dancing, cooking, etc. Just ask around, check your *gemeentegids* or give your *gemeente* a call.

Furthermore, there are several sports organizations, the more popular ones being for tennis, field hockey, gymnastics – though there is also judo, basketball, baseball, soccer, dancing, singing, music-making, horseback-riding, cycling (of course) and much, much more.

SWIMMING

One very important extra-curricular activity (that is often also arranged through schools) is swimming, which should come as no surprise in this country of canals, rivers, lakes and the sea. Though your child does not *have* to take swimming lessons, there is a well-regulated system of classes to take and diplomas to aspire to – a program that virtually every child follows and takes pride in completing.

FILLING YOUR DAYS

A very popular item of entertainment for younger kids in the Netherlands is the petting farm, to be found in almost every town and city. They usually have goats, sheep, rabbits, guinea pigs, chickens, ducks, pigs, a pony, some cats and the occasional donkey. Kids love it, and are invited to pet, admire and learn about the animals.

Many towns also have a so-called *hertenkamp*; an enclosed area with deer to feed bread to and sneak a little pat on the nose.

Playgrounds are also to be found, with swings, slides, seesaws, etc. Most zoos (see further on) have *great* (and large) playgrounds for when your children can't bear to see another ostrich.

During the summer, there are traveling circuses and fairs (*kermis*) to go to. Their arrival is announced well in advance. You buy an admission ticket to the circuses. The fairs sometimes charge an entry fee, but mostly you pay for the rides and attractions you choose to enter.

For rainy days (of which there will be plenty), there are the covered playgrounds – called Ballorig, Play City or Kidz City – which are huge covered areas with an incredible amount of things to do: impressive slides, complicated rope-climbing, merry-go-rounds, trains, you name it. Some of the bigger cities have activity centers, where children learn to build tree houses, floats and other complicated constructions. A great source of these activities is the so-called *Kids Gids*, a book for the bigger cities (and one that covers all of the Netherlands, which is now also available in English), listing petting farms, indoor and outdoor playgrounds, child-friendly restaurants, birthday party activities, (puppet) theaters, courses (dancing, circus acts, acting) and dozens of other things to do.

SCOUTS AND OTHER CAMPS

Boy and Girl Scouts (called *scouting*) are very popular here. Mostly on Saturday afternoons, fun and educational activities are arranged for the kids. Occasionally, the groups go camping for an entire weekend (Saturday morning to late Sunday afternoon) and often week outings are arranged during summer vacation. Check the telephone book or your *gemeentegids* for the local chapter.

Other popular camps are for horseback-riding and sailing and you could of course also ask among some of the international schools whether they are arranging anything for the summer (or know of someone who is). Some municipalities arrange a day-camp during the summer vacations with a full program of activities for the children; drop-off time early in the morning, pick-up time late afternoon. Once again, your gemeentegids or someone at the municipal offices should be able to tell you whether there's something like that going on in your town or one nearby.

AMUSEMENT PARKS AND MUSEUMS

The Netherlands has some great amusement parks and museums, such as

DE EFTELING: a huge park offering several days' worth of entertainment with a trip into fantasyland, with fairytale woods, wild rides on rollercoasters, castles, fairytale figures and more.
Address: Europalaan 1, Kaatsheuvel (near Tilburg)
tel.: 0416 273 35 35, Internet: www.efteling. nl.

THE OPEN AIR MUSEUMS (Openluchtmuseum): a trip through time. There are many, including, among others:
- *Nederlands Openluchtmuseum* (daily life in the Netherlands between 1600 and 1970): Schelmseweg 89, Arnhem tel.: 026 357 61 11, Internet: www.openluchtmuseum.nl
- *Bijbels Openluchtmuseum* (Biblical Open Air Museum, for a glimpse of the world 2,000 years ago in the Middle East): Profetenlaan 2, Heilig Landstichting, tel.: 024 382 31 30 Internet: www. bijbelsopenluchtmuseum.nl
- *Zuiderzeemuseum* (life in a fishing village around 1900): Wierdijk 16, Enkhuizen, tel.: 0228 35 11 11 Internet: www.zuiderzeemuseum. nl.

NEMO: a scientifically oriented play/educational center; a discovery trip through fantasy and reality.
Address: Oosterdok 2, Amsterdam, tel.: 0900 919 11 00
Internet: www.e-NEMO.nl.

LAND VAN OOIT: where children are the boss in a fantasy world filled with castles and princes.
Address: Parklaan 40, Drunen, tel.: 0416 37 77 75
Internet: www.ooit.nl.

SAFARI PARK BEEKSE BERGEN: a drive (or walk) among more than 100 wild animals, a trip that could take more than a day!
Address: Beekse Bergen 1, Hilvarenbeek (near Tilburg)
tel.: 013 536 00 32
Internet: www. beeksebergen.nl.

DUINRELL: a fantastic water festival, with attractions, a ski valley, a wild pool and lots of entertainment.
Address: Duinrell 1, Wassenaar, tel.: 070 515 52 58
Internet: www.duinrell.nl.

PONY PARK SLAGHAREN: life in the Wild West, with an amusement park, a shopping street, Wigwam World, Colorado City and lots of entertainment. Address: Zwartedijk 37, Slagharen tel.: (0)523 68 30 00, Internet: www.slagharen.org.

PLANETARIUM FRANEKER, where, more than 200 years ago, Eise Eisinga made a scale model of the solar system in his living room, with a mechanism that keeps planets and pointers in motion and that works to this day.
Address: Eise Eisingastraat 3, Franeker, tel.: 0517 39 30 70
Internet: www.planetarium-friesland.nl.

CHILDREN'S MUSEUM AT THE TROPICAL INSTITUTE (Koninklijk Instituut voor de Tropen), where contemporary non-Western cultures are brought to life for children between the ages of 6 and 12. Also available for children's parties.
Address: Linnaeusstraat 2, Amsterdam, tel.: 020 568 83 00
Internet: www. kit. nl/tropenmuseumjunior.

SIX FLAGS: a huge outdoor swimming and water paradise; 'a world of fun, excitement and thrilling speeds'.
Address: Spijkweg 30, Biddinghuizen, tel.: 0321 32 99 91. Visit the Internet, www.sixflags.nl for instructions in English on how to get there.

ANNE FRANK HOUSE: a moving visit to the house where Anne Frank and her family were in hiding during a large part of World War II, with descriptions of their lives there and a contemporary exhibition with themes relating to what occurred during this war.
Address: Prinsengracht 263, Amsterdam, tel.: 020 556 71 00
Internet: www.annefrankhuis. nl.

MADURODAM: a miniature version of the Netherlands and of portions of other countries.
Address: George Maduroplein 1
The Hague, tel.: 070 355 39 00
Internet: www.madurodam.nl.

This is but a small selection (see also Chapter 10 for tourist attractions). Ask around among other parents or at the vvv (Tourist Information Office; there is one in almost every municipality, but you will find a list of vvvs at the end of chapter 10) what other tips they may have. A great site is: www.uitmetkinderen.nl (a day out with children), where you can search for museums, amusement parks, pools, zoos, playgrounds, etc. according to age, zip code, price range, and alphabet.

ZOOS

Animals are always a great success with children and what makes the Netherlands such a wonderful 'zoo country' is that there are several zoos, for such a small country, and that a lot of effort is put into recreating the natural habitats of the animals – so that you have a feeling you are watching truly contented animals. All zoos have very extensive playgrounds as well, for when your kids need to blow off steam, as well as indoor facilities for rainy days and child-friendly cafeterias.

APENHEUL: Apenheul has thirty species of apes, monkeys and prosimians – some of which are allowed to roam free! Their group areas are extensive and imaginative, providing them with familiar surroundings and all manner of activities to keep them occupied. But monkeys and apes are not the only animals you will meet at Apenheul. The 'zoo' also provides a home to macaws, capybaras, otters, tortoises, and many other creatures.
Address: Apen-Natuurpark Apenheul, J.C. Wilslaan 21-31 (Park Berg en Bos), Apeldoorn, tel.: 055 357 57 57,
Internet: www.apenheul.nl.

ARTIS ZOO: Artis was founded more than 160 years ago and its winding paths, majestic trees and the monumental historical buildings still give it a special, 19th century atmosphere. There are more than 8,000 animals in the zoo, as well as two museums, the Zoological Museum and the Geological Museum, a very sophisticated Planetarium and a magnificent, recently renovated Aquarium.
Address: Plantage Kerklaan 38-40, 1018 CZ Amsterdam,
tel.: 020 523 34 00, Internet: www.artis.nl.

AVIFAUNA: Avifauna is one of the largest bird parks in the world. The birds come from the tropics or from the cold Northern Hemisphere. There are more than 450 species of birds, in beautiful settings, which are expertly and lovingly taken care of. Avifauna is not only a bird 'zoo', it is also actively involved with endangered species breeding programs and bird protection activities. In 2003, it opened a Philippines area (in honor of several types of birds that only exist there) in its tropical hall, aimed at educating the children on nature protection programs.
Address: Vogelpark Hotel Rederij Avifauna, Hoorn 65, 2404 HG Alphen aan den Rijn, 0172 48 75 75, Internet: www.avifauna.nl.

BLIJDORP ZOO: At Rotterdam Zoo you can walk from continent to continent, meeting fascinating animals that feel perfectly at home in the surroundings that emulate their natural habitat. The covered facilities, in case of rain, include Taman Indah, the bat cave, the nocturnal house and the Rivièrahal complex with a wide range of fresh and saltwater fish, reptiles, amphibians, birds and tropical plants. Recently, the Rotterdam Zoo added the 'Oceanium', a huge water paradise for fish.
Address: Rotterdam Zoo / Blijdorp, Van Aerssenlaan 49, Rotterdam, tel.: 010 443 14 95 (you will get a Dutch selection menu, but if you hang on, an operator will come on the line who can help you in English). Internet: www.rotterdamzoo.nl.

BURGERS' ZOO: Burgers' Zoo is a modern, but genuine jungle! This zoo, located near Arnhem, covers more than 45 hectares and houses more than 3,000 animals. The zoo has a spectacular tropical rain forest, a living desert and a large animal population, such as bighorns and red lynxes, to be admired in their natural surroundings. Furthermore, a large number of hoofed animals and birds live with the lions in the 'Safari Park' and there is a wonderful indoor water world.
Address: Burgers' Zoo, Schelmseweg 85, 6816 SH Arnhem, tel.: 026 442 45 34, Internet: www. burgerszoo.nl.

DOLFINARIUM HARDERWIJK: At Dolfinarium, you can visit the new Lagoon, a new biotope with dolphins, fish, seals and sea lions all living together. The Lagoon is a 15 million-liter closed saltwater ecosystem. Also, you can touch and feed the stingrays at the Ray Reef, walk through the Seal Wetlands, visit the modern rescue and research center for sick or injured dolphins or see the walrus and seal shows. If the weather is wonderful, everyone can sunbathe, swim or ride in a paddle boat near the Park Beach. Dolfinarium's program is continually changing and in 2003, Dolfinarium won two international awards for two of its shows.
Address: Dolfinarium Harderwijk, the World of the Sea, Strandboulevard Oost 1, 3841 AB Harderwijk, tel.: 0341 46 74 67, Internet: www.dolfinarium.nl.

EMMEN ZOO: Emmen Zoo is famous for the manner in which the park's habitats reflect the continents of the world. The animals reside in the part of the world where they belong. The zoo has a very spacious feel about it and all the animals enjoy a great amount of freedom in their enclosures, allowing them to behave as naturally as possible. You can spend hours enjoying the butterfly and hummingbird garden, the rats' sewer, and the exciting exhibitions in the natural history museum.
Address: Noorder Dierenpark Emmen, Hoofdstraat 18, 7801 BA Emmen, tel: 0591 61 88 00. Internet:www.zoo-emmen.nl.

NATURALIS: At Naturalis, nature is exhibited in all its colors and diversity and the museum is truly a combination of natural history and high-tech multi-media in a modern, artistic and technologically advanced setting, representing but a selection of two centuries' worth of collecting animal and plant specimens, fossils, stones and minerals. Exhibition rooms have seven permanent displays (including a walk through the Ice Age, with dinosaurs), while Naturalis hosts many fascinating temporary displays as well. There is also a Nature Information Center where amateur researchers can search through a wide range of books, magazines, slides, photographs, videotapes, computer files and reference collections.
Address: Naturalis, National Museum of Natural History, Darwinweg, Leiden, tel.: 071 568 76 00, Internet: www.naturalis.nl

REFERENCES

RECOMMENDED READING

BABIES AND TODDLERS
Published by ACCESS
Information for parents of babies and
toddlers in the Netherlands, starting with
pregnancy and covering child health and
safety, activities, support groups, childcare
services, recommended reading and much
more.
Internet:
www.euronet.nl/users/access
www.access-nl.org
ISBN 90 74109 18 7

WHEN ABROAD DO AS LOCAL CHILDREN DO
ORI'S GUIDE FOR YOUNG EXPATS
By Hilly van Swol-Ulbrich & Bettina
Kältenhauser
Published by XPat Media
This book reaches out to international
mobile families with children between 8
and 12 years old.
The activities and assignments in the book
encourage the taking of initiatives in
exploring the opportunities connected with
the new environment.
Internet: www.xpat.nl-www.hollandbooks.nl
- www.ori-and-ricki.net
ISBN 90 5594 262 6

**THE THIRD CULTURE KID EXPERIENCE –
THE EXPERIENCE OF GROWING UP AMONG
WORLDS**
By David C. Pollock and Ruth E. Van Reken
Internet: www.interculturalpress.com
ISBN 1 85788 295 4

WEBSITES

www.parentsplace.com: provides a wealth
of knowledge regarding prenatal and postpartum issues of interest
www.babycenter.com: comprehensive site
with lots of relevant information for
pregnancy and beyond
www.thebabynet.com: baby names, birth
announcements, message boards, baby
shower ideas, etc.
www.thefamilycorner.com: ages & stages,
family & kids, pets, travel, parenting,
education, etc.
www.childbirth.org: ask the pros, pregnancy
photos, pregnancy calendar, birth plans,

birth stories as well as links to other home
pages

(for more websites see also Chapter 9 -
Having a Baby)

DAY CARE

**MINISTRY OF PUBLIC HEALTH, WELFARE
AND SPORTS:**
Internet: www.minvws.nl

ACCESS publishes a fact sheet with information regarding non-Dutch day care options
Plein 24, 2511 CS The Hague
Tel.: 070 346 25 25
E-mail: info@access-nl.org
www.euronet.nl/users/access
www.access-nl.org

KINDEROPVANG ALCIDES
An independent organization with 74 day
care centers in the Randstad and Emmen
Headoffice
P.O. Box 22070, 1100 CB Amsterdam
Hullenbergweg 379, 1101 CR Amsterdam
Tel.: 020 398 61 00
Internet: www.kinderopvangalcides.nl

**HET NEDERLANDS INSTITUUT VOOR ZORG
EN WELZIJN / NIZW:**
www.nizw.nl

**STICHTING KINDEROPVANG NEDERLAND
(SKON)**
has a national network for *kinderopvang,
naschoolse opvang* and *buitenschoolse*
opvang
P.O. Box 1246, 3600 BE Maarssen
Energieweg 1, 3542 DZ Utrecht
Tel.: 0346 55 95 00
Internet: www.skon.nl

**NATIONAL INFORMATION BUREAU
KINDEROPVANG
(LANDELIJK INFORMATIEBUREAU
NETWERK KINDEROPVANG - LINK)**
P.O. Box 1575, 3500 BN Utrecht
Tel.: 030 231 79 79
Internet: www.kinderopvang.net

STICHTING KINDEROPVANG HUMANITAS,
has approximately 70 *kinderdagverblijven* in
the Netherlands as well as *gastouder centers.*

It also has a national registration point for
kinderopvang (Landelijk Meldpunt
Kinderopvang) that can help you find a
day care spot.
Headoffice:
P.O Box 591, 6400 AN Heerlen
Meezenbroekerweg 1a, 6412 VK Heerlen
Tel.: 045 561 53 53
Internet: www.humanitas-kov.nl

PLAYGROUPS/
KINDERGARTENS

THE ACTIVITY SHOP
Private English-Language Pre-School/
Kindergarten
Hallekenstraat 28A, 2242 VD Wassenaar
Tel.: 070 514 15 46
Internet: www.tasid.nl

ENGLISH-SPEAKING PLAYGROUP
Sixlaan 4, 2252 CG Voorschoten
Tel.: 071 576 56 64
Internet: www.english-playgroup-
voorschoten.nl

KINDERGARDEN
Herengracht 244, 1016 BT Amsterdam
Tel.: 020 423 54 22
Internet: www.kindergarden.nl

THE WINDMILL PLAYGROUP
Elzendreef 6, 2272 EB Voorburg
Theresiastraat 310, 2593 AZ Den Haag
Tel.: 070 327 20 88
Internet.: www.thewindmillplaygroup.com

AU PAIRS/NANNIES

AU PAIR & NANNY WORLD WIDE
Burg. Hogguerstraat 785, 1064 EB Amsterdam
Tel.: 020 411 60 10
Internet: www.worldwideaupair-nanny.com

AU PAIR AGENCY MONDIAL
Cornelis de Wittlaan 39, 2582 AB The Hague
Tel.: 070 365 14 01
Internet: www.aupair-agency.nl

ACTIVITY INTERNATIONAL
P.O Box 7097, 9701 JB Groningen
Tel.: 050 313 06 66
Internet: www.activityinternational.nl

NANNY ASSOCIATION
Heuvelpoort 310, 5038 DT Tilburg
Tel.: 013 543 78 85
Internet: www.nanny.nl

FINANCIAL ISSUES

**NATIONAL BUDGET INSTITUTE
(NATIONAAL INSTITUUT VOOR BUDGET-
VOORLICHTING NIBUD)**
P.O. Box 19250, 3501 DG Utrecht
Tel.: 030 239 13 50
Fax: 030 239 13 99
Internet: www.nibud.nl
(the site is in Dutch and allows you to order
a booklet on the costs of *kinderopvang*.)

KINDEROPVANG:
Internet: www.skon.nl, (in Dutch) gives you
the actual national average rates for all types
of *kinderopvang*.

SOCIAL INSURANCE BANK
(SOCIALE VERZEKERINGSBANK), for the
Child Benefit (*kinderbijslag*):
tel.: 071 512 90 00
Internet: www.svb.org

SPECIAL NEEDS CHILDREN

**AUTISM ASSOCIATION FOR OVERSEAS
FAMILIES (NL)**
Parents and professionals working together
for children with autism
Tel.: 070 354 72 77 (Tee Lamb)
e-mail: mail@aaof.info
Internet: www.aaof.info

SAFETY

www.babyproof.com
www.babysafe.com/tips.htm
www.safekids.org

FUN THINGS TO DO

www.uitmetkinderen.nl: search by location,
age, alphabet and more for fun things to do

www.uitgaan.nl: (in Dutch) Select: *jongeren-
vakantie, jeugdherberg, dagje uit, jongeren,
kinderlinks*

Vinea, tel.: 0515 469 777 (summer camp
activities for children age 10-17)
Internet: www.vinea.com

Holiday Camps for kids: www.holiday-
camps.nl

Kidsgids (English Language Edition)
Published by Kidsgids
Activities for kids, shops, museums, outings,
sports in the Netherlands
Tel.: 020 672 35 38
Internet: www.kidsgids.nl (with an event
calendar in Dutch)
ISBN 90 76691 22 3

If you have come to the Netherlands with children, then there are a few questions you might like to see answered. One of the big questions is: shall I send my child to a local or an international school? The pros and cons of these options are discussed in this chapter, as well as the Dutch educational system. As there are so many different types of international schools in the Netherlands, each often based on the national system of the country of origin, we advise you to contact the various international schools for more information on their program. You can find their addresses through the websites listed at the end of the chapter.

However, this chapter has not only been written with parents in mind, but also with (international) students, who will find issues that are of interest to them in the second half of the chapter: housing, financing, government grants, student organizations, seeking on-the-side employment and more.

Education

CONTRIBUTING AUTHORS: STEPHANIE DIJKSTRA, RENÉ HOFMA AND HAN VAN DER HORST

LOCAL OR INTERNATIONAL SCHOOL?

When moving from one country to another, there are several issues that come to mind when trying to decide on what type of school to send your children to, such as language, culture and, of course, curriculum. However, there are two other very important factors that should not be overlooked: belonging and continuity. Depending on the age of the child, either the one or the other could play an important role in your decision whether to send your child to an international or a local school.

BELONGING
Elementary school age is an age in which belonging to the local culture is very important. Riding your bicycle around and knowing (and communicating with) every schoolchild, shop owner and parent in the neighborhood is vital. At that age, for your basic sense of security in later life, belonging is what matters. In principle, this is best achieved by attending a 'national' school, speaking the local language and playing with local children.

TEENAGERS: CONTINUITY
The world at large, with raging hormones, a body that is spinning out of control, new expectations when it comes to dress codes and behavior, and new standards of coolness, are strange and bewildering enough at home. They are almost insurmountable in a new country, where culture and language are 'undecodable', and your child will almost certainly be at a total loss. At this age, therefore, continuity is of importance. For the sake of continuity, if this is your first move, it would be advisable to place your child in a school that approaches your home school as much as possible, be this German, French, Japanese, American or whatever else you can find. Particularly if you expect to go back to your home country after your stint here is over. If there is no such school, and there is no way to guarantee continuity, then there are many factors that will determine whether you want to send your child(ren) to an international school, a local school with an international department or just plain a local school – such as location, scholastic and language aptitude, whether you want to become a part of the local community, whether and where your child wants to study after completing high school, and of course, whether you expect to be transferred to yet another country after this.

If your move to Holland is one in a chain of transfers, and you want to keep the aim of achieving continuity at the basis of your decision, you will most likely end up placing your child(ren) in an international school – or, if you are confident that you will find a 'home school' (a school that teaches in keeping with the school system and in the language of your home country) in your subsequent countries, a home school. Your career path, and particularly the countries you will move to next, are important factors in this decision. Even so, continuity will only be partly achieved: without a doubt, international schools and home schools also differ (to a greater or smaller) degree from country to country.

And then there is one final issue to consider here, and that is the issue of isolation: whichever school you choose to send your child to, but particularly if you are going to send your child to an international school, try to live close by it, so that your child lives close to friends.

GOING TO UNIVERSITY

Another factor to consider, once your child is of high school age, is whether and where your child will go to university. If your child would like to go to university, you should look into whether the school you are planning to send your child to offers the type of high school diploma that universities in the country of destination will accept. Almost all, if not all, universities accept an IB (International Baccalaureate)-diploma.

WAITING LIST

In some schools, there is a shortage of places for children and you are strongly advised to place your child on a waiting list as soon as you know which school you would like to send your child to.

FEES AND TAXES

It must be noted that the fees of the various schools vary considerably. In order to obtain information on these fees, please contact the schools in question (for a list of all international schools in the Netherlands, visit the following website: www.sio.nl, of Stichting Internationaal Onderwijs, the International Education Foundation). Many companies pay or reimburse tuition fees, and the payments and reimbursements are exempted from income tax. However, it is important to know that (reimbursed) tuition fees for attendance at an international stream of a local school are not always tax-exempt. Tuition fees and taxes are a complicated issue, as there is also the 30%-reimbursement ruling, under which tuition fees are deductible (though, again, not for all Dutch schools with an international stream!). To be brought entirely up-to-date on this issue, we advise you to contact your tax consultant.

THE EDUCATION SYSTEM

The education system in the Netherlands is, with certain important exceptions, governed at all levels by national legislation. The Ministry of Education, Culture and Science is responsible for the implementation of educational legislation for most types of education, except for study programs in the fields of health care and agriculture, which are governed by the competent ministries. There is an increasing trend at all levels of education towards fewer rules and regulations from the national government, whose primary role it is to provide a framework regarding educational objectives, admissions requirements and funding, within which institutions operate.

PRIMARY EDUCATION

Children from age four through twelve go to primary school in the Netherlands. As of the age of five, they have the so-called *leerplicht* (learning obligation) which means that you can not keep them out of school and take them back to your home country for extended periods of time, outside of school vacations. You have to ask permission to do so and in principle it will not be granted for a period exceeding two weeks.

Primary education lasts eight years (including kindergarten), in the last year of which pupils are advised as to the type of secondary education they should pursue.

The Three Types of Primary Education

- Approximately one third of the Dutch children goes to *openbare school*, or PUBLIC SCHOOL. These schools are run under the authority of the municipality and are not based on any particular religion or conviction, though they do teach religion-related subjects upon request.
- A much smaller group of children goes to schools that are based on certain EDUCATIONAL PHILOSOPHIES, such as Montessori, Jenaplan, Dalton, Freinet and Iederwijs. For more information on these schools, you can contact the Association for Public Education (Vereniging voor Openbaar Onderwijs), see the telephone number at the end of the chapter.
- Approximately two thirds of the Dutch children goes to school with a particular DENOMINATION, such as Roman Catholic or Protestant/Christian. However, there are also Jewish, Islamic, Hindustani, Humanistic and so-called Free schools. Combinations of denominational schools and a particular educational philosophy can also be found.

CHILDREN REQUIRING SPECIAL CARE

For children who need special care and attention, there are 'special' schools, both public and denominational, such as for physically, hearing or sight impaired/challenged children, children who are sick for a long period of time and children with learning or behavioral problems.

GOVERNMENT FUNDING

Primary school is funded by the government. Each child costs them approximately € 3,900 per year (more in the case of special schools). Parents are only asked to pay a contribution for certain special activities such as events arranged by the school, swimming or cultural activities.

SECONDARY EDUCATION

In the Netherlands, after a child has completed primary school, the parents and child together choose what type of secondary school the child will go to. This decision is based, in part, on the recommendation given by the primary school during the last year.

There are three types of school they can choose from. All three start with a sort of 'basic package' that usually lasts three years and consists of subjects that all students should, in principle, follow. After those first three years, the three types of schools become quite different:

The Three Types of Secondary Education

1. *Vocational Education*, which has two phases:

- The first phase is called *Voorbereidend Middelbaar Beroeps-onderwijs* (VMBO), or preparatory secondary vocational education. It has four learning tracks differing in content and level. (The most theoretical track is known as MAVO.) VMBO also has four 'sectors' with fixed subjects. The four sectors are technology; health and personal care and welfare; economics; and agriculture. The student chooses a sector at the end of the second year. VMBO takes four years to complete.

- After completing VMBO, a pupil goes on to MBO (*Middelbaar Beroepsonderwijs*), or secondary vocational education. This consists of four types and levels of training courses, which are taken in sequence and increase in terms of difficulty: training to be an assistant (6 months to 1 year), basic vocational training (2-3 years), vocational training (3-4 years), and middle management training (3-4 years). Generally, pupils must complete a course at one level before moving on to the next. Pupils who complete vocational training can go on to specialist training (1-2 years), and those who complete either specialist training or middle management training can go on to a university of professional education (also known as HBO, see further on).

2. *Senior General Secondary Education, or HAVO (Hoger Algemeen Voortgezet Onderwijs)*

This lasts five years and is meant as preparation for study at a university of professional education (HBO). Pupils choose one of four subject clusters (*profielen*): nature and technology, nature and health, economics and society, and culture and society. Each cluster has a portion in common with the other clusters, a specialized portion, and a portion consisting of elective subjects.

3. *University preparation, or VWO (Voorbereidend Wetenschappe-lijk Onderwijs)*

This lasts six years, at the end of which the pupil is qualified to enter either university education (also known as WO, or *Weten-schappelijk Onderwijs*) or a university of professional education (HBO). Pupils choose one of the same four subject clusters (*profielen*) as in HAVO, and here too, the clusters consist of common portions, specialized portions, and elective subjects. VWO is more academically oriented than HAVO, however.

Studiehuis

For pupils in HAVO and VWO, the government recently introduced a reform that is supposed to transform schools into 'study centers' (*studiehuizen*) where pupils learn to pursue knowledge on their own or in groups rather than merely passively receiving transferred knowledge. Teachers act more as supervisors than instructors. The idea is that young people 'learn to learn', which will equip them with skills needed not only for higher education but also for tomorrow's 'learning society'.

Types of Schools

As is the case for primary schools, also secondary schools can be divided into public schools and schools based on a particular denomination (for instance, Roman-Catholic, Protestant, Jewish or Islam) or educational philosophy (for instance, Montessori or Jenaplan). Of course, there are also schools for students requiring special care, often in combination with an educational philosophy, such as Montessori, Jenaplan or Dalton.

The Obligation to Go to School and Government Funding

As long as a child is obligated to go to school (*leerplicht*), which is the case for any child that has not yet reached the age of 16 at the beginning of the school year, school is funded by the government. This costs the government approximately € 5,600 per year. Parents can be asked to make a contribution to the school. As of the age of 12 – up until and including the school year during which they reach the age of 17 – children are jointly responsible for their attendance of school. This is primarily based on the premise that children do not skip school without a reason and might require guidance for a particular problem. Between the ages of 16 and 18, children are partially *leerplichtig*, and once they turn 18, they are not at all *leerplichtig*. As of the school year after the child turns 16, education is no longer government funded. The parents (or, after its 18th birthday, the child) then owe a tuition fee of € 936 a year (school year 2004-2005).

HIGHER EDUCATION

The Netherlands has an elaborate system of higher education that has not been adopted from elsewhere but is firmly rooted in its own traditions. However, the European ministers of education have accepted a declaration in which the countries have agreed to introduce (their own version of) the Bachelor's/Master's degree program. First we will go into the traditional education system of the Netherlands. In a separate box you can read about the (intended) Bachelor's/Master's program.

Approximately 27% of the population between the ages of 15 and 64 has a higher education.

THREE STREAMS

The Netherlands has three streams of higher education that exist alongside each other:

- *Universities*. There are 14 universities including the Open University. In principle these institutes train students to be scientists and scholars, although many study programs also have a professional component and most graduates indeed find work outside the research community. The universities vary in size, with enrolments ranging from 6,000 to 30,000. Together they enroll some 187,600 students (another 18,900 attend the Open University).
- *Universities of Professional Education*, or UPE (*hogescholen*). The study programs offered by universities of professional education are, above all, geared to specific professions. The country has more than 50 such higher education institutions. The largest enroll 25,000 to 30,000 students; others are much smaller. Altogether some 334,500 students are enrolled in this form of higher education, which is known as HBO, or *hoger beroepsonderwijs*.
- *International Education*. A considerable number of institutes for International Education offer postgraduate courses in a wide range of fields. The courses are conducted in English and have been designed with foreign students in mind. For admission to most of the courses, a degree is required as well as several years of practical work experience. The International Education institutes have a total enrolment of several thousand students. The universities and the universities of professional education also offer courses that fall in this category.

PROBLEMS WITH STUDIEHUIS

The Study Center-principle has received a lot of criticism over the years. Its implementation is taking place slowly, partially because the teachers have had to change their system of teaching (which has become more 'guiding' in nature) and partially because it requires more of the students. It also requires more of the teachers as, aside from the changes, as they are now expected to come up with individual tasks for their students, whereby they must guide them, while still remaining in charge of the whole class.

This has led to a number of changes, aimed at lightening the load for both students and teachers. The course material has been made less strenuous, particularly at the expense of history and social sciences and of a newer cluster course – bearing the name of algemene natuurwetenschappen or general sciences. In the new system, these subjects are no longer obligatory. Furthermore, students are no longer required to learn another language – reading and writing – aside from English. They are expected to either drop the third language or to learn to read, write and speak the language.

The changes have created more room for the students to put together their own curriculum, so that they are no longer strictly limited to the four fixed study 'profiles'.

The changes have been received with mixed feelings. The teachers want to be left in peace, instead of having to cope with the ministerial urge to introduce changes. And here and there dissatisfaction has been expressed at the abolishment of history and social sciences as required courses.

Universities

Currently, the transition is being made, in the Dutch education system, to the Bachelor's/Master's system – inspired by the British and North American approach. You can read more about this on pages 200-201. The transition is going smoothly, but has not yet been completed. For this reason, we are including a description of the soon-to-be old structure, which remains of relevance as you might, as an employer, be faced with CVs based on the old system, in which case it would be good to know how it was constructed.

Propedeuse and Doctoraal

Under the 'old' (but still current) system, only one degree can be obtained; that of *doctorandus*. Everyone pursues the *doctoraal* degree, which requires four years of full-time study in many fields, or five years of full-time study in engineering, the natural sciences, mathematics, and agriculture. Integrated study programs in medical and health sciences last either five years (dentistry) or six years (medicine, pharmacy, and veterinary medicine). The *doctoraal* is an initial degree even though it is considered equivalent to a Master's degree.

The first year of every university program is called the *propedeuse*, and consists of required subjects introducing the field in question. Exams in all of these must be passed before a student may go on to complete the other requirements for the *doctoraal*. An academic career that is terminated before a person fulfills all the requirements for the degree is considered incomplete.

University course material in the Netherlands is strongly concentrated on the major field in which the degree is earned. Even the first years of study do not include any components that could be classified as liberal arts. These are covered in the stream of secondary school which qualifies young people for university study (vwo).

Independent research is an important part of every university program. The *doctoraal* thesis is a major requirement. This is a report written on the basis of the student's own original research. The best *doctoraal* theses find their way into scientific journals in abbreviated form, as articles.

Persons with a *doctoraal* degree use the academic title *doctorandus* (drs) unless their field is engineering, in which case the title is *ingenieur* (ir), or law, in which case the title is *meester* (mr). As mentioned earlier, the doctoraal degree is considered to be at the same level as Master's degrees in the Anglo-Saxon systems of the United Kingdom, Canada and the United States, for example.

The Doctorate or Ph.D.

A *doctoraal* degree confers eligibility for the pursuit of a doctorate through a process known as the *promotie*. This entails four years of full-time research under the supervision of a *promotor*, who must be a full professor at a university. To earn the title of 'doctor', a student must write a dissertation based on his or her own research project, and then successfully defend it in a public ceremony before a committee of professors. The Dutch doctorate is equivalent to a Ph.D.

Most students working on doctorates are in fact paid employees rather than students. They apply for positions as AIOS, or research assistants. These positions are advertised in the same way jobs are, and candidates approach the supervisor directly. Foreign nationals may apply for these positions and ask for permission to write their dissertation in another language. Candidates may also contact a university faculty at their own initiative and write their own research proposal. Sometimes the research for a dissertation can be conducted in the candidate's own country.

Universities of Professional Education

The universities of professional education, or *hogescholen*, also have a system unlike the two-degree system of American and British institutions – though some are introducing the two-tier Bachelor's and Master's degree system. Most confer only one degree, and all study programs require four years. Programs are available in seven sectors: agriculture, engineering and technology, economics and business, health care, fine and performing arts, education, and social work.

All programs have a *propedeuse*, or introductory year, the requirements of which must be completed first. Internships, or periods of work placement in a company or other organization, are important components of all HBO programs, which are always strongly oriented towards specific careers. Unlike the traditional universities, the universities of professional education do not conduct fundamental research and they do not offer possibilities for pursuing a doctorate. HBO graduates who wish to pursue a doctorate need to transfer to a traditional university to do so.

Persons who earn a diploma from a university of professional education may use the title *baccalaureus* (bc), or, in engineering and agriculture, the title *ingenieur* (ing – note the difference in abbreviation from a university-graduated engineer: ir). All graduates may also use the title Bachelor. Their degree makes them eligible for postgraduate study, either in a *post-doctoraal* program or Master's degree program, or in pursuit of a doctorate.

Alongside their regular Dutch degree programs, some of the universities of professional education also offer Anglo-Saxon-style Master's degree courses. Many of these are conducted in English in response to global demands and to facilitate the enrolment of non Dutch-speaking students in these courses. These programs last one or two years, and are open to graduates from either traditional universities or universities of professional education in the Netherlands. For foreign students, the admission requirement is usually a Bachelor's degree or its equivalent.

Admission Requirements

For admission to a degree program at a traditional university, students either must have a vwo diploma or they must have completed the first year of an HBO program. For admission to a degree program at a university of professional education, either a HAVO diploma or an MBO diploma (in middle management) is required although approximately 40% of applicants have a vwo diploma. Specific subjects in secondary school are also required for admission to many university and HBO programs.

Credit System and Grading

Workload is measured in *studiepunten*, or credits. One credit represents one week of full-time study (40 hours), including both contact hours and hours spent studying and preparing assignments. Four-year degree programs require a total of 168 credits, or

42 credits per year. The academic year is 42 weeks long. Grades are given from 1 (very poor) to 10 (outstanding). The lowest passing grade is 6; 9s are seldom given and 10s are extremely rare.

Independent Quality Assurance

All Dutch degree programs are regularly evaluated by committees of independent experts appointed by the associations of the two types of institutes of higher education (universities and universities of professional education). The committee reports are made public. If they are unfavorable, the Minister of Education, Culture and Science can take the steps he deems necessary. Even the most favorable of these reports generally make recommendations for improvement, which are taken seriously by the departments and institutions concerned.

This system of quality control, together with the official recognition of study programs (see below), guarantees that the education offered at all the institutions meets the same high standards. When Dutch students choose where they want to study, they are not thinking of which university or university of professional education is best, but instead are looking at which specializations are offered and which emphasis or academic tradition is featured. Each institution has its own atmosphere and style. They distinguish themselves in this way, and not through any absolute measure of quality. For these reasons, employers in the Netherlands look first at the degree a person has earned. Where this degree was earned is not so important.

Until recently the Inspection Higher Education of the Ministry of Education, Culture and Science was responsible for the quality control. In order to guarantee the transparency and independence of this control it was decided that it should be entrusted to an independent organization, which now is responsible not only for the quality control of higher education in the Netherlands but also in the Flemish part of Belgium. This organization, the Nederlands Vlaamse Accreditatie Organisatie (www.nvao.net) is currently reevaluating higher education for both these areas. Whenever you are looking into following a higher education in the Netherlands, you had best check what role the NVAO has played in evaluating it.

Institutes for International Education

All programs and courses that fall under International Education are conducted in English. They vary in length from three months to one or two years. In most cases, students are required to have completed a program of higher education in their own country. Usually this is a Bachelor's degree or its equivalent. The longer International Education courses lead to a Master's degree. Some of the International Education institutes have an arrangement with a Dutch university pursuant to which students can go on to pursue a doctorate after earning their Master's degree. In fact, the five largest International Education institutes are gradually being absorbed into their partner universities.

More and more institutes of higher education are offering International Education in addition to their Dutch degree programs. This most often takes the form of Master's degree courses. These have all the main features of the education offered at the institutes for International Education:

- they are taught in English
- diplomas and degrees are awarded that follow the Anglo-Saxon model (Master's degrees and Ph.D.)

THE NEW BACHELOR'S / MASTER'S SYSTEM

The most spectacular proof of the unification of Europe is the euro. However, unification is taking place in numerous other areas as well. Whereas the Treaty of Maastricht – in which the basis was laid for the introduction of the euro – has played an important role for the economy, the so-called Declaration of Bologna has played a pivotal role for higher education. In this Italian city, in 1999, all the European ministers of education joined in a conference in which they discussed how they could make the various national systems of higher education more compatible. They decided to introduce a Bachelor's/Master's system in their countries. This is the crux of the Bologna-declaration.

The Dutch minister of Education, Culture and Science, Loek Hermans, was an enthusiastic supporter of this reformation of the European higher education system and he found little resistance in the Netherlands. For this reason, with the blessing of parliament, he allowed the higher education institutes to start working out the new structure, even before the new legislation – which was only approved at the start of 2003 – had been introduced. The objective is for all higher education institutes to have implemented the new structure – which, in the Netherlands, goes by the dubious name of Ba-Ma – at the latest by the end of the year 2009. It is expected, however, that it will have been implemented much sooner – just as the Dutch relinquished their beloved guilder much quicker than even the most die-hard optimists had hoped for.

One must keep in mind, though, that schooling and education are very important elements of a national identity and of the uniqueness of a country's people and culture. There is no fixed rate for the exchange of degrees and diplomas. Particularly now that the European unification is progressing at such a steady pace, the emphasis on national identity is increasing. This is not a paradox: the European ideal explicitly does not entail a homogenizing of the cultures. A better way to describe the aim is to say that the purpose of a narrower cooperation is to create more room for variety. The next step, after the introduction of the new coin, will not be one unified European education. Also this was explicitly stated by the ministers who were party to the Bologna-Declaration. Each member state is allowed to define and implement the Bachelor's/Master's system in its own way. Often, the words 'Anglo-Saxon Model' are used in this context. However, this does not mean that the American or British examples will be copied blindly. At the most, they will be a source of inspiration for the various countries.

Having said this, it remains a fact that the new systems must have recognizable points – otherwise the whole European education reformation will have missed its purpose – and these are the following: a) those who have obtained a European-style Bachelor's degree must have broad knowledge in their area of study; b) those who have obtained a Master's degree must have pursued a specialization and have done some form of scientific research. Clearly, there is a lot of room for variation here. In the following paragraph, you will read about the Dutch variety.

UNIVERSITIES OF PROFESSIONAL EDUCATION

In the new system, the four-year studies completed at a university of professional education will lead to a Bachelor's degree. As traineeships traditionally are such an important part of this type of education, it is to be expected that most holders of this degree will immediately be able to launch a career upon completing their studies. More and more universities of professional education are also offering Master's degrees. These are generally expensive, as the Ministry of Education, Culture and Sciences has not been inclined to subsidize these studies to a great degree. Consequently, the students will have to bear the actual costs themselves, which means that they will have to pay between € 8,000 and € 10,000, or sometimes even more, annually. It is not yet clear whether students who have obtained a Bachelor's degree at a university of professional education will be able to go on to obtain a Master's degree at a 'regular' university, afterwards. It would appear that the regular universities will be given plenty of room to determine their rules and conditions for admission.

UNIVERSITIES

At the 'regular' universities, it will take three years to obtain a Bachelor's degree, followed by two years to obtain a Master's degree. The system of education at universities is more theoretical in nature than at universities of professional education. Traineeships do not play as important a role and are usually entirely absent during the first years at university. This is why the Bachelor's phase at regular universities can be so much shorter. Theoretically, the focus of a university study can be seen as more oriented towards a future in (scientific) research than towards a career in the corporate world or with the government – though it has to be said that the great majority of Dutch university graduates ends up outside the world of research and in the corporate world. Minister Hermans has made clear that the Master's phase is to be available to all those who have obtained a Bachelor's degree at university. The Master's phase is a phase in which the students will pursue a specialization. An important part of this phase is the final thesis, which must be primarily theoretical (requiring research) in nature. The final terms of the Master's degree will be practically the same as those for the traditional doctoraal degree (which one obtains at university according to the traditional system) – and will last one to two years. In most cases, this will be two years, as it is simply not possible to complete a two-phase academic study in a total of four years; up till now, students following the traditional system usually have proven to require five to six years to fully complete their academic studies.

The system for obtaining a Ph.D. will remain the same.

CONSEQUENCES

What will the university Bachelor's degree be worth on the labor market? Will many students be happy to finish their studies at that point? The answers to these questions are hard to give. They depend entirely on how prospective employers will react to the new system. Companies and organizations that make use of 'scientific' personnel, are long used to employing doctorandussen (considered equivalent to those who have a

Master's degree). Therefore it is likely that they will prefer holders of a university Master's degree to holders of a university Bachelor's degree.

It bears repeating that the situation for graduates of universities of professional education is entirely different: the corporate world is used to graduates of these institutes; Bachelor's degrees obtained at these universities already are a reliable passport into the corporate world.

WHAT DOES THIS MEAN FOR YOU?

As said earlier, all institutes for higher education have three years to implement the new structure. There will be those who run ahead and those who lag behind and those who will belong to the middle group. If you are looking for a place to pursue a higher education, you had best look into how the institute is faring with its introduction of the Bachelor's/Master's system. This is not because, as they may be behind in this area, this means they will be lagging in all other areas or that the quality of the education they offer will be inferior: the degree to which they have implemented this intended change in structure has nothing to do with that at all. It is rather because the holding of a Bachelor's or Master's degree is a desirable aim for those cosmopolitans among you who wish to complete their studies in another country. They/you can now show recognizable diplomas when applying to another institute of higher education (or for a job), which will greatly simplify integration – which is precisely what the aim of the unification was.

• courses are at an advanced level and tend to be in subjects in which the Dutch have special expertise.

Approximately 1,000 International Education courses are offered in a wide range of fields. They can be found in the Catalogue of International Courses published by Nuffic, which is also available online (see: www.studyin. nl).

Official Recognition and Student Grants

Regular higher education, which means the Dutch degree programs offered at universities and universities of professional education, is regulated by law in the Netherlands. The Higher Education and Research Act of 1993 officially recognizes the regular study programs offered by these institutes and the degrees and titles associated with them. All recognized programs are listed in the central register known as CROHO. All government-subsidized programs (approximately half of those listed by CROHO) have the same relatively low annual tuition fee (€ 1,476 for 2004-2005), the rest are free to set their own tuition fees. Students enrolled in these programs who meet the necessary requirements qualify for a monthly student grant from the government until they reach the age of 34 (called *studiefinanciering* – see page 204). International students who do not qualify for *studiefinanciering* can apply, under certain conditions, for a restitution of their tuition fees (see further on).

International Education falls largely outside this system and its subsidies. Tuition fees more often reflect real costs, and students enrolled in international courses do not qualify for Dutch student grants. Depending on which country they are from, they might be eligible for a scholarship, however.

The Master's degree programs at universities of professional education are usually validated either by a British partner university or by the Dutch Validation Council.

STUDENT LIFE

TYPES OF STUDY AND UNIVERSITY TOWNS

There are approximately 500,000 students in the Netherlands. However, the term 'students' covers two types: those who go to university (referred to as *Wetenschappelijk Onderwijs* or WO) and those who go to a university of professional education (referred to as *Hoger Beroeps Onderwijs* or HBO). The main difference between these two is the admission requirements, which are higher for a university (WO) education. Also the type of education is very different: that at university focuses more on science and theory, while HBO focuses more on practical experience and specific professions.

There are twelve cities in the Netherlands that have a university: Amsterdam, Rotterdam, Delft, Leiden, Utrecht, Wageningen, Groningen, Enschede, Nijmegen, Tilburg, Eindhoven and Maastricht. Some of these universities are very old, creating an atmosphere that you can feel when walking around in their old buildings – which are naturally also filled with the required amenities for modern-day students. A wonderful example of this is the University of Nijenrode in Breukelen, which has not yet been mentioned here (and is not a university in the traditional sense of the word, but a business school). The courses used to be taught in Nijenrode Castle, which was built in the 12th century. Nowadays, one can still take classes in the old armory, situated in the top of the castle. However, new buildings have been added.

On the other hand, there are more than 50 universities of professional education. They are more recent than the classical universities, such as those of Leiden and Utrecht, which are centuries old, but because of the sheer numbers of their students, they generate the feel of a student town in many of their home locations. In many cases, they are a very important employer and an asset to the local community. Universities of professional education, incidentally, often share a city or town with a classical university, while other cities house only universities of professional education, such as 's-Hertogenbosch, Diemen, Alkmaar and Haarlem. Almost all the student towns have a real student atmosphere. For instance, in Utrecht and Leiden you will find many student cafés, restaurants, etc., making it easy to have a 'cheap' night out on the town.

HOUSING

All student towns share one problem: it is hard to find proper housing. It is already hard enough for Dutch students, let alone for foreign students who do not have their own network and who will not be staying here long. Therefore, tip # 1 is: approach any and everybody to let them know you are looking for housing. You might be lucky. However, there is some help: every town or city has an organization that helps those looking for a place to live. The only problem here is the waiting lists. You might do better to try your luck with an organization such as 'Students for Students' (tel.: 020 618 64 25). This is a fairly new organization that helps students, and particularly foreign students, find housing and can be found in Amsterdam, Leiden and Utrecht – where it is hardest to find a place to live.

Perhaps the best help is available from the institutes of higher education themselves. They often have special departments that help students find a suitable place to live. Often they even have a special department for foreign students. These are the following:

- *the University of Amsterdam* (Universiteit van Amsterdam, or UvA), which has as its central telephone number 020 525 91 11, and has a Department for Foreign Students (Bureau Buitenland), which can be reached at 020 525 23 73. You can also contact the Guest Housing Department (*gastenverblijven*)
- *the Free University*, (Vrije Universiteit) in Amsterdam, which has as its central telephone number 020 444 77 77. It also offers help via an external organization in Amstelveen: Intermezzo, 020 543 11 00
- *Erasmus University* (Erasmus Universiteit) in Rotterdam (central telephone number: 010 408 11 11) has its own organization for these matters, ICIR, which can be reached at 010 408 16 49
- *the University of Twente* (Universiteit Twente) in Enschede (central telephone number 053 489 91 11) supports its foreign students via the ACASA Student Foundation (ACASA Huisvesting), 'Campus Drienerlo' in Enschede. They can be reached at 053 489 40 00
- *Wageningen University* (Wageningen Universiteit & Research) (central telephone number 0317 48 91 11) has two options. You can try the Student Housing Foundation Wageningen (Stichting Studenten Huisvesting Wageningen or SSHW) at 0317 47 25 01 or 0317 42 61 61, but you could best start out at the Dean's Office, as it coordinates everything
- *the Catholic University Brabant* (Katholieke Universiteit Brabant) in Tilburg (central telephone number 013 466 91 11) arranges these matters through the Foreign Students Service Bureau (Service Bureau Buitenland), which can be reached at above number
- *the University of Maastricht* (Universiteit Maastricht) (central telephone number 043 388 22 22) arranges housing through the Rooms Department (Kamerbureau), which can be reached at 043 388 53 00
- *the University of Groningen* (Rijksuniversiteit Groningen) (central telephone number 050 363 91 11) has a department called the Foreign Student Housing Foundation Groningen (Stichting Huisvesting Buitenlandse Studenten Groningen, or SHBSG). They can be reached at 050 571 04 97
- *the University of Utrecht* (Universiteit Utrecht) (central telephone number 030 253 91 11) also has a Department Foreign Student Housing (Bureau Buitenlandse Studenten Huisvesting). They can be reached at 030 253 26 96
- *the Catholic University of Nijmegen* (Katholieke Universiteit Nijmegen) (central telephone number 024 361 61 61) uses its Foreign Department (Externe Relaties) to arrange housing for foreign students (024 361 20 65)
- *the University of Leiden* (Universiteit Leiden) (071 527 27 27) has the University Guesthouse for visiting professors and researchers. They can be reached at 071 527 74 97.
- *the Technical University of Eindhoven* (Technische Universiteit Eindhoven) (040 247 91 11) has Vestide that can be reached at 040 247 91 11
- *the Technical University of Delft* (Technische Universiteit Delft) (015 278 91 11) uses the Student Housing Department (*Studenten Huisvesting*) to help students find housing. It can be reached at 015 219 22 00.

Incidentally, it is not always easy to reach these departments. This is why the central telephone numbers have been included so as not to end up taking the endless route of answering machines.

The last option might be less direct, but is an option for those who want to become a member of a student organization anyway. Many of these organizations have fraternities and sororities that often have their 'own' houses. The advantage to this is that you share a house with people you socialize and study with. However, on the other hand, you have to become a member of the organization first, which can take a lot of time. You would have to find housing for the interim and be coming to the Netherlands for a longer period of time.

Four websites where you can look for more on housing are: www.studentenkamers.nl (where you click on the town or city in which you are looking for a place to live), http://kamers.pagina. nl/ (which allows you to click on the university at which you will be studying, from where you click on the housing organization, if they have one), http://studenten.pagina.nl and http://studenten. boogolinks.nl (though the information may be in Dutch, they are fairly simple to navigate. Housing is *huisvesting*; anything with the word *kamers* – meaning 'rooms' – also refers to housing).

STUDENT ORGANIZATIONS

Not many Dutch institutes of higher education have a campus whose atmosphere is created by the fraternities/sororities and student organizations. This does not mean to say, however, that student organizations do not influence the atmosphere in these student towns. Young students become a member of these organizations to find a network, particularly for extracurricular activities and going out. Every student town has a number of student organizations that do or do not have their own buildings, and that have their own traditions, rules, atmosphere and culture. Their great advantage is that you meet many new people in a short period of time, and their buildings are a regular place to visit when going out. This is where their members meet to party or to have a drink with their fellow-students.

Becoming a member does, however, often include going through hazing. This costs a lot of time, particularly with the so-called Student Corps, where it can take weeks or even months before you are officially a member. If you are not going to be here long, you might prefer to check out the smaller student organizations that do not have any hazing traditions, or only a short one. These are often organizations that have been founded by the institutes of higher education themselves, but there are also organizations that are organized around a sport, religion or other common interest. It would be virtually impossible to list them all here, but you can visit the following website: http://studenten-verenigin-gen. pagina.nl or http://studenten.boogolinks.nl, which will give you an overview of all the student organizations per city and most international student organizations. And of course, you can ask anyone at your institute of higher education.

Aside from the so-called free time organizations (*gezelligheids-verenigingen*) there are the so-called faculty organizations (*stu-dieverenigingen*). Also these organize many activities, only more related to the subject of your studies. They organize lectures, workshops and, for instance, the sale of textbooks at a reduced price. These organizations are faculty-based and can be found via the institute of higher education. They are definitely worth visiting, as they allow you to meet many people who can help and advise you with your study and other important student life issues. An overview of these can be found on http://universiteiten-studieverenigingen.pagina.nl/.

And last but not least, there are a few national and international student organizations that can help you find work placements and temporary jobs as well as fun and interesting activities. The most important ones are AEGEE and AIESEC. AEGEE is a general European student organization, while AIESEC is an international organization for students studying economics. They can be found at www.aiesec.nl or www2.eur.nl/studeren/aegee/respectively.

SPORTS FOR STUDENTS

All student towns have facilities for the more popular sports, which are sometimes a part of the regular sports organization, but are sometimes affiliated with the institute of higher education. Unfortunately, sport life in the Netherlands is not at all comparable to that in the US, for instance, where students get to make free use of the facilities or even receive a scholarship if they are a member of a particular sports team. The Dutch student sports organizations are more about sporting together and less about competition. Membership is often not expensive, keeping it affordable.

One of the most important and more competitive student sports in the Netherlands is rowing. Most Dutch rowing clubs are student clubs, either affiliated with the larger student organizations, or independent. Many students take up this sport during their first year and stop after graduating. Its main event is the Varsity, a huge rowing tournament to which the larger student rowing clubs send their best teams to compete. While all the competing is going on, thousands of students sit and stand by the water to watch, picnic, drink and party – a party which is continued in the building of the student organization of the winning team of the so-called Old Four Race.

However, rowing is not all there is. There is soccer, rugby, tennis and more, most of which have their own organization. You can find out more about these at your faculty or you can visit the website of the Dutch Students' Sports Foundation (*Nederlandse Studenten Sport Vereniging* or NSSS), which represents the interests of student sports. Many student sports organizations are a member of NSSS, which also organizes national and regional sporting events and Dutch student championships. Its website is: www.nsss.nl.

A NIGHT OUT ON THE TOWN

Where to go for fun and socializing? Some of the Dutch student towns are the largest towns/cities in the Netherlands and have enough to offer in terms of cafés, restaurants, discos and other places. The answer to the question of where to go is obvious: wherever you want. Still, the most fun would be to go where you find other students and where things are not too expensive. Luckily, there are many student cafés and restaurants and designated student cafeterias, where, at little cost, you can buy a meal. But don't overlook the (student) 'eat-cafés', which have a pleasant atmosphere and cheap food. Go out and investigate, and ask others what they recommend. This search alone is already half the fun.

If you are looking for a cultural night out on the town, you might be interested in obtaining a CJP (pronounced say-yay-pay: *cultureel jongeren paspoort*, or cultural youth pass). The CJP is the Dutch equivalent of the Euro <26 card, costs € 12.50 and can be bought at the VVV or via www. cjp.nl. With this you not only obtain reductions on tickets for theater and concert events, but also on the entrance fee for exhibitions and films. If you visit www.cjp.nl and click on *agenda*, you can type in the place where you would like to do something cultural, and the date. The site will then tell you what's on.

FINANCES

The word alone is intimidating, because who wouldn't want more spending money? Here is some advice on arranging a loan, arranging insurance, and finding a job.

Banks

Most banks will probably be willing to support you financially and to answer any finance-related questions you may have. Ask about their loans. The following banks have special programs for students: ABN Amro, Postbank, Fortis, Rabobank and SNS. These programs include special interest rates, a maximum loan, the use of a credit card, special repayment programs, the 'leasing' of equipment (such as computers) and certain extras, such as a CJP (*Cultureel Jongeren Paspoort*).

Several banks (certainly in the cities where there is a substantial international student population) are fully aware of the situation of foreign students and are quite flexible in working out an arrangement that will help you cover your costs and pay back your loan once you have completed your studies and have a job. The banks will certainly ask to see your student registration and for you to find a guarantor. Approaching one of the banks listed above would be your best bet.

Insurance

Also, do not forget about insurance. If you have done about this in your home country, there is no problem. And sometimes your institute of higher education will already have arranged insurance for you (or have a collective package on offer for you to participate in). Otherwise, you can ask the banks about their student insurance plans as anything might happen and the last thing you want to return home with is a hefty hospital bill.

Jobs

Many students have on-the-side jobs in cafés and restaurants. However, there are also other sources of jobs; if you are looking for a job you can also go to an employment agency, which you can find at the end of chapter 2.

Of course, you can also go find a job yourself. If you do not feel your Dutch is up to snuff, then you can certainly try the bigger multinationals in the Netherlands: they often have international projects that can be carried out without having to speak faultless Dutch. You can find these companies on www.jobnews.nl. And then there are the Irish and English pubs, where everything is done in English.

Don't forget: unless you are planning to work illegally, you will need a residence permit, a work permit and a sofi-number! You can read more about these on pages 66 and 112-115.

GRANTS

Studiefinanciering

If are younger than the age of 30 and are starting your studies at a university or university of higher education, you have a right to the so-called *studiefinanciering*, which is made up of a basic grant, and additional grant, and an interest-bearing loan. The loan will be converted into a 'gift' if you successfully complete

The advantage of studying in Holland

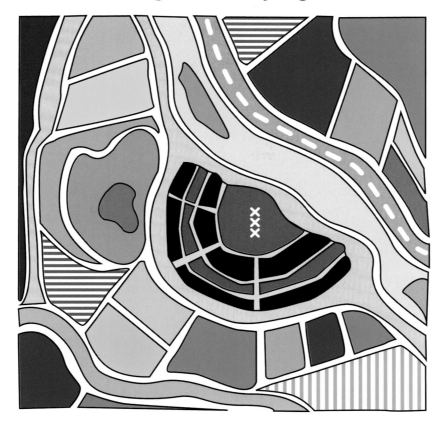

It's colourful either way you look at it

INTERNATIONAL MBA PROGRAMME

Our parttime and fulltime International MBA programmes are aimed at those who are willing and eager to invest in their human capital. This MBA offers you a complete programme based on the accepted fundamentals of the science of business intertwined with the art of doing business. Your knowledge as a MBA student will be enriched by core, functional and cross-cultural business disciplines in a dynamic, international environment.

Starting dates:

Fulltime: March & October, 13 months, € 12.995,-.

Parttime: March & October, 2 years, € 6.985,- per year

• Focus on Entrepreneurship and Innovation

• Accreditation by Dutch Validation Council

FOR MORE INFORMATION

www.hasb.nl
info@hasb.nl
Phone: +31 (0)20-523 64 29

HES AMSTERDAM SCHOOL OF BUSINESS
Post-Graduate Programmes

your studies. If you thus have a right to *studiefinanciering*, you will continue to receive it until you reach the age of 34.

The basic grant does not depend on your parents' income, but it does depend on whether you live at home or not (it is lower if you do). The additional grant does depend on your parents' income, whether you have brothers or sisters in school/pursuing higher education (and who receive a grant) and whether you have private or *Ziekenfonds* medical insurance (see more on *Ziekenfonds*-coverage on page 123). On top of these two grants, you can take out the loan, over which you pay an annually fixed amount of interest.

If you have a right to *studiefinanciering*, you also have a right to the *ov-studentenkaart*, with which you can travel by public transportation for free either during the weekend or on weekdays (your choice) and at reduced rates during the other days.

The monthly amounts of *studiefinanciering* that you will receive are the following (2005): basic grant € 233.08 (if you live independently) or € 75.70 (if you live at home). The additional grant amounts to a maximum of € 239.76 (if you live independently and have private insurance) or € 221.37 if you live at home. If you are covered by Ziekenfonds, the amounts are approximately € 35 lower. The further loan of € 258.69 is available at a fixed interest rate.

Visit: www.ib-groep.nl and click on *international visitors* for more on study grants, the restitution of tuition fees and other information.

Also contact your university in the Netherlands to find out whether it has a grant for international students, as some have their own grant programs.

Studiefinanciering for Non-Dutch Nationals

If you are a non-Dutch national, legally residing in the Netherlands, you have a right to *studiefinanciering* if:

- you are an EU/EEA national and work(ed) in the Netherlands during at least 32 hours a month or one of your parents is an EU/EEA national and works here
- you have a temporary residence permit issued in connection with family (re)unification. The parent or other family member must also have residence permit, type I,II,III or IV (temporary, permanent or refugee)
- you have a permanent residence permit or a residence permit for refugees (temporary or permanent)
- you or your parents have already received a study allowance at an earlier point in time.

You do not qualify if:

- you are an EU/EEA national other than in the situation above, *however* you do have a right to restitution of your tuition fee, see further on
- you are a refugee who has received a postponement on your deportation
- you have a document issued to embassy and similar personnel.

Refugees

Those who have refugee status, are starting a higher education and are 27, 28 or 29 years of age, can approach Stichting UAF Steunpunt (www.uaf.nl, in Utrecht, 030 252 08 35) for more information on the possibilities of a grant.

Study Grants for EU/EEA Nationals

If you are an EU/EEA national (listed below), but do not qualify for *studiefinanciering*, you can receive a one-time grant in the form of tuition fee restitution per year of study.

Pupils of secondary education and students at universities of professional education are eligible for an annual grant of up to € 670.20 per school year (2004-2005), while students of higher education are eligible for an annual grant of € 889.32 (2004-2005). To qualify for this, you must meet the following conditions:

- you are from: Austria, Belgium, Cyprus, the Czech Republic, Denmark, Estonia, Finland, France, Germany, Great Britain, Greece, Hungary, Iceland, Ireland, Italy, Latvia, Liechtenstein, Lithuania, Luxembourg, Malta, Norway, Poland, Portugal, Slovakia, Slovenia, Spain, Sweden or Switzerland
- you are following a course of study in the Netherlands which entitles you to a grant for tuition fees or a student grant (*studiefinanciering*)
- you have paid the tuition fees
- you are not eligible for the Dutch *studiefinanciering* grant
- you have your own bank or *giro* account in the Netherlands
- you have completed a 'Restitution of tuition fee' form.

To get this form, write or phone: Informatie Beheer Group, Productgroep Studiefinanciering, P.O. Box 30151, 9700 LB Groningen, tel.: 050 599 77 55. Forms can be downloaded from www.ib-groep.nl, click on *international visitors*, then on *brochures and forms*.

Apply for restitution one year at a time, always for the current year of study, and never later than on January 1.

LIVING ON A SHOESTRING
WELL-FED AND WELL-DRESSED

It would be nicest, if your employer were to send you to the Netherlands within the context of a jointly agreed career move in order to hone and show your professional talents at a local branch. Then, you would be welcomed by the Human Resource Department who would probably arrange suitable (though maybe comparatively cramped, compared to your home country – the Dutch are not into huge houses) housing for you and help you with your accommodation expenses. Many employers contribute to the tuition fees of your children. And a lease car – maybe not as large and comfortable as you are accustomed to (the Dutch are not into showy cars, either) – would be ready for you.

THE OTHER EXPAT

However, most of you who come to the Netherlands will not find such a 'neatly made up bed' – to use a Dutch expression. You've come here, driven by ambition; to study, or to find a job. Or possibly to seek protection from persecution. Or maybe your multinational employer has not yet caught on to your talents.

You've come to the Netherlands to make a change in your life. To 'lay the first bricks' of your career – you're ready to make a go of it.

A SHOE AND A SLIPPER

Also to this situation, a Dutch expression applies: you've come here on a shoe and a slipper. And it's going to stay that way, for the time being, also financially. Your income will lie somewhere between € 475 and € 950 a month, sometimes less. This will quite likely be the case if you have come here as a student.

And that brings us to another Dutch expression: to turn over each dime, before you spend it.

If this is your situation, how do you deal with it? In giving you the following tips, we are working on the assumption that you do

SCHAKELJAAR – LINK YEAR

Refugees, asylum seekers and other non-Dutch nationals who come to study in the Netherlands, often go through a period of cultural and language adjustment that conceivably prevents them from getting everything they can out of their studies – or giving it all they have. Luckily, a number of institutes of higher education now offer a so-called schakeljaar (link year), created specifically for non-European, non-Western students, who are planning on following a study at a Dutch university (of professional education).

During this year, you are offered a course in the Dutch language (including the specific terminology that you will run across during the course of your studies), English, computer science and study techniques, as well as a preparatory course for the study of your choice. Furthermore, you are familiarized with the Dutch university system; for instance, how you are expected to approach your studies, how classes are given, how to give a presentation and how to work on group assignments.

Schakeljaren are offered in Rotterdam, The Hague, Amsterdam, Utrecht, Groningen, Diemen, Maastricht, Nijmegen, Zwolle, Enschede and Deventer. For more information, visit the website of the Foundation for Refugee Students (www.uaf.nl) – here you click on publicities and then on folder schakeljaren, which is in Dutch, but does have a list, at the end, of universities that offer the course and how to contact them), or www.schakeljaar.nl. What the costs of the schakeljaar are, depend on your personal situation, as well as any agreements reached between your university and the municipality on financing and whether you have a right to studiefinanciering. For more information, approach your university.

have a place to live and, therefore, a mailbox. Many of the following tips may not be new to you, but to be complete, we will give them anyway.

YOUR MAIL BOX

For starters, you will find that your mailbox is full of publications that you have not asked for. In most cases, this will be promotional material for your local stores and supermarkets. Furthermore, you will receive one or two local (regional) newspapers. These are called 'house-to-house' papers (*huis-aan-huis bladen*), and contain, aside from local news, a lot of locally relevant advertising.

Don't throw them away; pay attention to them, as they can mean savings for you, even if your Dutch is not yet up to snuff. Here are a few words to remember:

- *Reclame*. This means that the product (of which there is hopefully a picture) is being sold at a reduced price
- *Aanbieding*. Same thing

- *Korting*. Also same thing
- *Bon, kortingsbon, coupon*. You are to fill in the coupon and take it to the store, where they will give you a reduction on the products advertised
- *Op = op, weg = weg*, or *op is op, weg is weg* (finished = finished, gone = gone). This means that a limited amount of a certain product is being sold at a reduced price
- *Occasion*. This is a second-hand (or 'pre-owned') item, almost always used for cars and computers.

FOOD

It is a good idea to take a look at above publications before going shopping. Most Dutch people shop for their daily needs at supermarkets that, in the 60s and 70s, chased away the local mom and pop stores. They are part of the larger chains – such as Albert Heijn, Aldi and Plusmarkt – and focus on a particular segment of the market. If you want to spend less money, go to a supermarket that targets a wide segment of the consumer market that has relatively little spending money. The quality of the products will be comparable, as the Netherlands has a very strict and effective Inspectorate for Consumer Goods. The things that will tip you off in your selection of a supermarket are through-put, variety and presentation. Luxurious-looking supermarkets are usually more expensive than their modest-looking competitors.

In the store, always be on the look-out for the word *aanbieding*. And check whether the supermarket sells goods under its own label, as these are usually cheaper than other, world-renowned, brands. The quality will almost always be the same; only the packaging will be cheaper. Pay attention if there is a reduction for buying more than one package (*2 halen, 1 betalen* – buy two, pay for one).

When buying food, pay attention to the 'best before'-date: *tenminste houdbaar tot*, sometimes merely *t.h.t.*

STREET MARKETS

But don't limit yourself to the supermarkets; the local street markets, which are organized once or twice a week, have plenty to offer. As they say in the Netherlands: at the street market, your guilder is worth one-and-a-half (the same, presumably, applies to your euro). Also here, shop around and compare.

The Dutch go to the street markets to spend less money and the market vendors know that. There are two main segments at the market: food and textile (but also flowers and plants – to buy those, you should go at the end of the day, when the vendors want to 'get rid' of their stuff and sell it at greatly reduced prices). And you can buy quite a decent wardrobe at the street market.

SMALLER SHOPKEEPERS

A third, good, source of supplies is the local 'exotic' food stores. Already since a long time, this country has had a good supply of *tokos* (Indonesian) and Chinese stores and supermarkets. Since it has become even more multi-cultural, the smaller shopkeepers have been making an admirable niche for themselves, especially those from the Middle and Far East. They have taken on the challenge of opening small butcher stores, bakeries and grocery stores – with success. With the added advantage that they often sell goods and spices that cannot be found in the traditional supermarkets (but can also be found at the street markets).

GOING OUT TO EAT

The best way to save money on food is by doing your own cooking, of course. But this is not always as much fun as going out for a bite to eat. If you decide to go out, focus on *eet-café's* rather than restaurants and check out the price of their *dagschotel* (meal of the day), which should not be more than € 8. They are served on a large plate and are sufficiently filling and nutritious. Even cheaper are the Surinam take-outs, which you can find in most big cities, and their Turkish and Moroccan competitors, who mostly advertise their shoarma. Or you can go to the traditional Dutch *patatzaak*, where they sell French Fries (*patat*), *kroketten* (which have a soft, meat-based filling, rolled in bread crumbs and fried) and other fried meat products. McDonald's can also be found in almost any city or larger town, though they are not necessarily the cheapest.

DURABLE GOODS

But food is not all you want. You also want durable goods, such as a radio, a television, a CD player and loudspeakers. You want to furnish your apartment. You might, one day, want a car. When it comes to owning a car, do not forget that the Netherlands is a country of traffic congestion and traffic jams. Buy a car only if you really need it, as taxes are high (both on the purchase price and on fuel) and the road tax (which is unavoidable) is considerable. The amount of road tax you pay depends on where you live, and the weight and fuel of your car. If you live in a city, be prepared to walk long distances as you can seldom park near your destination (or home). Consider whether you might not be better off with a bicycle (and public transportation) – in which case, don't forget a sturdy lock as bicycle theft is a thriving industry in the Netherlands! Stall your bicycle inside if you can. If you want a car anyway, check out the used cars market. The *huis-aan-huis* (house-to-house) papers contain many small ads for used cars, as do the larger newspapers, particularly the Saturday edition of *De Telegraaf* and *Algemeen Dagblad*.

CLASSIFIED ADS

For the purchase of durable goods, it is always worth your while to buy a particular type of newspaper. These are filled with free ads and notices and can be bought at tobacco stores and newspaper stalls. They contain thousands of *aanbiedingen* – cheap buying opportunities – and can be found all across the Netherlands. The largest and best-known is called *Via Via* (which also has its own website: www.viavia.nl).

Here, you can also place your own ads, offering whatever you want (including your services if you want to start a – free-lance – business from home). They even have a romantic section. The ads are classified and most often mention the price and the telephone number of the seller. You name it, you can find it. Cars, televisions, furniture, bicycles, gardening tools, baby items, pets, toys, computers, printers ... But be careful that you are not taken advantage of. And you can try to bargain, but keep in mind that not all Dutch people are used to bargaining and will tenaciously stick to their original price.

USED ITEMS

In so-called working class neighborhoods you can find many stores for used items, including clothing, though you should always check the quality. And there are the so-called recycle-centers, an initiative of the environmental organizations. These organizations object to the throw-away mentality of the well-to-do. You can fill your house with very useful items with the help of these organizations and the *Via Via*-like papers. And you might pick up a thing or two, of which you recognize the value and significance that the seller might not have.

Another great source of 'pre-owned' goods is www.marktplaats.nl, where you type in the brand name or simply the item you are searching for, indicate in which area of the Netherlands (if necessary all of the Netherlands) you wish to find it, and wait for the results. Keep a dictionary at hand, as it is in Dutch and will not find anything in the category 'couch', but will under *zitbanken*.

BEWARE OF VERY CHEAP PRICES

One final word of warning: many drug-addicts support their habit by selling stolen goods. Since the arrival of hard drugs, many people have installed extra locks and safety-locks – as should you. There are quite a few stolen goods on the market, such as electronic ware, scooters and bicycles – and their prices are very attractive. But beware of the fact that there are often well-concealed registration numbers on these items and that if the police find such a number (corresponding to a stolen good) on your purchase, then you have a problem. *The buyer of stolen goods is worse than the thief*, is their motto and they – nor the judge – will be much impressed by your defense that you bought the item in good faith. They operate on the principle that if an item has been sold at a 'ridiculously' low price, then you should have known better and cannot have been acting in good faith.

INSURANCE

In order to register in the Netherlands, you have to show that you have insurance, which is not always cheap. Therefore, it is good to know that if you have a relatively low-income job, or are receiving a benefit, you qualify for coverage by the *Ziekenfonds*. The *Ziekenfonds* covers visits to your family doctor (*huisarts*), specialists, physical therapy, pregnancy and childbirth costs, home care after birth, hospitalization, most prescription drugs and medical equipment. You can read more about this on page 123.

STUDENT

If you have come here as a foreign student, keep in mind that you can approach many of the larger banks for (low interest) loans and a student insurance package (if your educational institution has not already arranged one for you).

LEGAL AID

If you are in need of (cheap) legal advice, you can approach a so-called *Juridisch Loket*, which offers free consultation for elementary issues that can be dealt with in less than an hour, or else answers legal questions and then sets you up with legal aid. The *Juridisch Loketten* were introduced to replace legal aid societies and currently you can still find both, though the latter will swiftly disappear over the course of 2005, their tasks having been handed over to new legal offices. You can read more about this, and financial aid, on page 125.

COLD AND LONELY?

And if there is a lot of month left, after your change purse has been depleted of its last dime and you are feeling cold and lonely? Go to a library; entry is free and you can read anything you want, in several different languages. When reading, you are never alone and... there's central heating.

SCHOOL HOLIDAYS

MAY 2005

ELEMENTARY, MIDDLE
AND HIGH SCHOOLS
All Regions: April 30 – May 8

SUMMER 2005

ELEMENTARY SCHOOLS
Northern Region: July 23–September 4
Middle Region: July 2 – August 14
Southern Region: July 9 – August 21

MIDDLE AND HIGH SCHOOLS
Northern Region: July 16 – September 4
Middle Region: July 2 – August 21
Southern Region: July 9 – August 28

AUTUMN 2005

ELEMENTARY, MIDDLE AND HIGH SCHOOLS
Middle and Southern Region:
October 15 – 23
Northern Region: October 22 – 30

WINTER 2005–2006

ELEMENTARY, MIDDLE AND HIGH SCHOOLS
All Regions: December 24 – January 8

SPRING 2005

ELEMENTARY, MIDDLE AND HIGH SCHOOLS
Northern and Middle Region: February 18 – 26
Southern Region: February 25 – March 5

REFERENCES

ORGANIZATIONS

MINISTRY OF EDUCATION, CULTURE AND SCIENCES (*MINISTERIE VAN ONDERWIJS, CULTUUR EN WETENSCHAP*)
Information provided by the Ministry of Education, Culture and Science
www.minocw.nl/english

ASSOCIATION FOR PUBLIC EDUCATION (*VERENIGING VOOR OPENBAAR ONDERWIJS*)
P.O. Box 10241, 1301 AE Almere
Tel.: 036 533 15 00
Internet: www.voo.nl

INFORMATIE BEHEER GROUP
Education in Dutch and regular student grants
P.O. Box 30151, 9700 LB Groningen
Tel.: 050 599 77 55
Internet: www.ib-groep.nl

HBO-RAAD
Information or the higher professional education and the universities of professional education in the Netherlands
Internet: www.hbo-raad.nl

THE ROYAL TROPICAL INSTITUTE (**KIT**)
An independent center of knowledge and expertise in the areas of international and intercultural cooperation
Mauritskade 63, 1092 AD Amsterdam
Tel.: 020 568 87 23
Internet: www.kit.nl

INTERNATIONAL EDUCATION

For more information on primary and secondary education, denominational schools, special schools and schools based on a certain teaching and learning philosophy:
MINISTRY OF EDUCATION, CULTURE AND SCIENCES
P.O. Box 16375, 2500 BJ The Hague
Tel.: 070 412 3456
Internet: www.minocw.nl/english

INTERNATIONAL HIGHER EDUCATION

NUFFIC, *THE NETHERLANDS ORGANIZATION FOR INTERNATIONAL COOPERATION IN HIGHER EDUCATION*, is a clearing house for information about higher education. Its website www.nuffic.nl acts as a gateway to many other sources in addition to the information Nuffic itself generates.

NUFFIC
Kortenaerkade 11
P.O. Box 29777
2502 LT The Hague
Tel.: 070 426 02 60
Fax:. 070 426 03 99
E-mail: nuffic@nuffic.nl
Internet: www.nuffic.nl

NUFFIC PUBLICATIONS

See the complete list of Nuffic´s publications in English: www.nuffic.nl/publications

STUDY IN THE NETHERLANDS: COURSES AND STUDY PROGRAMS IN ENGLISH

STUDY IN THE NETHERLANDS: DUTCH DEGREE PROGRAMS
Updated annually, these two booklets offer general descriptions of International Education and of the regular programs offered at the universities and universities of professional education, as well as general information and tips about admission procedures, scholarships, and other practical matters. They contain lists of the courses and programs and the addresses of the institutions that offer them.

CATALOGUE OF INTERNATIONAL COURSES IN THE NETHERLANDS
This detailed catalogue contains complete listings and descriptions of more than 600 courses conducted in English, most of which are at postgraduate level. There is also a chapter on scholarships. Updated annually. Also available online:
www.nuffic.nl/publications

WEBSITES

STUDY IN THE NETHERLANDS
www.studyin.nl
http://studenten.pagina.nl or
http://studenten.boogolinks.nl, for an overview of all the student organizations per city and most international student organizations.

INTERNATIONAL SCHOOLS
www.intschools.nl: National organization for Dutch schools with an international stream
www.sio.nl: Stichting Internationaal Onderwijs (International Education Foundation) website with a list of all international schools (see also the next page)
www.usemb.nl: United States Embassy Internet which contains links to American international schools in the Netherlands

VISA FOR STUDENTS
www.study-visa-holland.nl

HOUSING FOR STUDENTS
http://come.to/kamergids
www.studentenkamers.nl
http://kamers.pagina.nl
for more references see page 202 - 203

STUDENT ORGANIZATIONS (*STUDENTEN-VERENIGINGEN*)
http://universiteiten-studieverenigingen.pagina.nl
http://studenten-verenigingen.pagina.nl

THE NACEE (**NETHERLANDS AMERICA COMMISSION FOR EDUCATIONAL EXCHANGE**)
provides information on study, research and internships in the United States of America and promotes the exchange of students, scholars and teachers between the Netherlands and the United States.
Internet: www.nacee.nl

INTERNATIONAL HIGHER EDUCATION INSTITUTES

FION
The Federation of Institutes for International Education in the Netherlands: www.fion.nl

EUROPEAN UNIVERSITY
Laan van Meerdervoort 20,
2517 AK The Hague
Tel.: 070 360 44 79
Internet: www.euruni.edu

HENLEY MANAGEMENT COLLEGE
Bergwijkdreef 10, 1112 XD Diemen
Tel.: 020 495 16 60
Internet: www.henley.nl

HES AMSTERDAM SCHOOL OF BUSINESS
Fraijlemaborg 133, 1102 CV Amsterdam
Tel.: 20 523 64 29
Internet: www.hasb.nl

INHOLLAND UNIVERSITY
with locations in Alkmaar, Delft,
Diemen/Amsterdam, Haarlem and Rotterdam
Internet: www.inholland.com

MAASTRICHT SCHOOL OF MANAGEMENT
Endepolsdomein 150, 6229 EP Maastricht
Tel.: 043 387 08 08
Internet: www.msm.nl

**NIMBAS GRADUATE SCHOOL OF
MANAGEMENT**
Nieuwegracht 39, 3512 HD Utrecht
Tel.: 030 230 30 50
Internet: www.nimbas.com

NYENRODE UNIVERSITY
Straatweg 25, 3621 BG Breukelen
Tel.: 034 629 12 91
Internet: www.nyenrode.nl

ROTTERDAM BUSINESS SCHOOL
Kralingse Zoom 91, 3063 ND Rotterdam
Tel.: 010 452 66 63
Internet: www.rotterdambusinessschool.nl

SAXION HOGESCHOLEN
with locations in Deventer, Apeldoorn and
Enschede
Internet: www.saxion.nl

**WAGENINGEN UNIVERSITY & RESEARCH
CENTRE**
Postbus 9101, 6700 HB Wageningen
Tel.: 0317 477 477
Internet: www.wageningen-ur.nl

UNIVERSITY OF PHOENIX
1e Riviumstraat 1, 2909 LE Capelle a/d IJssel
Tel.: 010 288 63 40
Internet: www.uop.nl

ROTTERDAM SCHOOL OF MANAGEMENT
Burgemeester Oudlaan 50,
3062 PA Rotterdam
Tel.: 010 408 22 22
Internet: www.rsm.nl

WEBSTER UNIVERSITY
Boommarkt 1, 2311 EA Leiden
Tel.: 071 514 43 41
Internet: www.webster.nl

TSM BUSINESS SCHOOL
International graduate school of the
University of Twente
Hengelosestraat 583, 7521 AG Enschede

Tel.: 053 489 80 09
Internet: www.tsm.nl

OPEN UNIVERSITY IN EUROPE
Eldon House
Regent Centre
Gosforth
Newcastle-upon-Tyne
NE3 3PW England
Netherlands co-ordinator,
tel.: 0044 191 284 1611
Internet: www.open.ac.uk

DUTCH UNIVERSITIES

VSNU
The Association of Universities in the
Netherlands
Internet: www.vsnu.nl

UNIVERSITEIT VAN AMSTERDAM
Sarphatistraat 104, 1018 GV Amsterdam
Tel.: 020 525 91 11
Internet: www.uva.nl

VRIJE UNIVERSITEIT AMSTERDAM
De Boelelaan 1105, 1081 HV Amsterdam
Tel.: 020 444 77 77
Internet: www.vu.nl

UNIVERSITEIT LEIDEN
Rapenburg 70, 2311 EZ Leiden
Tel.: 071 527 27 27
Internet: www.leidenuniv.nl

ERASMUS UNIVERSITEIT ROTTERDAM
Burgemeester Oudlaan 50,
3062 PA Rotterdam
Tel.: 010 408 11 11
Internet: www.eur.nl

KATHOLIEKE UNIVERSITEIT NIJMEGEN
Comenuslaan 4, 6525 HP Nijmegen
Tel.: 024 361 61 61
Internet: http://kunweb.hosting.kun.nl

RIJKSUNIVERSITEIT GRONINGEN
Broerstraat 5, 9712 CP Groningen
Tel.: 050 363 91 11
Internet: www.rug.nl

UNIVERSITEIT MAASTRICHT
Minderbroederweg 46, 6211 LK Maastricht
Tel.: 043 388 22 22
Internet: www.unimaas.nl

UNIVERSITEIT UTRECHT
Lundlaan 12, 3584 EA Utrecht
Tel.: 030 253 91 11
Internet: www.uu.nl

UNIVERSITEIT VAN TILBURG
Warandelaan 2, 5037 AB Tilburg
Tel.: 013 466 91 11
Internet: www.uvt.nl

TECHNISCHE UNIVERSITEIT EINDHOVEN
Den Deloch 2, 5612 AZ Eindhoven
Tel.: 040 247 91 11
Internet: www.tue.nl

TECHNISCHE UNIVERSITEIT DELFT
Julianalaan 134, 2628 BL Delft
Tel.: 015 278 91 11
Internet: www.tudelft.nl

UNIVERSITEIT TWENTE
Drienerlolaan 5, 7522 NB Enschede
Tel.: 053 489 91 11
Internet. www.universiteittwente.nl

WAGENINGEN UNIVERSITEIT
P.O. Box 9101, 6700 HB Wageningen
Tel.: 0317 477 477
Internet: www.wau.nl

OPEN UNIVERSITEIT NEDERLAND
P.O. Box 2960, 6401 DL Heerlen
Tel.: 045 576 28 88
Internet:www.openuniversiteit.nl

INTERNATIONAL SCHOOLS

1. THE RANDSTAD AREA

BRITISH SCHOOL OF AMSTERDAM
Anthonie van Dijkstraat 1
1077 ME Amsterdam
Tel.: 020 679 78 40
Internet: www.britams.nl

**AMSTERDAM INTERNATIONAL
COMMUNITY SCHOOL**
Wodenstraat 3, 1076 CC Amsterdam
Tel.: 020 577 12 40

INTERNATIONAL SCHOOL OF AMSTERDAM
Sportlaan 45, 1185 TB Amstelveen
Tel.: 020 347 11 11
Internet: www.isa.nl

REFERENCES

**INTERNATIONAL SCHOOL HILVERSUM
'ALBERDINGK THIJM'**
Emmastraat 56-58, 1213 AL Hilversum
Tel.: 035 672 99 31
Internet: www.klg.nl/ish

**VIOLENSCHOOL INTERNATIONAL
DEPARTMENT**
Rembrandtlaan 30, 1213 BH Hilversum
Tel.: 035 621 60 53
Internet: www.violenschoolintdept.nl

**RIJNLANDS LYCEUM OEGSTGEEST
INTERNATIONAL SCHOOL**
Apollolaan 1, 2341 BA Oegstgeest
Tel.: 071 519 35 55
Internet: www.isrlo.nl

**ELCKERLYC MONTESSORI PRIMARY SCHOOL
WITH INTERNATIONAL PTREAM**
Klimopzoom 41, 2353 RE Leiderdorp
Tel.: 071 589 29 45
E-mail: elckerlycIS@wish.net

AMERICAN SCHOOL OF THE HAGUE
Rijksstraatweg 200, 2241 BX Wassenaar
Tel.: 070 512 10 60
Internet: www.ash.nl

**INTERNATIONAL DEPARTMENT OF
HAAGSCHE SCHOOL VEREENIGING**
Nassaulaan 26, 2514 JT The Hague
Tel.: 070 36 385 31

INTERNATIONAL SCHOOL OF THE HAGUE
Theo Mann Bouwmeesterlaan 75
2597 GV The Hague
Tel.: 070 328 14 50
Internet: www.ishthehague.nl

BRITISH SCHOOL IN THE NETHERLANDS
Admissions Office: Tarwekamp 3
2592 XH The Hague, tel.: 070 315 40 77
Junior School Vlaskamp: Vlaskamp 19
2592 AA The Hague, tel.: 070 333 81 11
Junior School Diamanthorst: Diamanthorst
16, 2592 GH The Hague, tel.: 070 315 76 20
Senior School: Jan van Hooflaan 3
2252 BG Voorschoten, tel.: 071 560 22 22
Foundation School: Tarwekamp 3
2592 XH The Hague, tel.: 070 315 40 40
Internet: www.britishschool.nl

**AMERICAN INTERNATIONAL SCHOOL OF
ROTTERDAM (AISR)**
Verhulstlaan 21, 3055 WJ Rotterdam

Tel.: 010 422 53 51
Internet: www.aisr.nl

**ROTTERDAM INTERNATIONAL SECONDARY
SCHOOL (RISS)**
*BLIJBERG: DUTCH AND INTERNATIONAL
DEPARTMENTS*
Gordelweg 216-217, 3039 GA Rotterdam
Tel.: 010 466 96 29
Internet: www.blijberg.nl
WOLFERT VAN BORSELEN
Bentincklaan 280, 3039 KK Rotterdam
Tel.: 010 46 735 22 / 46 603 22
Internet: www.wolfert.nl

2. OUTSIDE THE RANDSTAD

AFNORTH INTERNATIONAL SCHOOL
Ferdinand Bolstraat 1, 6445 EE Brunssum
Tel.: 045 527 82 20
Internet: www.afnorthschool.com

**INTERNATIONAL DEPARTMENT OF
GRONINGSE SCHOOLVERENIGING**
Sweelincklaan 4, 9722 JV Groningen
Tel.: 050 527 08 18

ARNHEM INTERNATIONAL SCHOOL
PRIMARY DEPARTMENT:
DR. ALETTA JACOBS SCHOOL, Slochterenweg 27
6835 CD Arnhem, tel.: 026 323 07 29
SECONDARY DEPARTMENT:
LORENTZ COLLEGE, Groningensingel 1245
6835 HZ Arnhem, tel.: 026 320 01 10
Internet:
www.arnheminternationalschool.nl

EUROPEAN SCHOOL BERGEN
Molenweidtje 5, 1860 AB Bergen N.H.
Tel.: 072 589 01 09
Internet: www.eursc.org

INTERNATIONAL SCHOOL EERDE
Kasteellaan 1, 7731 PJ Ommen
Tel.: 0529 45 14 52
Internet: www.eerde.nl

**INTERNATIONAL SCHOOL
MAARTENSCOLLEGE**
Rijksstraatweg 24, 9752 AE Haren
Tel.: 050 534 00 84
Internet: www.maartenscollege.nl

HELEN SHARMAN BRITISH SCHOOL
Lottingstraat 17, 9406 LX Assen
Tel.: 0592 344 590
Internet: www.britishschool.nl

JOPPENHOF
Kelvinstraat 3, 6227 VA Maastricht
Tel.: 043 367 13 35
Internet: www.joppenhof.nl

REGIONAL INTERNATIONAL SCHOOL
Humperdincklaan 4, 5654 PA Eindhoven
Tel.: 040 251 94 37
Internet:www.rischool.nl

**INTERNATIONAL SECONDARY SCHOOL
EINDHOVEN**
Henegouwenlaan 2A, 5628 WK Eindhoven
Tel.: 040 264 59 99
Internet: www.dse.nl

OTHER-LANGUAGE SCHOOLS

**GERMAN INTERNATIONAL SCHOOL
(DEUTSCHE INTERNATIONALE SCHULE)**
Van Bleiswijkstraat 125, 2582 LB The Hague
Tel.: 070 354 94 54
Internet: www.disdh.nl

DEUTSCHE SCHULE BUDEL (GRUNDSCHULE)
Europalaan-Noord 16, 6021 EH Budel
Tel.: 0495 491 776

THE JAPANESE SCHOOL OF AMSTERDAM
Karel Klinkenbergstraat 137
1061 AL Amsterdam
Tel.: 020 611 81 36
Internet: www.jsa.nl

**STICHTING THE JAPANESE SCHOOL
OF ROTTERDAM**
Verhulstlaan 19, 3055 WJ Rotterdam
Tel.: 010 422 12 11

LE LYCÉE FRANÇAIS VINCENT VAN GOGH
Scheveningseweg 237
2584 AA The Hague
Tel.: 070 306 69 20
Internet: www.lyceefrancaisdespaysbas.fr.fm

INDONESIAN SCHOOL
Rijksstraatweg 679, 2245 CB Wassenaar
Tel.: 070 517 88 75

IRANIAN COMMUNITY SCHOOL
Laan van Meerdervoort 158
2517 BG The Hague
Tel.: 070 346 10 41

Study in
the Netherlands

your gateway to Europe

The Netherlands offers more courses **taught entirely in English** than any other country on the European continent. There are almost 500 international courses on offer, ranging from short courses to full-fledged programmes for bachelor's, master's or Ph.D. degrees. All are of the **highest quality**, but **tuition fees are low** thanks to government support for higher education.

For more information about studying in the Netherlands, you can visit the Nuffic website (http://www.nuffic.nl) or request one of the 'Study in the Netherlands' publications from:

Nuffic
PO Box 29777
2502 LT The Hague
The Netherlands
Phone: +31 (0)70 42 60 260
Fax: +31 (0)70 42 60 229
E-mail: nuffic@nuffic.nl

Online information about studying in the Netherlands:
http://www.nuffic.nl

Nuffic

Netherlands organization for international cooperation in higher education

Few things are more distressing than becoming sick abroad. Do the doctors have the same wealth of knowledge as they do in your home country? What are the health facilities? Will you be able to communicate with them? Many expats take great consolation from the fact that medical care in the Netherlands is in a league with the best of the world. Not only that, but (almost) all doctors speak English, which is also very reassuring. Whether you have a common cold, a serious illness or are expecting a baby, medical care is excellent and thorough.

There are, of course, differences, as this is a different culture. For this reason, we have selected a number of relevant topics (finding a family doctor, going to the hospital, having a baby and other medical issues) to help familiarize you with the careful, caring, though nonetheless Dutch approach to health care.

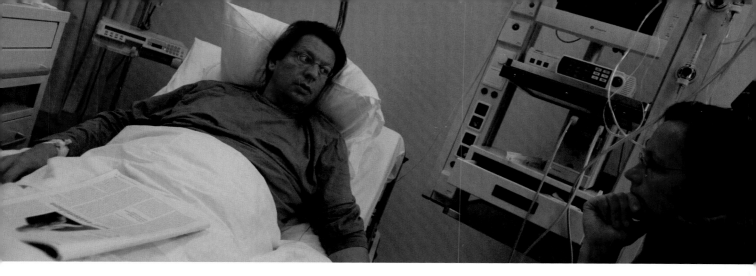

Health Care &
the Medical System

CONTRIBUTING AUTHORS: STEPHANIE DIJKSTRA, ADA HENNE KOENE AND LEE TOLMAN

THE FAMILY DOCTOR

HUISARTS – FAMILY DOCTOR

The Dutch word for family doctor or GP is *huisarts* – which literally translates into 'house doctor'. This does not mean that he or she will come to your house if you are sick – though *huisartsen* do make house calls in the case of emergencies; either after hours or during specifically allotted hours in their schedule. The name 'neighborhood doctor' would have been closer to the truth, as most people in the Netherlands go to a *huisarts* in their neighborhood.

FINDING A HUISARTS

The best place to start looking for a *huisarts* is in fact in your neighborhood – and the way to find out which doctor lives in your neighborhood is to visit your *gemeentehuis* or city/town hall. There you can ask for a *gemeentegids* (a booklet issued by your municipality containing information on just about everything relevant to the town or city you live in, such as doctors, sports schools, lawyers, day care, churches, etc.), which will have a list of all the local *huisartsen*. If you feel a bit hesitant about leafing through this booklet and finding your way, someone at the *gemeentehuis* will probably be glad to help you out. Of course, you can also simply ask those living in your neighborhood or other expats which doctor they go to. Or you can check the Yellow Pages of your phone book under *Artsen – huisartsen*.

In no way are you obligated to go to the *huisarts* who lives nearest to you. Nor can you expect him (or her) to accept you, should you approach him: sometimes a *huisarts* will turn you down – how-ever, this is not because you are a foreigner but rather because he has more patients than he can handle. And this happens quite often. Once you have settled on a *huisarts*, ask him if you can meet to discuss your needs and expectations and to establish compatibility – especially as you are from abroad and might have different expectations. It is hard to change your *huisarts* and it is rarely done.

SPREEKUUR – VISITING HOURS

If you have any medical questions or need help, your *huisarts* will be the first one you call. For colds and lesser illnesses, the *huisarts* usually sets aside a certain hour every morning (*inloop spreekuur* – walk-in hours) where you can sit in his waiting room without appointment with, on occasion, a room full of other patients. You will be called in according to the order in which you arrived. Other *huisartsen* do not have *inloop spreekuur*; you simply call ahead to their assistant and make an appointment. Be forewarned how-ever, that the doctor's practice may be very busy and that he might not be able to see you till the next day.

For simple questions, or to request a refill for your prescription, most doctors have a *telefonische spreekuur,* whereby you can call in and speak to the doctor (or, at times, his assistant, who has fol-lowed special training) with your question or request.

Speaking of questions, most *huisartsen* do not necessarily volun-teer any extra information. They like to keep things short. If you are feeling a little insecure about your illness, or would like some background information, do not hesitate to ask your questions, as this is likely the only way you will be getting any extended answers.

IF YOU NEED TO SEE A SPECIALIST

The *huisarts*, if he thinks you need more specialized expertise, will recommend you to a specialist. Most often, this will be someone at the nearest hospital. He will give you a referral notice (containing, among others, a history of your ailment) for the hospital and specialist he feels you should see. This does not mean that you do not have a say in what (type of) specialist you get to see or which hospital you would like to go to. Most *huisartsen* are quite flexible and all you have to do is say what (or who) it is you want.

Keep in mind that, for your insurer to cover the expenses involved in your visit to the specialist, they will want to see a copy of the referral notice (see page 217).

EMERGENCIES

Should you have a medical emergency of the type that requires first aid, you can go straight to the hospital to the EHBO (*Eerste Hulp bij Ongelukken* – First Aid) for assistance. In the case of other types of emergencies, you can either dial 1-1-2 (the emergency telephone line), or you can call your *huisarts*, who – if he feels you should indeed head straight for the hospital – will call ahead to the hospital and make sure someone is aware of the problem and ready to receive you.

IF YOUR DOCTOR IS AWAY

If your *huisarts* is away on a skiing vacation in the Austrian Alps or is out for an evening at the opera, he will leave a taped message in Dutch giving you the number of an on-duty doctor. The taped message might also give you the number of the emergency line, the *doktersdienst*. The actual name of the *doktersdienst* depends on where you live, as does the telephone number. Once you dial this number, they will ask what your problem is and where you live, after which they will give you the telephone number of a doctor on duty near you, or have a doctor call you.

THE REGIONAL DOCTOR'S OFFICE

Another alternative is the so-called *Regionale Huisartsenpost*. Often, the *huisartsen* in a particular regional area will join forces to cover the evenings, nights and weekends. To consult a doctor outside of office hours, all you need to do is call one central number. The phone will be answered by a doctor's assistant or *huisarts*, and, if need be, you can visit the *Huisartsenpost*. If, for whatever reason, this is not possible, a doctor will visit you.

In all likelihood, your doctor will also be on duty at some point, but if you want to be sure, check with him or his assistant, as not all *huisartsen* participate.

MEDICATION

The *huisarts* can recommend medication and give you a prescription (*recept*). If you live in a country where you leave the doctor's office with a prescription for at least three types of medicine no matter what you have, then you had best be prepared. Chances are, your doctor will recommend that you simply go home to bed with some toast and a cup of hot tea, which is the Dutch panacea for most minor illnesses. He probably will not prescribe antibiotics, as Dutch doctors are of the opinion that the more frequently you take them, the less effective they become. Furthermore, if truth be told, the thought that suppressing the symptoms (in the case of the millions of cold viruses running rampant in the winter) might bring you more comfort is not something that occurs to most of them.

If you very much would like to be given medication, the best thing is for you to say so. Your doctor might not be in complete agreement, and might make you feel like a bit of a wimp, but to clear away any misunderstandings, you can explain that this is the treatment you receive in your home country and that it makes you feel more secure (or better!).

For medication refills, simply call your *huisarts* and he will forward your request to the pharmacy of your choice, or you can pick up the prescription at his office. He will, of course, charge you for an office call.

PAYMENT

You will receive a periodic statement from your doctor that you can forward to your insurance company for payment or you can request that he bill your insurance company directly.

OTHER SERVICES

If you need to see a dentist, eye doctor, physical therapist, need other help with physical disabilities, or need advice on your sexual health, ask your huisarts for referrals. See more about these topics further on.

THE SPECIALIST

If you have received a referral to see a specialist from your *huisarts*, you will then have to make an appointment. Usually, your *huisarts* will have written down the relevant phone number on your referral notice. Depending on the type of specialist you need to see and the urgency of your condition, you can see him/her the same day or only months hence (certain specializations, such as orthopedics and ophthalmology, are known to have considerable waiting lists). Once you arrive at the hospital for your appointment, you give the referral notice to the specialist's assistant – this ensures that the insurance company will accept the charges. Along with the referral notice you will hand in an envelope containing a short description of your ailment, allowing the specialist to gain some preliminary insight into your condition.

THE REFERRAL NOTICE – INSURANCE COMPANY

As mentioned under *The Family Doctor*, do keep in mind that, for your insurer to cover the expenses involved in your visit to the specialist, they will want to see a copy of the referral notice (proving that your doctor thought it was necessary for you to go to the specialist). Often, the hospital keeps your referral notice and forwards a copy to the insurer along with the bill they submit on your behalf. If, however, you declare your own expenses with the insurer (either after paying them yourself, or along with a request for your insurer to pay the bill), then you will have to send a copy (and sometimes the original) of the referral notice yourself. Without this referral, the insurer will likely not pay the bill.

POLIKLINIEK AND PONSPLAATJE

Often, specialists work out of hospitals. In that case, when you come to visit him/her at the hospital, you look for the sign *Poli-*

klinieken, and the correct department. If this is your first visit to the hospital, you register at the front desk. There you will be asked a few initial questions (your name, address, insurer, *huisarts*, and a few other questions). This information will go into the computer and also onto a little credit card-sized plastic card, called a *ponsplaatje*, which you must bring with you every time you go to the hospital as it is used, among others, to find your records, mark forms, send your bills to your insurance company, and to print out labels for lab tests.

YOUR VISIT WITH THE SPECIALIST

When you visit the specialist, he will read your referral notice, discuss your situation with you, arrange the necessary tests and prescribe a possible treatment. Again, medical care in the Netherlands is in a league with the best of the world – so you are in excellent hands.

In most cases, you will not be filling out four pages of your own (and your entire family's) medical history before the visit – but this really depends on the medical problem at hand. If you have any allergies to medicine, be sure to mention this of your own accord. And, as with the *huisarts*, if you have any questions, ask. And if you expect some type of treatment or medicine, discuss this. Dutch doctors are not circumspect out of meanness; they simply believe that the patient will ask what he wants to know. Depending on the seriousness of your illness and the urgency of your lab tests, you may be referred to an emergency room of the hospital.

ARRANGING HOSPITALIZATION

If your illness requires hospitalization, the specialist calls ahead and makes the appropriate arrangements. If the lab tests he needs are urgent, he may also refer you to the emergency room in a hospital or send you straight to the laboratories. He will call ahead so that the doctors on duty will be waiting for you. In addition to the hospital doctors, your *huisarts* might check on you from time to time, though he might wait till you have come home from the hospital and pay you a house visit.

HOSPITALS

GENERAL

There are many fine hospitals in the Netherlands, all with the latest in technology – eight of them are university hospitals and others are run by the community or religious organizations. In principle, all Dutch hospitals offer the same specializations so that going to one hospital is as good as going to the next. The only thing that can be said about university hospitals versus community or religious hospitals is that, on the whole, more research is carried out at university hospitals so that they can be more up-to-date on recent medical developments. When it comes to hospitals specializing in treating a certain type of medical condition: some hospitals may have more (advanced) equipment and doctors specialized in certain treatments. One can consider these to be specialized in this area. However, these are not always university hospitals: ask your *huisarts* whether there is a hospital that is specialized in your condition.

Keep in mind that for some surgeries, such as heart bypasses, there might be a long waiting period.

BEING ADMITTED TO THE HOSPITAL

We mentioned earlier that you should not expect to go through your entire medical history when visiting the specialist. This *does* happen, though, when you are admitted to a hospital, particularly if you are going to be operated on. You may even find yourself going through your whole history three times: with the admitting doctor, with the anesthesiologist and with the doctor who will be operating you. Anything vital, such as allergies to medicine, is definitely worth repeating each time.

ROOMS

Don't expect a private room during a hospital stay. You might be offered a double room but also be prepared for a room for six. The rooms here also can be co-educational so don't be surprised if they ask you if you object to sharing a room with patients of the opposite sex.

Take your pajamas, toothbrush, toothpaste and other toiletries that you might need for any overnight or weekend stay. Also take along your prescription medicines.

Most, if not all, hospitals allow you to have your own telephone line and have a television set hanging over your bed. You do not have to make use of either; if you do, you are charged a daily fee (and given headphones for the television).

Dutch hospital roommates can be quite chatty so that, if you are fond of your privacy and want your curtains closed all the time, they might be a bit disappointed. This could particularly be the case if they find out you are a foreigner, as they are naturally curious to start with and even more so if they find you are from another country. They not only want to know more about where you're from, they also want to be sure you appreciate what a fine country you have come to live in.

CHILDREN'S HOSPITALS

While all hospitals have children's wards, there are also several excellent children's hospitals in the country. You can give your *huisarts* your preference. Don't forget to take your records along that describe the child's previous illnesses and a list of immunizations taken. Children's hospitals put a lot of effort into keeping the children entertained and many offer the opportunity to keep up with school, so that the child does not get too far behind.

LODGING FOR THE RELATIVES

Some hospitals, but particularly children's hospitals, have lodging possibilities if you or your relatives want to be close at hand. This is of particular importance if you are still nursing a baby that is being hospitalized. There are also Ronald McDonald houses (for parents of sick children) in the larger cities.

VISITING HOURS

Do not forget to check on visiting hours, as they are different in every hospital. Some hospitals can be very strict about enforcing these hours.

HAVING A BABY

SAFE

Many newcomers to the Netherlands are taken aback by the non-interventionist approach to perinatal care and are often told that everyone delivers at home with a midwife. In fact, only about 30%

of deliveries take place at home, the rest take place in a hospital under the guidance of a midwife or gynecologist. You may also find it reassuring to know that, according to the World Health Organization, the Netherlands is one of the world's safest places to have a baby. Mothers-to-be receive excellent care throughout pregnancy, labor and delivery as well as during the postpartum period – as do their babies.

SO YOU'RE PREGNANT...

Congratulations! The first step is to make an appointment with your local *verloskundige* (midwife). This should be done by week 8-10 as most practices are quite busy. Look in the Yellow Pages under *verloskundigen* or confer with your *huisarts*. Although you do not officially need a referral to visit a midwife, your *huisarts* will be able point you in the right direction.

A midwife is an independent practitioner who can legally practice obstetrics without the supervision of a medical doctor. And unless complications arise or there is a previous medical problem – in which case you will be referred to a gynecologist – the midwife will be your sole health care provider during pregnancy, labor, delivery (see page 220, *Where Will You Have Your Baby?* for more on this) and the initial postpartum period. The midwife may work alone or in a group practice, in which case you will be seen by different midwifes during routine check-ups. One word of advice: as the Dutch feel that pregnancy and childbirth are very

normal, natural occurrences, they might not anticipate your need for information or reassurance. Make sure you have a list of questions ready and don't let yourself be thrown by what might appear to be a casual approach to and/or dismissal of your concerns. If need be, explain that there is more (hospital) guidance in your country, and stand your ground.

ROUTINE CHECK-UPS

Your first visit will take place around week 12. The midwife will take your and your partner's medical history as well as that of your family. Your weight and blood pressure as well as fetal growth, position and heart beat will be monitored. Blood iron levels will also be checked. She will also inquire whether you plan to have a *thuisbevalling* (home birth) or a *poliklinische bevalling* (out-patient in a hospital). You will visit the midwife approximately 12 times during pregnancy and except for the first visit which should last about a half an hour, most visits will be no longer than a quarter of an hour. As most midwifes do not have ultrasound equipment, you will be referred on to a hospital should it become necessary. It is also possible to have a so-called *pret-echo* (an ultrasound for fun) or video made of your baby *in utero*. Inquire about this option during your routine visit.

In approximately 10% of the cases, an expectant mother is cared for by her *huisarts.*. This holds true in small villages where there is no midwifery practice. The *huisarts*, in effect, takes over the midwife's normal responsibilities.

Although it is not standard Dutch practice, should you prefer to be cared for by a *gynaecoloog* (gynecologist) during your pregnancy, labor and delivery – and therefore in a hospital setting – then you will need a referral from your *huisarts*. First check with your medical insurer regarding reimbursement policies, as most medical insurance policies do not cover hospital birth unless there is a *medische indicatie* (medical condition warranting special gynecological care).

It is important that you feel at ease and can communicate your needs to your practitioner – whether this be a *verloskundige, huisarts* or *gynaecoloog*. Should you feel that your best interest is not being met, move on. There are other midwifes and other doctors.

PRENATAL TESTING

Prenatal testing and genetic screening are not performed on a routine basis in the Netherlands. Genetic screening, for example, is generally conducted only when the pregnant woman is found to be in a high-risk category for fetal chromosomal defects such as Down's Syndrome, Cystic Fibrosis, Spina Bifida or Muscular Dystrophy. In the Netherlands, a pregnant woman is considered at high risk if she is 36 years or older, if she has previously had a child with a congenital defect or if she has a history of chromosomal problems in either her or her partner's family. Should you not fit into one of the above categories but have personal concerns, discuss this matter over with you midwife or gynecologist. The following are the most standard tests available:

Echoscopie (Ultrasound)
Ultrasound is used in screening for fetal defects between 16-20 weeks, whereby an image of the fetus is projected onto a screen by means of sound waves. It can diagnose some, but not all, fetal abnormalities. If in doubt, it can also be used to detect twins or to determine the due date.

The Triple (Screen) Test
This is a blood test done between 15-18 weeks to measure three different protein levels associated with fetal abnormalities. This test can only estimate the risk of a woman having a baby with a chromosomal defect. Should the results be positive for an increased risk, one of the following two tests may be advised. It is not done on a routine basis.

Vlokkentest (Chorionic Villi Sampling)
This can be done through the cervix at 10-12 weeks or through the abdomen at 12-13 weeks. Both methods aspirate chorionic villi – minuscule, naturally occurring, finger-like projections – from the fetal membrane. The results are back within 7-10 days. This test can be performed at any major medical center.

Vruchtwaterpunctie (Amniocentesis)
This test is done between 15 and 17 weeks by aspirating amniotic fluid through the abdomen. It takes several weeks to get the test results back. This test must also be performed at a major medical center. Since there are potential risks involved with both the *vlokkentest* and the *vruchtwaterpunctie*, you should discuss these options with your practitioner.

Nekplooimeting (Neck Fold Measurement)
The measurement of the fetus's neck fold is performed during an ultrasound around 10-14 weeks, when the fetus is 4-8 cm long. Research has shown that an enlarged neck fold may be indicative of defects such as Down's Syndrome. This test may be performed in conjunction with the Triple Test.

Doptone (Fetal Heart Monitor)
The heartbeat of the baby can be monitored for irregularities. This is also carried out during routine check-ups and is therefore not only used to detect potential abnormalities.

ZWANGERSCHAPSCURSUSSEN
(CHILDBIRTH PREPARATION CLASSES)
The Netherlands offers several types of prenatal exercise and birthing classes. Here is a list of the most common approaches to preparing for childbirth:

Zwangerschapsgymnastiek (Childbirth Gym)
This 8-10 week class is given by a physiotherapist and is usually offered through your local *Thuiszorg* organization (for more information on this organization see page 223). A combination of exercises, breathing and relaxation techniques and informal lectures is used to help prepare you for the big day. One of the classes is a 'partner' evening where spouses/birthing coaches can learn hands-on techniques useful during labor and delivery. Classes start in the last trimester.

Yoga
The emphasis of this course is on mastering simple yoga positions, increasing body awareness and learning breathing techniques to promote relaxation in order to better deal with labor pain. Classes are available for women only and/or expectant mothers with their (coaching) partners. This course is usually offered as of the second trimester.

Samen Bevallen ('Delivering Together')
This nine-week course helps couples prepare for labor and delivery. The role of the partner as well as breathing and relaxation techniques are covered. Available through some *Thuiszorg* organizations.

Haptonomische Zwangerschapsbegeleiding (Haptonomy Childbirth Class)
Haptonomy is the art of touching and feeling. Through stroking and rocking, couples learn to make contact with their baby *in utero*. Breathing and relaxation techniques are also taught in order to better cope with labor pain. These private lessons usually start in the fourth or fifth month and are given by a physiotherapist specialized in Haptonomy.

Oefentherapie Mensendieck voor Zwangeren (Mensendieck Prenatal Exercise Class)
This group class focuses on exercising muscle groups stressed during pregnancy and delivery. Emphasis is placed on improving postural awareness and movement in order to avoid discomforts or pain which may occur during pregnancy. Breathing and relaxation techniques are also thoroughly covered. This course is made up of 8-10 lessons with one partner evening and one postpartum session. Usually initiated by the sixth month.

Zwangerschapszwemmen (Swimming during Pregnancy)
Most local pools offer special classes for expectant mothers. The water temperature is usually warmer, which promotes general relaxation.

WHERE WILL YOU HAVE YOUR BABY?
As previously mentioned, there are several options available when giving birth in the Netherlands: either at home under the guidance of a *verloskundige* or *huisarts* or in the hospital with a *verloskundige* or *gynaecoloog*. Keep in mind that if you decide to have your baby at home, this is not irreversible. You have the right to change your mind at any point during pregnancy or delivery, although the latter may be more difficult. And rest assured, you will be taken to the hospital by ambulance should the *verloskundige* detect any complications during the delivery.
If you have been under specialist (hospital) supervision during your entire pregnancy, then you will most likely deliver your baby at the hospital. If you have been under non-hospital *verloskundige* supervision, you will only deliver in the hospital if there are complications (detected either prior to or during delivery). However, you can also opt for what the Dutch call a *poliklinische bevalling* attended either by a midwife or gynecologist; you then voluntarily have a hospital delivery, but are in and out of the hospital within 24 hours – barring complications. You will be required to stay longer in the case of medical complications or a (planned) Caesarean section (5-7 days). As mentioned earlier, a

voluntary hospital delivery will, in most cases, not be covered by your insurance company – unless complications arose during or after delivery. In all other cases, hospital deliveries are covered by your insurance.

ZWANGERSCHAPSVERLOF (PREGNANCY LEAVE).

If you are currently working and plan to do so following delivery, you will need to obtain a *zwangerschapsverklaring* ('pregnancy statement') from your midwife or gynecologist. This document confirms your estimated due date and is used to determine when you are eligible for *zwangerschapsverlof*. In the Netherlands, women have the right to 16 weeks paid leave. This may be initiated between 4-6 weeks prior to the estimated due date. The law states that you may not work from four weeks before, until six weeks after delivery. Should the baby arrive early, you still have a right to the full 16 weeks. If it is late, and you have used up the 6 weeks beforehand, you still have the right to a 10-week leave following the baby's birth. You can read more about pregnancy leave on page 184. And don't forget, Dads also have their own *verlof*. The law stipulates that fathers are entitled to two paid days off following the birth of their child (see page 184).

THE BIG DAY HAS COME!

Call the *verloskundige* or hospital once your waters have broken and/or your contractions have reached a certain frequency. In the case of a *thuisbevalling* (delivery at home), the *verloskundige* will either come right over or within a few hours, depending on the stage of labor you're in. She will stay with you throughout the delivery, and once the baby is born, will examine the baby and perform the APGAR-test. During delivery, the *verloskundige* is assisted by a *kraamverzorgster* (maternity aid – see further on). Generally speaking the *verloskundige* will leave your house within an hour of the delivery. The *kraamverzorgster* will, on the other hand, stay on to dress and care for the baby, prepare the crib, help the mother take a shower and clean up the house. If the baby was born during the night, she will leave a list of instructions and her phone number – urging you to call if you have any questions. If the baby is born during the day, she will stay a few more hours (see section *Kraamzorg* for more details).

If you have opted for a *poliklinische bevalling* (out-patient hospital delivery), then you will have to phone either your midwife (who will then in turn call the hospital) or the hospital directly – depending on what has been agreed upon. The hospital will discuss with you whether or not you should come in straight away. Once in the hospital, you will be given a birthing room and they will palpate and examine you to determine how much you are dilated. The heartbeat of the baby will also be monitored.

Depending on how busy it is, be prepared to spend much of the time on your own with your (coaching) partner – another reason to take a childbirth class to prepare you both for this period of waiting and coping with contractions. You will of course be checked on regularly, but it is usually not until the actual delivery – attended by either an in-house *verloskundige*, your own *verloskundige*, or a gynecologist – that you will have full-time supervision. And bear in mind that you may be assisted by the *verloskundige* or *gynaecoloog* on duty, and not the practitioner who followed you throughout the pregnancy.

PAIN MEDICATION DURING DELIVERY

As mentioned earlier, the Dutch have a rather 'level-headed' attitude towards pregnancy and delivery and feel that it is a natural process that should not be interfered with. Consequently, pain medication is not offered during a home birth and only rarely during delivery in a hospital. *Verloskundigen*, on the whole, are not even allowed to administer pain medication. Be sure to discuss with your doctor or *verloskundige* what types of medication or pain relief options are available. Be tactful, but persistent! If need be, explain your concerns and let them know that labor and delivery are handled differently in your home country.

Learning to deal and cope with pain is one of the keys to a successful labor and delivery. Research has shown that the more you know about labor and delivery, the better you are able to deal with both pain and any complications which may occur. So sign up for a childbirth preparation class early on – and take your partner along! Other so-called 'alternative' pain relief options are hypnosis, acupuncture and TENS (Transcutaneous Electrical Nerve Stimulation). Ask your doctor or *verloskundige* or call the phone numbers at the end of the chapter for details.

KRAAMZORG (MATERNITY HOME CARE)

The Netherlands provides wonderful maternity home care subsequent to either a home birth or hospital delivery. Depending on your insurance coverage, you are entitled to 8-10 days of home care provided by a *kraamverzorgster* (maternity aid). She will visit daily to assess the health status of both the mother and child. Full or part-time care is available (8 hours, 5 hours or two 1 1/2 hour visits per day) although full-time care is becoming more and more difficult to book due to a shortage of *kraamverzorgsters*. Check in the Yellow Pages under *kraamzorg* or with friends and/or your *verloskundige* or gynecologist for a list of organizations in your area. And be sure to apply during the first trimester – you certainly do not want to miss out on this unique care.

The *kraamverzorgster* teaches parents/care-givers how to bathe, change and care for the baby. She will also assist with breastfeeding and will, depending on how many hours per day she works, tend to housekeeping, cooking, shopping and caring for the other members of the family.

BABY IN THE HOSPITAL

If your baby needs to stay in the hospital for a while, check with your hospital what options are available in terms of lodging for you. Also check with your insurance provider what is covered. Many hospitals have some type of maternity lodging option whereby you do not officially take up a hospital bed but still can spend the night – and nurse/be there with your baby.

THE FIRST WEEK AFTER BIRTH

During that first week at home you will be visited 2-3 times by your *verloskundige* and/or *huisarts*. to check on the health status of you and your baby. They will also confer with the *kraamverzorgster*. You must arrange for this service prior to delivery, especially if you are planning to give birth in a hospital – the gynecologist does not make house calls! On day 3 or 4 they will also administer the *hielprik* ('heel shot') to check for several metabolic and thyroid diseases – whereby a small amount of blood is drawn from your baby's heel and sent to a laboratory for testing. Within the first 14 days, the *Consultatiebureau* (Well Baby Clinic, see next section) will send a *wijkverpleegster* (neighborhood nurse) to your home to check on the baby. Depending on where you live, the *hielprik* may be performed by this nurse, rather than by your midwife or GP.

As you can see, you will have quite a full house that first week: the *kraamverzorgster*, the *verloskundige*, the *huisarts*, the *wijkverpleegster* and last but not least, the *kraamvisite* (visitors). And believe me, they will come in droves! In the Netherlands, once a baby is born, everyone comes to admire your little person: neighbors, colleagues, friends, relatives...

THE CONSULTATIEBUREAU (WELL-BABY CLINIC)

Whereas in most countries routine check-ups are carried out by a *huisarts* or *kinderarts* (pediatrician), in the Netherlands this service is provided to parents by the local *Consultatiebureau* up until a child is 4 years of age. The *Consultatiebureau* is a community-based, country-wide network of clinics providing preventative health care to infants and toddlers. Your first contact with the *Consultatiebureau* will take place by phone with the registration of your infant. This should be done soon after delivery. The local office will follow up by sending a *wijkverpleegkundige* (neighborhood nurse) to your home within 10-14 days after delivery. During this initial visit the nurse will observe your baby, discuss with you your initial experiences with (breast)feeding and schedule the first check-up at your local clinic. You will also be given a *Groeiboek* (Growth book), which you should take with you to each appointment at the *Consultatiebureau*. An English version is available, so be sure to ask for one at the time of registration.

During the first year you will visit the *Consultatiebureau* approximately ten times. Preventative care is the *Consultatiebureau's* main goal. Through screening – motor and cognitive development, speech, hearing and sight – abnormalities can be detected early on and followed up. But the *Consultatiebureau* doctor may not treat your child. If need be, your child will be referred to your *huisarts* who, in turn, will refer you on to a specialist when appropriate.

You will be seen by either the *Consultatiebureau* doctor and/or nurse during each visit and your infant will be weighed and measured at each appointment by the *Consultatiebureau-assistent*. You will have sufficient time during these visits to discuss any other issues of concern (nutrition, up-bringing, etc.).

One of the more important responsibilities of the *Consultatiebureau* is carrying out The Ministry of Health, Welfare and Sports' vaccination program. Although it is not mandatory, 95% of all parents do indeed opt to have the clinic perform this service.

After that initial year, you and your child will visit the *Consultatiebureau* on a yearly basis. Prior to each visit you will be asked to complete a questionnaire regarding your child's health, living situation, development and behavior. The results are discussed during your visit with both the doctor and the nurse. They will also follow-up with the vaccination program.

SCHOOL-AGE CHILDREN

Once your child has reached school age, this health service is transferred to the local health office of the *Gemeentelijke Gezondheidsdienst*, better known as the GGD (Municipal Health Service). Both the *Consultatiebureau* and the GGD-services are offered free of charge.

REGISTERING YOUR BABY

Your baby needs to be registered within three working days after birth at the *gemeentehuis* (town hall) in the city or town where the baby was born. You can read more about this on page 184.

POSTPARTUM CLASSES

Postpartum exercise classes are available through the *Thuiszorg* organization (see section on *Thuiszorg*). If you participated in their *zwangerschapsgym* during pregnancy, you will be invited to attend these classes. During these sessions you will have the opportunity to strengthen muscles which have taken a beating during pregnancy and delivery (abdominals and pelvic floor) as well as all other major muscle groups. Both the *zwangerschapsgym* and the postpartum classes present a wonderful chance to exchange pleasure and pain. In most cases the group of women is the same, so that you get the opportunity to exchange birthing experiences and compare notes. The first class is usually a 'baby show' where you come together with all the babies and show off your new off-spring!

English-language postpartum classes are offered through ACCESS (see section at the end of the chapter).

SIX-WEEK CHECK-UP

You will go back to either your midwife or gynecologist for a check-up around six weeks postpartum. They will examine the position of your uterus, the healing of any ruptures or exterior incisions and – if you had any medical complications – discuss your general recovery. This is a good time to bring up any particular issues of concern such as postpartum blues and anti-conception, although these may also be discussed with your *huisarts*.

(OUDERSCHAPSVERLOF (PARENTAL LEAVE)

The law stipulates that both working parents have the right to take a non-paid leave of absence to care for a child (adoption or foster child included). You can read more about this on page 186.

MEDICAL ORGANIZATIONS

THUISZORG (HOME CARE) ORGANIZATION

For services leading up to the birth of your baby and for follow-up care (*kraamzorg*), check out your local *Thuiszorg* organization. Some services provided by the *Thuiszorg*, such as the *Consultatiebureau*, are now covered under the *Algemene Wet Bijzondere Ziektekosten* or AWBZ (Exceptional Medical Expenses Act – general law concerning special medical costs) and are free of charge. Others, such as home care, are covered by your insurance (check your particular policy or insurer for details). And whereas some lectures are offered to the general public free of charge, others must be paid for.

The *Thuiszorg* offers many other health care services in addition to the prenatal and postpartum courses which we have already mentioned, such as:

- courses: First Aid for Children, baby massage, coping with a toddler and bladder training (in Dutch)
- rental of *bedklossen* (metal frames that raise the bed; required for home birth/first week following delivery) and baby scales
- home care following a serious illness or accident
- home care for the elderly or handicapped
- rental of crutches, wheelchairs, special beds, bed pans and lifting devices (these will be brought to your house and installed if necessary)
- household help, if due to illness or handicap you are no longer able to do this yourself
- hairdresser and pedicure at home, plus the possibility of buying new clothing from your home.
- dietary and nutritional advice.

To find your local *Thuiszorg*, check the telephone book or ask your *huisarts* or *verloskundige* (see also the listing at the end of this chapter). Some of the services are offered in the same building as the *Consultatiebureau*.

The *Thuiszorg* system is divided into geographic regions, with services and costs differing from one organization to another. In most regions the *Consultatiebureau* falls under the responsibility of the *Ouder en Kind* (parent and child) department of the *Thuiszorg* organization. Amsterdam is one exception. In most areas within Amsterdam it is the *Gemeentelijke Gezondheid & Geneeskundige Dienst* or GG&GD (Municipal Health & Medical Service) that is responsible for the coordination of the *Consultatiebureau* and its services, though there are also *Thuiszorg* organizations that have a *Consultatiebureau*.

MEDICATION

THE PHARMACY AND THE DRUGSTORE

Prescription drugs are filled at an *apotheek* (pharmacy or apothecary). They computerize your prescriptions and keep a close watch on the drugs you are taking in order to avoid drug interaction. Many bill your insurance company directly for the costs of prescription medicine. Opening hours are much the same time as for other establishments, but there is always an *apotheek* open in the evenings and on weekends. The name(s) of *apotheek(en)* open during after-hours is posted on your *apotheek's* door or you can obtain a copy of their schedule at any local pharmacy.

Pharmacies also carry over-the-counter (non-prescription) drugs, vitamins, homeopathic medicines, infant formulas and some baby foods as well as medical supplies such as bandages and thermometers – albeit at a higher price than at your local *drogisterij* (drugstore) such as ETOS, Kruidvat, DA, etc. Drugstores, on the other hand, do not carry prescription drugs, but handle over-the-counter remedies such as throat lozenges, syrups, homeopathic medicines, and pain relievers, as well as toiletries, cosmetics, cleaning supplies and baby formulas and foods.

ALTERNATIVE MEDICINE

Alternative medicine such as acupuncture and homeopathy are also very popular in the Netherlands. For more information, get in touch with the *Alternatieve Geneeswijzen Infolijn* or look in the *Gouden Gids* (Yellow Pages) under *Alternatieve Geneeswijzen*. Some alternative medicines are covered by insurance policies and others not. Check your particular insurance policy for details. Homeopathic medicines can be purchased at either an *apotheek*, *drogisterij* or a *reformhuis* (health food store).

OTHER MEDICAL ISSUES

DENTIST
Many expats save their visits to the dentist for when they go back 'home'. However, also dental emergencies cannot be predicted and it is better to know whom you want to call *before* your gums have decided to call it quits. As when looking for a *huisarts*, the *gemeentegids* is a good source of addresses. However, now that you have a *huisarts*, you can also simply ask him to recommend you one. Other sources are the Yellow Pages under *Tandartsen*, or colleagues, friends or neighbors. In the Yellow Pages you will also find orthodontists (*Tandartsen – specialisten orthodontie*) and dentists specializing in surgery and other mouth afflictions (*Tandartsen – specialisten mondziekten en kaakchirurgie*).

As is the case with your *huisarts*, if you have an emergency after hours (evening, night, weekend), simply call your *tandarts* and you will hear a recording telling you which *tandarts* in your neighborhood is on duty.

PHYSICAL THERAPY
For physical therapy, manual therapy, haptonomy, chiropractics, cranial-sacral therapy and more, check the Yellow Pages under *Fysiotherapeuten*, or ask your *huisarts*. Check with your insurance company whether they cover the costs; those that do often require that you hand in a referral notice from your *huisarts*, stating that you need this type of therapy, before they are willing to cover the costs.

PHYSICAL DISABILITIES
The Netherlands has an excellent record when it comes to dealing with individuals with certain physical disabilities. If you are in this position and require special help, contact the city hall (*gemeentehuis*) to see what they are prepared to do for you. In some cases, they have been known to assist in adapting your home to meet your requirements. There are also many ways in which the organizations in the Netherlands, such as *Thuiszorg* (see earlier on), can assist. All you have to do is ask.

Check page 68 for information on the Exceptional Medical Expenses Act (AWBZ), which covers all persons living or working in the Netherlands and pages 68-71 for information on the employee insurance schemes (and self-employed persons insurance schemes).

PUBLIC AND SEXUAL HEALTH
If you are traveling to Third World countries and need injections before you go, you will get them at the city clinics/Municipal Health Service (referred to as the GGD – *Gemeentelijke Geneeskunde Dienst* – or GG&GD – *Gemeentelijke Gezondheid & Geneeskundige Dienst*). They will advise on what is required as opposed to what is recommended plus they are responsible for advising the community at large on PAP smears, mammograms, sexually transmitted diseases and vaccinations for babies and older children.

For information on sexual health and birth control, you can contact *Rutgers Stichting*, which has branches in several of the bigger cities across the Netherlands. For information on AIDS, you can contact the AIDS Foundation, which you will find at the end of the chapter.

MENTAL HEALTH CARE AND ADDICTIONS
Mental health care is available for children and young people, adults, the elderly, addicts, and so-called forensic-psychiatric patients. For more information on the services available, you can contact the Regional Institutions for Ambulatory Mental Health Care (RIAGG). They have several offices in the Netherlands; check your local telephone book to see if they have a listing where you live, call information or ask your *huisarts*. If you wish to see a private psychologist or psychiatrist, you can also ask your *huisarts* to refer you to one.

For problems with addictions, there are also several options: there are ambulant centers for alcohol and drugs (Centrum voor Alcohol en Drugs), institutions for social work that focus on care for people with drug problems, clinics for treatment and outpatient clinics with special departments for addicts. Ask your *huisarts* for more information.

DEATH
In case of death in the family or a visiting friend or colleague, it is best to call on your *huisarts* who can certify the death. He can walk you through what is required in the Netherlands. Then you will have to call the embassy or consulate of the country of which the deceased is a passport holder. They will help take care of the required formalities of their country and help notify the next of kin.

REFERENCES

GENERAL

MINISTRY OF HEALTH, WELFARE AND SPORTS (*Ministerie van Gezondheid Welzijn en Sport*) Parnassusplein 5, P.O. Box 20350, 2500 EJ The Hague
Tel.: 070 340 79 11
Internet: www.minvws.nl

RECOMMENDED READING

THE ACCESS GUIDE TO HEALTH CARE IN THE NETHERLANDS
Published by ACCESS
This publication concisely covers a wide range of health topics from birth to death, insurance to legal rights, home care to hospitals, special services to social services.
Internet: www.access-nl.org
ISBN 90 74109 20 09

BABIES AND TODDLERS
Published by ACCESS
Information for parents of babies and toddlers in the Netherlands. Topics include pregnancy, child health and safety, activities, support groups, childcare services,recommended reading, etc.
Internet: www.access-nl.org
ISBN 90 74109 18 7

EMERGENCIES
In case of an emergency, call the national emergency number 112. State whether you need an ambulance, the police or the fire department and they will connect you with the correct department

MEDICAL SERVICES

LANDELIJKE MAATSCHAPPIJ TER BEVORDERING VAN DE TANDHEELKUNDE (Dutch Dental Organization), tel.: 030 607 62 76

VERENIGING GEHANDICAPTENZORG NEDERLAND (Netherlands Association for the Care of the Disabled), tel.: 030 273 93 00

HAVING A BABY

www.parentsplace.com: a good place to start, providing a wealth of knowledge
www.babycenter.com: comprehensive site with lots of relevant information for pregnancy and beyond
www.thebabynet.com: baby names, birth announcements, message boards, baby shower ideas, etc.
www.thefamilycorner.com: ages & stages, family & kids, pets, travel, parenting, education, etc.
www.childbirth.org: ask the pros, pregnancy photos, pregnancy calendar, birth plans, birth stories as well as links to other home pages

INTERNATIONAL CONFEDERATION OF MIDWIVES
Supports the interests of pregnant women, mothers and midwives.
Eisenhowerlaan 138, 2517 KN The Hague, tel.: 070 306 05 20
Internet: www.internationalmidwives.org

LANDELIJKE VERENIGING VOOR THUISZORG (National Home Care Association)
tel.: 030 659 62 11
internet: www.thuiszorg.nl

THUISZORG THE HAGUE, tel.: 070 379 51 50 (customer service number)
Stichting Rijn-, Duin- en Bollenstreek (all types of home care, social work and Well-baby clinics for Katwijk, Wassenaar, Lisse, Noordwijk, Noordwijkerhout, Sassenheim, Oegstgeest, Hillegom, Rijnsburg, Valkenburg, Voorhout, Voorschoten and Warmond):
071 409 33 33 (general number)

LA LECHE-LEAGUE (Nursing), tel.: 045 32 48 84

BABYECHOCENTRUM DRIEBERGEN,
Korte Dreef 9-G, 3972 EB Driebergen, www.babyecho.nl, (one of the largest organizations where you can have an 'ultrasound for fun' (pret-echo) made): tel.: 030 289 48 28, e-mail: info@babyecho.nl

ACCESS (tel. 070 346 25 25) offers An English-language lecture / information session 'Having a Baby in Holland' four times a year

for couples interested in learning more about this subject. ACCESS also offers English-language Childbirth Preparation Class for couples as well as Prenatal and postpartum exercise classes

PRENATAL AND POSTPARTUM CLASSES are offered by Physiotherapist and Childbirth Educator, Lee A. Tolman, MSPT, who also teaches Childbirth Preparation Classes for ACCESS of The Hague. Baby massage and TENS rental and consultation also offered. Partners in Movement, tel.: 071 523 70 77, e-mail: latolman@yahoo.com

HAPTONOMY
The Academy for Haptonomy, tel.: 0343 515 178
Academie voor haptonomie en kinesionomie: www.haptonomie.nl

MENSENDIECK
Nederlandse Vereniging voor Oefentherapeuten Mensendieck: www.mensendieck.nl

HYPNOTHERAPY
Hypnotherapy by doctors, tel.: 030 234 13 54
Dutch Professional Organization of Hypnotherapists (*Nederlandse Beroepsvereniging van Hypnotherapeuten*), tel.: 0318 580 470
Dutch Guild of Hypnotherapists (*Nederlandse Gilde van Hypnotherapeuten*): tel.: 020 676 14 32

PREGNANCY YOGA (*zwangerschapsyoga*)
Central Registration of yoga-teachers qualified to teach pregnancy course Samsara, tel.: 075 687 17 57
internet: www.yoga-nl.nu

ACUPUNCTURE
Dutch Association for Acupuncture (*N.V.A. Nederlandse Vereniging voor Acupunctuur*), tel.: 033 461 61 41, e-mail: acunva@wxs.nl

ALTERNATIVE MEDICINE

INFORMATIE EN DOCUMENTATIECENTRUM ALTERNATIEVE GENEESWIJZEN (Information and Documentation Center Alternative Medicine), tel.: 0348 437 600

NEDERLANDSE VERENIGING VAN KLASSIEK HOMEOPATHEN (Dutch Association for Classic Homeopathy), tel.: 0172 48 88 99

SEXUAL HEALTH

AIDS FOUNDATION, tel.: 020 626 26 69, internet: www.aidsfonds.nl

AIDS/SOA INFORMATION LINE: 0900 204 20 40

AMSTERDAMS CENTRUM VOOR SEXUELE GEZONDHEID,tel.: 020 624 54 26
RUTGERSHUIS ROTTERDAM, tel.: 010 477 32 44
RUTGERSHUIS THE HAGUE, tel.: 070 363 09 63
RUTGERS NISSO GROEP, tel.: 030 231 34 31, Internet: www.rng.nl

NL MINISTRY OF FOREIGN AFFAIRS: www.minbuza.nl/english See items: drugs- and euthanasia policy

MENTAL HEALTH AND ADDICTIONS

ALCOHOLICS ANONYMOUS, tel.: 020 610 46 56

PARNASSIA, (Psycho medical centers in the The Hague region), tel.: 070 391 63 91, internet: www.parnassia.nl

ADDICTION AND MENTAL HEALTH, Trimbos Instituut: www.trimbos.nl (which also has English-language information)

10

From world-famous museums to an ice-skating extravaganza equaled by none, the Netherlands is one of the best-kept travel secrets and, now that you're living here, it's all right at your doorstep. Considering that the entire country is only 310 kilometers at its longest stretch, you should have no excuse for not exploring this rich cultural realm from top to bottom. This chapter will set you on your way with an up-to-date selection of events for 2005 and beyond, the top ten tourist attractions, an exclusive list of extra haunts favored by the Dutch themselves, plus a special section for antique lovers intent on pursuing the perennial trail of the Netherlands' treasures. Finally, for those of you desiring a more steady diet of activity, our club section will provide you with a wealth of friendly persuasions from which to choose. *Veel plezier*! (Enjoy!)

Things to do in Your Free Time

BY SHIRLEY AGUDO, STEPHANIE DIJKSTRA, ALMAS MAHMUD, CONNIE MOSER AND STEVEN STURP

CULTURAL LIFE

Small on land but big on culture, the Netherlands is filled to the brim with a rich blend of visual and performing arts steeped in history. Home to almost 1,000 museums, the most famous of which are the Rijksmuseum and the Vincent van Gogh Museum in Amsterdam, the Kröller-Müller Museum in Otterlo, and Boijmans van Beuningen and the Kunsthal in Rotterdam, the Netherlands offers a cultural pick-me-up just waiting for you to imbibe. With such a rich history of Golden Age painters and other artists, including Rembrandt, Vermeer, Van Gogh, Jan Steen, Frans Hals, M.C. Escher, Karel Appel and Piet Mondriaan, Dutch museums are bulging with homegrown legacies. Even the small Mauritshuis Museum in The Hague, which is known for, among others, the famous 'Vermeer' and 'Rembrandt by Himself' exhibitions, has made a name for itself.

From art palette to architectural palette, the Netherlands is home to no less than 55,000 historic monuments and buildings officially protected by preservation laws. These ancient buildings, some several centuries old, can be found not only in the larger inner cities of Amsterdam, Leiden, The Hague and Delft, but virtually everywhere, villages included. On the flip side, the Netherlands is also renowned for its modern architecture, and there are many modern-day architects such as Herman Hertzberger, Aldo van Eyck and Jo Coenen, whose designs are admired by people the world over.

Performing arts venues, such as the various theater groups, both 'mainstream' and experimental, are active all year round in theaters, parks and on the streets. Dance groups that are invited to perform across the globe include the Nederlands Dans Theater, Scapino Ballet and the National Ballet. Every year, The Hague hosts the Cadance Festival and Utrecht hosts the annual Springdance Festival. Every other year, you will find the Holland Dance Festival in The Hague.

Throughout the whole month of June, you can visit the Holland Festival in Amsterdam, combining all of the performing arts, while the Baroque Festival in Utrecht is famous for its medieval and baroque music. All the major cities have concert halls (such as the Concertgebouw in Amsterdam), where you can enjoy classical concerts and operas. And then there is Pinkpop, and Parkpop, both for popular music, and last, but definitely not least, the wild and woolly North Sea Jazz Festival.

And for movie buffs who want to see more than just the million-dollar-grossing movies or merely want to acquire a taste of Dutch culture, there are the Dutch film festivals, such as the Rotterdam Film Festival in February, the Dutch Film Festival in September, the World Wide Video Festival in April, and the International Documentary Film Festival in December.

And while you're on the 'expat' trail, be sure to catch a glimpse of Rotterdam, the busiest seaport on earth. Countering a World War II history of utter devastation, Rotterdam's modern splendor is a striking testimony to Dutch ingenuity, earning it the designation of 'cultural capital of the world' in 2001.

GETTING IN

For most entertainment and cultural events, tickets are usually available through the network of local information offices (vvvs) throughout the country, a roster of which you'll find at the end of this chapter. For Amsterdam in specific, the Amsterdam Uit Buro (0900 0191, AUB Uitlijn) offers a simple way of ordering tickets from your own home. Other than that, you can always buy your tickets at the respective theaters, well in advance, we might add, for the more popular shows. For movies, you can find an overview for the whole of the Netherlands on the website listed at the end of this chapter, as well as in the larger newspapers.

If you are particularly interested in museums, you might want to buy a *museumkaart* (museum pass, formerly known as the *museumjaarkaart*), which you can purchase at all participating museums (or via their website, www.museumkaart.nl), giving you either free or discounted admission to more than 400 museums throughout the country. If you are older than 24, it will cost you € 25 (plus € 4.95 administrative costs), if you are younger than 25, it will cost you € 12.50 (again, plus € 4.95 administrative costs). Also if you purchase a two-year rail pass, known as the *Voordeel-urenkaart* (€ 49), you not only get a 40 percent discount on off-peak train travel but also, with the right subscription, a 50% reduction on admissions to the same 400-plus museums. There are several types of rail passes, so inquire as to which one gives you this reduction. If you're a regular train traveler and museum-goer, the savings will quickly outweigh the cost.

In order to encourage younger people – ages 12 through 27 – to take an interest in culture, the *cultureel jongeren paspoort* (CJP – Cultural Youth Pass) has been introduced. It costs € 12.50 and can be bought at the VVV, at theaters and through their website (www.cjp.nl). The CJP offers you considerable reductions for many of the events listed above, as well as an overview of what is happening on the culture scene in the Netherlands on their website.

SELECTED CULTURAL EVENTS IN 2005

No matter what language you speak, the following selected cultural events for 2005 are sure to please.

THE EUROPEAN FINE ART FAIR – TEFAF
Dates: Mar. 4 – 13, 2005 (in 2006 TEFAF will take place from March 10 – 19)
See page 240 for a description of this event.
Location: MECC Maastricht, Forum 100, Maastricht.
For information, tel.: (in advance) 0411 645 09 01; (during the Fair) 043 383 83 83
Internet: www.tefaf.com

NATIONAL MUSEUM WEEKEND
Dates: Apr. 9 – 10, 2005
This is a weekend on which many museums open their doors to the public. There will be more than 100 organized excursions, ranging in distance from 5 to 8 km, in the neighborhood of these museums. Furthermore, there will be free films, slide shows, extra tours, a look behind the scenes, demonstrations, workshops and treasure hunts for children. You can recognize the participating museums by the special red-white-and-blue flags of the Museum Weekend.
Location: across the country, various museums
For more information, tel.: 0900 40 40 910
Internet: www.museumkaart.nl and www.museum.nl

HAAGSE KONINGINNENACH
Dates: Apr. 29, 2005
The night before the biggest public holiday in the Netherlands is customarily celebrated in The Hague, the home of the Queen. The night before her birthday celebration, the city turns into one big, access-for-all music and dance festival with performances on dozens of indoor & outdoor stages all across town.
Location: The Hague City Center
For more information, tel.: 070 364 19 33
Internet: www.internach.nl

DUNYA FESTIVAL
Dates: May 29, 2005
The largest multi-cultural world music festival in the Netherlands.
Location: Euromast, Parkhaven, Rotterdam
For more information, tel.: 010 233 09 10
Internet: www.dunya.nl

PINKPOP
Dates: May 14 – 16, 2005
Large international open-air festival with various pop artists performing their hits.
Location: Landgraaf
For more information, contact VVV Landgraaf, tel.: 045 532 29 29 or the organizers: 046 475 25 00
Internet: www.pinkpop.nl

HOLLAND FESTIVAL
Dates: Jun. 1 – 25, 2005
Innovative stage performances in Amsterdam. The world's most celebrated artists perform one whole month in, among others, the Stadsschouwburg, the Muziektheater and the Concertgebouw. Visitors can enjoy opera, theater, music, dance and film.
Location: various theaters in Amsterdam
For more information, tel.: 020 530 71 10
Internet: www.hollandfestival.nl

FESTIVAL MUNDIAL
Dates: Jun. 18 – 19, 2005
Multicultural festival with, among others, theater and music from all corners of the world, a Novib exposition and The Parade of the Future.
Location: Tilburg Leijpark
For more information, tel.: 013 543 13 35
Internet: www.festivalmundial.nl

PASAR MALAM BESAR
Dates: Jun. 8 – 19, 2005
The largest Eurasian festival in the world. For twelve days, the Eurasian culture and its global context are put in the spotlight on a 20,000 m² festival site in The Hague.
Location: The Hague, Malieveld
For more information, tel.: 0900 72 72 762
Internet: www.pasarmalambesar.nl

THE HAGUE SCULPTURE
Dates: Jun. 7 – Sep. 4, 2005
The Hague Sculpture (Den Haag Sculptuur) is without a doubt the most public outdoors exhibition of all Dutch cultural events. With

Prinsenhof, Delft Chamber Music

beautiful, old houses reflecting The Hague's and the Netherlands' history, the sculptures exhibited during the summer months on Avenue Lange Voorhout transform this elegant sightseeing spot in The Hague into an open-air museum.

Every year, over half a million visitors from the Netherlands and abroad experience by day and night the inspiring combination of art and city life, without having to pay an entrance fee.

Location: Lange Voorhout, The Hague
For more information, tel.: 070 346 94 86
Internet: www.denhaagsculptuur.com

OEROL FESTIVAL
Dates: Jun. 10 – 19, 2005
10 days of theater on location: street theater, world music and visual arts.

Various locations on Terschelling (one of the Wadden Islands, north of the Netherlands), for more information, contact the VVV of Terschelling.
For more information, tel.: 0562 44 84 48
Internet: www.oerol.nl

36TH POETRY INTERNATIONAL
Dates: Jun. 18 – 24, 2005
International cultural festival of poets, with participants from various countries. Includes, among others, a translations project, discussion programs, expositions, film and video presentations – and, when all is said and done, a huge final party.
Rotterdam Schouwburg, Schouwburgplein 25, Rotterdam
For more information, tel.: 010 282 27 77
Internet: www.poetry.nl

PARKPOP
Date: Jun. 26, 2005
The largest free open-air pop festival in Europe with contributions by local and foreign pop groups on two stages. There will also be a pop market and a playground for children.
Location: Zuiderpark, The Hague
For more information, tel.: 070 361 88 88
or call: VVV The Hague, tel.: 0900 340 35 05
Internet: www.parkpop.nl

30TH NORTH SEA JAZZ FESTIVAL
Dates: Jul. 8 – 10, 2005
One of the largest and best known international jazz festivals in the world which has, in its decades-long history, enjoyed performances by virtually all the jazz heroes of all time. More than 8 hours of music on 13 stages per day, with contributions by more than 1,000 jazz musicians.
Location: Nederlands Congrescentrum, Churchillplein 10, The Hague
For information tel.: 070 306 63 66, or the organizers: 015 214 83 93
Internet: www.northseajazz.nl

SOLERO SUMMER CARNIVAL
Dates: Jul. 29 – 30, 2005
An exotic music, dance and float parade, which turns the inner city of Rotterdam upside down. Dancers in fantastic costumes and many swinging orchestras on decorated floats are followed by thousands of dancing visitors.
Location: Center of Rotterdam.
For more information, contact the VVV of Rotterdam, tel.: 0900

403 40 65 or call 010 414 17 72
Internet: www.solerozomercarnaval.com

DELFT CHAMBER MUSIC FESTIVAL
Dates: Jul. 29 – Aug. 7, 2005
A unique chamber music festival with 16 different Chamber Music concerts.
Location: Stedelijk Museum, Delft
Internet: www.delftmusicfestival.nl

GRACHTENFESTIVAL
Dates: Aug. 17 – 21, 2005
Five days of more than 70 classical concerts on the canals of Amsterdam.
Location: Prinsengracht, Amsterdam
Internet: www.grachtenfestival.nl

LOWLANDS
Dates: Aug. 19 – 21, 2005
Lowlands is Holland's biggest and most adventurous outdoor music festival. It offers a choice of the best alternative music, theater, film, stand-up comedy, visual arts, literature and more.
Location: Six-Flags, Biddinghuizen
Internet:www.lowlands.nl

PREUVENEMINT
Dates: Aug. 25 – 28, 2005
Four-day culinary event, with over thirty stands acting as restaurants. Beer and soft drinks available at four separate large stands. Live music on a permanent open-air stage.
Location: Vrijthof Square, Maastricht
Internet: www.preuvenemint.nl

UITMARKT AMSTERDAM
Dates: Aug. 26 – 28, 2005
Opening of the new cultural season with shows on indoor and outdoor stages. Also an information market and a book market.
Location: Museumplein, Amsterdam
For more information, contact vvv Amsterdam, tel.: 0900 01 91 or call 020 621 13 11
Internet: www.uitmarkt.nl

HA-SCHI-BA
Date: Aug. 21, 2005
The Ha-Schi-Ba is a large multicultural festival in the Schilderswijk (painter's district) of The Hague, a nationally recognized urban renewal area with the highest concentration of immigrants in the Netherlands.
Location: Schilderswijk, The Hague
For more information, contact tel.: 070 364 19 33
Internet: www.doenevents.nl

WORLD HARBOR FESTIVAL
Dates: Sep. 2 – 5, 2005
Experience daily life in the biggest harbor in the world. This festival is all about maritime, educational and cultural activities in which the harbor of Rotterdam and its industrial area are the main feature.
Location: Harbor of Rotterdam
For more information, contact tel.: 010 209 21 11
Internet: www.wereldhavendagen.nl

HAAGS UIT FESTIVAL
Date: Sep. 3, 2005
At this festival, music ensembles, dance companies, orchestras and theater groups give you a taste of what is to come in the new season. The performances are held on various stages of the theaters on the Spui and there is a literary, cultural, theater and information market.
Location: Spuiplein, The Hague
For more information, contact vvv The Hague, tel.: 0900 340 35 05
Internet: www.denhaag.com

CROSSING BORDER FESTIVAL
Dates: Nov. 10 – 13, 2005
A refreshing look at poetry, writing and music, with approximately 120 performances on various stages by poets, writers and musicians.

Various locations in The Hague
For more information, contact tel.: 070 346 23 55
Internet: www.crossingborder.nl

INTERNATIONAL DOCUMENTARY FESTIVAL (IDFA)
Dates: Nov. 24 – Dec. 4, 2005
One of the biggest documentary film festivals in the world, with more than 150 documentaries and an extensive workshop program.
Location: Leidseplein , Amsterdam
Internet: www.idfa.nl

INTERNATIONAL FILM FESTIVAL ROTTERDAM
Dates: Jan. 26 – Feb. 6, 2005 (dates may change)
International film festival with non-commercial films from all across the world, amounting to approximately 200 movies, documentaries, short films and videos.
Location: Schouwburgplein, Rotterdam.
For more information, tel.: 010 890 90 90
Internet: www.filmfestivalrotterdam.com

EXPATS' TOP TEN
TOURIST ATTRACTIONS

THE TOP TEN PLACES THAT DRAW THE MOST FOREIGN VISITORS
Tourists and expatriates alike come to the Netherlands to admire the beautiful manifestations of its cultural heritage, with lyrical wind- mills, spectacular fields of tulips and renowned Dutch artists such as Van Gogh, Rembrandt, Vermeer, Hals and Steen completing the picture.
Below you will find the ten most popular sites visited. While Amsterdam remains the biggest draw with its rock-and-roll reputation, some of the best-kept travel secrets lie well beyond this hub, and there's much more to see within a very short reach.
To locate these attractions, simply refer to the map on the right.
For the main zoos and other children's attractions, see Chapter 7, page 188.

1. VAN GOGH MUSEUM
Amsterdam's top tourist attraction is devoted almost entirely to the work of one of the most popular artists that the world has ever known, spanning his early years in South Holland, through his Impressionist years in Paris, to his last years in St. Rémy. This museum is a perfect size for those short on time. Temporary exhibits also on tap.
Address: Paulus Potterstraat 7, Amsterdam, tel.: 020 570 52 00
Internet: www.vangoghmuseum.nl

2. ANNE FRANK HOUSE
Possibly the most deserving of all the Netherlands' major tourist attractions, the Anne Frank House, gives a fascinating insight into the Frank family's life in hiding from 1942 until 1944 during the Nazi occupation. The museum also gives information on the plight of the 100,000 Dutch Jews who were killed in the Holocaust.
Address: Prinsengracht 267, Amsterdam, tel.: 020 556 71 05
Internet: www.annefrank.nl

TOURIST ATTRACTIONS

1   DE EFTELING, KAATSHEUVEL [NEAR TILBURG]
2   KINDERDIJK, KINDERDIJK
3   KEUKENHOF, LISSE
4   VAN GOGH MUSEUM,
    ANNE FRANK HOUSE,
    THE TROPEN MUSEUM, AMSTERDAM
5   ZUIDERZEE MUSEUM, ENKHUIZEN
6   MADURODAM, THE HAGUE
7   DELFT

8   DELFSHAVEN, PORT OF ROTTERDAM
9   THE KRÖLLER–MÜLLER MUSEUM, OTTERLO [NEAR ARNHEM]
10   BIESBOSCH NATIONAL PARK
11   DE HAAR CASTLE, HAARZUILENS
12   FRANEKER PLANETARIUM, FRANEKER
13   THORN [NEAR ROERMOND]
14   BOSCHPLAAT NATURE RESERVE, TERSCHELLING
15   PALEIS HET LOO, APELDOORN
16   WATERLAND NEELTJE JANS, BURG-HAAMSTEDE
     [BETWEEN THE ISLANDS OF SCHOUWEN AND NOORD-BEVELAND]
17   NOORBEEK [NEAR MAASTRICHT]
18   HUNNEBEDDEN/DOLMENS, BORGER [BETWEEN ASSEN AND EMMEN]
19   VEERE [SOUTH-WEST PROVINCE OF ZEELAND]
20   WESTEREMDEN [GRONINGEN]

3. RIJKSMUSEUM AMSTERDAM
(Although only partly open during major renovation until mid-2008, this is actually one of the best times to visit this world-famous museum, as the most important pieces have been temporarily assembled in one wing.)
The largest museum in the Netherlands houses an internationally renowned collection based around the paintings of the 17th-century Dutch Republic, the 'Golden Age', including works by Rembrandt (the most famous of which is the imposing *Night Watch*), Johannes Vermeer, Frans Hals and Jan Steen. Silver, delftware, doll's houses, prints, drawings, Asiatic art and Dutch history are also featured.
Address: Jan Luikenstraat 1, Philips Wing (temporary entrance), Amsterdam, tel.: 020 674 70 47.
Internet: www.rijksmuseum.nl
(In inimitable Dutch style, the Rijksmuseum, in conjunction with Amsterdam Airport Schiphol, has opened the world's first, permanent airport museum exhibit center. A fly-through peek at Dutch art history features exhibits by the masters themselves, including Jan Steen, Pieter de Hoogh, Jacob van Ruisdael and, of course, Rembrandt. Entrance is free to this 'art on tap' situated behind passport control on the 'Holland Boulevard', the corridor between the E and F Pier.)

4. KEUKENHOF
From late March through the end of May, visitors come in droves to see the display of over 7,000,000 flowers in the famous Keukenhof Gardens. The 70-acre gardens offer a breathtaking, immacu-

ELFSTEDENTOCHT: ELEVEN CITIES MAGICAL ICE TOUR

If you happen to be in the Netherlands when a frigid winter takes hold, usually in January or February, and the canals and lakes freeze over enough for the Ice Master to give his blessing, then you won't want to miss the most feverishly anticipated event known to the Dutch: the world-famous, 200-kilometer ice skating marathon which winds its way through no less than 11 towns in the northwest province of Friesland. A grueling test of endurance with no equal, the Elfstedentocht (Eleven Towns Skating Race), begins and ends in Leeuwarden, the provincial capital, and passes through the picture-postcard-perfect towns of Sneek, IJlst, Sloten, Stavoren, Hindeloopen, Workum, Bolsward, Harlingen, Franeker, and Dokkum, in that order.

Of the 15 such races to date – the first official one taking place in 1909 and the last (as of this writing) being in 1997 – only the hardy Dutch have ever triumphed, although racers from other nations have tried. Record-breaker Evert van Benthem from the 1985 race still holds the fastest time at 6 hours and 47 minutes.

Of the 16,000 who actually participate in the tour itself, approximately 300 qualify for the competitive part of the race. The winner receives no prize money – just the coveted cross medal, a medallion, his or her name on a perpetual trophy and, above all, eternal fame. Thereafter, the memorabilia is kept in Het Eerste Friese Schaatsmuseum (The First Frisian Skate Museum) in Hindeloopen, where a once-frozen, amputated toe, donated following the 1963 race, is also on display.

Only those who are a member of the Elfsteden Association may participate in this infrequent event. You can, however, do your best to complete the course any other day of the year, along mapped-out bike and car routes, complete with replica tour cards to be stamped in each 'Elf' town. For those of you bent on precisely duplicating the fantasy, be aware that the official start time for the racers is 5:30 A.M.. All other tour riders, as opposed to racers, start later, and trickle in to the finish line, virtually frozen, until the clock strikes midnight. Hundreds of thousands of spectators go north to cheer on the participants, to the tune of oom-pah-pah bands, hearty Dutch pea soup (*erwtensoep*) and hot chocolate, capped off with insulating Beerenburg juniper liqueur. The majority of the other 16 million-plus inhabitants sit glued to their television sets for the one-day, magical mystery tour.

Elfstedentocht winners are seldom Olympic-trained skaters, but more often modest farmers who have trained between milking cows or growing crops, and whose proud fathers come out of retirement for a day to run the farm while their sons or daughters go up north to try to conquer a place in Dutch ice skating history. In fact, the Dutch generally prefer it when the hero(ine) of the day turns out to be the average man or woman next door.

ROTTERDAM: HOLLAND'S BEST KEPT SECRET

Rotterdam is the city of the present tense. The Netherlands' most modern city with the world's most modern port. Rotterdam is the city of progressive architecture and a dazzling skyline. With trendy cafés and renowned restaurants. Besides, Rotterdam is home to a myriad of museums, exciting sport events and fascinating festivals such as the International Film Festival Rotterdam, the Gergiev Festival, and Poetry International. And with one of the most beautiful zoos in Europe: Rotterdam Zoo. To find out more about the many things to do in Rotterdam, please visit www.rotterdam.info

OBR
City Development Corporation
City of Rotterdam

late display of tulips, hyacinths, daffodils and amaryllis planted by the Netherlands' leading flower growers. Not to be missed.
Address: Stationsweg 166a, Lisse, tel.: 0252 465 555
Internet: www.keukenhof.nl

5. DELFT
Famous for its distinctive blue and white porcelain, Delft continues to charm visitors – and shoppers. Once home to Dutch artist Vermeer, it has an abundance of beautifully preserved 17th-century buildings (including the imposing Town Hall and the Old Church), requisite tree-lined canals and a daunting array of porcelain shops.
For information, contact vvv Delft, Markt 85, tel.: 015 212 61 00
Internet: www.delft.nl

6. THE KRÖLLER-MÜLLER MUSEUM
Located in the wooded parkland of De Hoge Veluwe National Park, you can either drive your car or borrow white bicycles available at the park gates, free of charge, to travel the couple of kilometers to this museum, which ranks as the third most important collection of art in the Netherlands. Over 275 works by Van Gogh (roughly 50 of which are on display at any given time) and other artists such as Seurat, Monet and Picasso are featured, including a Sculpture Garden second to none and worth the trip in itself.
Address: Houtkampweg 6, Otterlo, near Arnhem, tel.: 0318 59 10 41
Internet: www.kmm.nl

7. DELFSHAVEN/PORT OF ROTTERDAM
Delfshaven is where the Pilgrim Fathers departed for the New World in 1620. The tiny harbor has been preserved to look much as it did in centuries past, with the addition of some trendy waterfront restaurants. Across the road at the Spido Landing Stage, tours by boat give a unique insight into modern life in the world's busiest seaport.
Delfshaven/Spido Landing Stage, Rotterdam, tel.: 010 41 35 400
For more information on Delfshaven: De Havenaar, Information Center for Historical Delfshaven, Voorhaven 38c, 3024 RN Rotterdam, tel.: 010 425 86 47, Internet: www.delfshaven.com
Historisch Museum Rotterdam, Korte Hoogstraat 31, 3011 GK Rotterdam, tel.: 010 217 67 67,
Internet: www.hmr.rotterdam.nl

8. MADURODAM
'All Netherlands in a day' is how to best describe this miniature scale-model town where you can see all of the Netherlands' major cities and landmarks up close and personal, with many mechanized exhibits, including busy motorways and sailing ships.
Address: George Maduroplein 1, The Hague, tel.: 070 416 24 00
Internet: www.madurodam.nl

9. KINDERDIJK
A UNESCO World Heritage Site and the most archetypal of all Dutch scenes with 19 windmills idyllically situated along a broad canal. Visitors' windmill opens March 21, with canal cruises beginning on May 1. During July and August the mills are put into action on Saturdays from 1:30 – 5:30 P.M. (National Windmill Day is May 7, when most windmills across the country are open to the public.)

Location: By the Lek River, southeast of Rotterdam
Visitors' Center Windkracht 4, Molenstraat 236, Kinderdijk, tel.: 078 693 09 25, or vvv Zuid
Holland, tel.: 078 613 28 00
Internet: www.kinderdijk.nl

10. DE EFTELING
With a fairy-tale theme, De Efteling Amusement Park has been charming both children and adults alike with its enchanted forest, haunted castle, roller coasters and 'white-water' boat rides, since the 1950s. There's also a pleasant hotel conveniently located on the premises.
Address: Europalaan 1, Kaatsheuvel (near Tilburg),
tel.: 0416 273 35 35
Internet: www.efteling.nl

PLACES UNDISCOVERED BY THE MASSES

Expatriates and tourists are not the only ones who like to enjoy what there is to see in the Netherlands, so here are some places recommended by the Dutch themselves. (Be sure to check websites or call for opening times, as some places are closed, for example, on Mondays.)

BIESBOSCH NATIONAL PARK
7,000 hectares of winding gullies, deep creeks and fields of rushes that were created in 1421 when the St. Elizabeth flood washed away sixteen villages and turned a prosperous agricultural region into a freshwater tidal area. Today visitors can explore the park on foot or by boat and observe a unique range of plants, animals and birds.
Location: near Dordrecht. For more information on boat rental /private tours, contact the Biesbosch Information Center, tel.: 078 630 53 53

THE SINGER MUSEUM
Laren (near Hilversum in the province of North Holland) became fashionable with painters in the 1870s, notably those of the Impressionist Hague School. The Singers, an American couple who moved to Laren in 1901, collected the paintings of visiting artists, and this delightful museum – situated in the residential area of a very chic town – is based on their collection. Upscale local shops complete the experience.
Address: Oude Drift 1, Laren, tel.: 035 531 56 56
Internet: www.singerlaren.nl

DE HAAR CASTLE
Although the original castle on this site dates from the 12th century, what stands today was rebuilt in 1634 after King Louis XIV destroyed it. It's a romantic, fairy-tale structure complete with moat and spiky turrets, and legendary curiosities, including the tiny carriage that Louis XIV rode in as a child. The stunning grounds are perfect for enjoying a picnic on a summer's day.
Address: Kasteellaan 1, 3455 RR Haarzuilens (near Utrecht), tel.: 030 677 85 15 (guided tours available)
Internet: www.kasteeldehaar.nl

FRANEKER PLANETARIUM
In 1774, Eise Eisinga, an amateur scientist, built a planetarium in his living room in order to calm the villagers' fears about the end of the world. Despite his limited knowledge about the conjunction of the planets, the planetarium is a masterpiece of engineering still functioning perfectly after 200-some years, making it the oldest one in the world.
Address: Eise Eisingastraat 3, Franeker (Friesland),
tel.: 0517 39 30 70
Internet: www.planetarium-friesland.nl

THORN
A favorite subject for posters advertising the province of Limburg, but a village relatively undiscovered by foreign visitors. Thorn is a wonderfully picturesque town with cobbled streets and white-washed houses and farms that intrude right into the main or 'high' street, giving the town a very rural atmosphere. The local abbey was founded at the end of the 10th century.
Location: Thorn, near Roermond. For information, contact the vvv Thorn, Wijngaard 14, tel.: 0475 56 27 61

ESCHER IN HET PALEIS
In the Lange Voorhout Palace in The Hague is this magnificent museum tribute to one-of-a-kind graphic artist, M.C. Escher (1898 1972), Dutch master of illusion from the Frisian town of Leeuwarden. Virtual reality takes you inside the magic as you attempt to visualize what went on in this ingenious man's mind. Seeing is believing in this kid-friendly museum with an almost complete collection of Escher's work.
Address: Lange Voorhout 74, The Hague, tel.: 070 338 12 41
Internet: www.escherinhetpaleis.nl

BOSCHPLAAT NATURE RESERVE (ISLAND OF TERSCHELLING)
Situated on the marshy land of the southern shore of Terschelling, one of the five 'Wadden' islands, this is where thousands of water-fowl and migrating birds gather. Nearby you'll also find lovely beaches where the sand is golden and the water clean.
Location: Terschelling, on the North Sea, tel.: 0512 58 50 00

THE TROPEN MUSEUM
Not as crowded as Amsterdam's other large museums, here you can stroll through the makeshift slums of Delhi, the markets of Vietnam and into Massai villages, discovering a world apart. An excellent restaurant serves unusual dishes from around the world, and temporary exhibits, such as a recent one about evil, are also featured. The adjacent Tropentheater presents a mind-boggling selection of cultural performances from around the world.
Address: Linnaeusstraat 2, Amsterdam, tel.: 020 568 82 15
Internet: www.kit.nl/tropenmuseum

PALEIS HET LOO
Once the favorite summer residence of the Dutch Royal Family from 1686 to 1975, this palace is now a museum reflecting the tastes and lifestyles of the Royal Family over three centuries. The Baroque gardens with perfectly clipped parterres and ornate fountains are a highlight.
Address: Koninklijk Park 1, Apeldoorn, tel.: 055 577 24 00
Internet: www.paleis.hetloo.nl

WATERLAND NEELTJE JANS (THE DELTA PROJECT)
In a fascinating exhibition and tour, find out about Zeeland's endless fight with the sea and the pragmatic Dutch response – a massive dam and flood barrier that literally closed off the sea. From April-October it is possible to visit a dolphin station and make a round-trip on the Oosterschelde (a portion of the sea that once stretched into the province of Zeeland, but that now, due to the dikes, has become brackish water and a unique nature area). Don't miss the hurricane simulator!
Address: D.M.A. Gelukweg 1, Burgh-Haamstede (between the islands of Schouwen and Noord Beveland), tel.: 0111 65 27 02
Internet: www.neeltjejans.nl

NOORBEEK
Popular with Dutch hikers, this tiny village nestles cozily in a valley (yes, they do exist) and still retains its authentic atmosphere with tractors chugging down the high street to deposit hay in the lofts above the farms.
Location: near Maastricht, tel.: 043 325 21 21
Internet: www.noorbeek.nl

ZUIDERZEE MUSEUM
This living museum of 130 buildings built on the banks of the IJsselmeer provides a snapshot of life between 1880 and 1932. Original houses, school, church and shops have been transported from 39 locations in the IJsselmeer region.
Address: Wierkade 12-22, Enkhuizen, tel.: 0228 35 11 11
Internet: www.zuiderzeemuseum.nl

OPEN AIR MUSEUM (Nederlands Openlucht Museum) ARNHEM
A 44-acre park representing a time capsule of Dutch provincial life with all the inherent customs and traditions in a living history setting, complete with a cross section of real historic buildings and houses literally transported from their actual settings. Windmills, fully furnished thatched-roof farmhouses and craft shops complete the melting pot.
Address: Schelmseweg 89, Arnhem (northern outskirts of town),
tel.: 026 357 61 11
Internet: www.openluchtmuseum.nl

FOAM FOTOGRAFIE MUSEUM - AMSTERDAM
A new kid on the block, Foam is described as 'a museum for photography, for a city like Amsterdam: inspirational, accessible, uncomplicated, yet critical'. Includes major exhibitions and discussions.
Address: Keizersgracht 609, Amsterdam, tel.: 020 551 65 00
Internet: www.foam.nl

GRONINGER MUSEUM – GRONINGEN
For a tour 'up north' which includes some of the following sites (see 'Hunebedden' and 'Helmantel'), include this eclectic museum that juts out into the canal and defies description, with exhibits ranging from arts and crafts to fashion. If the drawbridge entrance happens to be raised for a passing boat, be sure to look at the tongue-in-cheek tiles underneath. A zany place through and through.
Address: Museumeiland 1, Groningen, tel.: 050 366 65 55
Internet www.groninger-museum.nl

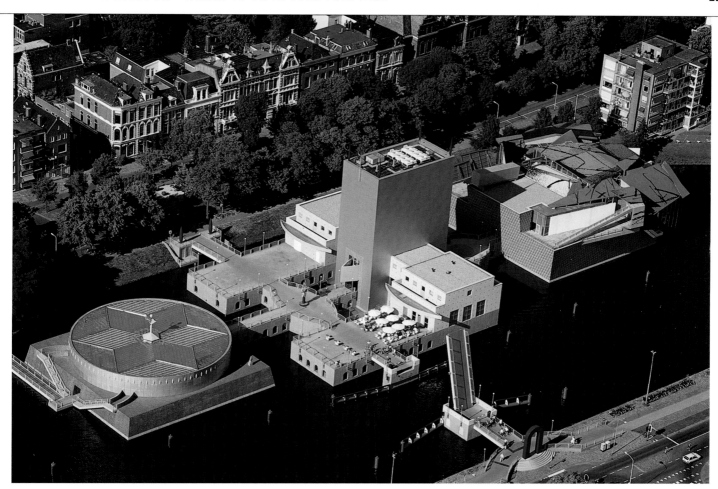

HUNEBEDDEN (DOLMENS)

One of the largest concentrations of Stone Age boulder forma-
tions exists in the idyllic province of Drenthe in the northeast,
where 54 dolmen configurations, one with a capstone weighing
an incredible 20,000 kilos, are scattered throughout the countryside and believed to be the megalithic skeletons of burial tombs
used by farmers in this most ancient area of the Netherlands.
Amazingly, these Fred-Flintstone-like structures are almost 2,000
years older than the famous Stonehenge in England, and 1,000
years older than the pyramids in Egypt. Even more amazing is
how they were transported and lifted into place. The Nationaal
Hunebedden Informatiecentrum (National Dolmen Information
Center) in Borger, where you can also see the largest *hunebed*, is
the perfect place to get the lowdown on theories.
Address of information center: Bronnegerstraat 12, Borger (between Assen and Emmen), tel.: 0599 23 63 74
Internet: www.tref.nl

'CUTE AND QUAINT VILLAGE' DESTINATIONS

While there are plenty of picturesque villages or *dorpjes* throughout the country, *The Holland Handbook* award goes first and foremost to five in the northern and heartland provinces: Sloten and
Hindeloopen in Friesland, Giethoorn and Staphorst in Overijssel,
and Bronckhorst in Gelderland. *SLOTEN*, about the size of a pano-
ramic snapshot, is the epitome of charm with its gabled houses
along a central canal. *HINDELOOPEN*, famed for its ornately hand-
painted furniture and interiors, as well as its ice skate museum
glorifying the Elfstedentocht race (see page 235), clings to the
IJsselmeer, cut off and preserved from its sailing prosperity by the
construction of the Afsluitdijk, or Enclosing Dike in 1932. *GIET-
HOORN*, the 'Venice of the North' where transportation is limited
to boats and bikes in the old part, is a punter's paradise and one of
the most stunning thatched-roof villages in all of the Netherlands, despite the yearly onslaught of camera-happy gawkers.
Staphorst, where locals still don their traditional garb, wins the
time warp prize of the bunch for its fiercely independent ad-
herence to Calvinistic ways. (Be wary of pointing and shooting
your camera at the traditionally outfitted residents here though,
as they consider it a serious invasion of privacy.) *BRONCKHORST*,
officially the smallest town in the Netherlands, is a precious mix
of cobblestone streets, farmhouses and local artisans, accented,
oddly enough, with a museum devoted to Charles Dickens, and a
Christmas festival bar none.
Other prizewinners in this category include Veere, in the south-
west province of Zeeland, and the previously-mentioned Thorn, in
the southeast province of Limburg. *VEERE* was a former sailing
port of major significance, although it's now blocked off from the
sea by a dike and sits ever-so-quietly but elegantly on the shore of
the Veerse Meer, one of the largest lakes in the Netherlands.
THORN, in contrast, is a rural haven known as the 'white village'

for its overabundance of white-washed, 18th-century houses. It makes for a pleasant respite on your journey either into or out of the bustling metropolis of Maastricht.

And for the quintessential daytrip, offering a combination of village charm and infusion of art, don't miss the glorious studio and gallery of destined-for-eternal-fame, Dutch still-life artist Henk Helmantel in his spectacular, 13th-century parsonage home in WESTEREMDEN in the northern province of Groningen. Open to the public on certain afternoons only from May through September (and by appointment throughout the year), the Helmantel gallery is a work of art in itself. (Address: Abt Emopad 2, tel.: 0596 55 14 15, Internet: www.helmantel.nl).

For more information on all of the above sites, contact the pertinent VVVs (whose phone numbers you can obtain from your local VVV or via 0900 8008).

THESE BOOTS WERE MADE FOR WALKIN'
'Let's see, shall we walk from one end of the country to the other, or to the islands today?' In the Netherlands, believe it or not, you can actually do both, but preferably not all in one day.

North to South on Foot: The Pieterpad Route
Bicycling is not the only cross-country sport in the Netherlands; walking on a well-laid-out path is another – 490 kilometers worth of walking, that is, from Pieterburen in the northern province of Groningen to the Pieterberg (Pieter Mountain) in Maastricht in the southernmost province of Limburg. Objective: to experience all that the Netherlands has to offer under one low sky and, of course, to commune with nature while getting a hardy dose of exercise. Different routes are detailed in a guidebook, a prerequisite for your journey and available at the VVV or ANWB offices. If you are feeling really ambitious, an extension of the trail continues on through France all the way to the Mediterranean Sea.

The Ultimate Adventure: Mud-Flat Walking to the Islands
For those of you with even more time to kill (well, at least a full day, anyhow), roll up those trousers, don your 'wellies' (that's Wellington boots to the Brits), and get ready to trudge through knee-deep to waist-high mud, at low-tide, of course, to the Dutch Wadden islands of Ameland or Schiermonnikoog. Recommended

ONLY with an official guide, as certain bravado types have, indeed, succumbed to its perils and drowned, Wadlopen takes place from mid-March to early October. To arrange a tour, call 0595 52 83 00 or 0519 56 16 56. For a private guide, contact Mr. Lammert at 0594 62 20 29.

FOR ANTIQUE LOVERS ONLY

The Netherlands is replete with a regular cache of antique fairs, exhibitions, shopping routes and auctions (veilingen) sure to satisfy the most discriminating antique lover and buyer. In fact, certain venues are world-renowned meccas for museum-quality pieces. Whether you're a professional buyer or an amateur with deep pockets and good taste, you won't want to miss these annual events. Here are a few of our favorites, beginning with the two biggest and best:

TEFAF MAASTRICHT: March 4 – 13, 2005
In the very southeast corner of the Netherlands in the city of Maastricht, The European Fine Art Fair (TEFAF) is an annual blockbuster event drawing more than 75,000 visitors from around the world. A paradise for antique buffs and buyers, the TEFAF is one of the world's most prestigious arts and antiques fairs, and a trendsetter in the field. Now in its 18th year, the works presented by the 203 art and antiques dealers from 14 countries are museum-quality and unrivaled anywhere in scale and diversity. Six separate sections include Old Masters' paintings, drawings and prints; modern art; antiques and decorative art; illuminated manuscripts, rare books and maps; classical antiquities and Egyptian art; and jewelry. (Up to 25,000 objects for sale)
Place: MECC, Forum 100, Maastricht
For information, tel.: (in advance) 0411 645 09 01; (during the Fair) 043 383 83 83
Internet: www.tefaf.com

PAN AMSTERDAM: December 3 – 11, 2005
Known as the best national art and antiques fair with prominent dealers and gallery owners from the Netherlands and Flanders, the PAN Amsterdam, now in its 19th year, is regarded as the most

important fair in the world for Dutch glass and silver. Equally attractive is its reputation for an excellent price/quality ratio, in other words, good value for your money.
Place: RAI, Amsterdam
For more information, tel.: 0411 64 50 90
Internet: www.pan-amsterdam.nl

AUCTION HOUSES

For those of you preferring the fast-action bidding scene, the Netherlands offers monthly opportunities to attend both major and minor auctions or veilingen, with CHRISTIE'S (Cornelis Schuytstraat 57, 020-575 52 55, www.christies.com) and SOTHEBY'S (De Boelelaan 30, 020 550 22 00, www.sothebys.com) leading the pack in Amsterdam. Watch for notices of their kijkdagen (open viewing days) where you can survey what will be auctioned in forthcoming days.
For a list of regular auctions, Roundabout magazine provides a monthly agenda as well as auction web links on www.roundabout.nl.

ANTIQUE SHOPPING

While delftware is often foremost on the shopping list for visitors, the Netherlands offers a plethora of antique treasures and pursuits for every budget. In almost every major town, the VVV information office can provide a brochure of antique shopping routes or, at the very minimum, suggestions on what streets have the largest concentration of such shops.
A good example of this is the world-famous SPIEGELKWARTIER, a very historic and picturesque neighborhood just across the bridge from the acclaimed Rijksmuseum in Amsterdam. Featuring over 80 specialized art and antique shops, this area has been the heart of the national art and antiques trade for more than a hundred years. From archaeological finds to 17th century furniture, glass and Dutch delftware, from oriental art to art nouveau, from tribal art to contemporary art, from old medical instruments and clocks to jewelry, icons, paintings and Old Master prints, the Spiegelkwartier has it all. It even has its own website at www.spiegelkwartier.nl.
Another great venue is the summer-long antique and book market held on the LANGE VOORHOUT plaza in The Hague where, on Thursdays (10 A.M. to 7 P.M.) and Sundays (11 A.M. to 5 P.M.) from mid-May to the beginning of October, you can immerse yourself in leisurely antique browsing with some requisite café-sitting on the perimeter. According to the VVV of The Hague, the street with the largest concentration of antique shops in the city is DENNEWEG, a curiosity-seeker's paradise, and also a very popular restaurant and bar area. The FREDERIKSTRAAT is also known for its proliferation of antiques shops – including antiquarian bookshops – as well as the JAVASTRAAT. For two days at the end of August, The Hague Art and Antique Days features open houses with antique and art dealers, galleries and auction houses, around a core antique and book market. For more information, contact the VVV – Den Haag, or The Hague Visitors & Convention Bureau, both listed at the end of this chapter.
For a more extensive antique shopping route, try the northeast province of GRONINGEN'S 'Antiek & Curiosa Route' that takes you through some of the prettiest countryside that the Netherlands has to offer. A brochure by that name is available from the VVV office in Groningen, and lists specific shops interspersed among the lyrical farmhouses and windmills. For other such routes, check with the VVV information offices in the areas you wish to visit.
Throughout the year, be on the lookout for antique fairs and special exhibitions, many of which take place in Dutch manor houses, such as the one featured around the second week of February each year at FRAEYLEMABORG, a stunning 17th-century, moated manor house just 20 kilometers northeast of Groningen. For more information, contact the VVV in Groningen, or visit www.borgen.nl/fraeylemaborg (Fraeylemaborg is located at Hoofdweg 30 in the northeastern town of Slochteren).
Another example is the fair that takes place in September at the historic country house Kasteel Amerongen (in Amerongen, between Utrecht and Arnhem).
For more information, call 0343 45 41 86.

INTERNATIONAL CLUBS

The real estate agents have found you the ideal place to live, the movers have brought over your possessions from another part of the world, an acquaintance or two at work has shown you the places around town, and you think you are on the road to settling in – but not quite! For those who like the company of others, either occasionally or often, it's the circle of like-minded friends that one needs in order to be able to enjoy the fairly long blustery winter of the Netherlands. Social clubs are a great place to meet other expatriates who have recently arrived, as well as those 'expats' and other members who have been around for a while. The women have the advantage of several women's clubs and neighborhood coffee mornings to content themselves with, and in most cases men are invited for an annual event or two, as mentioned in the following section on the Women's Clubs. However, there are a number of clubs where couples can join together, and where the events are mostly geared to the entire family. First, let's look at a list of Mixed Clubs in the Netherlands, and then a list of Women's Clubs, followed by English Theater Groups and some information about Sports Clubs.

MIXED CLUBS

- *The Commonwealth Club in Rotterdam*, founded in 1955, is open to all nationalities, and the official language of the club is English. To make it all-embracing, this club aims to provide social, cultural and sports activities for its members. Highly flexible in organizing events on a 'demand and supply' concept, it includes in its yearly activities visits to restaurants and theaters, day-trips within the Netherlands, BBQ weekend trips, and pub evenings; for the sports enthusiasts, tennis, badminton, golf and sailing are the popular activities. Their newsletter, *Communiqué*, takes you through the 'what's up' monthly schedule, whether it is to Rotterdam's best loved traditional fish restaurant, Kaat Mossel, or to a tombola stall at The Mission's Seamen's Annual Bazaar; while it also keeps you updated on happenings within the country.

- *The British Society of Amsterdam* offers members and their partners an opportunity to meet other English-speaking people and enjoy a large range of sporting, social and cultural events. With both new arrivals and long-term residents, the club proudly boasts a membership of several nationalities of varying ages. The society's very hectic yearly schedule includes both weekly and monthly activities, and also seasonal events such as a Bonfire Night, a Christmas Ball and summer trips. The family activities include 'mothers and babies' groups, car treasure hunts, cycle trips and visits around the country. The evening entertainment is packed with pub nights, gourmet restaurant visits; wine tasting, lectures, theater visits, and dance and film nights. Daytime activities are the popular coffee mornings, bridge, badminton and the club lunch. Sports enthusiasts can enjoy badminton, squash, tennis, sailing, horseback riding, skating, and for weekends, gear themselves to skiing, water sports, cultural trips and sightseeing.

- *In-Touch in Rotterdam* is a modest-size club with approximately 85 members with an intermingling of several nationalities and cultures. Meetings are held in its members' homes with activities to interest families with small kids, as well as lots of summer events and a Christmas party. A relaxing dine-out with partners, organized by the club on an on-and-off basis, is a pleasant change. In an effort to be different, men have started their own Out of Touch group event – a social weekly football evening!

- *The Commercial Anglo Dutch Society (CADS)* was established 30 years ago by the then-British Consul-General and a number of Anglophile business people and enjoys, at present, approximately 120 members. The association aims to provide a network of professionals and has as its members: bankers, diplomats, account- ants, journalists, hoteliers, lawyers, consultants and those work- ing for multinationals. A luncheon meeting is organized once a month, as well as a couple of social events during the year to meet partners.

- *Connect International* serves the international community in Friesland, Drenthe and Groningen, and offers three areas of service: relocation services, expatriate services with special events, activities and publications, and business services for networking via their International Business Club meetings.

- *Rotary International:* The Netherlands boasts two English speaking Rotary clubs, RCAI – Rotary Club Amsterdam International and RCMTH – Rotary Club Metropolitan The Hague. The Netherlands' group has about 18,500 Rotarians, spread out over approximately 413 clubs. All clubs meet regulary to develop 'Comrade Ship'. Rotterdam will shortly be chartered and the club in Utrecht will be chartered in March 2005. The Rotary Club of the Hague Metropolitan Area includes Scheveningen, Rijswijk, Voorburg and Wassenaar, and its membership reflects the cosmopolitan tapestry of the community. Professionally, the Club covers a wide spectrum of businesses, sciences and international relations. Both clubs have fund-raising events to support service projects both internationally and within the Netherlands. Very few Rotary clubs are listed in the telephone book, as membership is by invi-tation only.

WOMEN'S CLUBS

1. *THE INTERNATIONAL WOMEN'S CONTACT* has clubs in The Hague, Amsterdam, Maastricht, Breda, Eindhoven and Utrecht; all of which function independently but maintain contact within the Netherlands and internationally through the international coordinators.

- *IWC in The Hague* boasts a membership of approximately 400 women from some 60 countries. Its aim is to encourage friendship between expatriate women and those from the internationally-oriented Dutch community. The monthly meetings include films, cultural presentations and an occasional guest speaker. The club also organizes activities such as art appreciation, book discussion, bridge, computers, craft and needlework, a culinary odyssey, an international cuisine luncheon, a 'mothers and toddlers' group, Mah-jongg, golf, patchwork and quilting, and Dutch conversation.

- *IWC in Amsterdam* started in 1973 and now has about 400 members. To meet its objective of facilitating contact and fostering friendship between women of all nationalities living in and around Amsterdam, the club meetings are held the first Tuesday of each month. Besides a monthly outing, the club has a large number of special interest groups revolving around such subjects as: ceramic techniques, the art of listening to classical music, hatmaking and dressmaking, and body shape – all offering the members an opportunity to make new friends.

- *IWC of South Limburg* in Maastricht brings together the expatriate community not only in South Limburg but also in neighboring parts of Belgium and Germany. Coffee mornings take place every third Tuesday of the month and there is a 'happy hour' every second Tuesday. Set up in 1985, the club now has 185 members from 37 different countries and forges bonds of friendship among its members as they share country walks, museum visits, book discussions and bridge sessions – to name but a few of their activities.

- *IWC Amersfoort/Utrecht* serves to make life easier for expat women living in the Amersfoort/Utrecht area where the club started its activities in 1992. It now has some 65 members living in the areas in and around Hilversum, Arnhem, Utrecht and Amersfoort. As most of the members are working women, the club meets in the evening every second Tuesday of the month in Utrecht, with guest speakers as the draw. Cycling trips, monthly coffee mornings, craft workshops (with a popular spring and autumn series), book discussions and Dutch Practice evenings are also organized.

- *IWC in Eindhoven* is there for women both from an international background who want to settle in the Netherlands as well as for Dutch women who have lived abroad and would like to maintain international ties. The club's general meetings revolve around a speaker, a presentation, a particular theme or a luncheon. Special interest group activities include conversational practice in foreign languages, sports activities such as badminton and tennis, a meeting of minds over a good brisk walk, or a more relaxed book discussion.

2. *AMERICAN WOMEN'S CLUBS.*
Functioning independently in Amsterdam, The Hague and Rotterdam, these clubs are affiliated with the Federation of American

Women's Clubs Overseas (FAWCO). The AWC in Amsterdam has grown from an intimate group of friends in 1927 into an institution of over 500 women, both American and non-American but with close ties to the United States, from the greater Amsterdam area. The monthly General Meetings invite speakers who present talks of political, economic and cultural relevance, while there are also many interesting and educational club activities and social events spread over four geographic areas. Fundraising for local charities and community projects are an essential part of club involvement.

- *AWC in The Hague*: The club members of the AWC in The Hague can stroll into their lovely clubhouse anytime to look at the art exhibits that are changed every month, or use the library with over 10,000 volumes, CDs, DVDs and the popular audio-books. The Tulip Café, for members, offers light lunches and the large clubhouse provides a place for people to meet and organize activities. The club offers an excellent variety of classes, as well as outings to such places as Delft, Leiden, Bruges (Belgium) and Cologne (Germany). Their annual AWCH Holiday Bazaar features various art and craft vendors from all across Europe. The AWCH played an integral roll in helping to spearhead the Pink Ribbon Foundation and the Women's Walk for Breast Cancer in The Hague. Through its annual Pink Gala, the dedicated efforts of the group have raised over € 250,000 in the past two years for the Dutch national cancer association and for medical research.

- *American Netherlands Club of Rotterdam* (ANCOR), the third of the AWCs, was founded in 1955. ANCOR enjoys a very cosmopolitan fabric with a ratio of 40% American and 60% international and Dutch women. Other than its monthly meetings, the club arranges regular meetings and activities and has monthly evening meetings for professional women, with guests who speak on interesting topics.

3. BRITISH CLUBS
- *The British Women's Club* in The Hague, started in 1928 by a small group of friends, is equipped with its own club facilities on the Plein and organizes activities that include nature walks, and talks and visits to museums, and special sports arrangements for members. There are groups for bridge, mah jongg, tennis, keeping fit, Mums and Tots, Dutch conversation, crafts, book circle, hospitality for newcomers, coffee mornings, interesting speakers at the general meetings and excursions both within and outside the Netherlands.

- *The Pickwick Women's Club:* Charles Dickens' famous Pickwick Papers found its way to Rotterdam, if only in name, with the Pickwick Women's Club located here. Started in the 1950s, its aim is to develop a network of British women for social activities. Members of the club are British by birth, naturalization or marriage. Club activities include an annual Christmas and Spring Lunch, the Christmas Bazaar, tours and outings and monthly get-togethers where guest speakers are featured.

4. OTHER NATIONALITY-ORIENTED CLUBS
- *The Australian and New Zealand Women's Club* in The Hague updates its members by means of a monthly newsletter on significant news events in Australia and New Zealand, and features

community announcements and advertisements while the Out and About page meanders through the social calendar of upcoming events in the Netherlands.

- *The Canadian Women's Club* in The Hague is a dynamic club with good attendance at its annual events such as the Opening Hospitality Coffee Morning, the Family Picnic and the Thanksgiving Dinner. Events to look forward to are: 'Roving Pub Nights', where the CWC members try out new neighborhood pubs every month; golf, bridge and tennis sessions; and the Terry Fox Run in collaboration with the Canadian Embassy.

- *The Canadian Expatriates Club of Amsterdam* (CECA) organizes outings and activities for Canadians in the Amsterdam area and links them through their website.

- *The Irish Club Netherlands (ICN)* gathers together over 1,200 members for a variety of Irish activities. Since 1984, the club provides a focal point for Irish people living in the Netherlands. Anyone with shared interest in the Irish culture is welcome to attend activities, which include sports, Irish Step, Set and Ceili Dancing, traditional Irish music, Irish theater and Gaelic language.

- *The South African Women's Club* in The Hague aims to provide a social forum for both South African and non-South African women who have lived in that country. In addition to exciting day excursions, talks with guest speakers range from Power Communication to places of interest and available services. Weather permitting, the club organizes 'Braais', a typical South African barbecue. For those longing for a treat from home, the club can put you in touch with a supplier of goodies with everything from Niknaks to Ouma Rusks.
For a more extensive list of nationality-oriented clubs, please see the end of this chapter.

5. MORE CLUBS
- *Women's International Network* in Amsterdam provides professional women with a forum for meeting, networking and exchanging ideas, as well as getting down to business. Members have lived or worked internationally, have cross-cultural experience, and include company executives, entrepreneurs, independent professionals and representatives of international organizations. At the regular meetings, the women share new skills to adapt to their professions, and they find the informal monthly *borrels* (happy hours) a valuable asset. WIN aims to provide professional women in all fields of business, arts, science and politics a platform for communication and understanding, and to help them stimulate professional and personal growth while aiming to maintain the highest professional standards. WIN is an affiliate of the European Professional Women's Network.
- *Connecting Women in The Hague* operates along somewhat similar lines. Its objective is to provide a forum for motivating and supporting professional and internationally aware women in the paid and unpaid workforce, through the exchange of information and resources. The organization strives to build up contacts internationally with other professional women's organizations as well as to facilitate networking among members themselves. Members are encouraged to share their knowledge and skills

with the group through workshops or skill-building sessions, and there is always the opportunity to learn about jobs in the local workplace.

- *Petroleum Wives Club of The Hague:* The Petroleum Wives Club was founded in August of 1983 and though small by some standards, the group currently boasts just over 150 members of all nationalities. The wives/partners of anyone working in the petroleum industry, on or off shore, or previous members of Petroleum Wives' Clubs in other locations may become members.

- *The English Language Bond of Women (ELBOW)* Club, which is not limited to any particular nationality, meets on the first Friday of each month at the Cultureel Centrum Sterrenburg in Dordrecht. Like other clubs, ELBOW has a diverse range of activities such as coffee mornings, bowling evenings, boat trips, a car rally, a reading circle, 'busy fingers' for members who enjoy crafts, a drama group, and the lunch/dinner circle for members who enjoy gastronomic outings.

- *The English-Speaking Ladies' Club* at Uithoorn celebrates its 30th year with members reminiscing about what they were like and what they were doing way back in 1975. The club meets over coffee, cakes and a good chat every third Thursday of the month and has a newsletter that informs members of events to come.

- *Grapevine:* 'Put two women together and there is enough room for conversation for others to join in.' That was Grapevine's beginning twenty-five years ago, and today they meet every third Wednesday of the month at De Boulder, Groenhoff in Amstelveen, where they help English-speaking women adapt to life in the Netherlands. In a relaxed social set-up, members enjoy food nights such as the International Supper, and Summer Supper, sports events, a diners' club and film nights. The club is well known for its children's Easter and Christmas parties.

- *The Noordwijk & District Ladies' Club* gets together on a smaller and more informal level and is designed to meet the needs of women living around the Noordwijk area. Different members volunteer to host the meetings every second Tuesday of the month. The club has a reasonably sized library, arranges tours both within and outside the Netherlands and, through its activities, raises money for charity. For gourmet enthusiasts, a twice-yearly lunch is organized in style at a chic restaurant.

The above are but a few of the numerous clubs across the Netherlands. A good way to find out more is to get in touch with ACCESS (070 346 25 25 or at 020 423 32 17) For more international clubs, telephone numbers and websites see page 247.

ENGLISH THEATER GROUPS
Throughout the Netherlands, there is a smattering of independent English theater groups, as well as sporadic English-language productions by Dutch theater houses. Whether you're interested in attending or participating, following is a sampling of what's on offer:

- American Repertory Theater (ART), Rozengracht 117, Amsterdam, tel.: 020 627 61 62
- The In-Players International Drama Group, Amsterdam, tel.: 020 770 49 84
- The Stadhouderij Theater Company, Bloemgracht 57/1, Amsterdam, tel.: 020 626 40 88
- Anglo-American Theater Group (AATG), P.O. Box 10239, Den Haag, tel.: 070 394 59 88, Internet: www.aatg.nl
- Leiden English-speaking Theatre (LEST), Hooglandsekerkgracht 20a, Leiden, tel.: 071 513 00 02
- International Drama Group of English Speaking Associates (IDEA), tel.: 078 617 04 65.

SPORTS CLUBS

As you'll quickly realize, the hardy Dutch are avid sports enthusiasts with well-organized leagues and clean, modern facilities. Whether it's a bike touring group or a competitive, high-profile sport that you fancy, there's something for everyone here. As an expat, you'll have no excuse not to be fit during your sojourn in this country.

WHY JOIN A SPORTS CLUB?
Sports clubs offer a great outlet for meeting new people, staying (or getting) in shape, practicing the Dutch language and, in many cases, providing an indoor venue when the weather outside is frightful. The question is: what's the best way to find a sports club in your area that suits your interests and budget?

HOW DO I FIND THE RIGHT CLUB?
Depending on where you live:
- find out if your community publishes a guide titled *stadgids* or *gemeentegids*, or visit the local city hall, *gemeentehuis*. The sports clubs will be listed under *sportverenigingen*. Most of the titles should be understandable, but you may have to use your dictionary. Telephone the club's chairperson, secretary or contact person. Chances are good that they will speak English if your Dutch is not yet up to speed
- contact the Nederlands Olympisch Comité, Nederlandse Sports Federatie at 026 483 44 00 (in Amsterdam, 020 552 24 90; in The Hague, 070 353 7272; in Rotterdam, 010 417 28 86)
- call ACCESS at 070 346 25 25
- check the classified ads in the local newspapers (your dictionary may be necessary)
- search the Internet, as many clubs have their own websites
- try the sports facilities in your area. When you speak with people working in the facilities, be very specific that you want information about clubs (*sportverenigingen*). They may not be well informed about everything that takes place in the facility, so be prepared to persist. You can also check bulletin boards within the facility for club announcements.

Once you have found one or more clubs in the sport you like and made contact, ask if you can try out the training sessions a couple of times before you must become a member. There is no harm in shopping around if the community you live in has more than one of the particular sports clubs. Once you join, you are usually committed financially for a year.

COMPETITIONS

Dutch sports are unified into national 'bonds' or governing sports bodies, and competitions follow international rules and regulations.

JUST FOR KIDS

In the Netherlands, sports are not really part of the Dutch school curriculum as in many other countries. If students want to be active in sports, they must find a venue outside of school. International and American schools in the Netherlands, however, generally provide more opportunities. Additionally, in a country where most people live below sea level, children are required to earn a swimming diploma. Many clubs offer such a program. A good source of information on sports clubs (for kids) is the *gemeentegids* (or *stadsgids*), which you can pick up at your municipality (*gemeentehuis*). If your Dutch is reasonable, you can also try the local *Kids Gids*, or Kids' Guide, which has been published for cities and surrounding areas of The Hague, Amsterdam, Rotterdam, Utrecht, Amersfoort, Flevoland and all of the Netherlands. There is also an English-language *Kids Gids* available, covering the whole of the Netherlands. A special *Kids Gids* is *Kids Gids Speciaal* for families with children who are physically, visually, hearing or mentally challenged.

AMERICAN BASEBALL FOUNDATION

For nostalgic Americans and all those interested in 'batting up', this foundation has its own clubhouse and even branches out to feature interims of football, basketball and softball. For more information, see the reference pages.

AMSTERDAM ADMIRALS

The Amsterdam Admirals were founded in 1995 as part of the NFL Europe, the professional six-team European American football league featuring NFL talents. Other participating teams are Dusseldorf Rhein Fire, Frankfurt Galaxy, Barcelona Dragons, Berlin Thunder and Scottish Claymores.

An Admirals' game gives the NFL-stars of tomorrow the chance to prove their talent with the only professional football team in the Netherlands. They train in the US and come over to Europe during the 11-week-short season that starts in April and ends in June. Home games take place in the Amsterdam ArenA. If you want to know more about them, the cheerleaders or their schedule, visit their website, which you will find at the end of the chapter.

STUDENTS

For more information on sports activities for students, see page 204.

WEBSITES

The website www.holland.com/us/special/active/ is good source of (English-language) information on sports activities going on in the Netherlands: cycling, walking, barging, roller blading, soccer, marathons, the Elfstedentocht (ice-skating) and lots more (not only sports)!

For another complete, English-language overview of sports events for all ages and levels, check out www.expersport.nl, with, among others, baseball and softball, track and field, and basketball events.

SPORTS IN THE NETHERLANDS

Sometimes in the Netherlands it feels as if the world you know has been turned inside out. Consider sporting events. In countries such as the United States, these are family outings. A fight in the stands during a game is a major news story; reports of injuries are greeted with shock and outrage. People bemoan the loss of innocence. Outside the stadium, all bets are off. While the death of some of the spectators in a drive-by-shooting a few days later would still be awful, people would shake their heads and agree that these things happen.

REVERSE SITUATION: In the Netherlands, the situation is reversed. In spite of Dutch concerns that the country has become less safe, street violence remains rare. Whenever the odd incident of the much feared – and redundant – *zinloze geweld* ('senseless violence') occurs, the country has a collective nervous breakdown, with governmental hearings, newspaper editorials, massive protest marches and national moments of silence. On the other hand, news that fans rioted at a football (soccer) match would come as no surprise. If people were injured or even killed in such an incident, everyone would agree that, while it was a tragedy, these things happen.

UNCHARACTERISTIC: Sadly, violence at football matches in the Netherlands is not uncommon. If this seems strangely uncharacteristic, it is. While the perpetrators are a very small minority of the Dutch populace, they have made their presence known. Only English hooligans exceed the Dutch in their reputation for violence. As a consequence, a massive police presence that is just short of a major military operation helps keep the peace at games. This includes the Mobiele Eenheid ('Mobile Unit') or ME, the bad dudes of the normally pleasant Dutch police force: the riot police. Meanwhile, the fans, busy celebrating and singing their team's fight songs, seem oblivious to all of this. The collective atmosphere is bizarre: a festival parading through the middle of an armed camp. It is strange what people grow accustomed to.

HOBBIES: Given this level of enthusiasm for football, you won't be surprised to learn that sports in general are very popular in the Netherlands. During your stay in the country, you'll have an opportunity to take advantage of this at one of the seemingly innumerable local sports clubs and associations, which allow athletes of every age and caliber to participate in their favorite hobby or simply socialize.

NATIONAL PASTIMES: Alternatively, you can partake in one of the national pastimes, such as a pleasant bicycle ride. The Netherlands is filled with scenic routes running through forests or next to canals that practically beg to be peddled-down – and, invariably, lead to one of the bars and cafés that dot the countryside. Another perennial favorite is wandelen or walking, be it on (in?) the mud flats on the North Sea coast or during the *Vierdaagse van Nijmegen* (The Four Days in Nijmegen), an annual walking event. Or, if the local pond freezes over in the winter, you can dazzle (amuse) your neighbors with your ice-skating prowess (ineptitude).

FRISIAN SPORTS: Other options are provided by activities that are unique to the Netherlands. The northern province of Friesland is home to several. *Polsstokspringen* (pole-jumping) is a sort of aquatic pole vault where you try to jump over a canal – to a dry victory. Another, discussed on page 233, is the *Elfstedentocht* (Eleven City Tour). This classic Dutch event is a 125-mile (200-kilometer) ice-skating race. During the most recent *Elfstedentocht*, all other activity in the country came to a halt. The live television broadcast attracted almost three-quarters of the Dutch population! Never a people to let an excuse for a party pass, tens of thousands celebrated the whole weekend long. The race itself is not for the faint-hearted. For many it is a grueling experience. As a consequence, the winner is an instant, albeit temporary, national hero.

GO HOLLAND!: If you're less ambitious or a couch potato at heart, television offers an easy way out. The Netherlands provides numerous athletes and teams for you to cheer on. At the international level, the country is surprisingly competitive in a number of sports, including the superlative performances of athletes such as *Pieter van den Hoogenband* in swimming. Historically, notable areas of excellence include volleyball, field hockey, tennis, bicycle racing, football and speed skating.

THE 'CLAP' SKATE: In the last category, the Dutch are currently nothing less than a world superpower. Thanks in part to their invention of the so-called *klap* ('clap') skate, which has a hinged blade, they have dominated the longer distance events in recent years. To give you an idea how strong the Dutch skaters are, they swept the medals in the men's 10,000 m event at the Winter Olympics in 1998; all three skaters broke the existing world record and the new mark set by *Gianni Romme* shaved an incredible

fifteen seconds off the old record! And at the Winter Olympics in 2002, the Dutch were triumphant again, including a gold metal and a dazzling world record for *Jochem Uytenhaage*.

FOOTBALL/SOCCER: Football/soccer, however, is the sport the Dutch have consistently excelled at for the longest time, including seven World Cup appearances and two trips to the finals; but lacking the crucial final victory, the Dutch are still known as the best team never to win the World Cup. (Team sport or not, internal rivalries have on occasion been the Achilles heel of the Dutch squad.) It helps that football is immensely popular in the Netherlands, with numerous amateur and professional teams throughout the country. Allegiance varies from city to city: Rotterdam has *Feyenoord*, Amsterdam has *Ajax* and Eindhoven has PSV (the Philips Sports Vereniging, or Union). Dutch football stars are definitely in vogue these days. There are Dutch players on professional teams throughout the world.

TEMPORARY NATIONAL PRIDE
Dutch fans are no less legendary than the teams they support, although some are infamous, as we have seen. With the notable exception of the hyperactive hooligan minority, the Dutch bring a festive atmosphere to any sporting event. Stadiums resound with the sounds of *"Nederland, o Nederland"* ("Netherlands, oh Netherlands"), a fight song sung to the tune of "Auld Lang Syne" that is played by the small band of drums and trumpets that inevitably accompanies the Dutch fans. Now and then, you'll hear cries of *"Oranje boven!"* ("Orange Above!" or Orange Will Triumph!) and *"Hup Holland hup!"* (Go Holland!). This team spirit is reflected on the streets of the country in a sort of micro-nationalism phenomenon. Normally the Dutch aren't openly proud about their nationality, but on the day of a major contest or tournament there is an explosion of pride in the form of the royal color orange on the flags, balloons, shirts and hats that suddenly blanket the land. These disappear with equal rapidity after the game.

SMALL COUNTRY
But for all of their talent, the size of the country provides Dutch athletes and fans with one overriding advantage, a secret weapon for sporting events: no matter what you do, you just can't win. If you beat them, they will solemnly tell you, "What do you want from a small country?" If you lose, they will gleefully cry out, "See what a small country can do!"

WEBSITES

GENERAL

www.holland.com: the official Holland website of the Netherlands Board of Tourism & Conventions
www.aub.nl: very informative website of the Amsterdam Uitburo on outings and events in Amsterdam
www.uitlijn.nl: national event calendar and online ticket sales (tel.: 0900 0191)
www.belbios.nl: cinema reservations
www.concertgebouw.nl: for productions of the Concertgebouw in Amsterdam
www.rnw.nl/culture: English-language website, containing such items as politics, an interactive global youth radio station, art exhibitions, music productions and more
http://webshop.topticketline.nl: to order tickets online

MUSEUM WEBSITES

www.museum.nl: general museum website
www.amsterdammuseums.nl: about the 35 most important museums of Amsterdam

DINING OUT
Special Bite
Guide to Special Dining in Amsterdam, Rotterdam, The Hague, Utrecht, Haarlem and Maastricht.
Visit this site when you are looking for restaurants that are rated as 'special' by well-informed locals. The guide provides a local perspective to where to dine thus avoiding tourist restaurants.
Internet: www.specialbite.com

IENS INDEPENDENT INDEX
IENS offers an up-to-date and objective restaurant survey for Amsterdam, Rotterdam, The Hague, Utrecht, Maastricht and Groningen. IENS makes use of a large group of assessors. Each restaurant is evaluated according to their opinions.
IENS also publishes yearly updated off line restaurant guides. The Hague and Amsterdam guides are available in English.
Internet: www.iens.nl
Available in book stores and www.hollandbooks.nl

RECOMMENDED READING

THE HOLLAND EVENT DIARY 2005
Compiled by Mireille van der Sluis en Ilonka Haak
Published by Mercurius van Keulen
The ultimate tool for the expat who wishes to get the most out of a stay in the Netherlands.
Handily sorted by day, all of the many exciting upcoming activities for 2005 are listed in this colorful diary.
internet: www.hollandeventdiary.nl
ISBN 90 8087611 9

HERE'S HOLLAND
By Sheila Gazaleh-Weevers
Comprehensive guide to Dutch cities, villages, out-of-the-way places, museums, gardens, castles, dining out and settling in - with cultural and historical background. Recognizes the needs of families with children. Full of ideas for planning interesting excursions.
Internet: www.heresholland.com
ISBN 90 801255 2 0

ROUNDABOUT
A monthly English language guide to what's on in the Netherlands (the arts, clubs, sport, markets/gardens, cinema, classified ads, etc.).
Available by subscription and some book stores
P.O.Box 96813, 2509 JE The Hague
tel.: 070 324 16 11, fax: 070 328 47 00
E-mail: info@roundabout.nl
Internet: www.roundabout.nl
ISSN 1567 9799

THE XPAT JOURNAL
Published by xPat Media
A colorful magazine packed with information of interest to expats in the Netherlands. Articles cover topics such as housing, education, legal affairs and tax, as well as reviews of local sites of interest, culture and upcoming events.
Published quarterly, in English.
Available by subscription (visit www.xpat.nl) and some book stores
Van Boetzelaerlaan 153, 2581 AR The Hague
tel.: 070 306 33 10, fax: 070 306 33 11
E-mail: info@xpat.nl
Internet: www.xpat.nl
ISSN 1388 932 X

HOLLAND FROM THE TOP I AND II
Published by Scriptum, Photography Karel Tomei
This book gives you wings
Internet: www.scriptum.nl - www.hollandbooks.nl
ISBN 90 5594 302 9 (part I)
ISBN 90 5594 365 7 (part II)

THE NETHERLANDS
By Jeremy Gray & Reuben Acciano
Published by Lonely Planet Publications
For curious and independent travelers
Internet: www.lonelyplanet.com
ISBN 1 74059 303 0

HOLLAND
The Rough Guide
By Jack Dunford, Jack Holland & Phil Lee
Published by Rough Guides
Distributed by Penguin Travel Guide
Internet: www.roughguides.nl
ISBN 1 85828 229 2

AMSTERDAM CITY GUIDE
By Andrew Bender
Published by Lonely Planet Publications
A smart, stylish and streetwise guide which helps to connect with the real Amsterdam
Internet: www.lonelyplanet.com
ISBN 1 74104 002 7

AMSTERDAM IN PICTURES
Published by Scriptum, Photography Ben Deiman and Karel Tomei
This book is a wonderful memento, with short descriptions (in the introduction) of the city and its different neighborhoods, such as the Wallen, the Jordaan and de Pijp. The most important aspect, however, is the photographs.
Internet: www.scriptum.nl - www.hollandbooks.nl
ISBN 90 5594 326 6

AMSTERDAM ALWAYS
Published by Maestro Books, Photography Marcelo Bendahan
This book contains captivating color photographs on all aspects of Amsterdam
Internet: www.amsterdamalways.com
ISBN 90 9017 724 8

ROTTERDAM IN PICTURES
Published by Scriptum, Photography Ben Deiman, Text Han van der Horst

REFERENCES

This book shows the city and its people and what Rotterdammers do with their city
Internet: www.scriptum.nl -
www.hollandbooks.nl
ISBN 90 5594 275 8

KIDSGIDS (English Edition)
Activities for kids, shops, museums, outings, sports in the Netherlands
Tel.: 020 672 35 38
Internet: www.kidsgids.nl
ISBN 90 76691 22 3

Holland Books
Features a wide range of books and travel guides on Holland
Internet: www.hollandbooks.nl

INTERNATIONAL CLUBS

ENGLISH-SPEAKING CLUBS

American Women's Club,
General website: www.fawco.org
Amsterdam, tel.: 020 644 35 31,
internet: www.awca.nl
The Hague, tel.: 070 350 60 07,
internet: www.awcthehague.org
Rotterdam, tel.: 010 458 69 73,
internet: http://ancor.fawco.org/
AFNORTH International Club,
tel.: 045 527 42 73
Amersfoort British Club, tel.: 033 472 39 41
American Netherlands Club Rotterdam
(ANCOR), tel.: 010 438 65 27
Australian & New Zealand Women's Club,
The Hague, tel.: 070 317 98 81, internet:
anzwcnetherlands@hotmail.com
Australians in Holland,
internet:www.coolabah.com/oz/hollandsite
British Women's Clubs
The Hague, tel.: 070 346 19 73, internet:
www.bwclubthehague.demon.nl
Amersfoort, tel.: 033 472 39 41
Utrecht, tel.: 030 210 03 71
British Society of Amsterdam,
Amsterdam, tel.: 020 624 86 29,
internet:
www.britishsocietyofamsterdam.org
CADS (Commercial Anglo Dutch Society),
tel.: 054 682 32 44
Canadian Women's Club of The Hague,
tel.: 070 326 44 88
internet: http://groups.msn.com/Canadian-
WomensLeagueoftheNetherlands-Member-
ship

The Canadian Expatriates Club of Amster-
dam (CECA),
internet: http://www.spetz.ca/CECA.html
Commonwealth Club, The Hague,
tel.: 010 422 04 58
Connect International, Groningen, tel.: 050
521 45 41, internet: www.connect-int.org
Connecting Women, The Hague, tel.: 070 365
25 43, internet: www.connectingwomen.nl
English Language Bond of Women,
Dordrecht, tel.: 078 618 36 81
English Speaking Ladies Club,
Uithoorn, tel.: 029 756 52 74, internet:
www.geocities.com/eslcsite
English Speaking Contact Group,
Haarlem, tel.: 023 555 33 40
English Speaking Community in the Nether-
lands, internet: www.elynx.nl
ELBOW, Dordrecht, tel.: 078 618 36 81
Expat Lions Club,
The Hague, tel.: 070 350 86 93
Grapevine, tel.: 029 728 6604
International Contact,
The Hague, tel.: 070 383 08 58
International Women's Club of The Hague,
tel.: 070 355 8863
International Women's Contact
Amsterdam, tel.: 0297 56 30 27, internet:
www.euronet.nl/users/iwc_amst
Breda, tel.: 076 597 13 57,
internet: www.iwcbreda.info
Eindhoven, tel.: 040 253 96 99
South Limburg, tel.: 043 325 43 53
The Hague, tel.: 070 355 88 63, internet:
www.iwcthehague.nl
Utrecht/Amersfoort, tel.: 033 461 43 56,
internet: www.iwcu.non-profit.nl
Maastricht, tel.: 043 321 54 69
International Cultural Exchange Group (ICE)
internet: http://uk.groups.yahoo.com/
group/ice_thehague/
In-Touch, Rotterdam, tel.: 018 032 31 16
The John Adams Institute, Amsterdam, tel.:
020 624 72 80, internet: www.john-adams.nl
Irish Club of the Netherlands, The Hague,
tel.: 070 427 71 23, internet: www.irishclub.nl
Paddyish Irish Club of Amsterdam
tel.: 035 685 0344
internet:
www.egroups.com/group/PADDYISH
Lions Club The Hague Universal
Rijswijk, tel.: 070 394 83 70
My Haarlem, the social network for
professionals in Holland,
internet: www.myhaarlem.com
The Netherlands England Society
National contact tel.: 071 561 52 09
Amsterdam tel.: 075-6169936

Utrecht: tel.: 030-6991618
The Hague tel.: 070-3247888
internet: www.nederlandengeland.nl
Netherlands-India Association
internet: www.netherlands-india.nu
Noordwijk & District Ladies Club
Noordwijk, tel.: 0252 37 67 50
North Holland International Friendship
Club, internet: www.nhifc.org
UFDA (United Filipino Dutch Association),
tel.: 023 – 539 6312
Pickwick Women's Club
Rotterdam, tel.: 010 452 69 49,
internet: www.3kleur.nl/pickwick/index.
pickwickclub.htm
Petroleum Wives Club
The Hague, tel.: 070 517 7629,
internet:
www.globaloutpostservices.com/thehague
Rotary International
Amsterdam, tel.: 020 549 1440
Rotary International
The Hague, internet: www.rotary.nl
Royal Air Force Association
Amsterdam Branch, tel.: 020 696 0133,
internet: www.britian.nl (See Defence pages
– link to RAFA icon)
Russian Community in The Netherlands
tel.: 0900 90 90 000,
internet: www.ruscom.nl
Singapore-Netherlands Association,
tel.: 010 511 4400, internet: www.sna-nl.org
South African Women's Club, The Hague,
tel.: 070 328 15 12, internet: www.sawcnl.com
South Africa Club,
internet: www.southafricaclub.nl
St. Andrew's Society of the Netherlands,
Wassenaar, tel.: 070 511 81 51,
internet: www.standrews.nl
Scottish Coalition,
internet: http://scottish-coalition.org
Royal Scottish Dance – The Hague District,
(also information on other dance groups),
tel: 070 320 23 52
Scandinavia Club, tel.: 070 352 11 93,
internet: www.clubscandinavia.com
Swedish Women's International Network
SWEA, tel.:0343 516 122,
internet: www.chapters-swea.org/holland/
Twente Expatriates Club,
Enschede, tel.: 053 484 96 49
Women's International Network,
tel.: 020 683 88 62,
internet:www.womensinternational.net

FRENCH CLUBS

Accueil des Francophones de la Haye
Schoutenstraat 46, 2596 SL The Hague
Tel.: 070 365 05 63

Alliance Française, La Haye (also in Leiden, Amsterdam, Rotterdam & Utrecht)
Cultural activities and French courses.
Tel.: 070 362 15 23 or 071 515 54 57 (Leiden branch)
Amitié Club de la Haye
Tel.: 070 387 01 12
Amitié Club de Rotterdam
Tel.: 010 426 74 19
Amitié Club d'Amsterdam
Tel.: 020 699 47 61

To order a publication on organizations for French-speaking people in the Netherlands:
Union des Français à l'Etranger
Die 17, 1862 HW Bergen
E-mail: dravail@tip.nl
Délégation Générale de l'Alliance Française
Keizersgracht 635, 1017 DS Amsterdam
tel.: 020 627 92 71

The French Cultural Institute,
internet: www.maisondescartes.com

GERMAN CLUBS

Deutscher Klub in den Niederlanden
P.O. Box 65786, 2506 EB The Hague,
tel.: 070 391 41 07

Deutsch-Niederländischer Verein
P.O. Box 7933, 1008 AC Amsterdam,
tel.: 0297 582 522

Goethe-Institut Amsterdam
Herengracht 470, 1017 CA Amsterdam
Tel.: 020 623 04 21
Internet: www.goethe.org

Goethe-Institut Rotterdam
Westersingel 9, 3014 GM Rotterdam
Tel.: 0010 209 20 90

ENGLISH SPEAKING ART CLUBS

The Decorative & Fine Arts Society (DFAS) of The Hague
Popular, high quality and well-illustrated monthly lecture program, in English
Tel.: 070 517 90 03

International Art Club
Nieuwe Schoolstraat 22B, 2514 HZ The Hague
Tel.: 070 362 33 47
Internet: www.nadfas.org.uk

Images International Photo Club,
tel.: 070 354 59 64,
internet: www.imagesphotoclub.com

Studio Jean, drawing and painting lessons,
tel.: 070 392 16 72,
internet: www.studiojean.nl

Leiden English Speaking Theatre Group (LEST)
Hooglandskerkgracht 20a, Leiden
Tel.: 071 513 00 02
Anglo-American Theater Group (AATG)
P.O. Box 10239, 2501 HE The Hague
Tel.: 070 394 59 88
Internet: www.aatg.nl

American Repertory Theater (ART)
Rozengracht 117, 1016 LP Amsterdam
Tel.: 020 627 61 62

International Drama Group of English Speaking Associates (IDEA), tel.: 078 617 04 65

In-Players International Drama Group,
Amsterdam
Tel.: 020 770 49 84
Internet: www.inplayers.org

The Stadhouderij Theater Company
Bloemgracht 57/1, Amsterdam
Tel.: 020 626 40 88

The British Choir of The Hague,
tel.: 070 328 13 87

Sweet Adelines International,
internet: www.sweetadelines.nl

Society of English-Native-Speaking Editors (SENSE), internet: www.sense-online.nl

Toastmasters International
Amsterdam, internet: www.toastmasters.nl
The Hague, internet:
www.toastmasters.nl/thehague

Urban Learning
Interesting courses on just about anything,
internet: www.urbanlearning.com

ENGLISH-SPEAKING COMEDY THEATER

Boom Chicago
Not cabaret, and not stand-up, Boom Chicago is a mix of sketches and pure improvisation. Innovative visuals and music from first-class VJS, DJS and musicians make for a unique evening out. Boom Chicago resides in the Leidseplein Theater in Amsterdam
Tickets and reservations, tel.: 020 423 01 01
Internet: www.boomchicago.nl
Without Ties
Comedy trio of UK/USA humor performing weekly on Sundays at the Comedy Café on the Max Euweplein 43-45 in Amsterdam.
tel.: 020 638 3971,
internet: www.withoutties.com

Theater Diligentia
English-speaking performances, music and comedy in the beautifully restored Theater Diligentia in The Hague, tel.: 0900 414 41 04,
internet: www.theater-diligentia.nl

Xaviera Hollander
Avant garde English language productions in Amsterdam, internet: www.xavierahollander.com

SPORTS

ENGLISH SPEAKING SPORTS CLUBS

ABF - The American Baseball Foundation
This volunteer organization provides soccer, basketball and baseball programs for children from age 4 up. There are also opportunities to play adult soccer and softball. Sports programs are conducted in English, but the membership is composed of many nationalities.
Ammonslaantje 1, P.O. Box 133, 2240 AC Wassenaar
Tel.: 070 514 65 15
Internet: www.abfsport.nl

Amsterdam Admirals - American Football
The Admirals play all of their home games at the Amsterdam ArenA. This stadium is located in the south eastern area of Amsterdam.
Arenaboulevard 61 - 75, 1101 DL Amsterdam
Tel.: 020 485 05 50
E-mail: info@admirals.nl
Internet: www.admirals.nl

REFERENCES

Amstelveen RC 1890 (ARC 1890)
A international rugby club located just
20 minutes south of the Amsterdam city
center, right next to Schiphol Airport.
Sportlaan 25a, Amstelveen
Tel.: 020 643 89 79
E-mail: info@arcrugby.com
Internet: www.arcrugby.com

THE HAGUE HASH HOUSE HARRIERS,
'a drinking club with a running problem'
meets weekly.
Tel.: 020 699 05 19, Contact: Ronald Verboven,
Tel: 06 51391999
E-mail: rubberron@comprise.com or
info@haguehash.nl
Internet: www.haguehash.nl

Hash House Harriers Amsterdam,
internet: www.harrier.nl

The Hague Road Runners
Groenendaal 1, 2244 BK Wassenaar
Tel.: 070 328 10 25
Internet: www.hagueroadrunners.nl

The Randstad Harings Diving Club, internet:
www.randstad-harings.demon.nl

CRICKET

De Kieviten Cricket Club, The Hague, tel.: 070
354 23 14, internet: www.kieviten.nl/cricket
Voorburg Cricket Club, Voorburg,
tel.: 070 386 26 78
General info and clubs in the Netherlands,
internet: www.cricket.nl

GOLF

Nederlandse Golf Federatie,
De Meern, tel.: 030 662 18 88
Amsterdamse Golf Club,
Amsterdam, tel.: 020 497 78 66
Kennemer Golf Club, Zandvoort,
tel.: 023 571 28 36
Haagsche Country Club Groengeel,
The Hague, tel.: 070 517 93 71
Haagsche Golf and Country Club,
Wassenaar, tel.: 070 517 96 07
Rijswijkse Golf Club, Rijswijk,
tel.: 070 319 24 24
Utrechtse Golfclub Amelisweerd,
Utrecht, tel.: 030 254 66 48

For more golf clubs in the Netherlands:
www.golf.nl

CYCLING

Cycling vacations in the Netherlands:
www.tulipcycling.com
Cycling in Rotterdam:
www.rotterdambycycle.nl

WEBSITES

www2.holland.com/us/special/active/:
a good source of information on sports
activities going on in the Netherlands
www.expersport.nl: for another complete
(English-language) overview of sports events
for all ages and levels

TOURIST INFO

Tourist Information Office
You will find the vvv offices by following the
blue signs with the white letters

vvv Amsterdam
Stationsplein 10, 1012 AB Amsterdam
Tel.: 0900 400 40 40
Internet: www.vvvamsterdam.nl

vvv The Hague has 2 offices:
Kon. Julianaplein 30, 2595 AA The Hague
tel.: 0900 340 35 05
G. Deynootweg 1134, 258G BX The Hague
Tel.: 0900 340 35 05
Internet: www.denhaag.com

vvv Maastricht
Kleine Staat 1, 6122 ED Maastricht
Tel.: 043 325 21 21
Internet: www.vvvmaastricht.nl

vvv Rotterdam
Coolsingel 67, 3012 AC Rotterdam
Tel.: 0900 403 40 65
Internet: www.vvvrotterdam.nl

vvv Utrecht
Vredenburg 90, 3511 BD Utrecht
Tel.: 0900 1288 732
Internet: www2.utrecht.nl

OTHER ADDRESSES

Royal Dutch Touring Club ANWB,
Wassenaarseweg 220, 2596 EC The Hague,
General information, tel.: 0800 0503
Internet: www.anwb.nl

**Netherlands Board of Tourism &
Conventions**
Vlietweg 15, 2266 KA Leidschendam,
tel.: 070 370 57 05
Internet: www.holland.com and
www.rootsinholland.com

**Alliance Gastronomique Neerlandaise
(culinary club)**
De Pinckart 54, 5674 CC Neunen,
tel.: 040 263 11 53

CITY INFO

CITY OF AMSTERDAM
This site is in Dutch and English and provides everything you need to know about
Amsterdam, what's on, where to go as a tourist and even what the weather is like. There
are also good links to other interesting sites
Internet: www.amsterdam.nl

Amsterdam.info
Very informative website on Amsterdam:
Internet: www.amsterdam.info

The Internet Guide to Amsterdam
A non-commercial site, this is a personal
introduction to Amsterdam, designed to be
printed out and taken with you.
Internet:
www.cwi.nl/~steven/amsterdam.html

Time Out Amsterdam
Published by Time Out Group
Internet: www.timeout.com/amsterdam

For a virtual tour of Amsterdam
www.amsterdamhotspots.nl or
www.channels.nl

The Hague Visitors & Convention Bureau
P.O. Box 85456, 2508 CD The Hague, tel.: 070
361 88 88, fax: 070 361 88 50
Internet: www.denhaag.com

CITY OF THE HAGUE
The Hague City Council official website
offers city news, events and information in
Dutch, with a version in English
Internet: www.denhaag.nl or
www.thehague.nl

THE MUNICIPALITY OF THE HAGUE
The Hague Hospitality Center
City Hall, Spui 70, Rooms B01.13 and B01.14
(1st floor), The Hague, tel.: 070 353 50 37
The International Corner
City Hall, Spui 70, Atrium (gemeentelijk
ContactCentrum),
The Hague, tel: 070 353 30 00
Internet: www.thehague.nl and
www.denhaag.nl

City Mondial
Multicultural The Hague website with day
tours, outing tips and an event diary.
Internet: www.citymondial.nl

GEMEENTE ROTTERDAM
The Rotterdam City Council official website.
Internet: www.rotterdam.nl

GoRotterdam
Event calender with events, exhibitions,
festvals, general information, tips etc.
Internet: www.gorotterdam.com

Rotterdam Qualitime
Bi-yearly glossy magazine with news on
what's going on in the city when it comes to
working, shopping, cultural events, night life
in Rotterdam.
Including an agenda of cultural happenings
in the city, a number of sightseeing
suggestions and a map of the city. Written in
both Dutch and English
For more information:
www.rotterdamqualitime.nl

GEMEENTE UTRECHT
Internet: www2.utrecht.nl

GEMEENTE GRONINGEN
Internet: www.groningen.nl

CONTRIBUTING COMPANIES AND ORGANIZATIONS

C&G CAREER SERVICES
Peter P. Kranenburg
Edisonstraat 24, 2811 EM Reeuwijk
Tel.: 0182 300 745
E-mail: mail@cg-services.com
Internet: www.cg-services.com

GOUDA INTERNATIONAL INSURANCE
Inge Kool
P.O. Box 9, 2800 MA Gouda
Tel.: 0182 544 544
E-mail: ikool@goudse.com
Internet: www.expatriatesinsurance.com

KPMG
Luydert Smit, Marike Maas, Anton Steijn,
Erno Tonkes
P.O. Box 74600, 1070 DE Amsterdam
Tel.: 020 656 18 80
E-mail: smit.luydert@kpmg.nl
Internet: www.kpmg.nl

LENOS C.S.
Paul Lenos, Toon de Ruiter
Nieuwe Uitleg 21, 2514 BR The Hague
Tel.: 070 413 34 13
E-mail: info@lenos-vat.com
Internet: www.lenos-vat.com

LOYENS & LOEFF NV-ROTTERDAM OFFICE
Ruud Blaakman, Rina Driece, Yvonne
Sørensen
P.O. Box 2888, 3000 CW Rotterdam
Weena 690, 3012 CN Rotterdam
Tel.: 010 224 62 24
E-mail: ruud.blaakman@loyensloeff.com
rina.driece@loyensloeff.com
yvonne.sorensen@loyensloeff.com
Internet: www.loyensloeff.com

LOYENS & LOEFF NV-AMSTERDAM OFFICE
Nathalie Idsinga, Geeske Tuinstra
P.O. Box 71170, 1008 BD Amsterdam
Forum, Fred. Roeskestraat 100,
1076 ED Amsterdam
Tel.: 020 578 57 85
E-mail: nathalie.idsinga@loyensloeff.com
geeske.tuinstra@loyensloeff.com
Internet: www.loyensloeff.com

NUFFIC
The Netherlands Organization for International Cooperation in Higher Education
Han van der Horst
Kortenaerkade 11, 2518 AX The Hague
P.O. Box 29777, 2502 LT The Hague
Tel.: 070 426 02 60
E-mail: nuffic@nuffic.nl
Internet: www.nuffic.nl

RELOCATION ADVISERS
Dennis van Riet
Joh. Verhulststraat 14, 1071 NC Amsterdam
Tel.: 020 664 74 70
E-mail: info@relocationadvisers.nl
Internet: www.relocationadvisers.nl

BUREAU RIETMEIJER
Bert Rietmeijer
P.O. Box 60111, 1320 AC Almere
Tel.: 036 545 80 00
E-mail: info@rietmeijer.nl
Internet: www.rietmeijer.nl

RELOCATION CARE
Annette de Vreede
P.O. Box 152, 4650 AD Steenbergen
Tel.: 0167 56 52 48
E-mail: info@relocationcare.nl
Internet: www.relocationcare.nl

ADVERTISERS INDEX

PHOTO INDEX